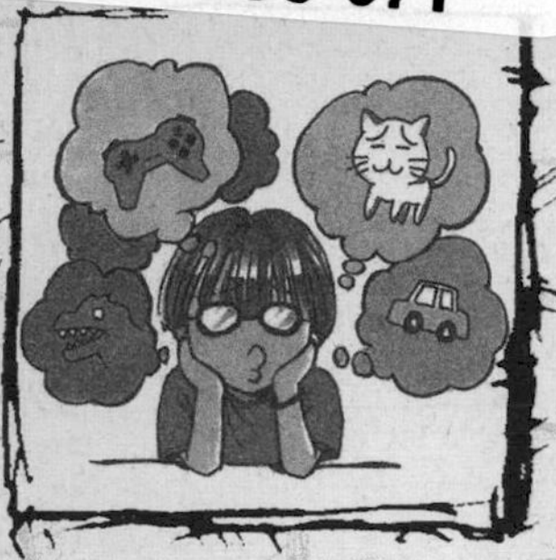

I once heard that cells have memories. I was born in 1980, but I'm drawn to photos of places and people that were taken long before I was born. Street shots of Japan at the height of the economic boom of the 1960s and 1970s leave me feeling nostalgic. Could these be genetic memories I've inherited from my parents? ...Or am I thinking like a manga artist again? It's a vocational hazard.

—Kentaro Yabuki, 2004

Kentaro Yabuki made his manga debut with ***Yamato Gensoki***, a short series about a young empress destined to unite the warring states of ancient Japan and the boy sworn to protect her. His next series, ***Black Cat***, commenced serialization in the pages of ***Weekly Shonen Jump*** in 2000 and quickly developed a loyal fan following. ***Black Cat*** has also become an animated TV series, first hitting Japan's airwaves in the fall of 2005.

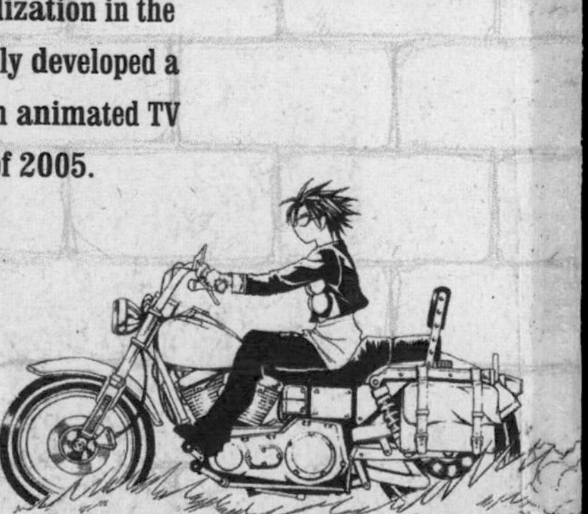

BLACK CAT VOL. 19
The SHONEN JUMP Manga Edition

STORY AND ART BY
KENTARO YABUKI

English Adaptation/Kelly Sue DeConnick
Translation/JN Productions
Touch-up Art & Lettering/Gia Cam Luc
Design/Courtney Utt
Editor/Jonathan Tarbox

Editor in Chief, Books/Alvin Lu
Editor in Chief, Magazines/Marc Weidenbaum
VP, Publishing Licensing/Rika Inouye
VP, Sales & Product Marketing/Gonzalo Ferreyra
VP, Creative/Linda Espinosa
Publisher/Hyoe Narita

Printed in the U.S.A.

Published by VIZ Media, LLC
P.O. Box 77010
San Francisco, CA 94107

SHONEN JUMP Manga Edition
10 9 8 7 6 5 4 3 2 1
First printing, March 2009

www.viz.com

THE WORLD'S
MOST POPULAR MANGA
www.shonenjump.com

TRAIN
HEARTNET

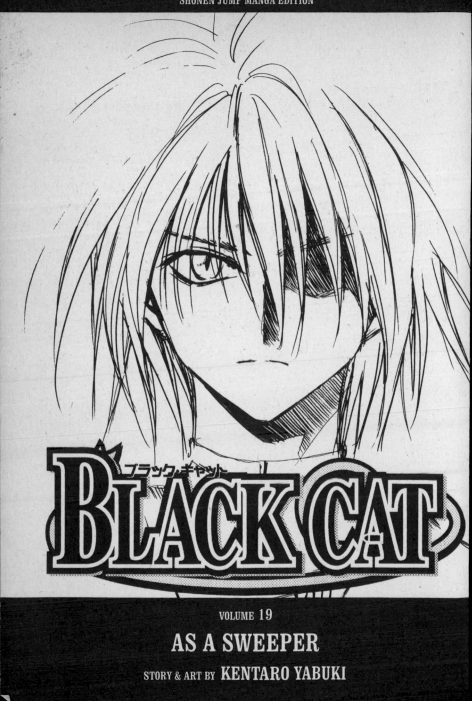

SHONEN JUMP MANGA EDITION

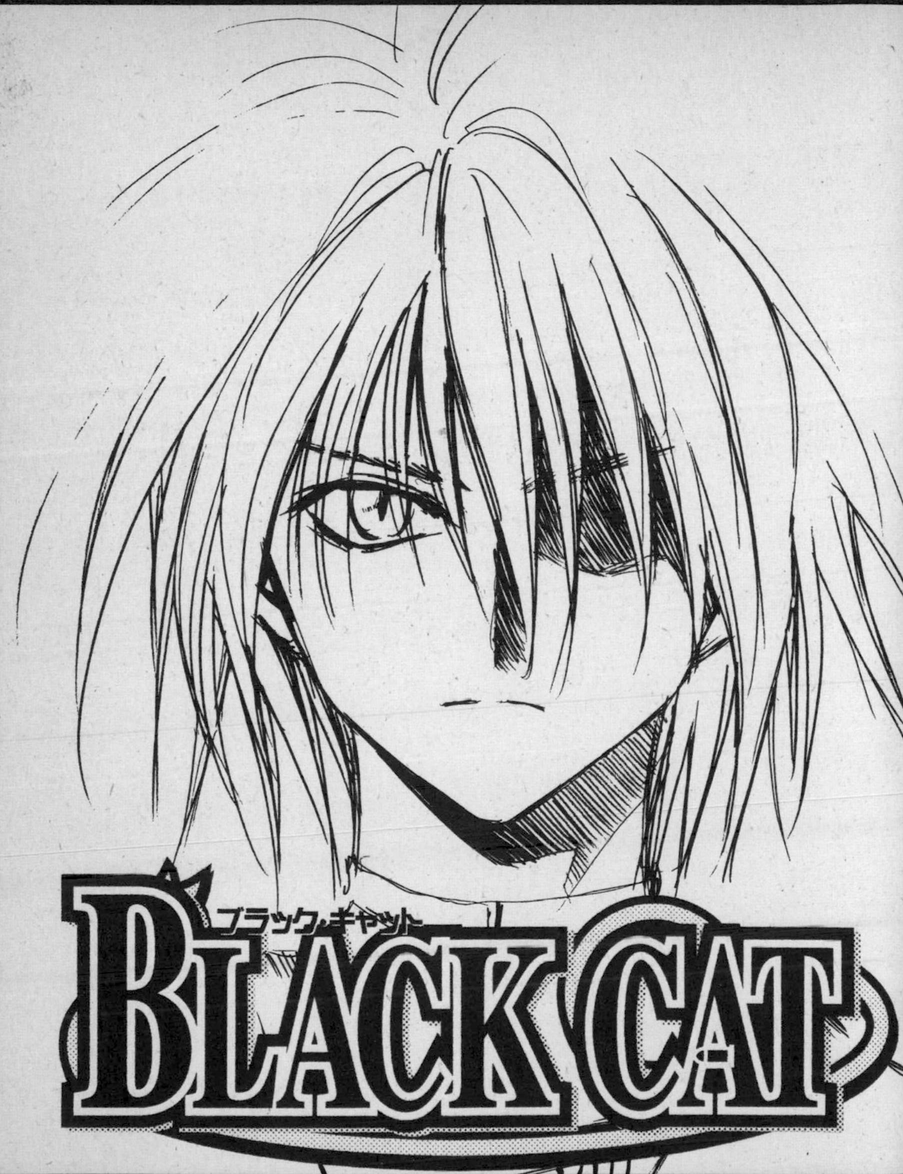

BLACK CAT

ブラック・キャット

VOLUME 19

AS A SWEEPER

STORY & ART BY KENTARO YABUKI

SVEN VOLLFIED

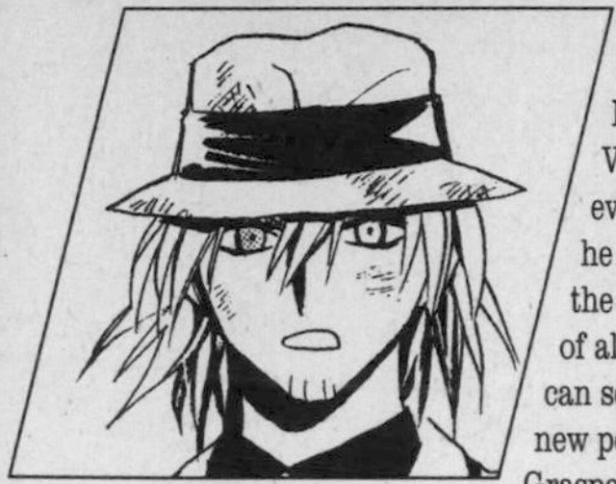

Train's partner Sven, a former IBI agent. His Vision Eye has evolved, and now he can slow down the movement of all objects he can see with his new power, the Grasper Eye.

SEPHIRIA ARKS

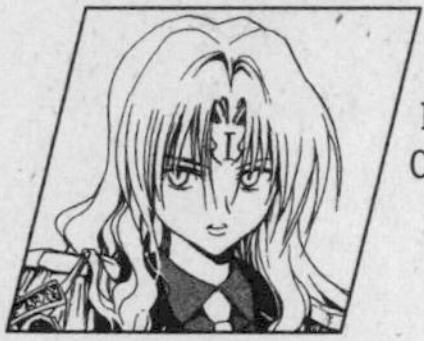

As Number I, Sephiria is the leader of the Chrono Numbers.

BELZE ROCHEFORT

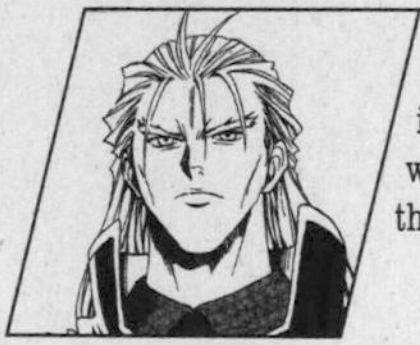

As Chrono Number II, Belze is equally adept with the pen and the sword.

JENOS HAZARD

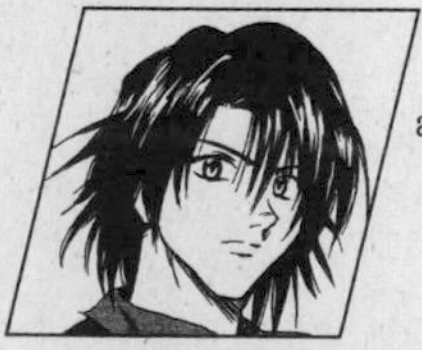

Chrono Number VII manipulates wires... and women.

LIN SHAOLEE

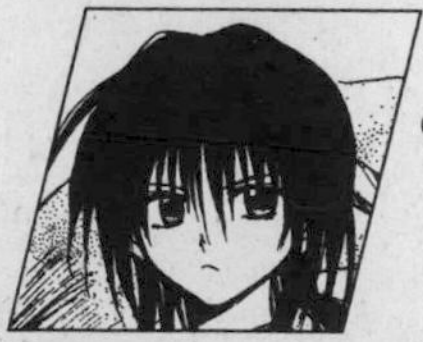

Chrono Number X is a master of disguise.

TRAIN HEARTNET

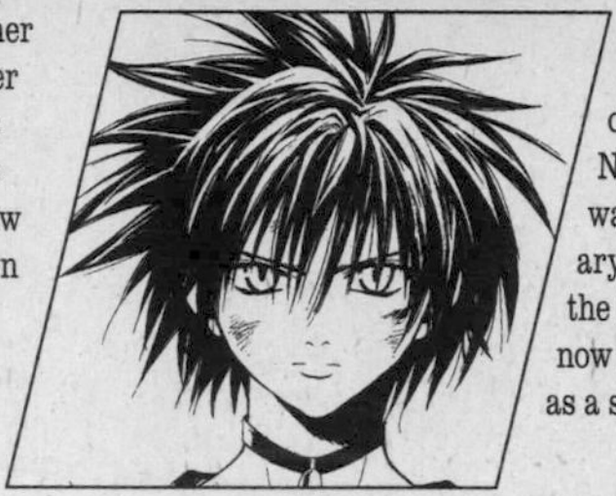

Formerly Number XIII of the Chrono Numbers, Train was once a legendary eraser called the Black Cat. He now pursues Creed as a sweeper.

EVE

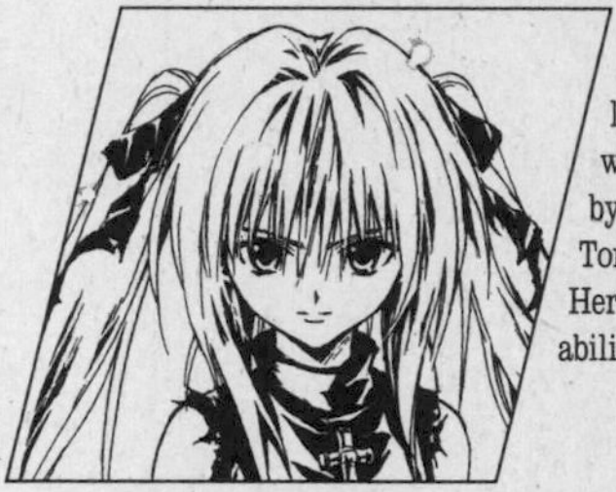

Part bioweapon and part little girl, Eve was manufactured by weapons dealer Torneo Rudman. Her power lies in her ability to transform.

RINSLET WALKER

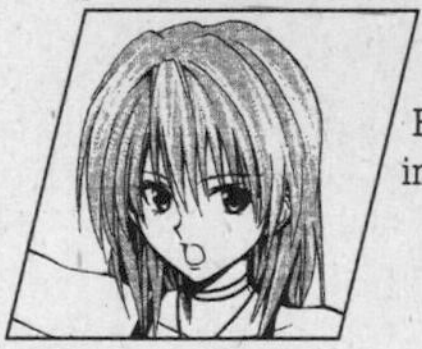

A self-styled thief-for-hire, Rinslet is fiercely independent.

SAYA MINATSUKI

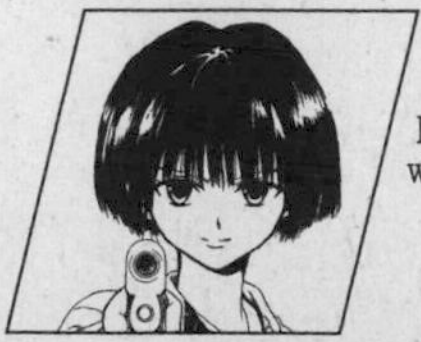

Saya is an important woman from Train's past who was fatally wounded by Creed.

A fearless "eraser" responsible for the deaths of countless men, Train "Black Cat" Heartnet was formerly an assassin for the crime syndicate Chronos. Train betrayed Chronos and was supposedly executed for it, but now, two years later, he lives a carefree wanderer's life, working with his partner Sven as a bounty hunter ("sweeper") and pursuing Creed Diskenth, the man who murdered his dear friend Saya Minatsuki.

Creed finally turns up, determined to lead a revolution against Chronos. He tries to convince Train to join his Apostles of the Stars, but fails at that and escapes once again.

Train decides Creed must be stopped, and for the first time, he tells his friends the story behind Creed and Saya.

In an effort to close the door on Train's past, he, Sven and Eve head out with a new resolve. They hook up with an elite band of bounty hunters to form a Sweeper Alliance and infiltrate Creed's island hideout. Once there, they confront formidable Apostles wielding the power of Tao.

Despite their many adversaries, Train and his comrades relentlessly pursue Creed. Meanwhile, the Chrono Numbers land on the island and begin their assault. At last, Sephiria Arks pits her weapon against Creed's terrifying Imagine Blade!

CREED DISKENTH

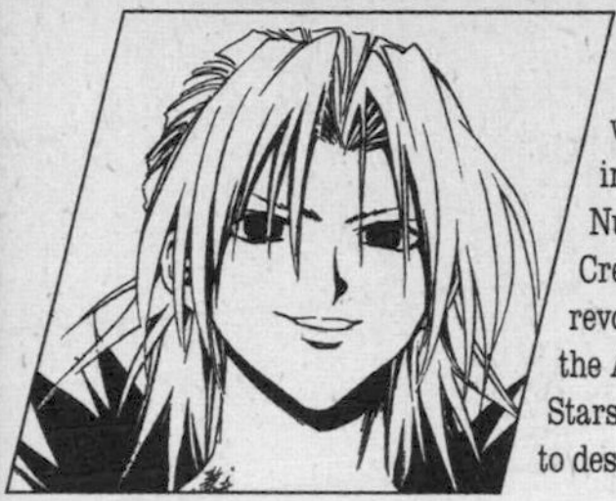

Though he and Train were associates in their Chrono Numbers days, Creed now heads the revolutionary group the Apostles of the Stars, whose goal is to destroy the world.

ECHIDNA PARASS

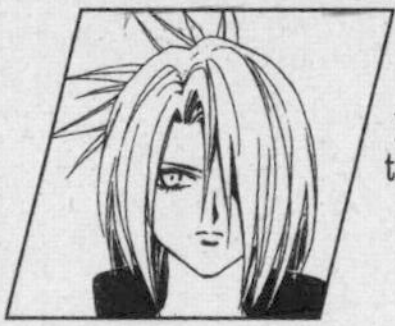

Echidna has the power to create portals in space and travel through them.

BALDORIAS S. FANGHINI

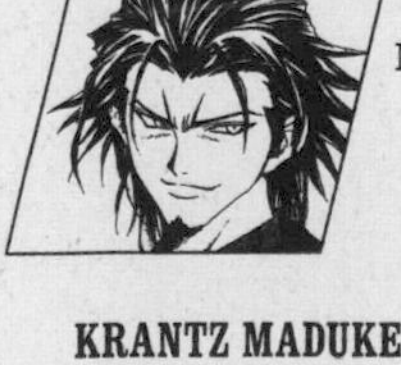

Nurtured by Chronos to fight as Chrono Number VIII.

KRANTZ MADUKE

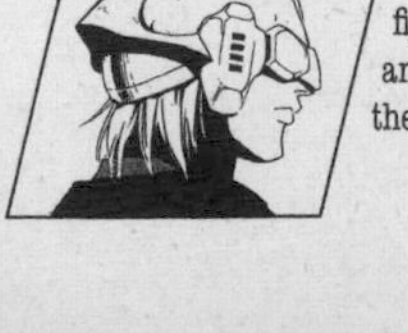

Blind warrior Chrono Number IV fights using sound and his keen sense of the air around him.

BLACK CAT

VOLUME 19 THE TRUTH ABOUT THE TAO

CONTENTS

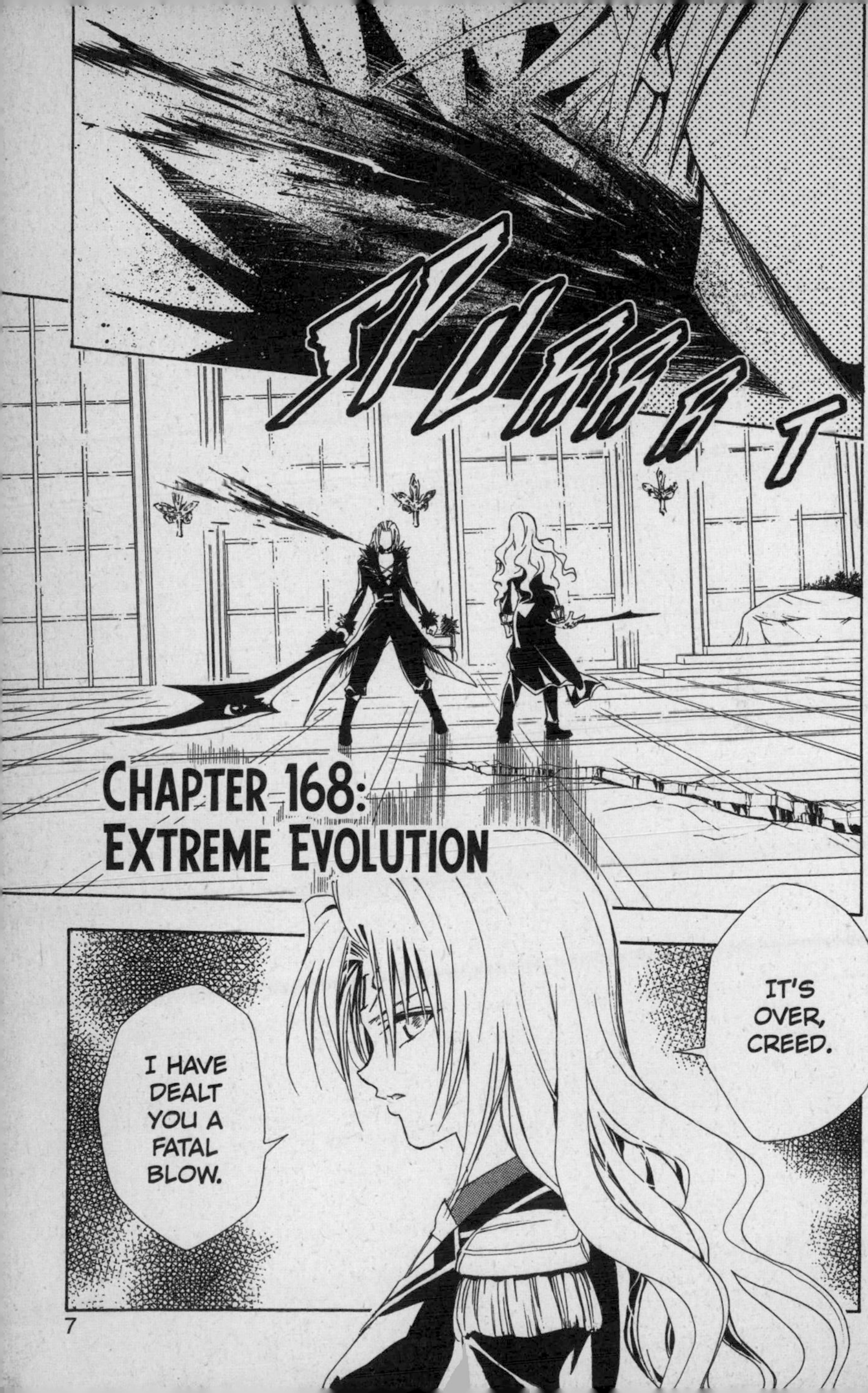
CHAPTER 168: EXTREME EVOLUTION
IT'S OVER, CREED.
I HAVE DEALT YOU A FATAL BLOW.

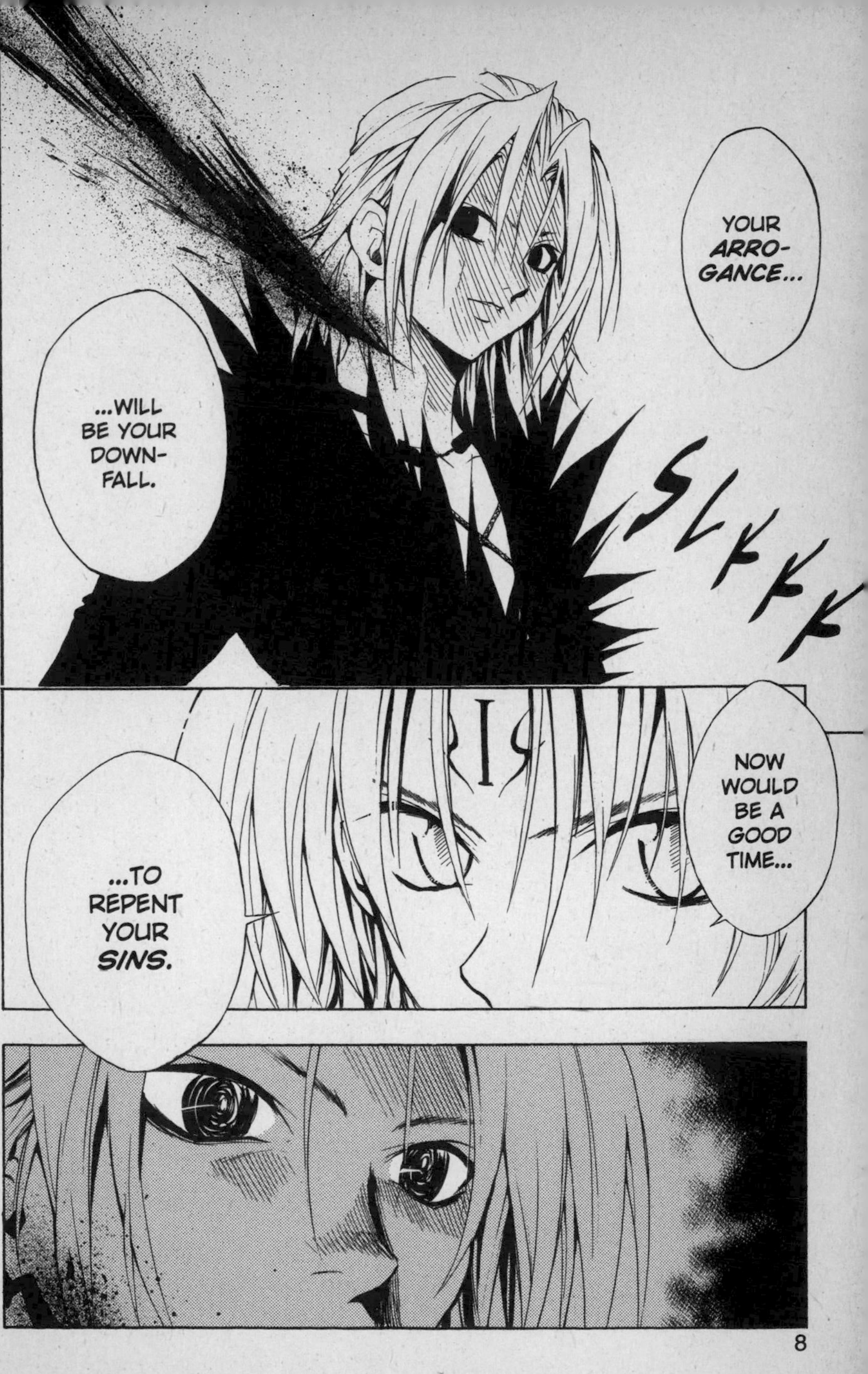
YOUR ARRO-GANCE...
...WILL BE YOUR DOWN-FALL.
SLKKK
NOW WOULD BE A GOOD TIME...
...TO REPENT YOUR SINS.

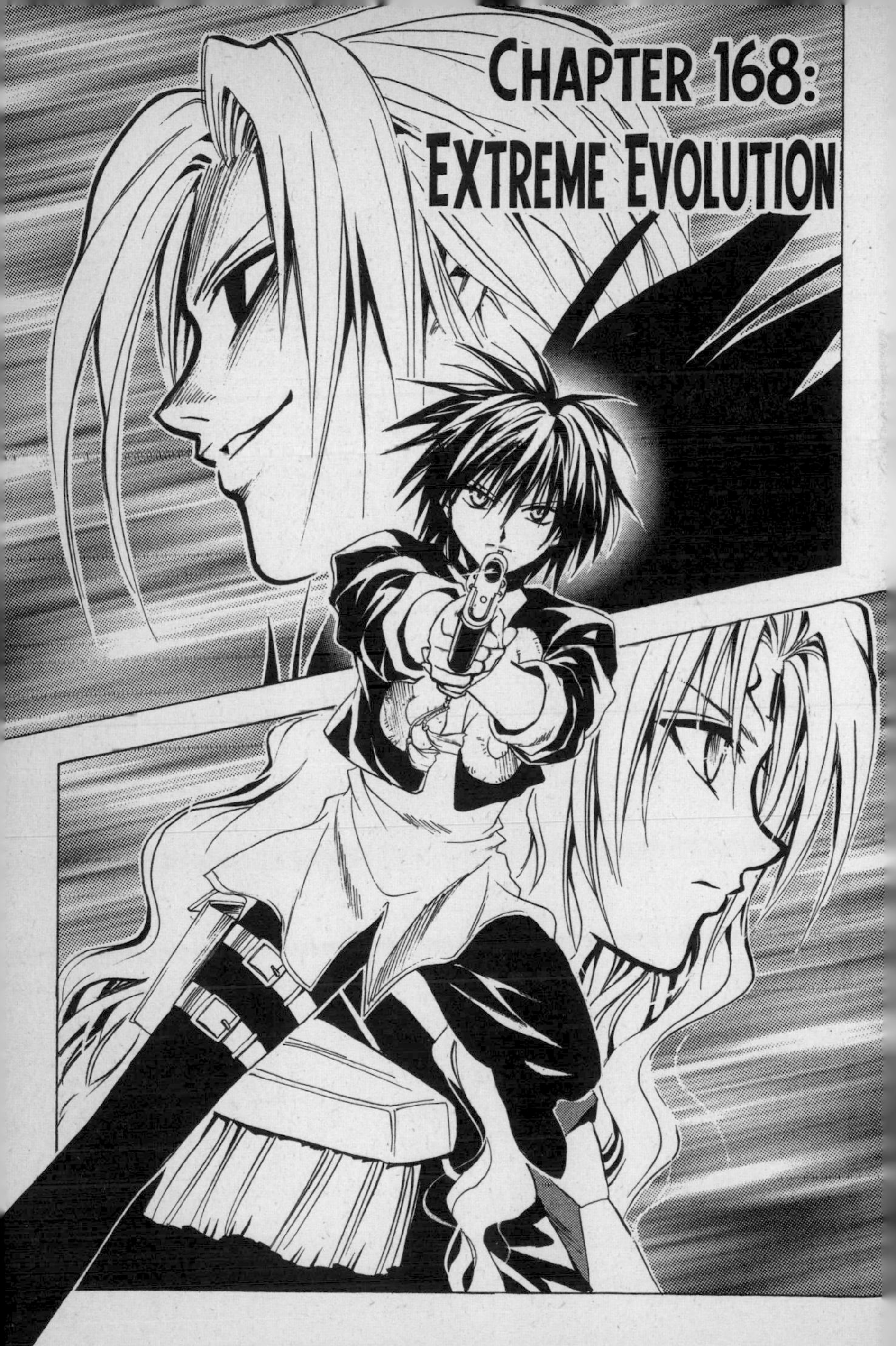
Chapter 168:
Extreme Evolution

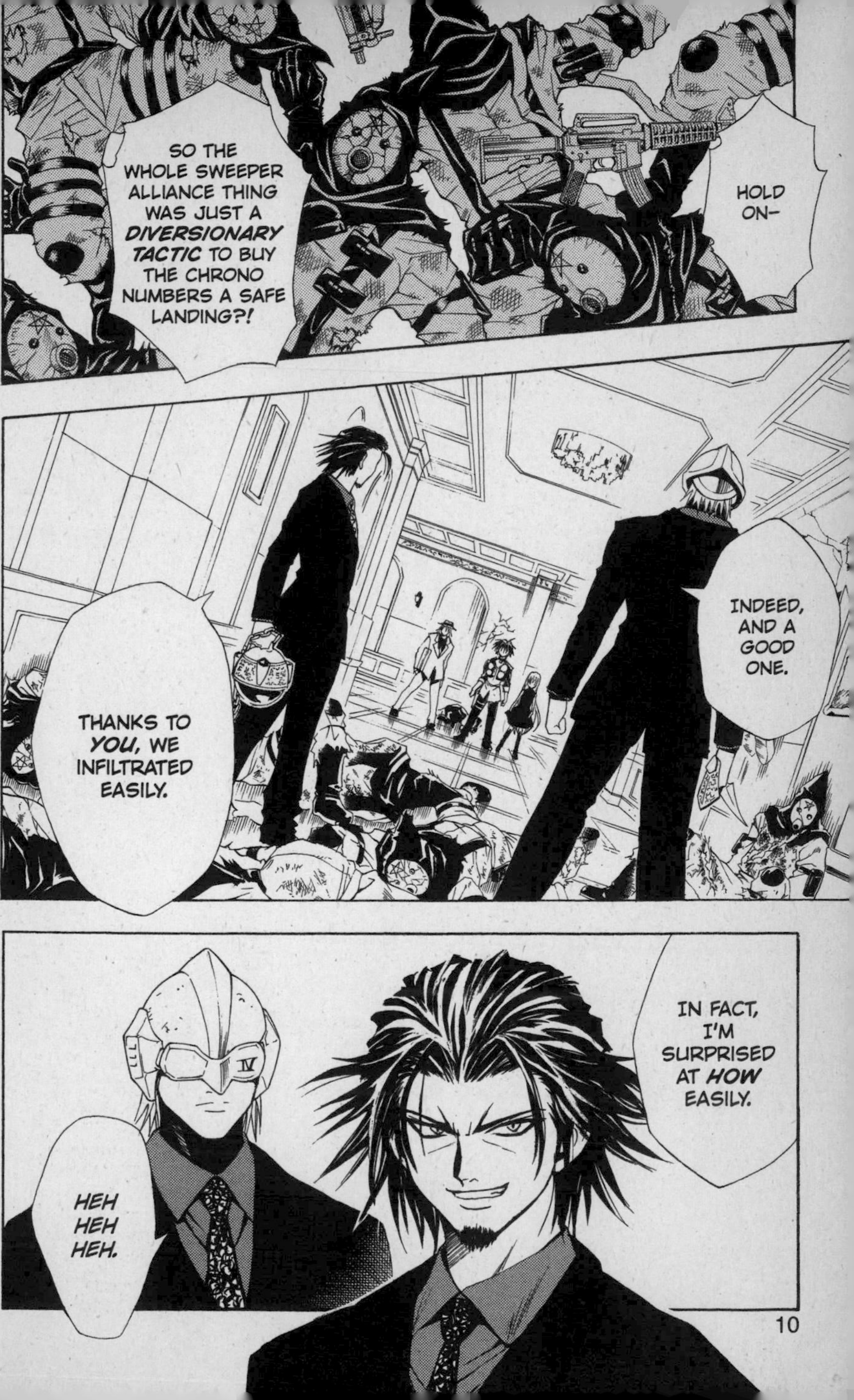
HOLD ON—
SO THE WHOLE SWEEPER ALLIANCE THING WAS JUST A *DIVERSIONARY TACTIC* TO BUY THE CHRONO NUMBERS A SAFE LANDING?!
INDEED, AND A GOOD ONE.
THANKS TO *YOU,* WE INFILTRATED EASILY.
IN FACT, I'M SURPRISED AT *HOW* EASILY.
HEH HEH HEH.

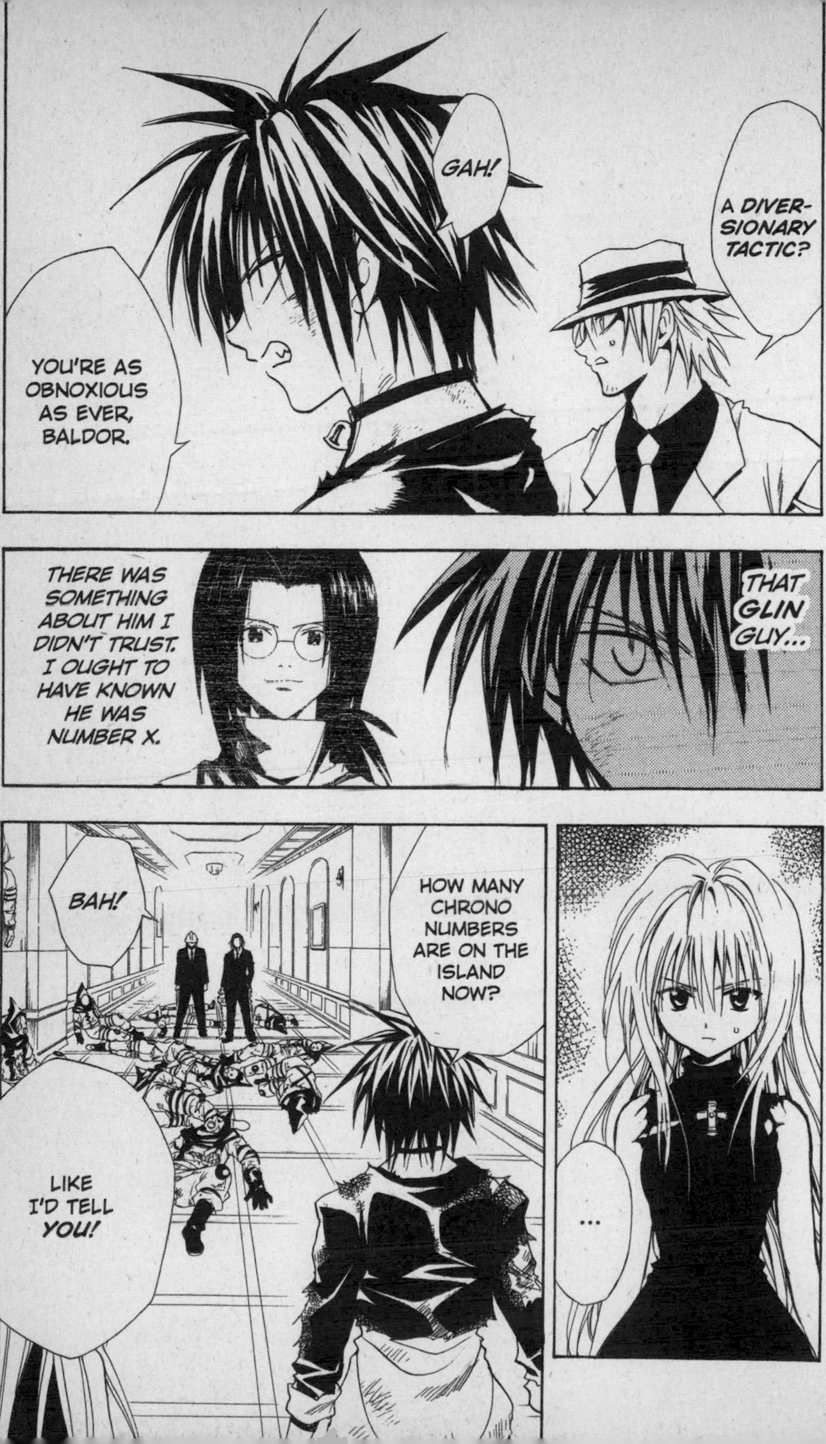
A DIVERSIONARY TACTIC?
GAH!
YOU'RE AS OBNOXIOUS AS EVER, BALDOR.
THAT GLIN GUY...
THERE WAS SOMETHING ABOUT HIM I DIDN'T TRUST. I OUGHT TO HAVE KNOWN HE WAS NUMBER X.
...
HOW MANY CHRONO NUMBERS ARE ON THE ISLAND NOW?
BAH!
LIKE I'D TELL YOU!

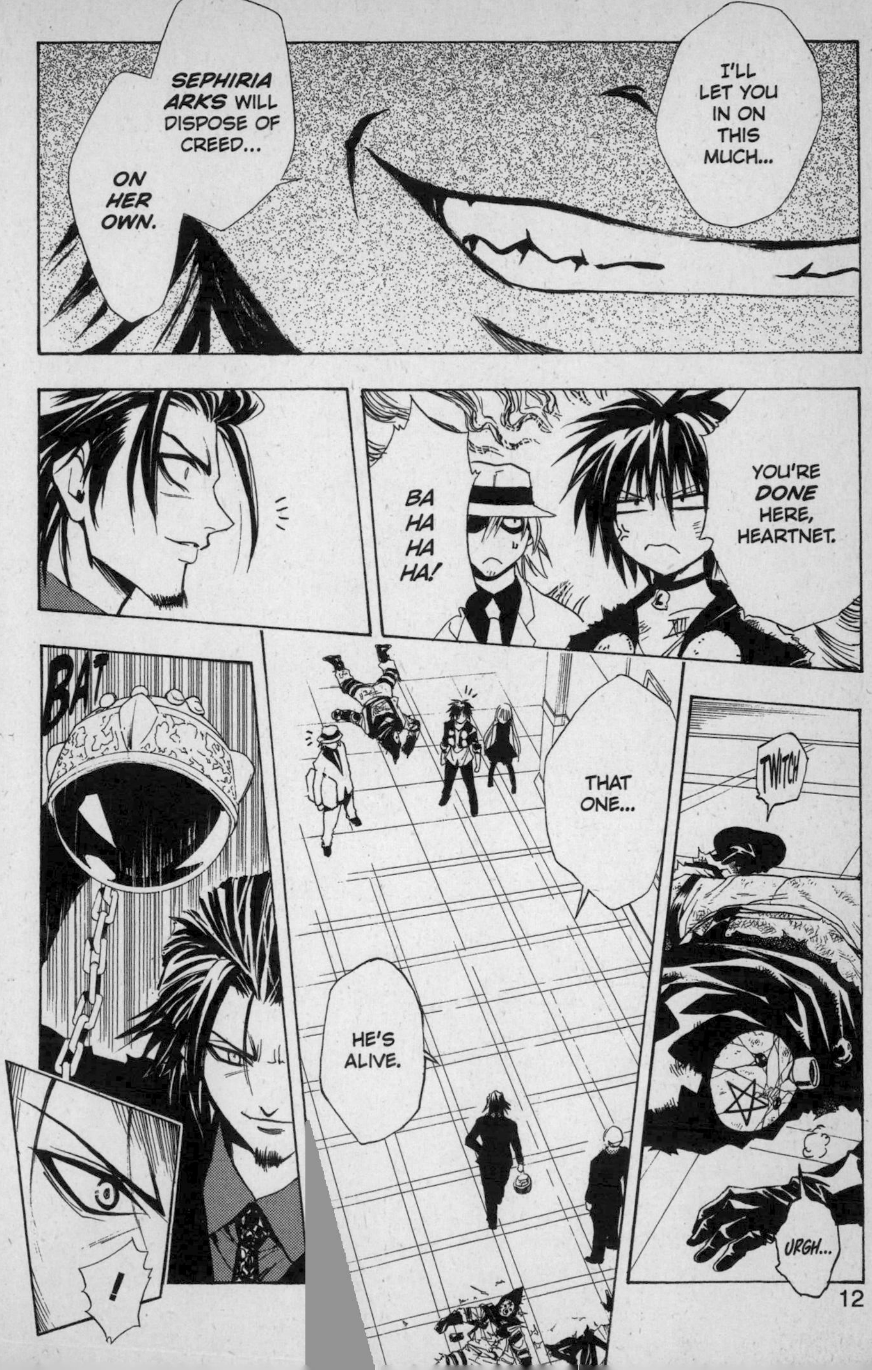
I'LL LET YOU IN ON THIS MUCH...
SEPHIRIA ARKS WILL DISPOSE OF CREED...
ON HER OWN.
YOU'RE DONE HERE, HEARTNET.
BA HA HA HA!
TWITCH
URGH...
THAT ONE...
HE'S ALIVE.
BAT
!

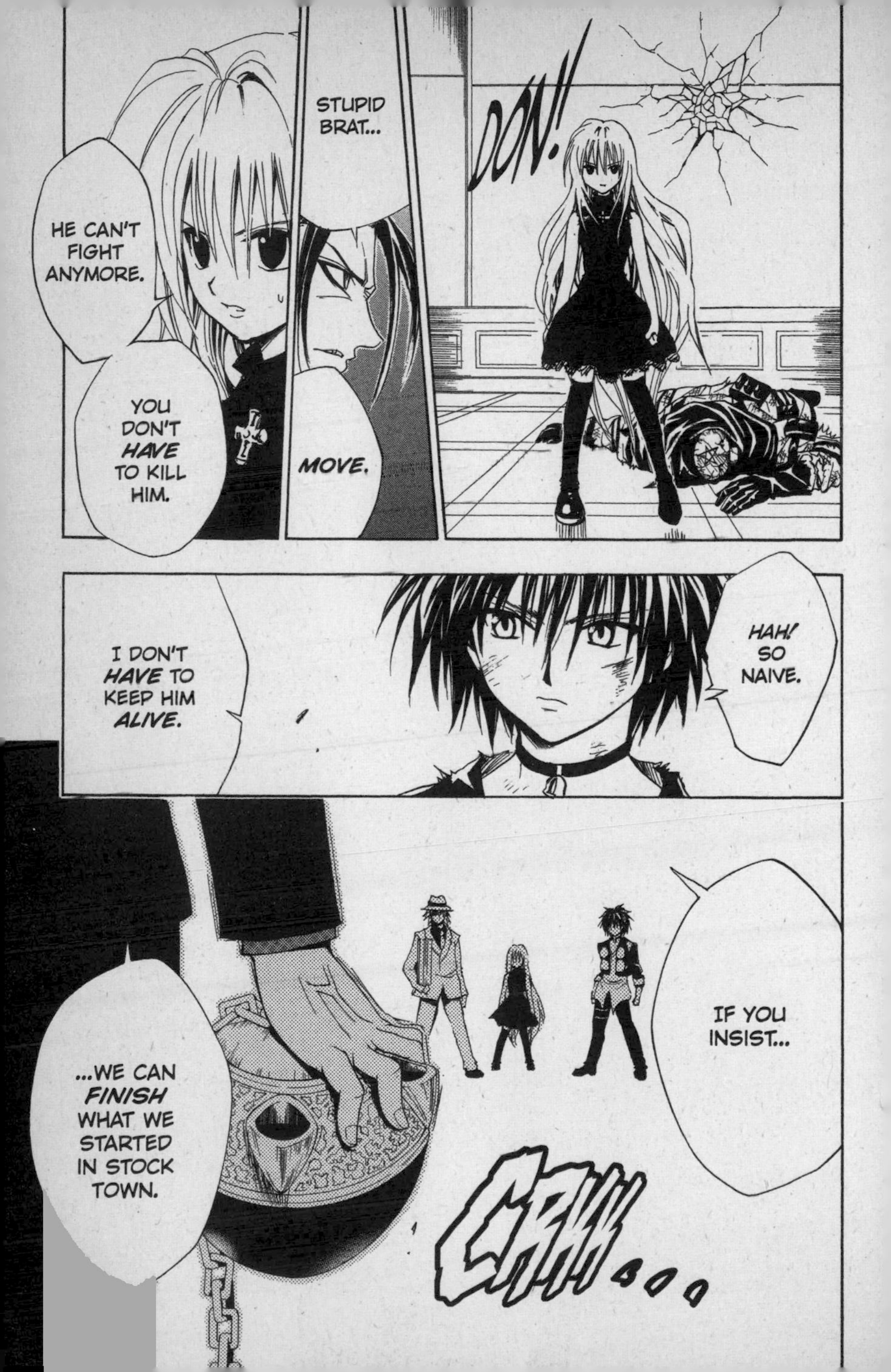
DON!
STUPID BRAT...
MOVE.
HE CAN'T FIGHT ANYMORE.
YOU DON'T *HAVE* TO KILL HIM.
HAH! SO NAIVE.
I DON'T *HAVE* TO KEEP HIM *ALIVE.*
IF YOU INSIST...
...WE CAN *FINISH* WHAT WE STARTED IN STOCK TOWN.

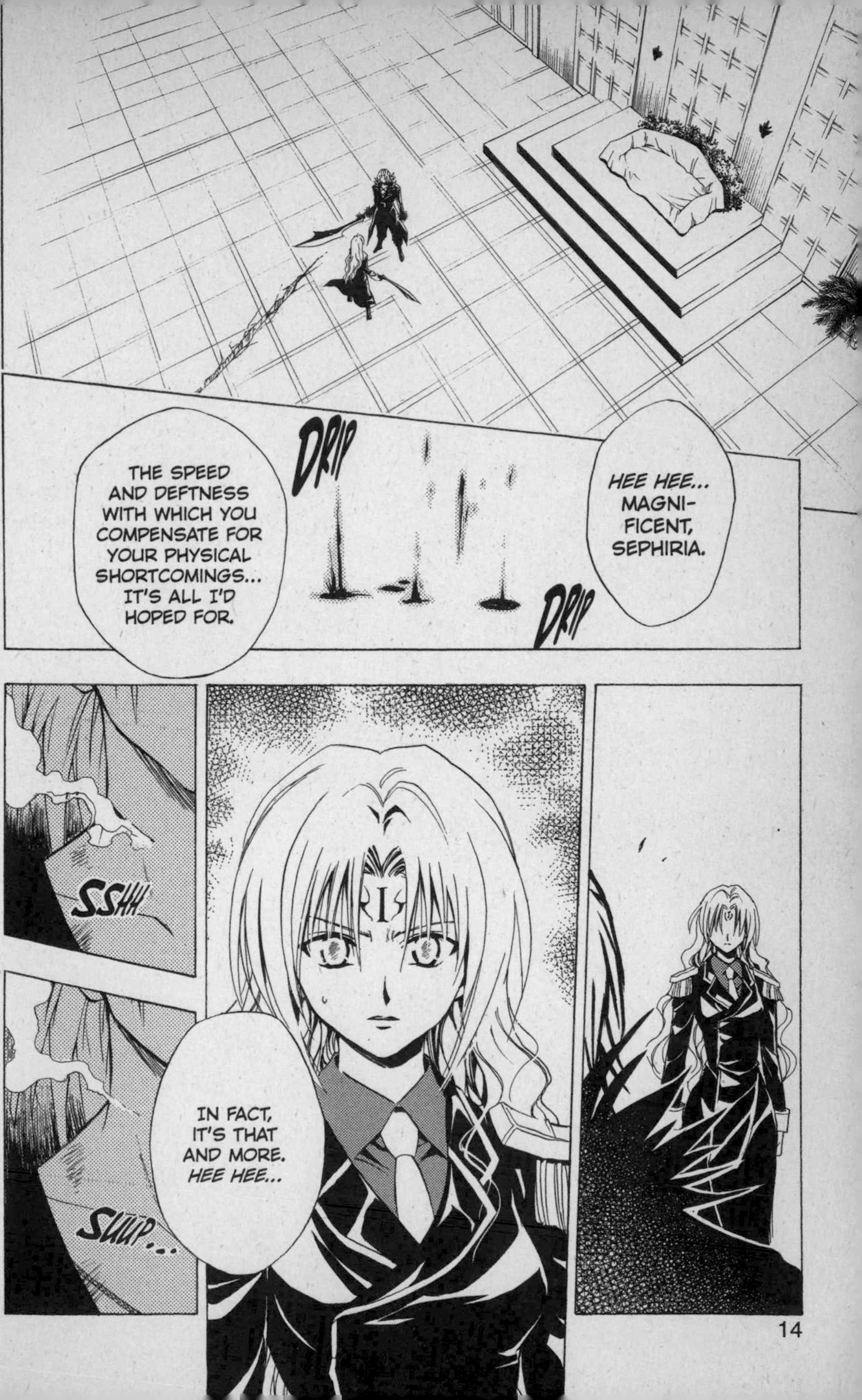
HEE HEE... MAGNIFICENT, SEPHIRIA.
DRIP
DRIP
THE SPEED AND DEFTNESS WITH WHICH YOU COMPENSATE FOR YOUR PHYSICAL SHORTCOMINGS... IT'S ALL I'D HOPED FOR.
IN FACT, IT'S THAT AND MORE. HEE HEE...
SSHH
SLUP...

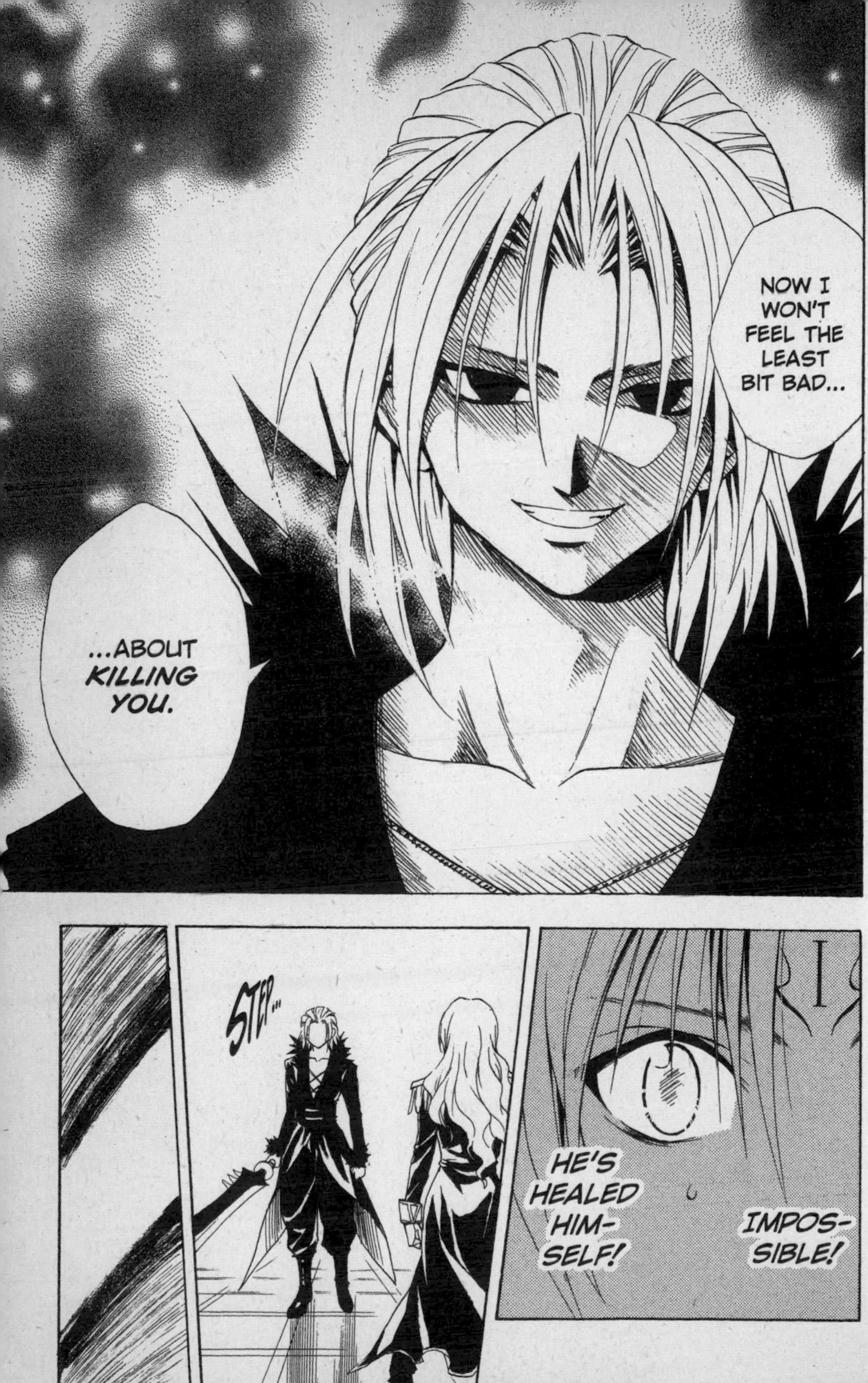
NOW I WON'T FEEL THE LEAST BIT BAD...
...ABOUT KILLING YOU.
IMPOS-SIBLE!
HE'S HEALED HIM-SELF!
STEP...

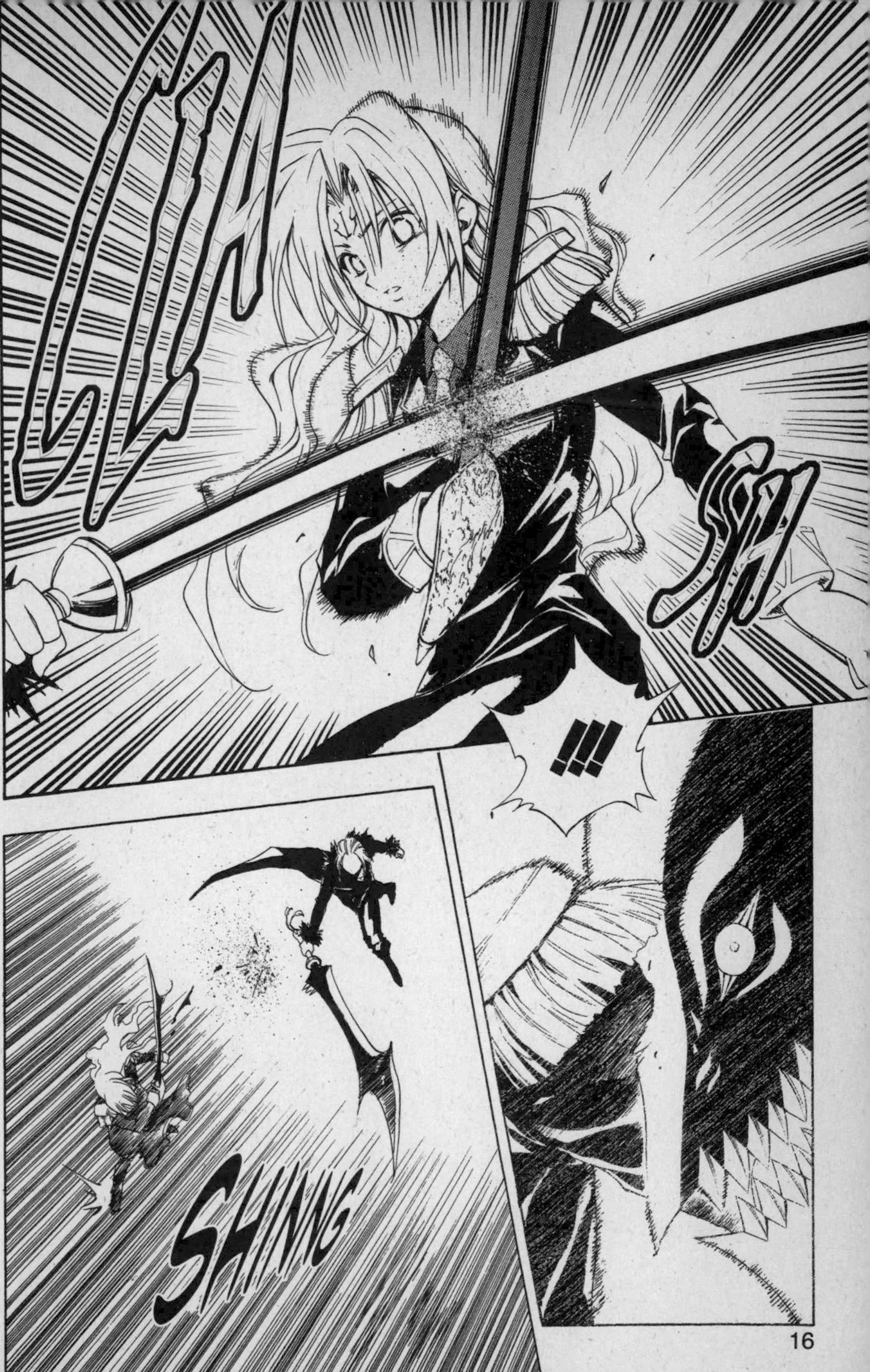
CLA
SH
!!!
SHING

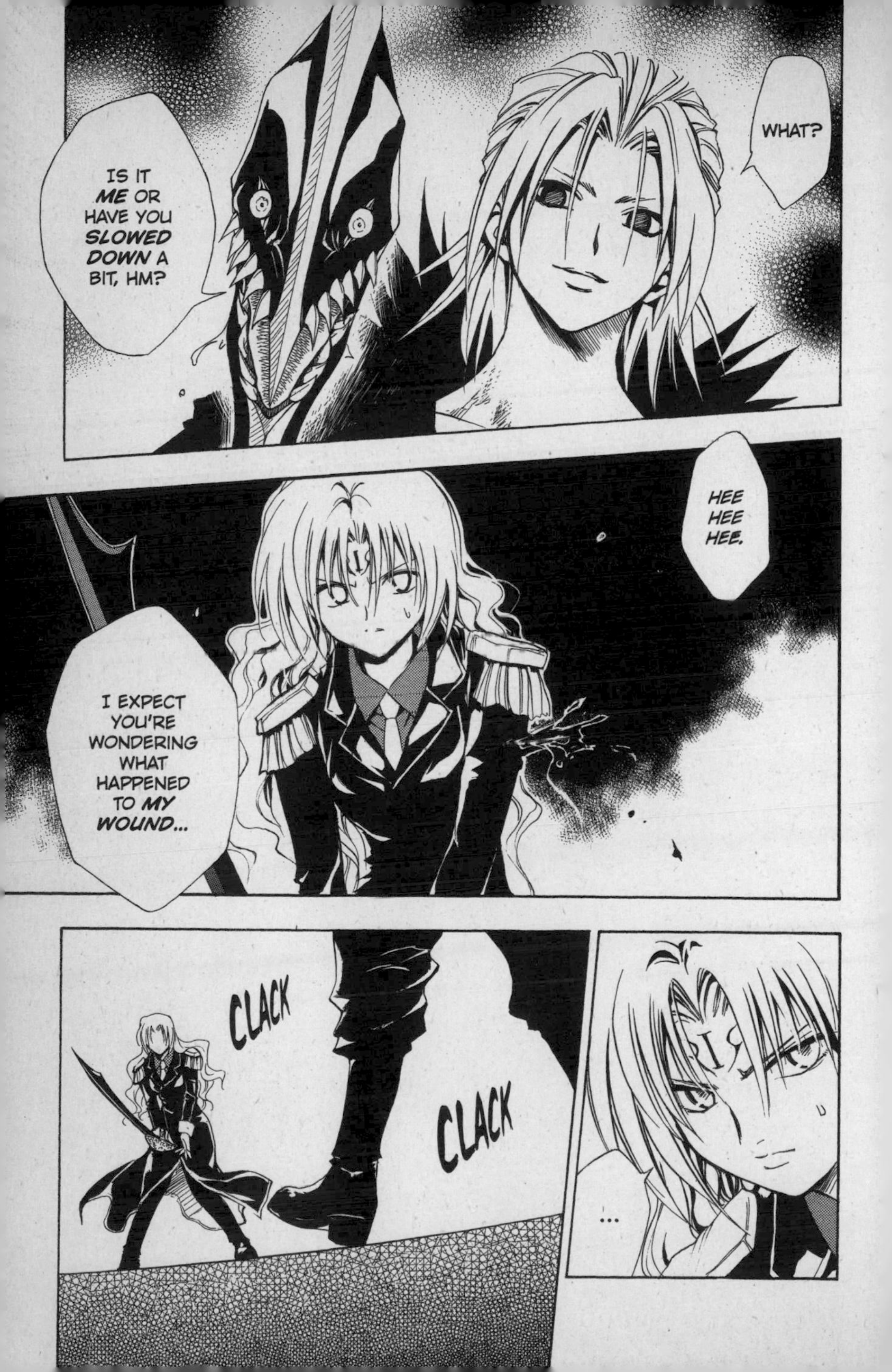
WHAT?
IS IT ME OR HAVE YOU SLOWED DOWN A BIT, HM?
HEE HEE HEE.
I EXPECT YOU'RE WONDERING WHAT HAPPENED TO MY WOUND...
...
CLACK
CLACK

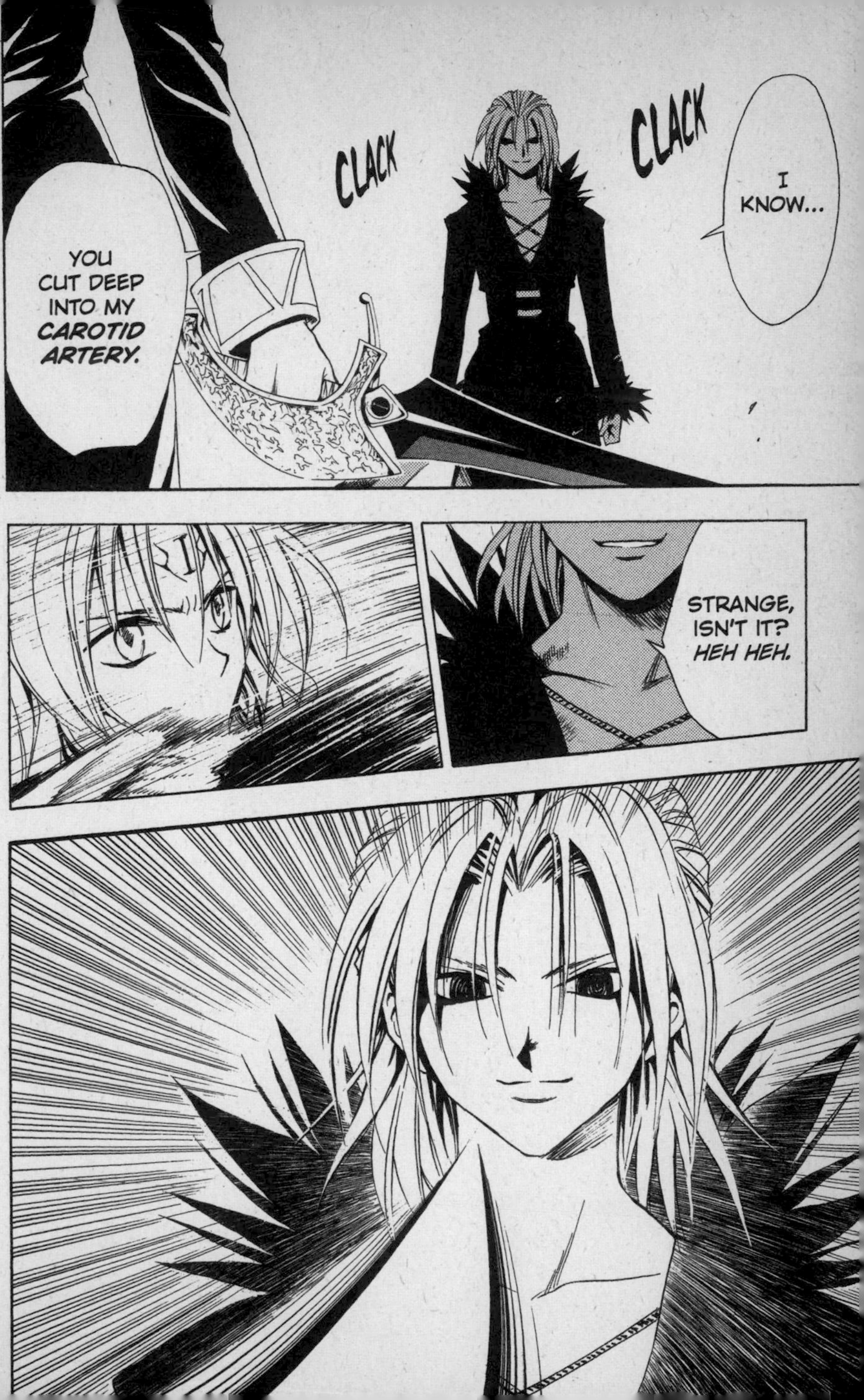
I KNOW...
CLACK
CLACK
YOU CUT DEEP INTO MY *CAROTID ARTERY.*
STRANGE, ISN'T IT? *HEH HEH.*

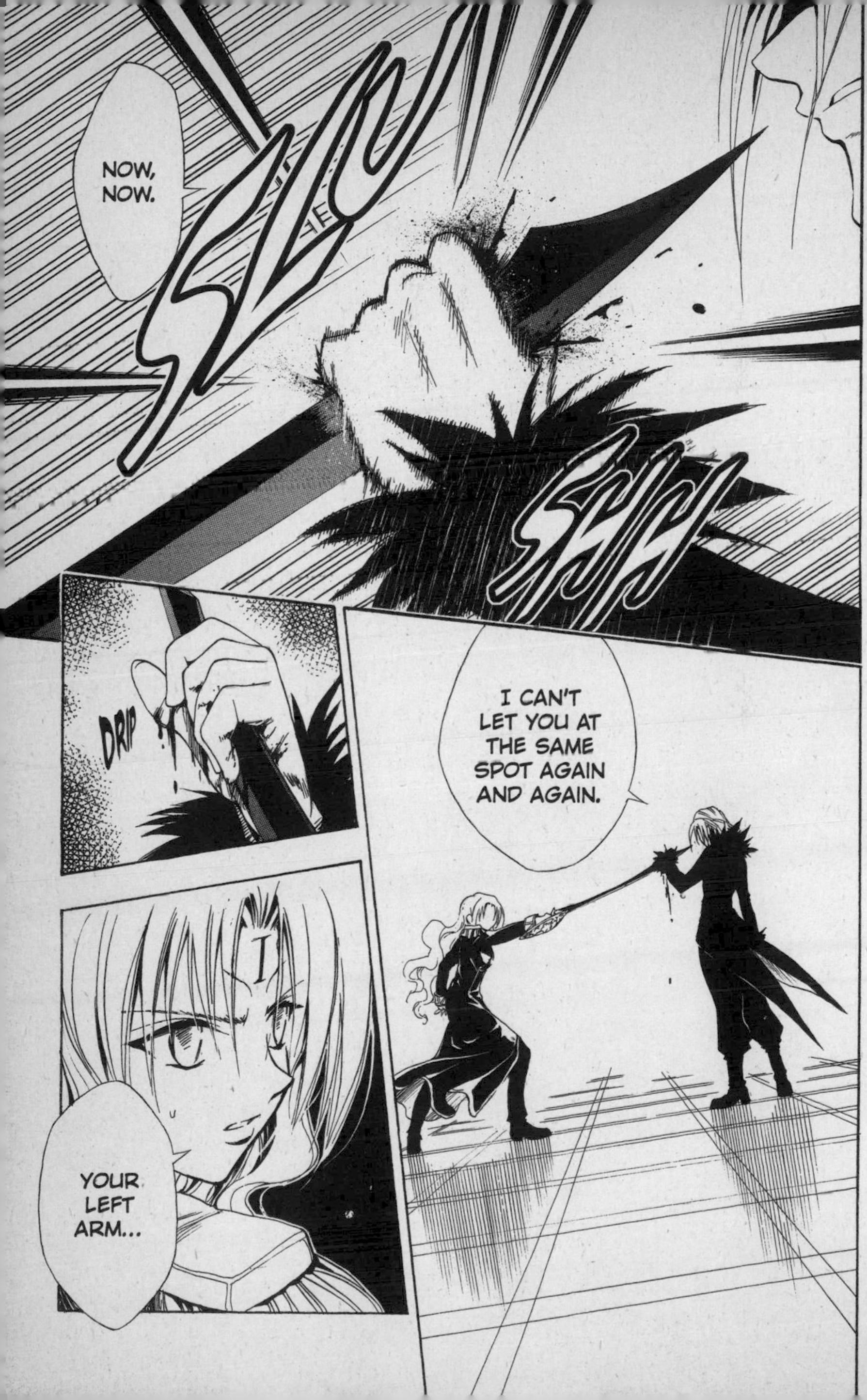
NOW, NOW.
I CAN'T LET YOU AT THE SAME SPOT AGAIN AND AGAIN.
DRIP
YOUR LEFT ARM...

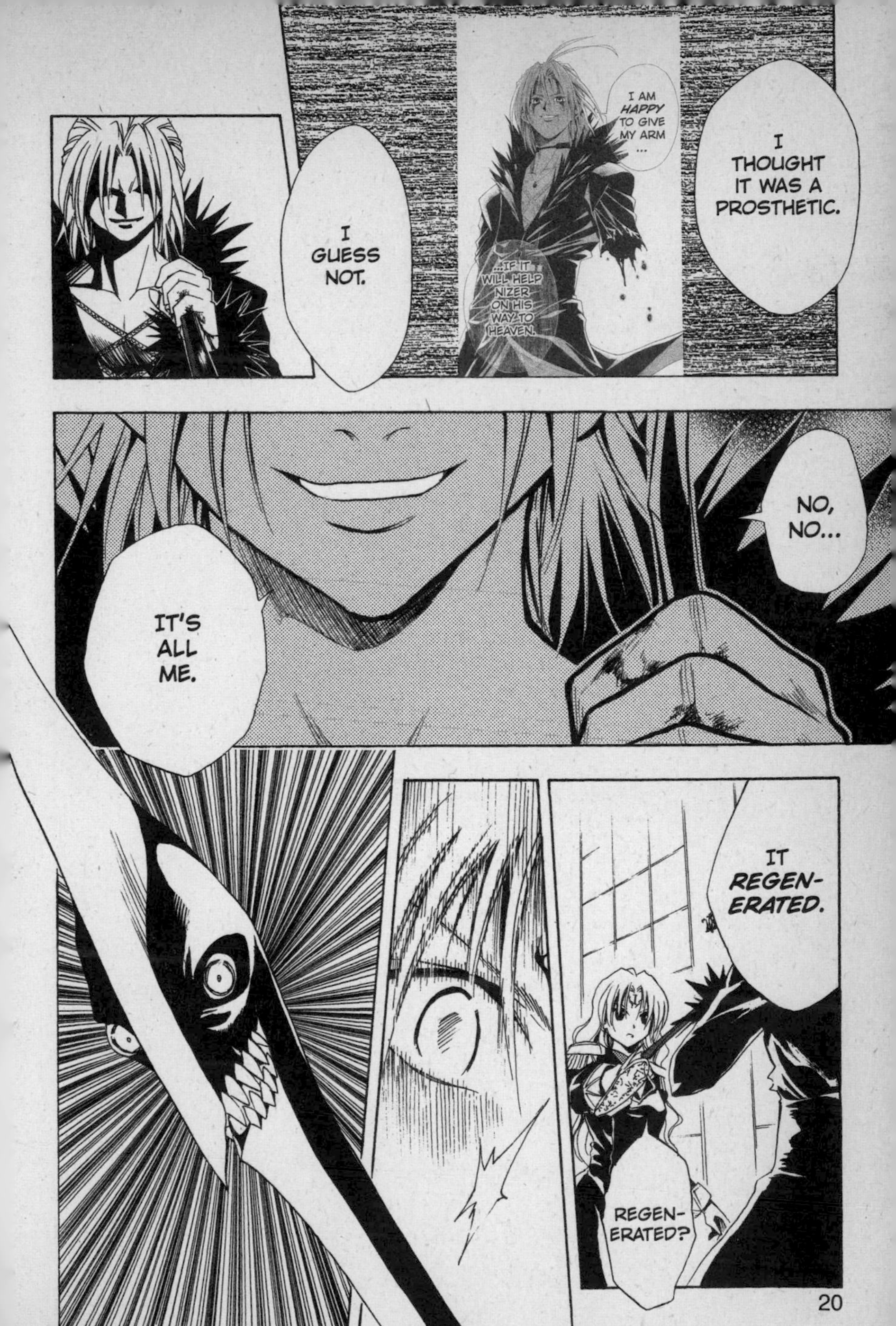

I THOUGHT IT WAS A PROSTHETIC.
I AM *HAPPY* TO GIVE MY ARM ...
...IF IT WILL HELP NIZER ON HIS WAY TO HEAVEN.
I GUESS NOT.
NO, NO...
IT'S ALL ME.
IT *REGENERATED.*
REGENERATED?

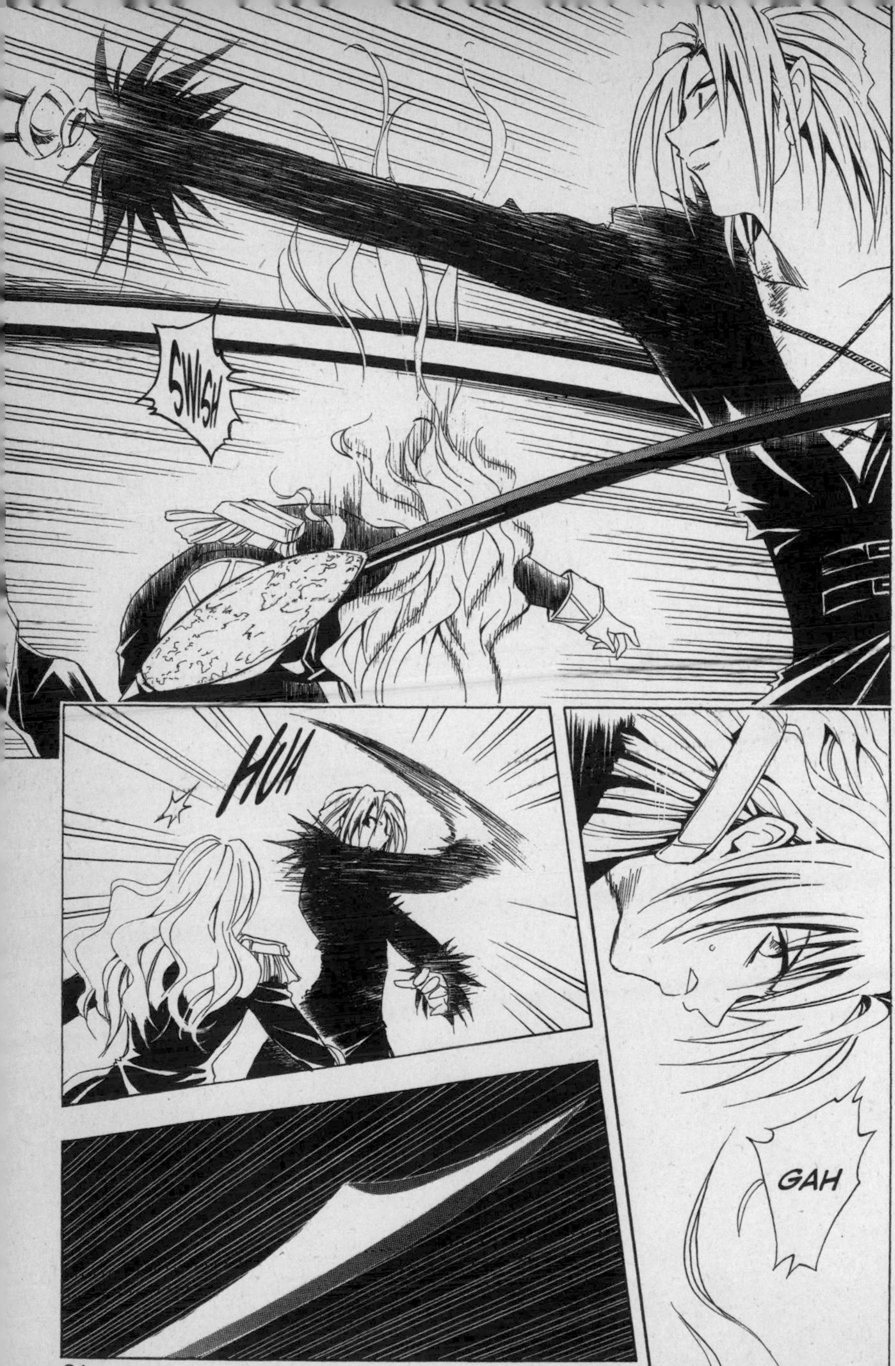
SWISH
GAH
HUA

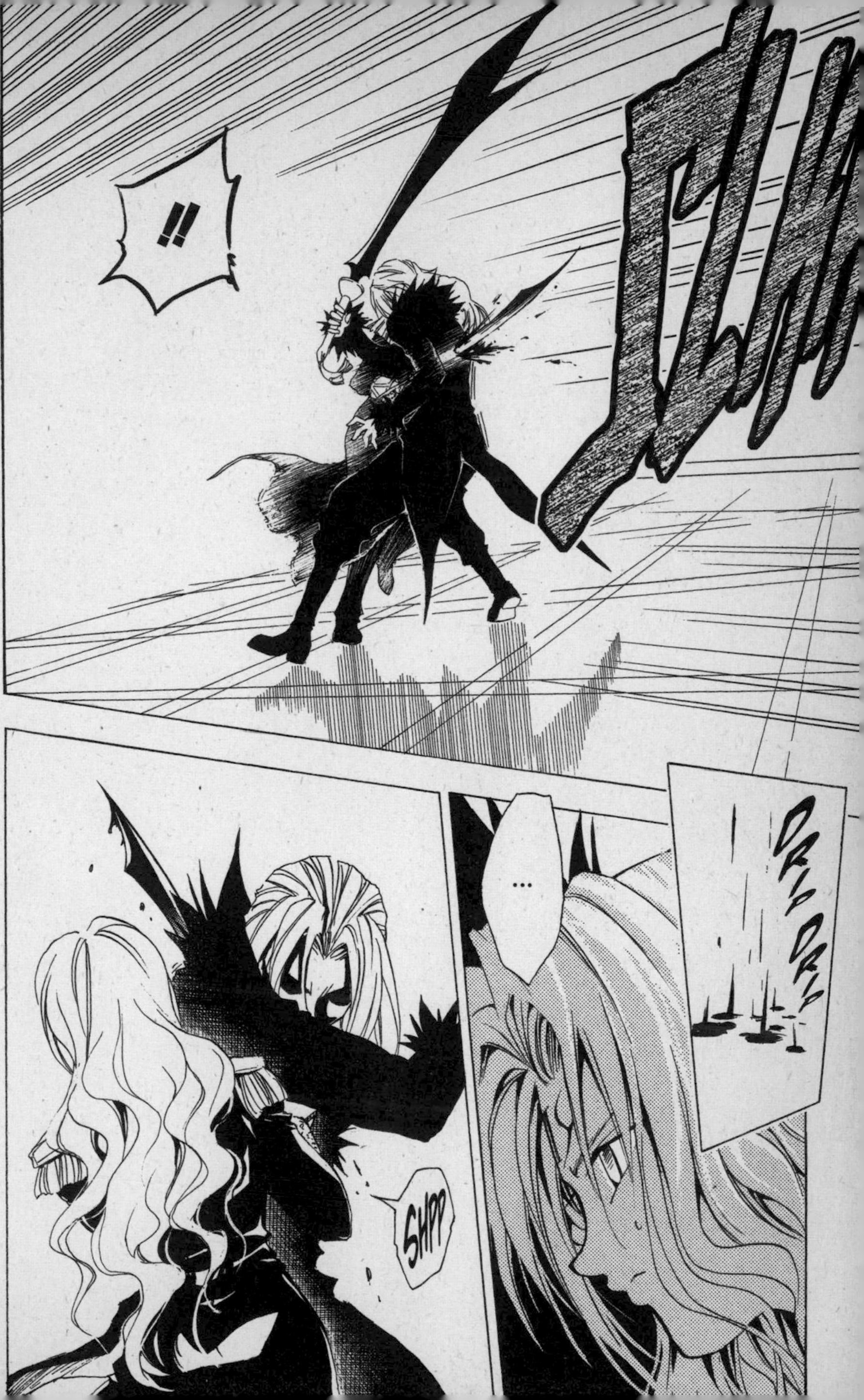
!!
DRIP DRIP
...
SHPP

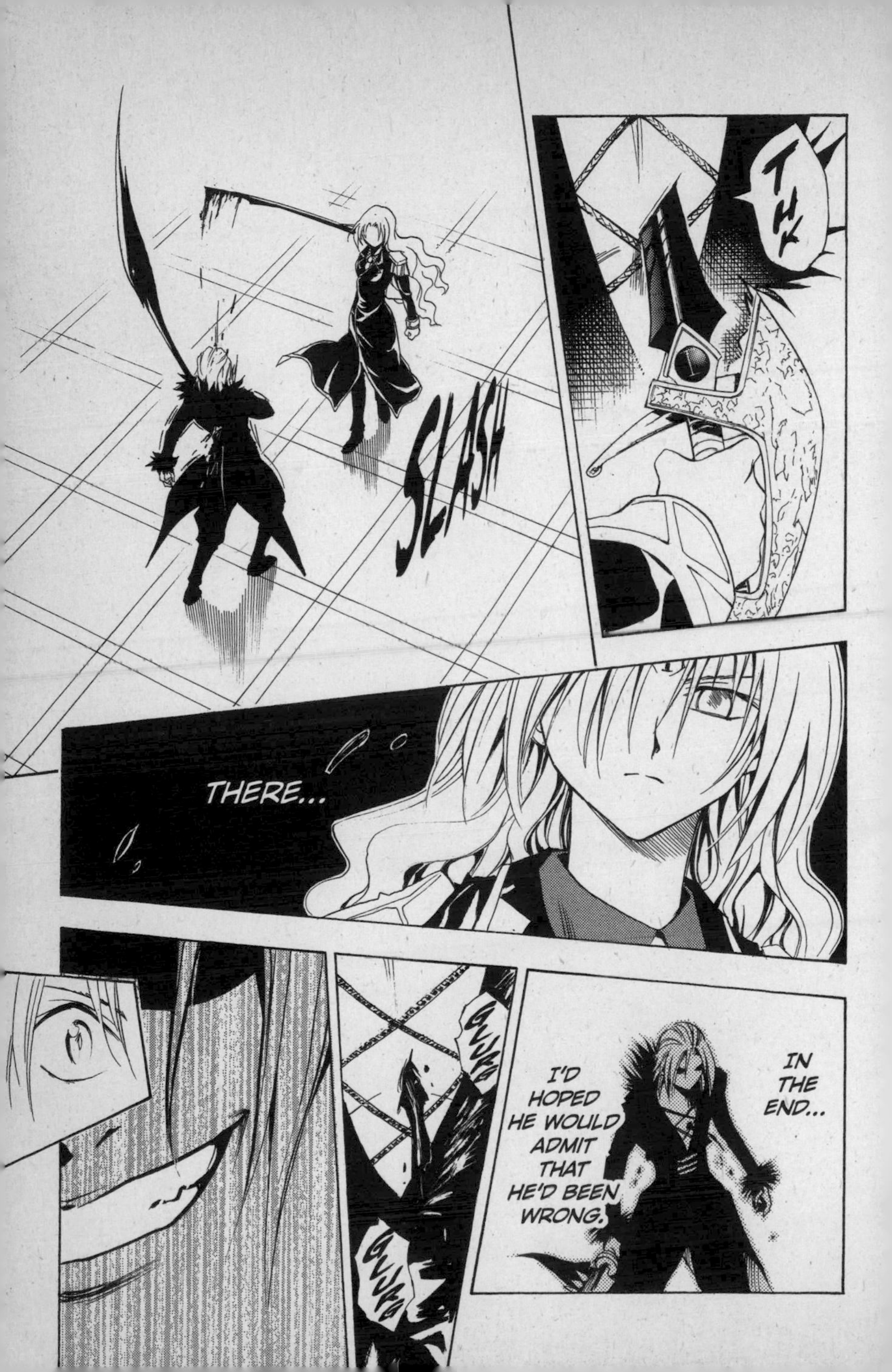
THK
SLASH
THERE...
IN THE END...
I'D HOPED HE WOULD ADMIT THAT HE'D BEEN WRONG.
GLURG
GLURG

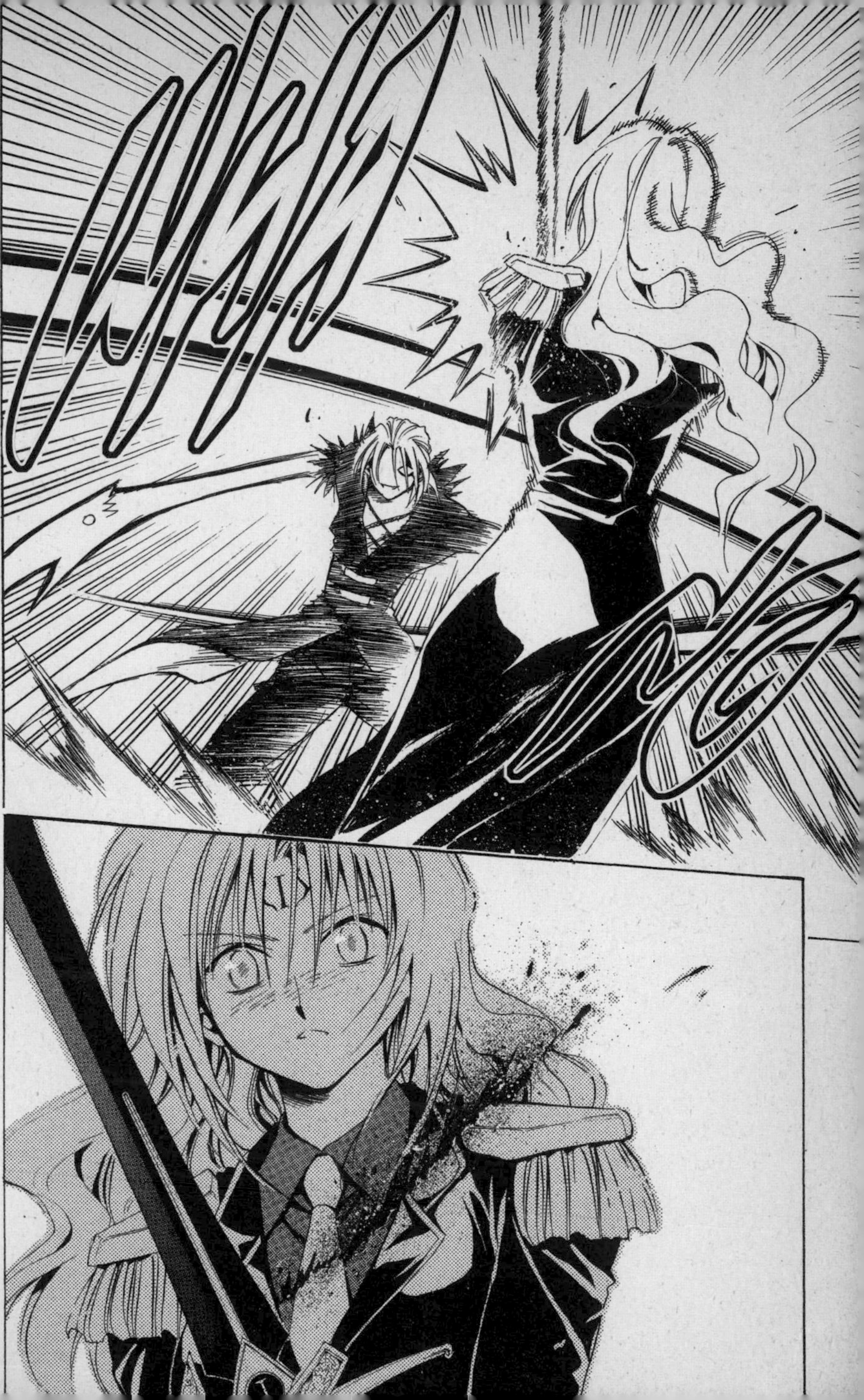

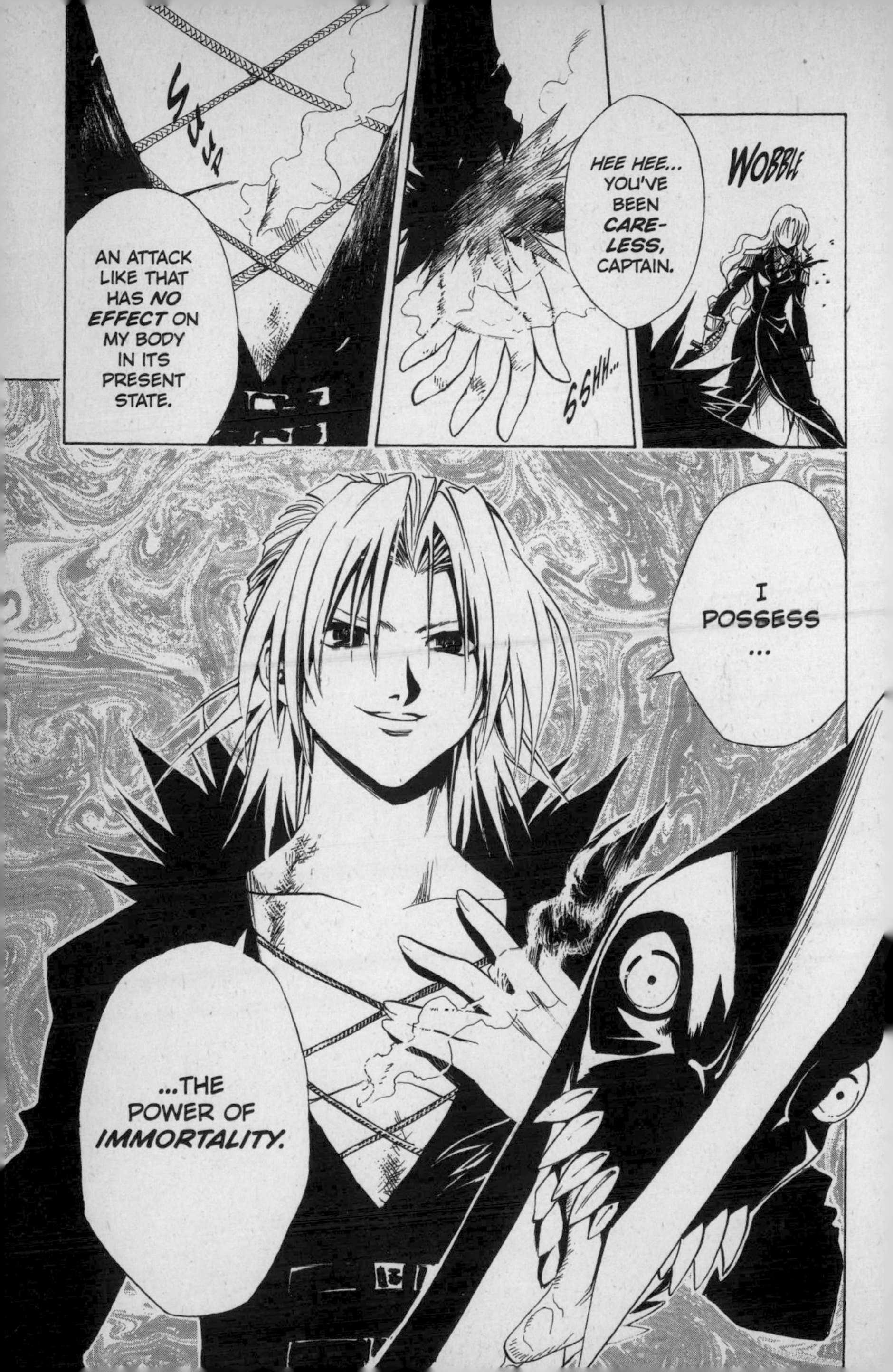
WOBBLE
HEE HEE... YOU'VE BEEN CARELESS, CAPTAIN.
SSHH...
AN ATTACK LIKE THAT HAS NO EFFECT ON MY BODY IN ITS PRESENT STATE.
I POSSESS ...
...THE POWER OF IMMORTALITY.

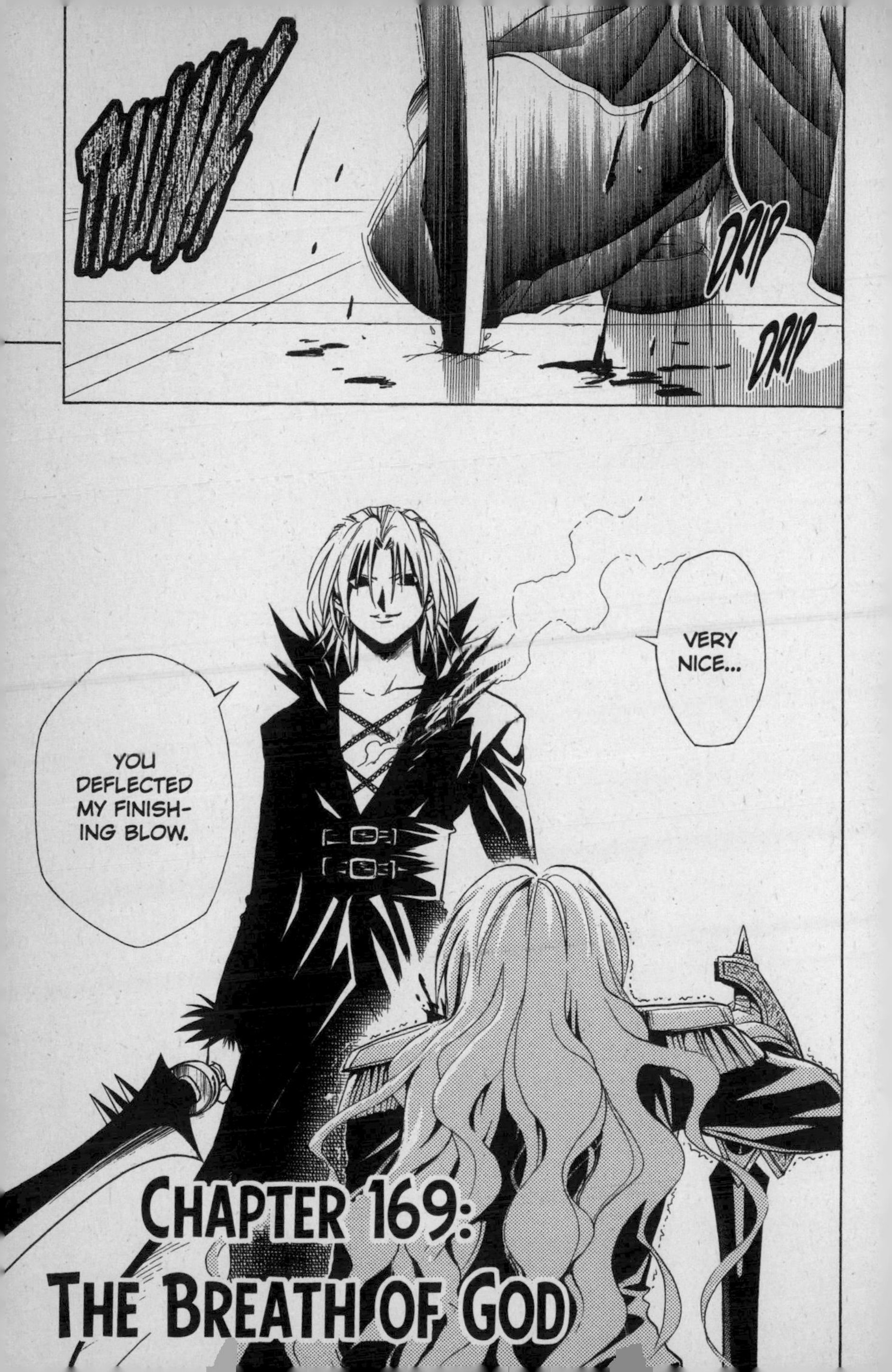
THUNK!
DRIP
DRIP
VERY NICE...
YOU DEFLECTED MY FINISHING-ING BLOW.
Chapter 169:
The Breath of God

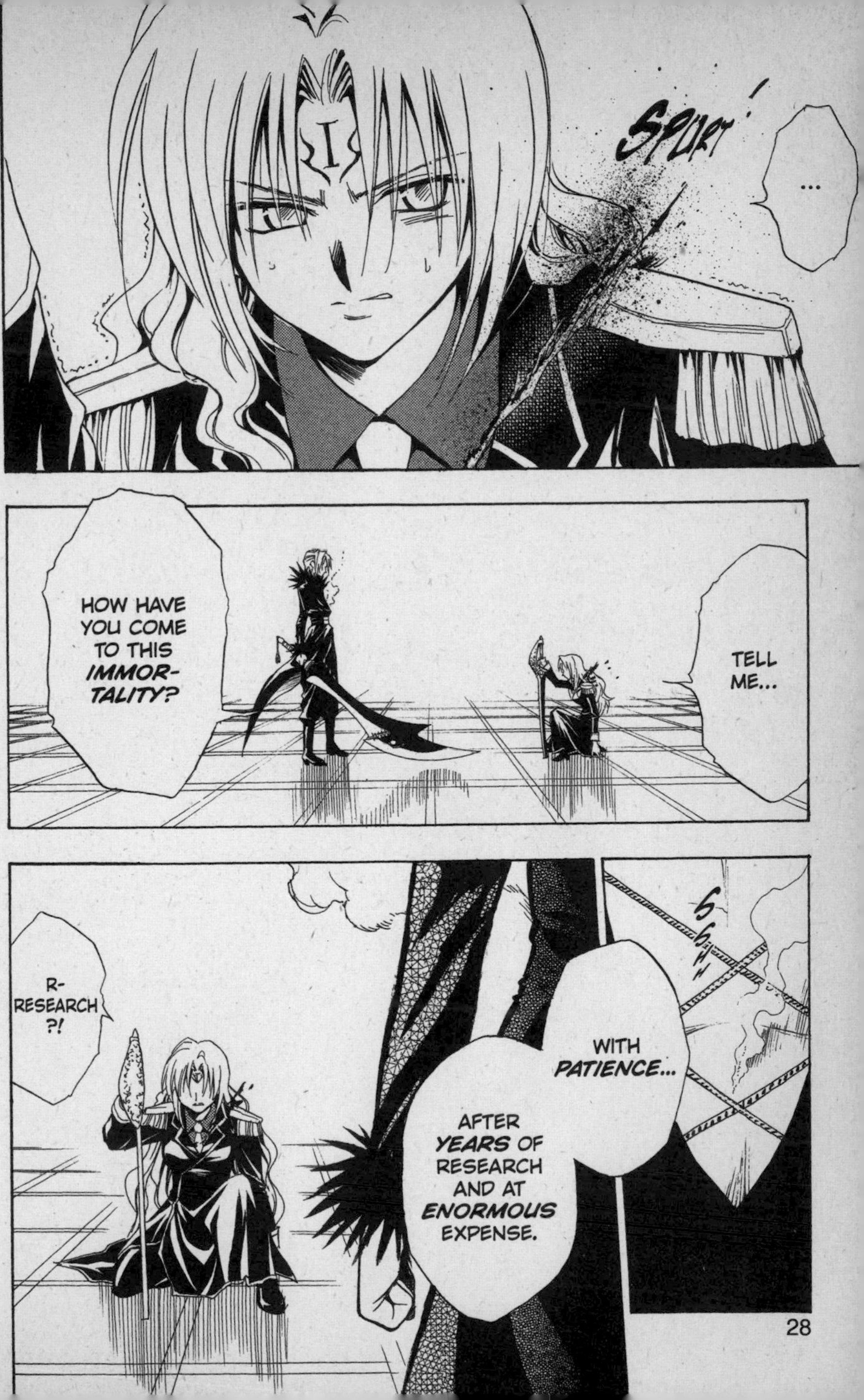
SPURT
...
TELL ME...
HOW HAVE YOU COME TO THIS IMMORTALITY?
WITH PATIENCE...
AFTER YEARS OF RESEARCH AND AT ENORMOUS EXPENSE.
R-RESEARCH?!

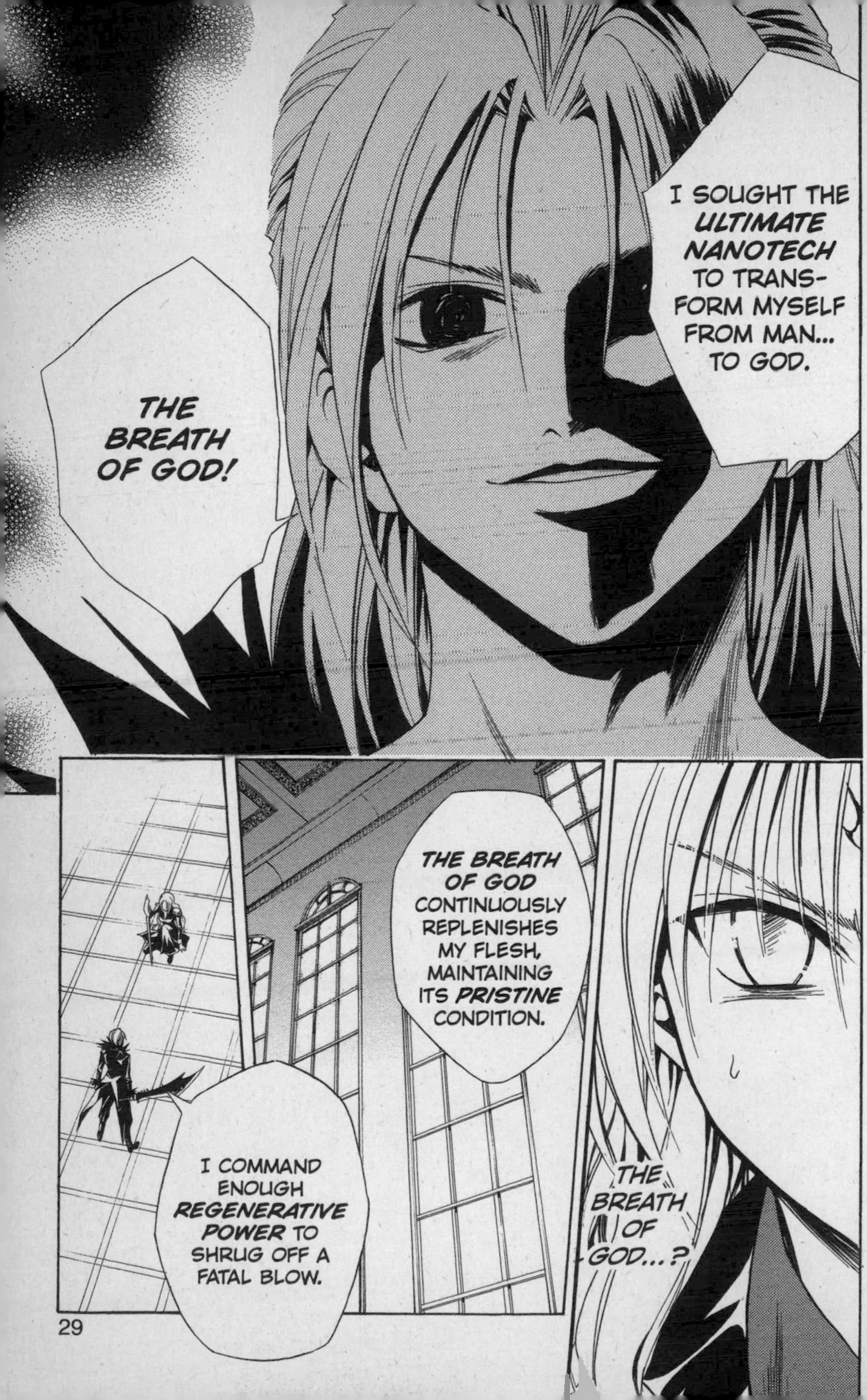
I SOUGHT THE ULTIMATE NANOTECH TO TRANS-FORM MYSELF FROM MAN... TO GOD.
THE BREATH OF GOD!
THE BREATH OF GOD...?
THE BREATH OF GOD CONTINUOUSLY REPLENISHES MY FLESH, MAINTAINING ITS PRISTINE CONDITION.
I COMMAND ENOUGH REGENERATIVE POWER TO SHRUG OFF A FATAL BLOW.

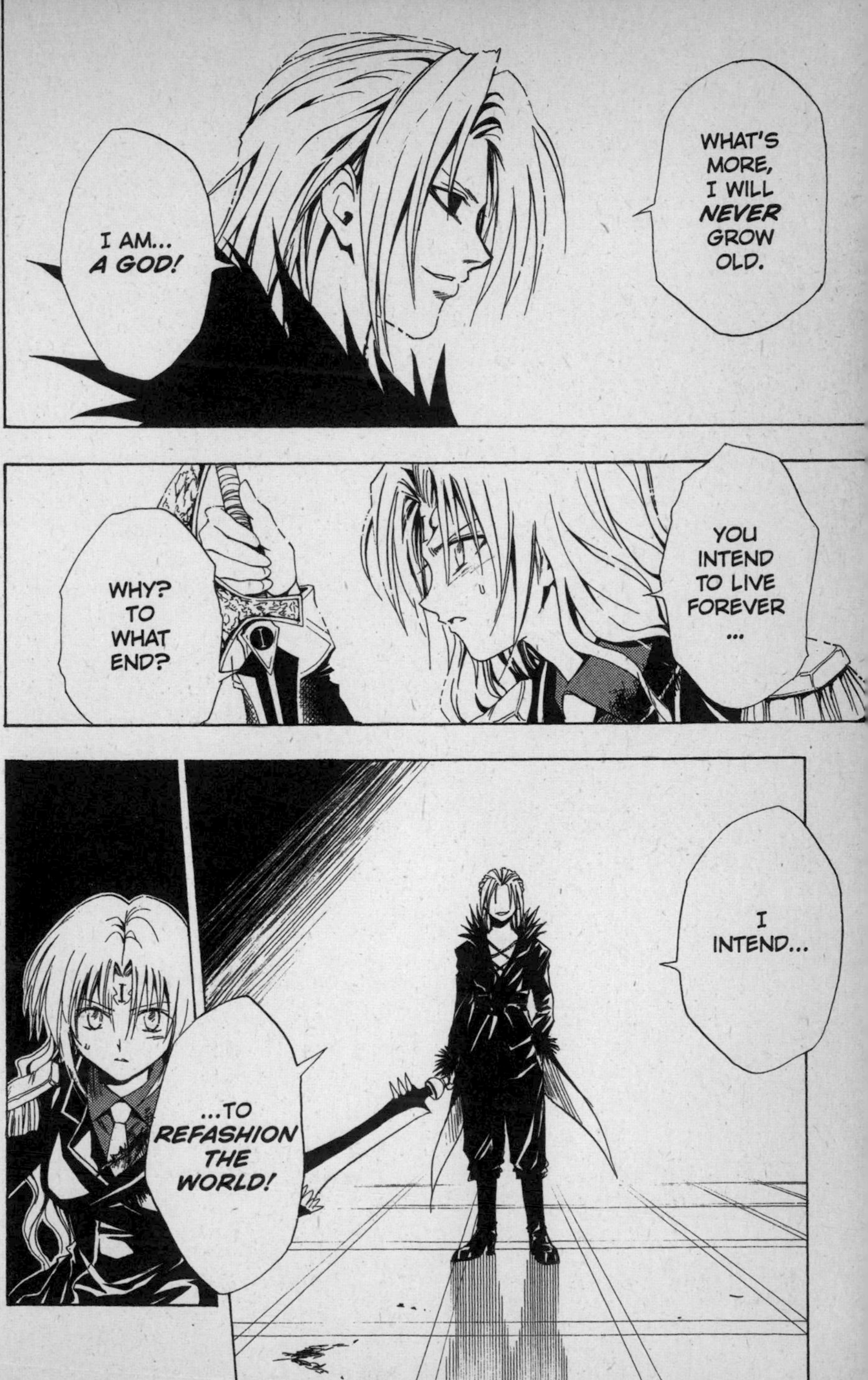

WHAT'S MORE, I WILL *NEVER* GROW OLD.
I AM... *A GOD!*
YOU INTEND TO LIVE FOREVER ...
WHY? TO WHAT END?
I INTEND...
...TO *REFASHION THE WORLD!*

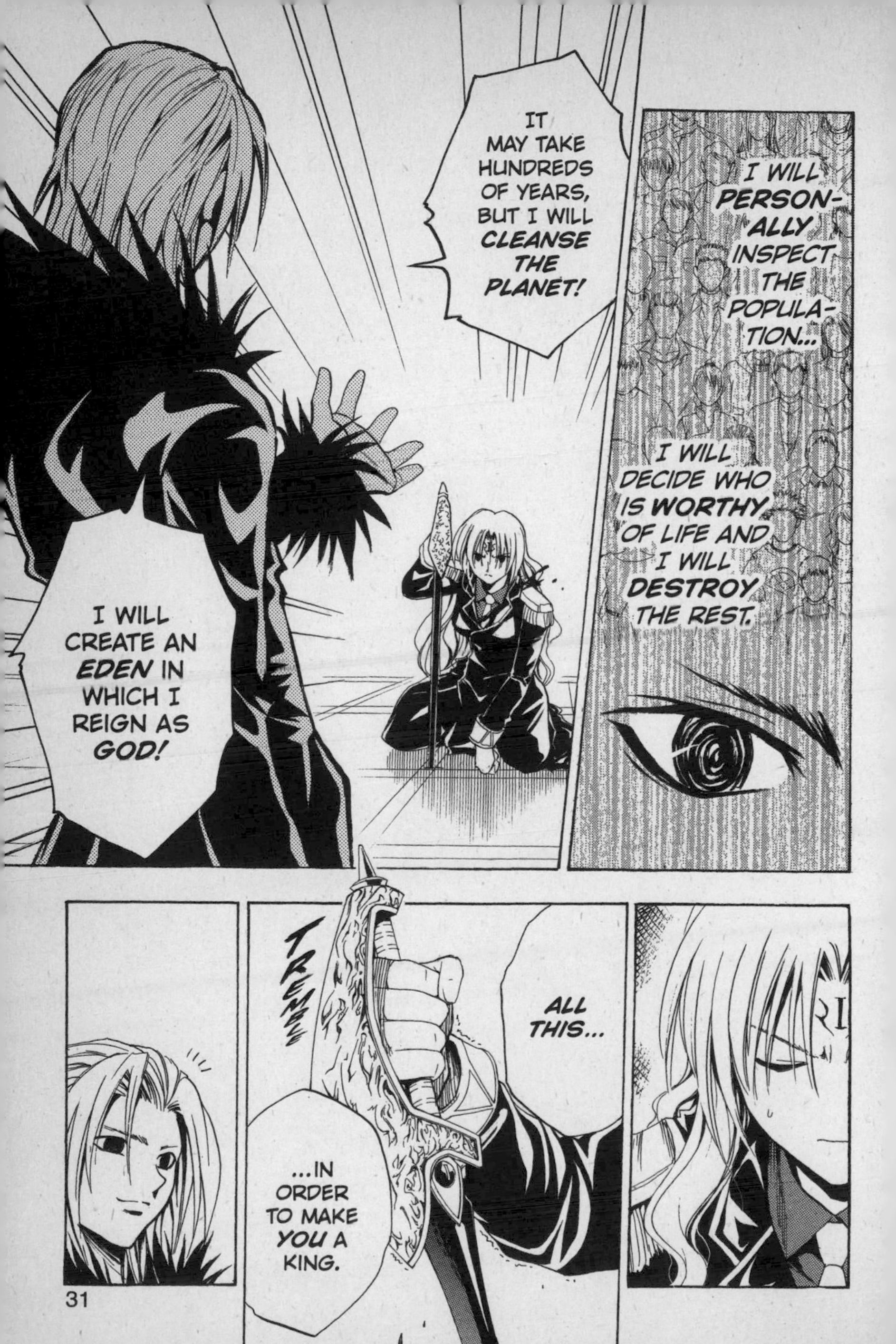
I WILL PERSON-ALLY INSPECT THE POPULA-TION...
I WILL DECIDE WHO IS WORTHY OF LIFE AND I WILL DESTROY THE REST.
IT MAY TAKE HUNDREDS OF YEARS, BUT I WILL CLEANSE THE PLANET!
I WILL CREATE AN EDEN IN WHICH I REIGN AS GOD!
ALL THIS...
TREMBLE
...IN ORDER TO MAKE YOU A KING.

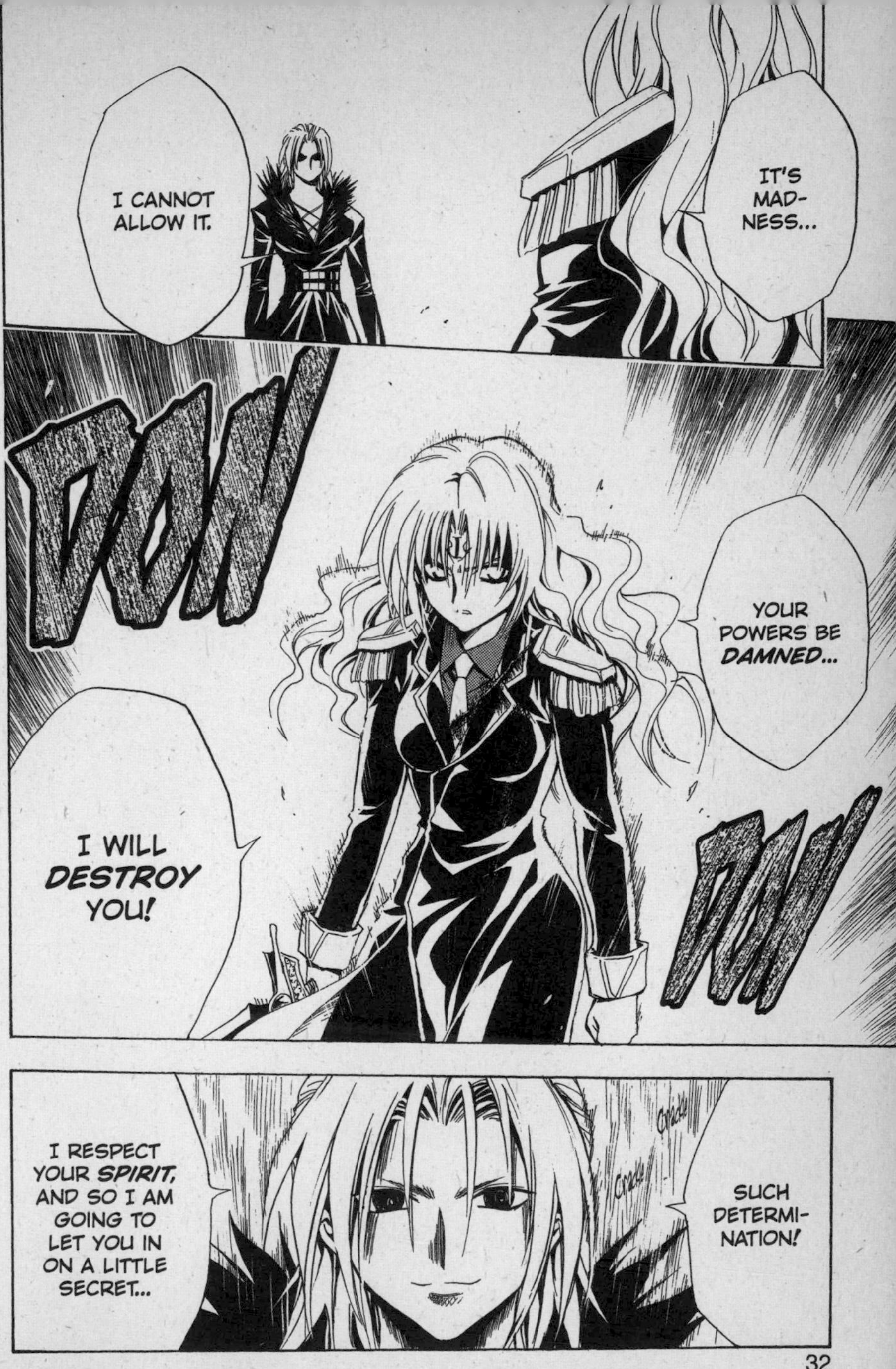
IT'S MADNESS...
I CANNOT ALLOW IT.
DON
YOUR POWERS BE *DAMNED*...
DON
I WILL *DESTROY* YOU!
Crack
Crack
SUCH DETERMINATION!
I RESPECT YOUR *SPIRIT*, AND SO I AM GOING TO LET YOU IN ON A LITTLE SECRET...

READ THIS WAY

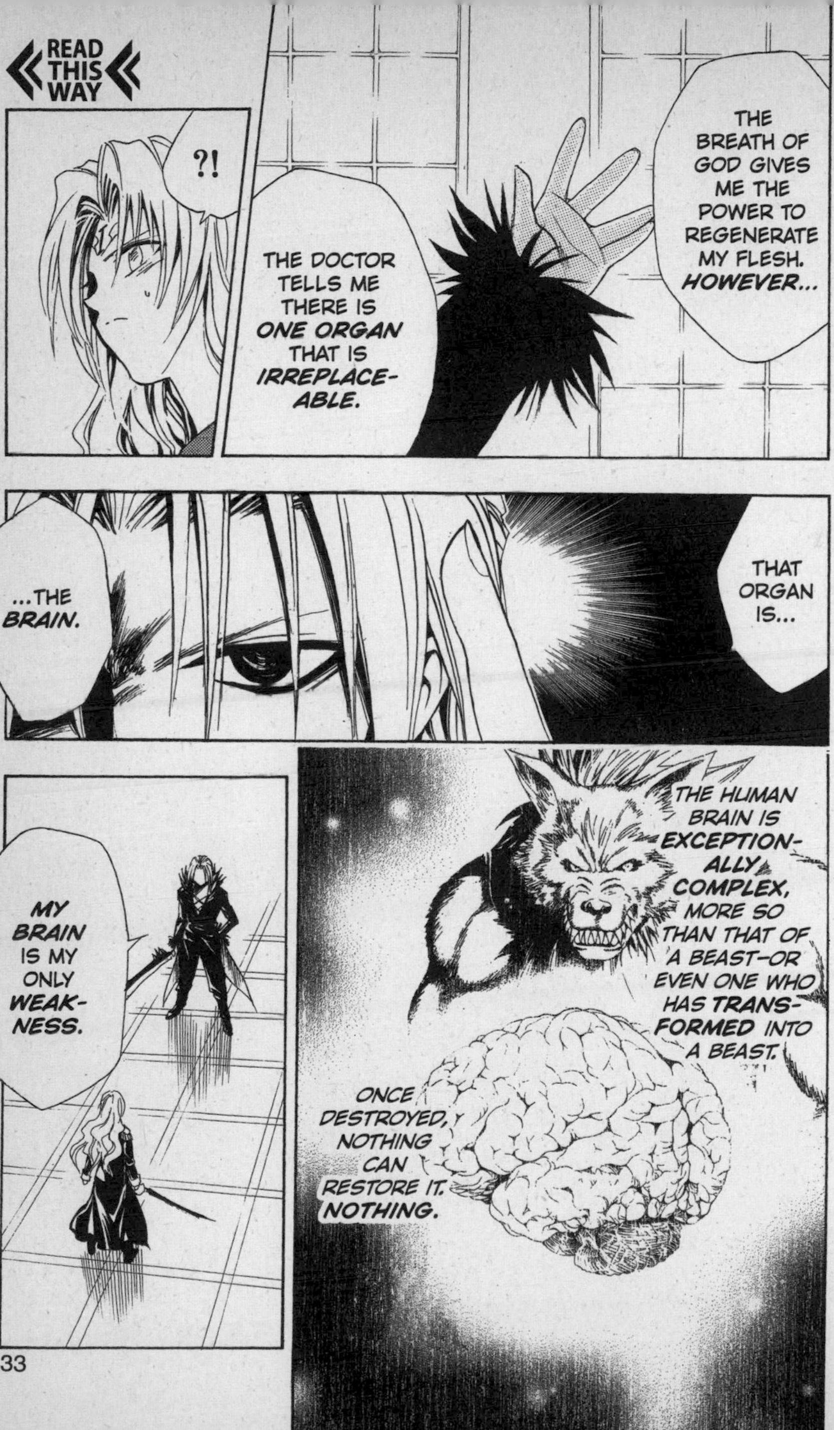
THE BREATH OF GOD GIVES ME THE POWER TO REGENERATE MY FLESH. HOWEVER...
THE DOCTOR TELLS ME THERE IS ONE ORGAN THAT IS IRREPLACE-ABLE.
?!
THAT ORGAN IS...
...THE BRAIN.
THE HUMAN BRAIN IS EXCEPTION-ALLY COMPLEX, MORE SO THAN THAT OF A BEAST--OR EVEN ONE WHO HAS TRANS-FORMED INTO A BEAST.
ONCE DESTROYED, NOTHING CAN RESTORE IT. NOTHING.
MY BRAIN IS MY ONLY WEAK-NESS.

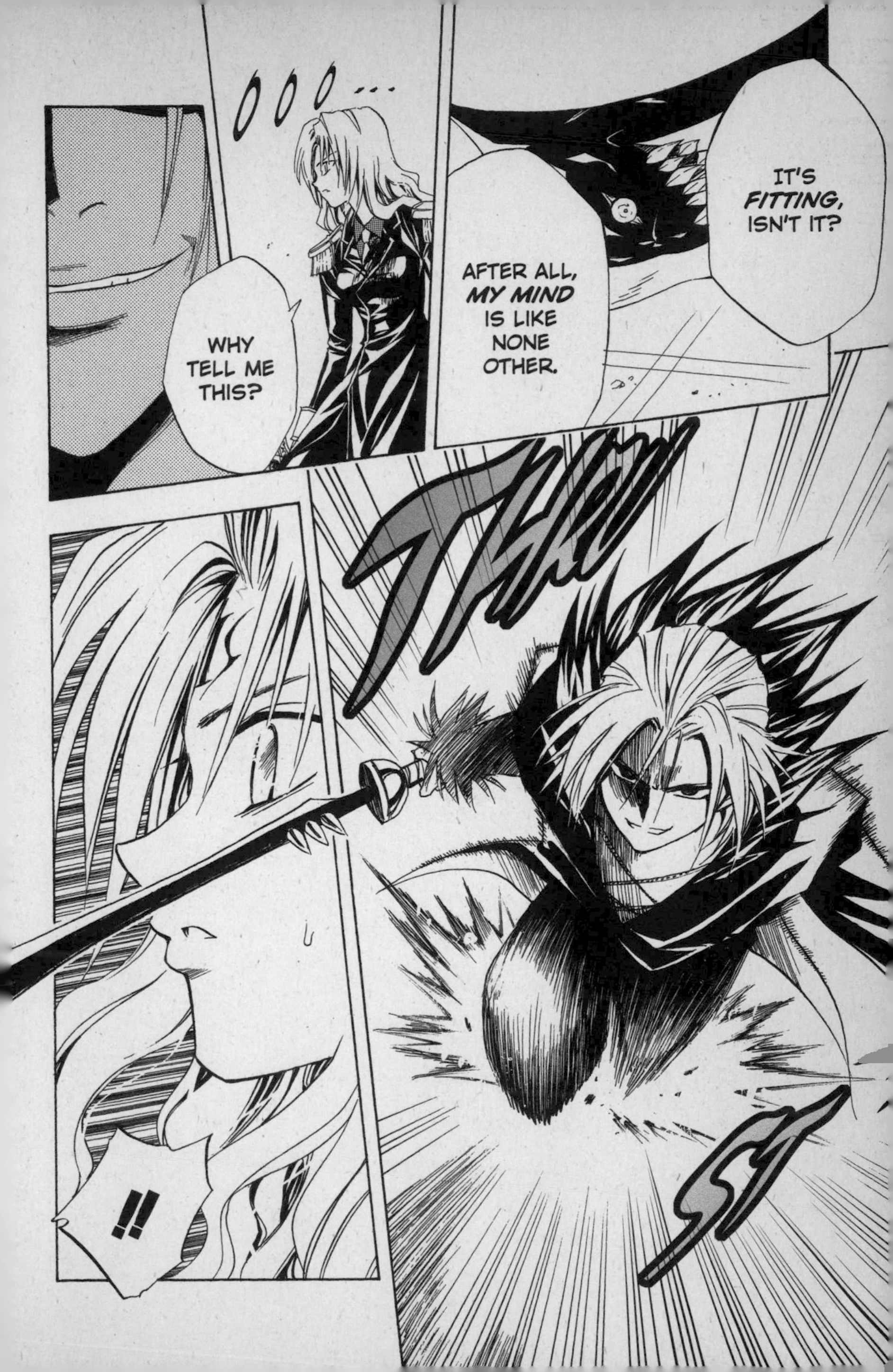
IT'S *FITTING,* ISN'T IT?
AFTER ALL, *MY MIND* IS LIKE NONE OTHER.
WHY TELL ME THIS?
!!

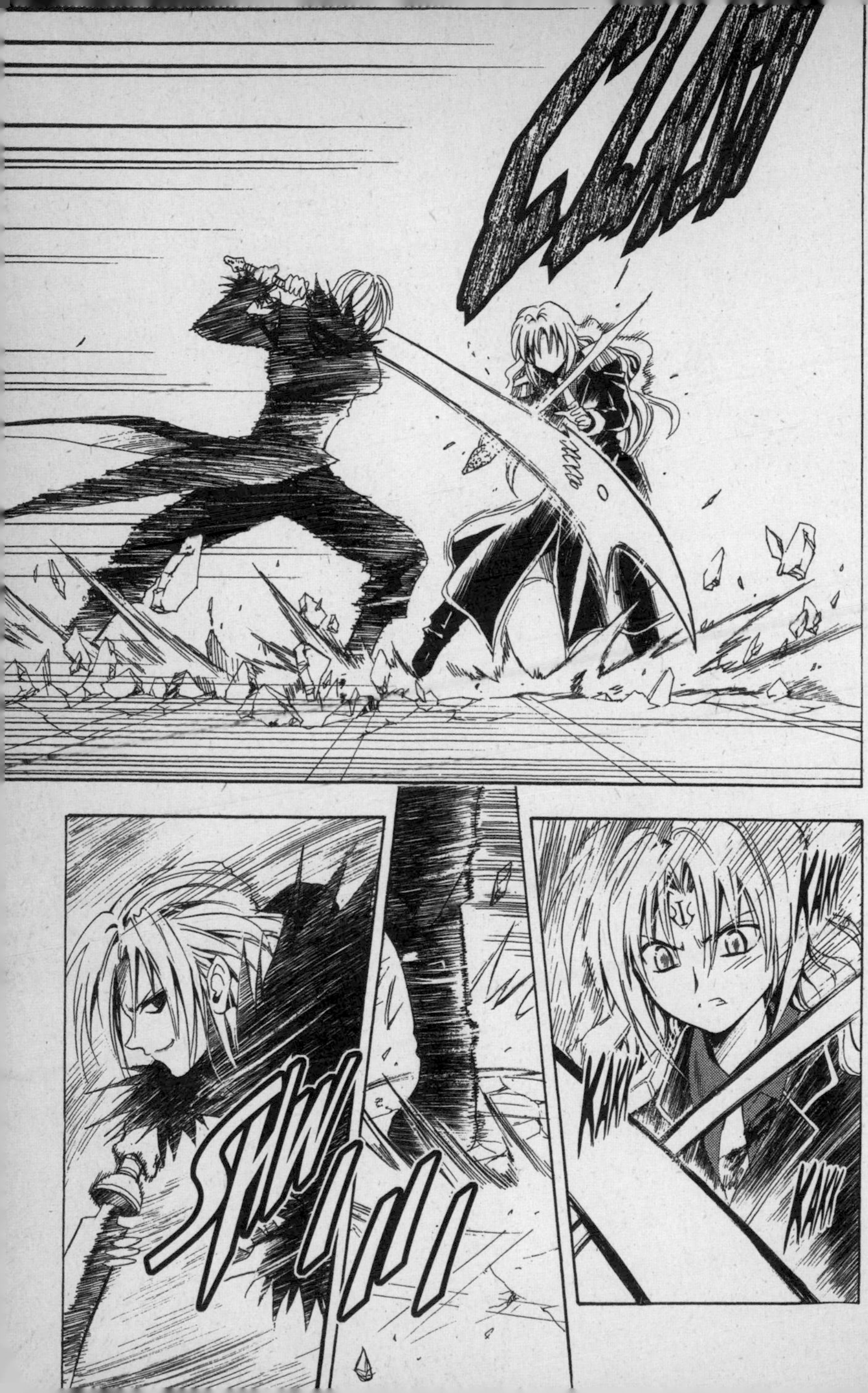

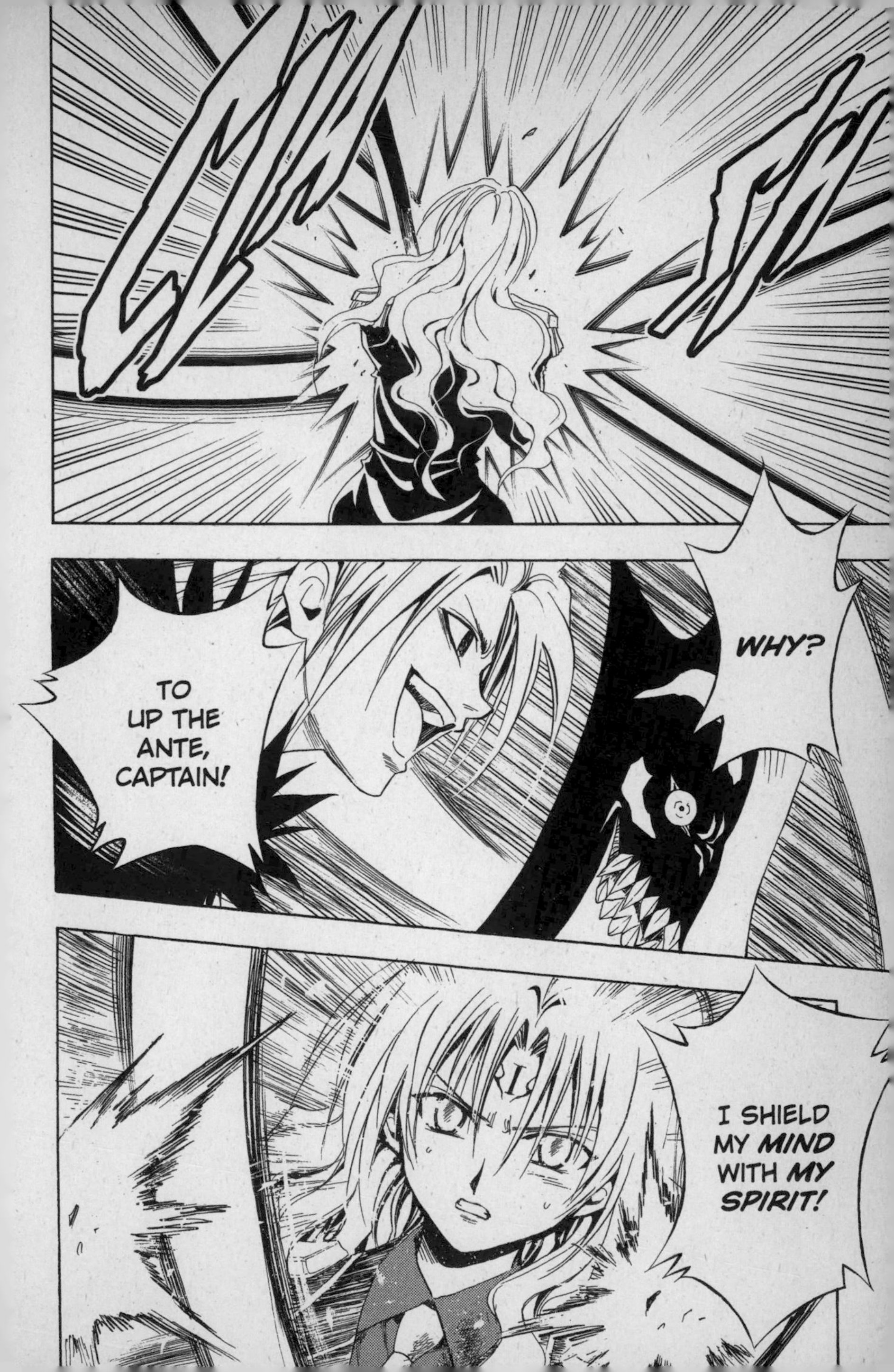
WHY?
TO UP THE ANTE, CAPTAIN!
I SHIELD MY MIND WITH MY SPIRIT!

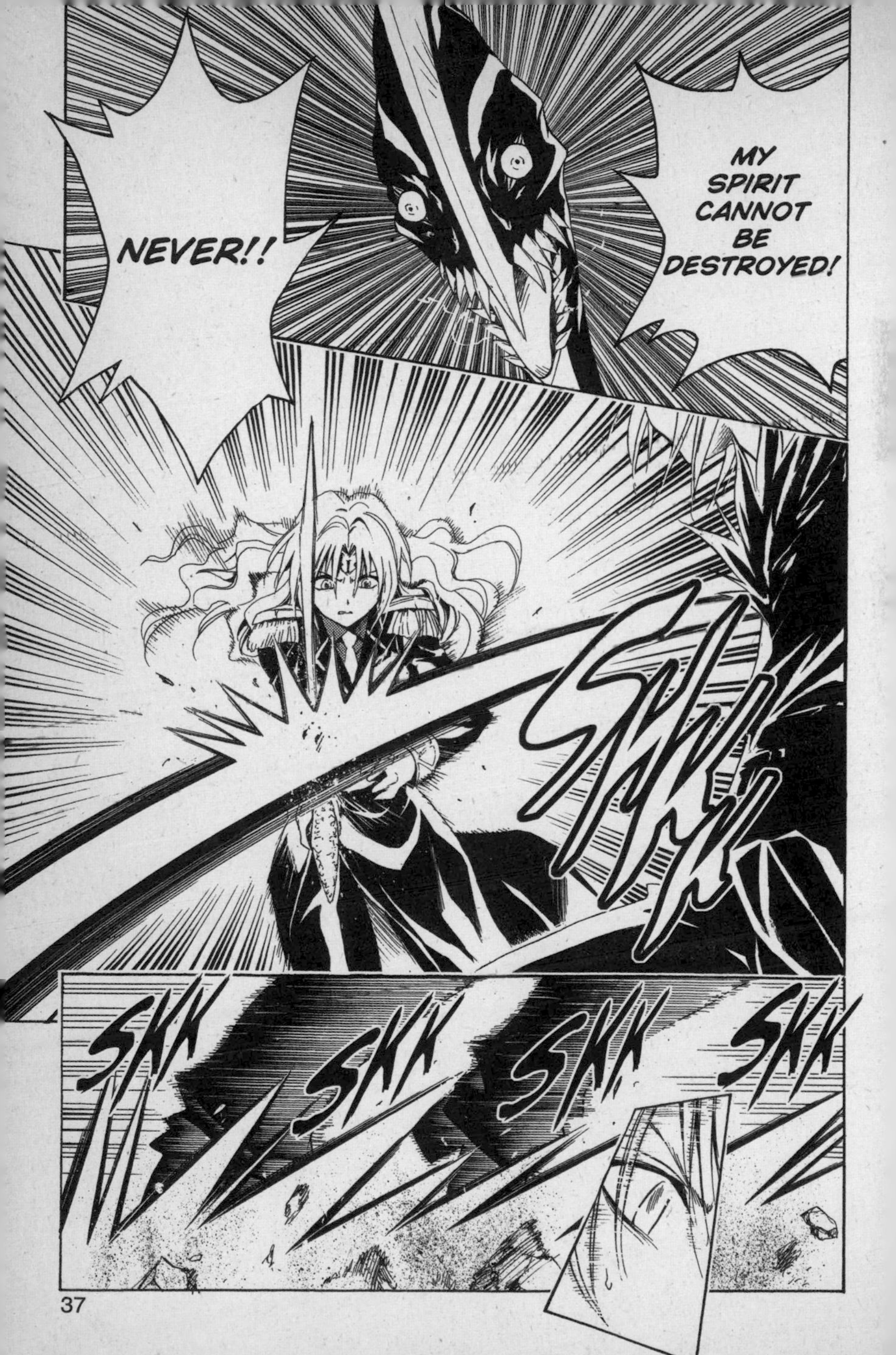
MY SPIRIT CANNOT BE DESTROYED!
NEVER!!
SPLT
SHK SHK SHK SHK

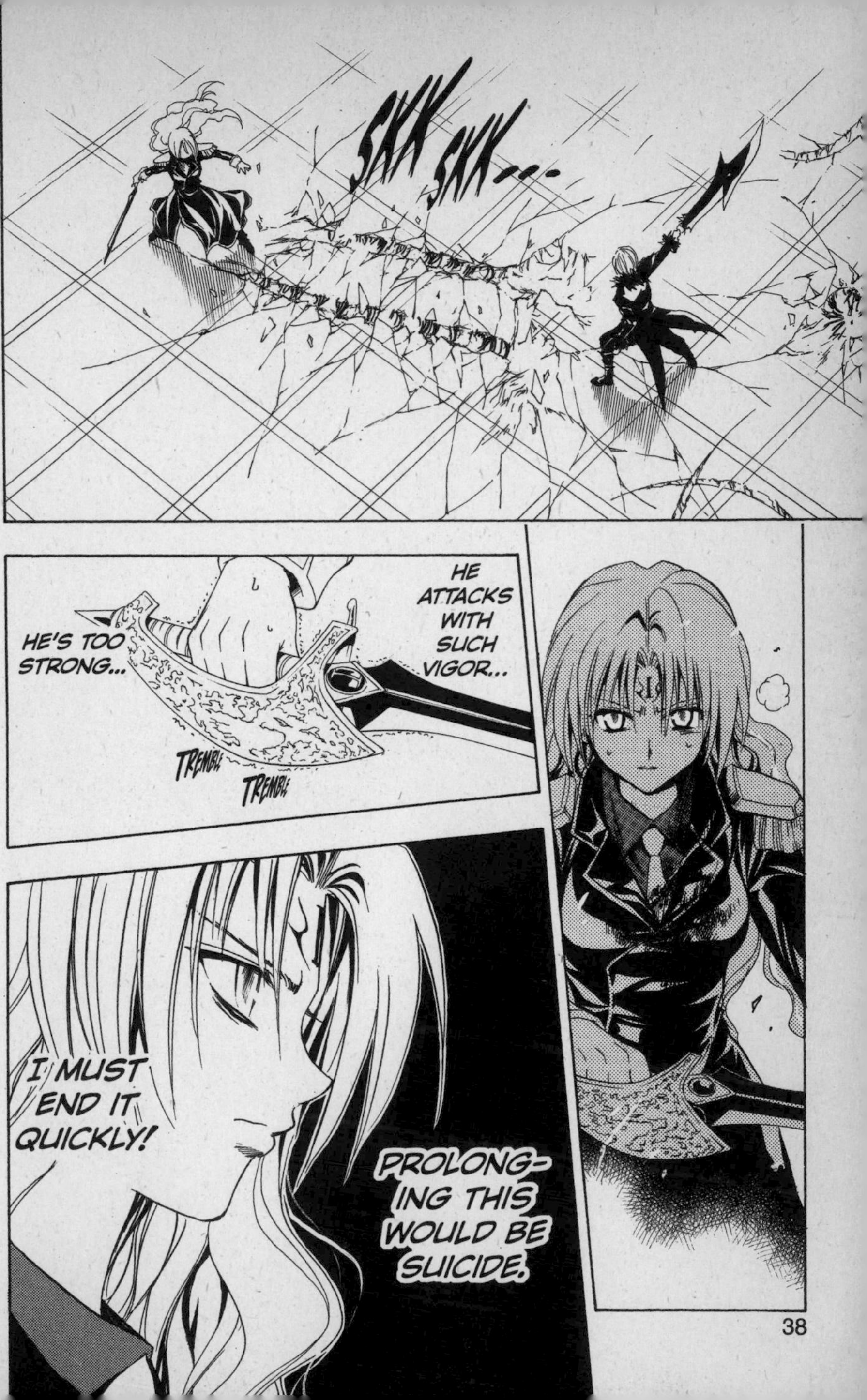
SKK SKK...
HE ATTACKS WITH SUCH VIGOR...
HE'S TOO STRONG...
TREMBLE
TREMBLE
PROLONG-ING THIS WOULD BE SUICIDE.
I MUST END IT QUICKLY!

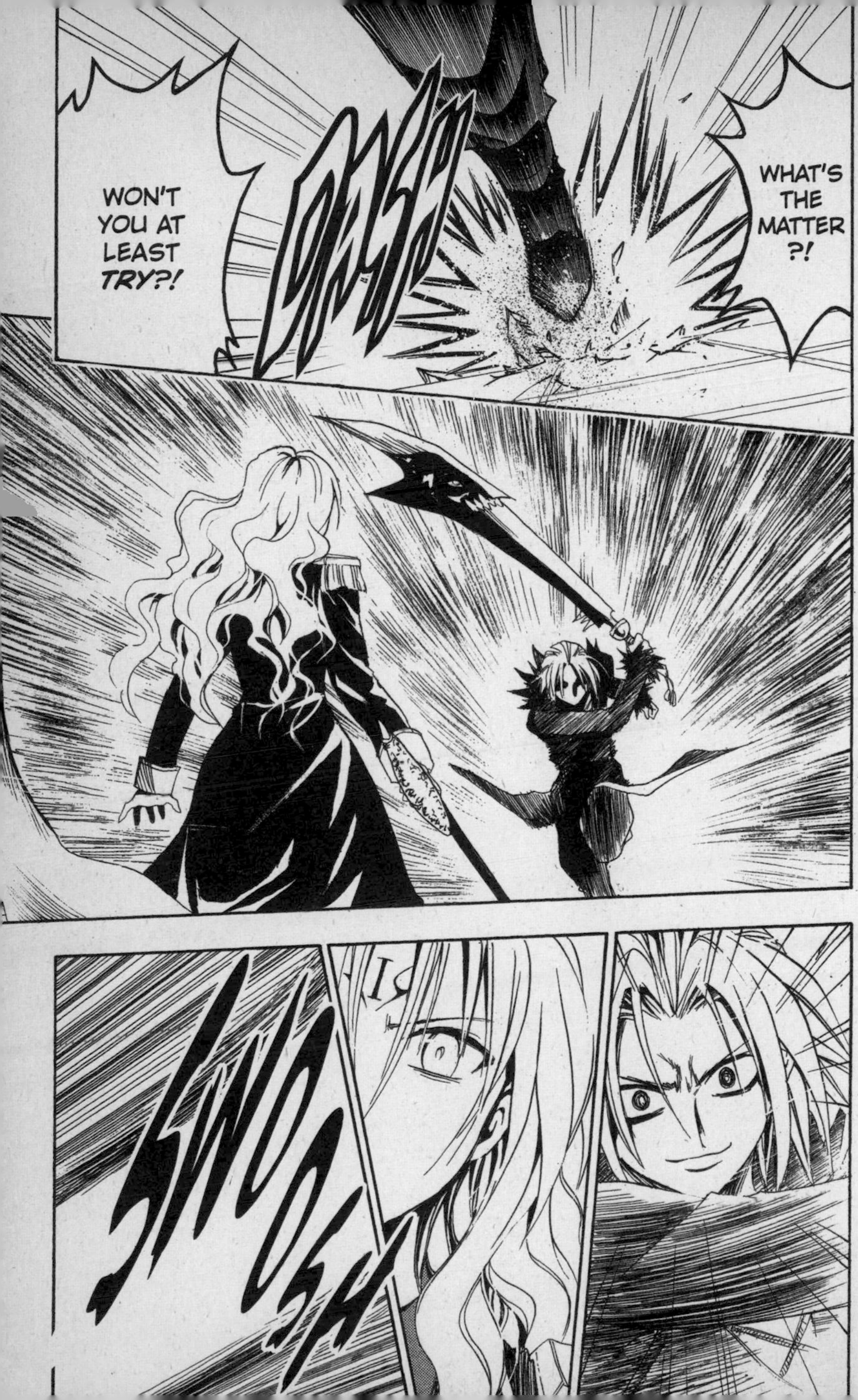
WHAT'S THE MATTER?!
WON'T YOU AT LEAST *TRY?!*

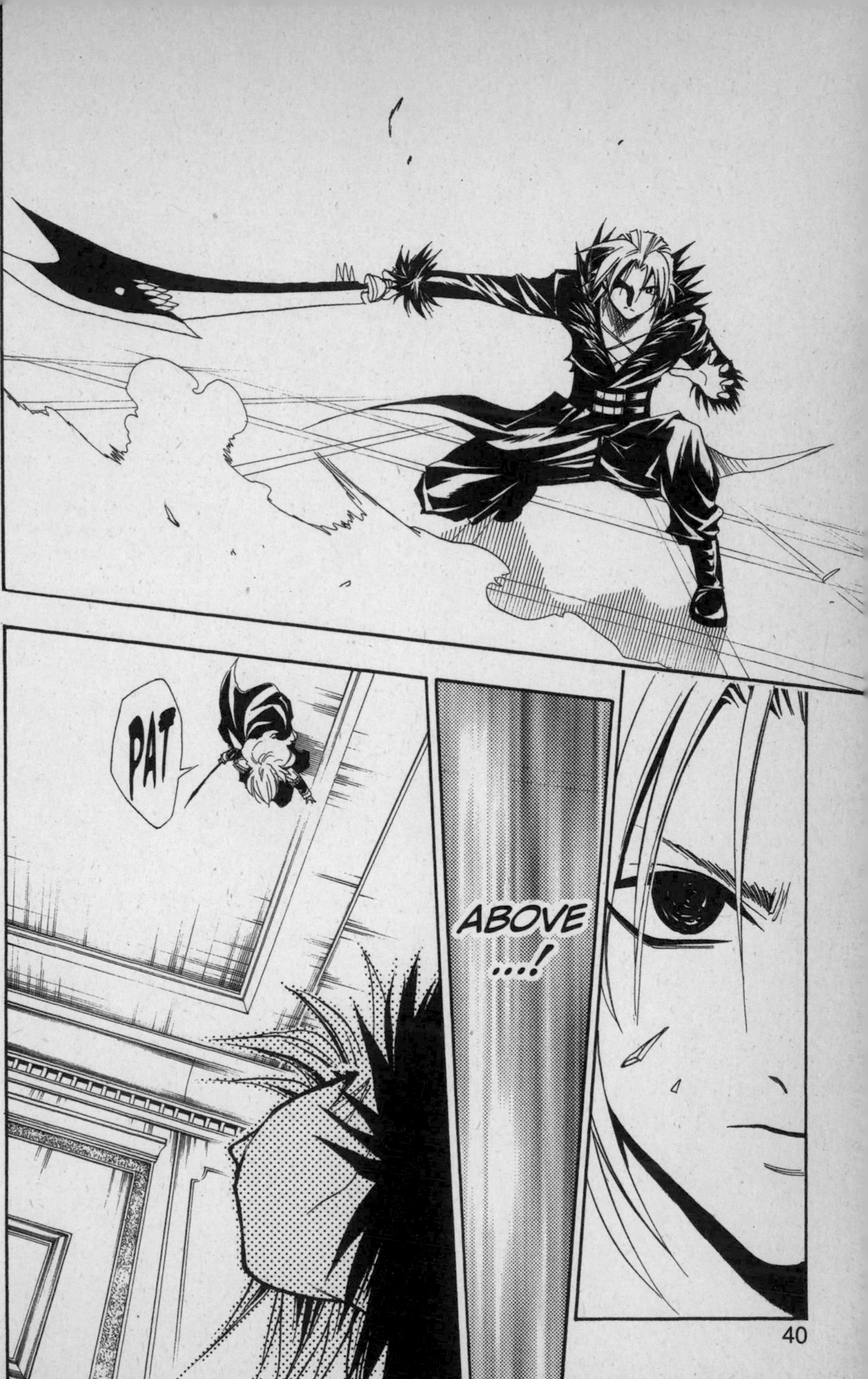
ABOVE
...!
PAT

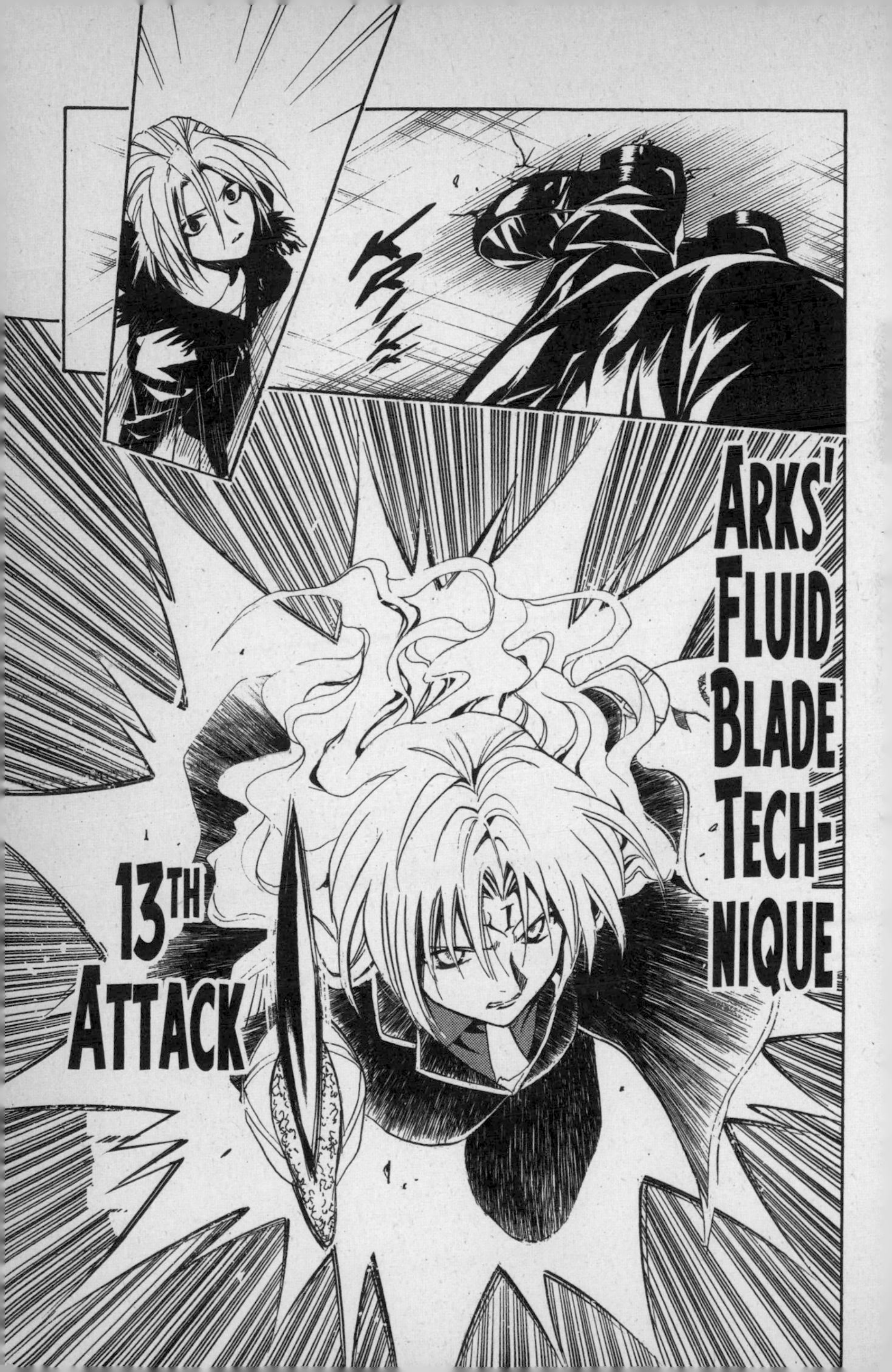
ARKS' FLUID BLADE TECH-NIQUE
13TH ATTACK

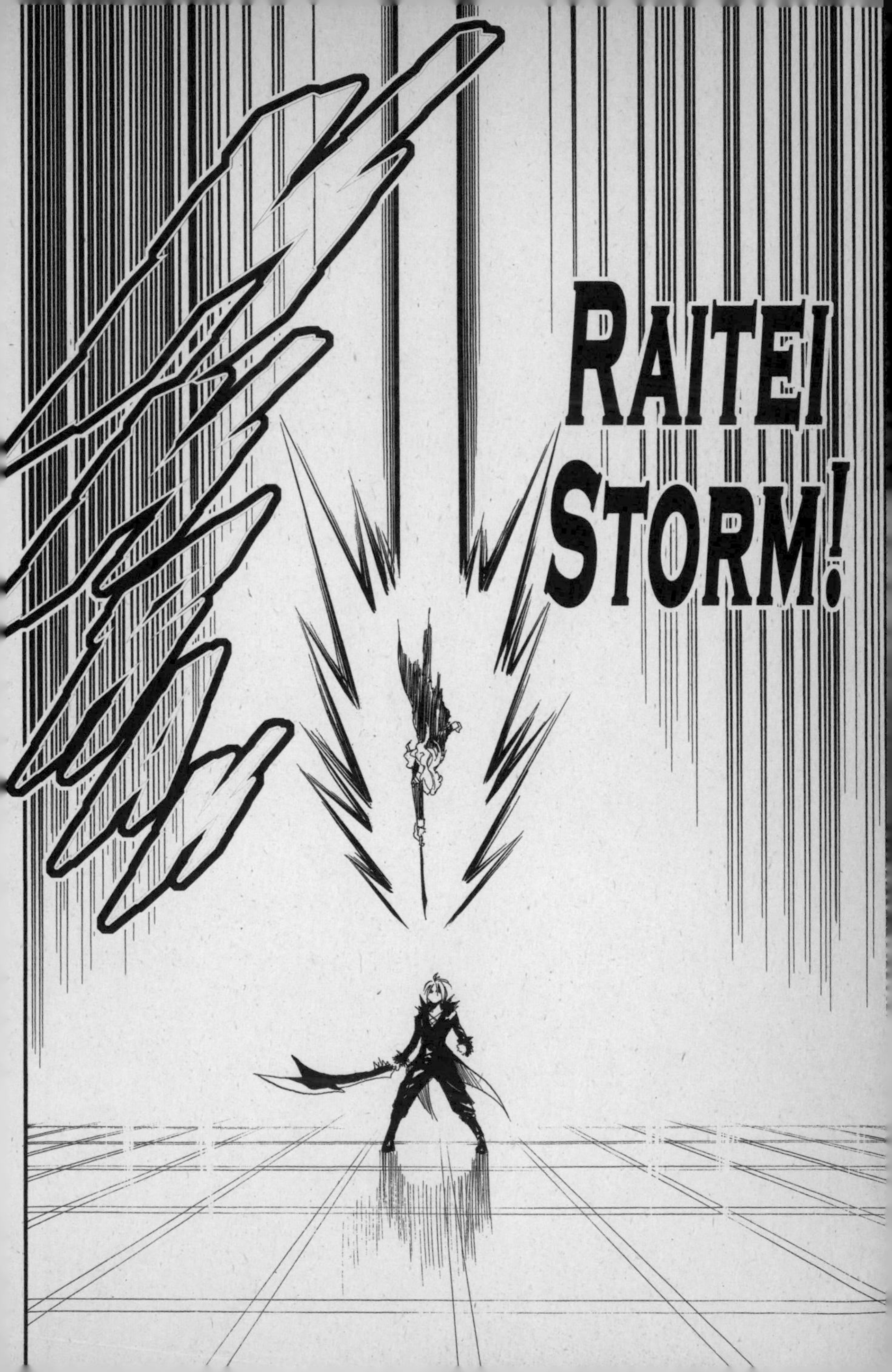
RAITEI STORM!

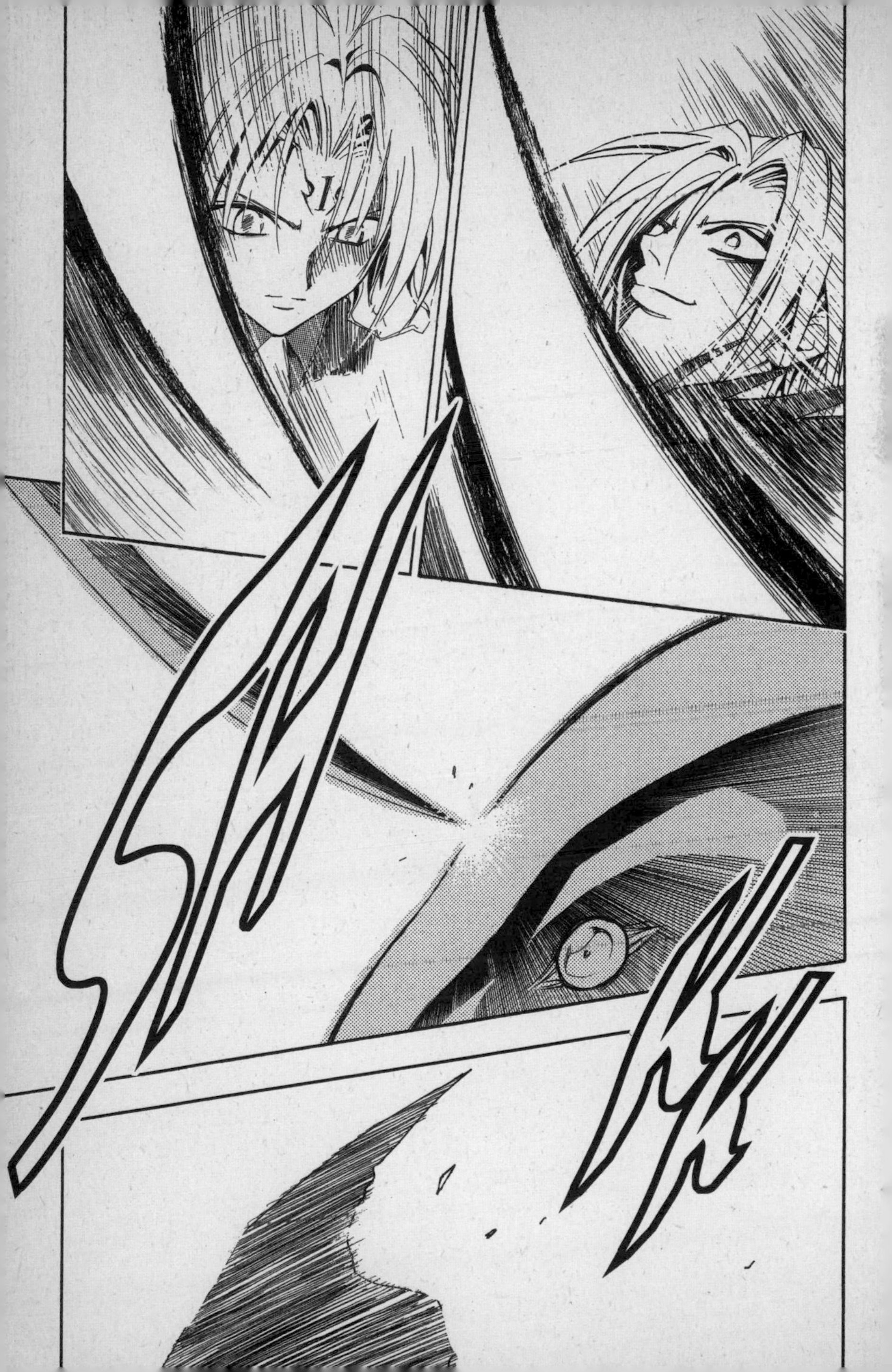

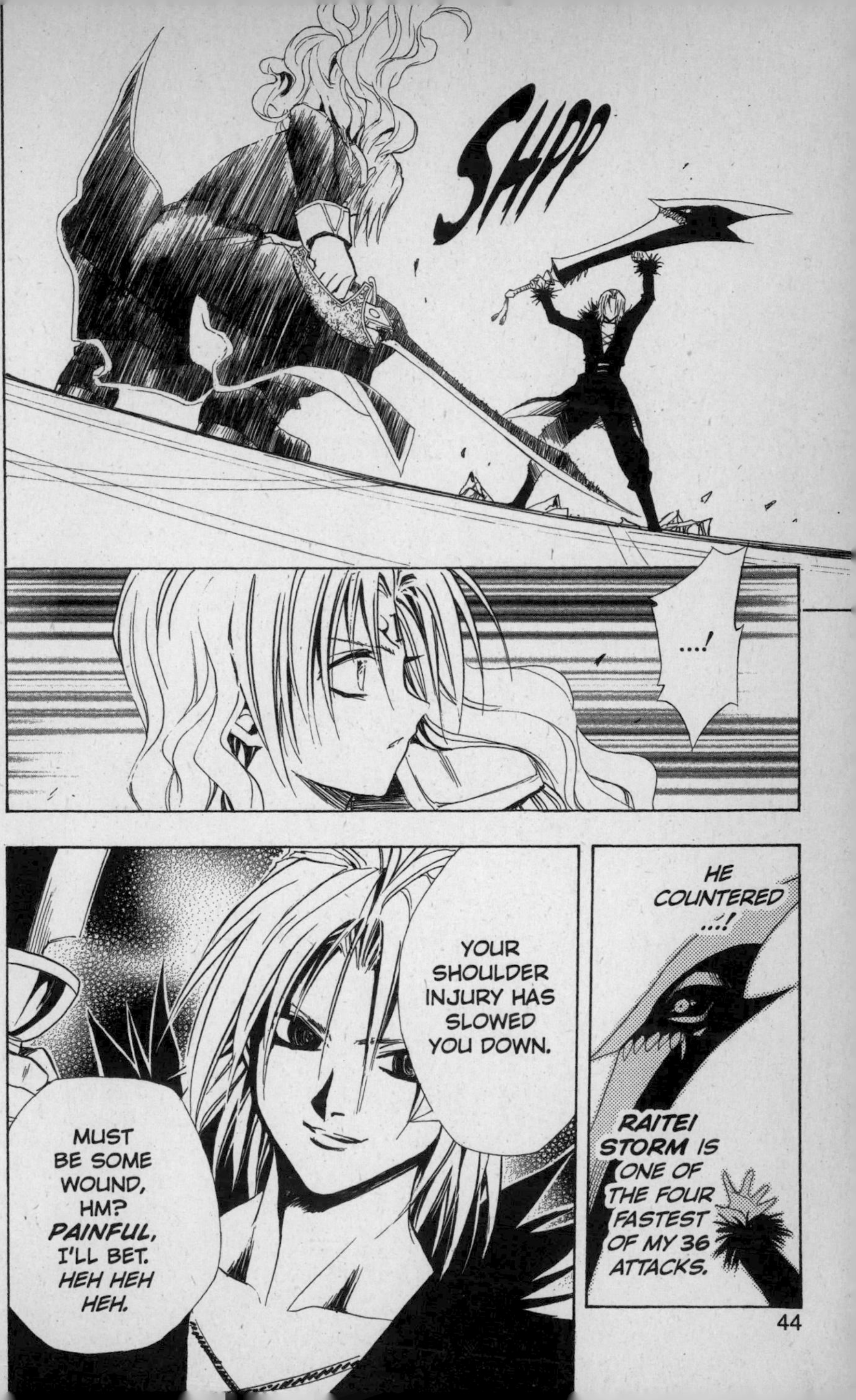
SHPP
...!
HE COUNTERED ...!
RAITEI STORM IS ONE OF THE FOUR FASTEST OF MY 36 ATTACKS.
YOUR SHOULDER INJURY HAS SLOWED YOU DOWN.
MUST BE SOME WOUND, HM? PAINFUL, I'LL BET. HEH HEH HEH.

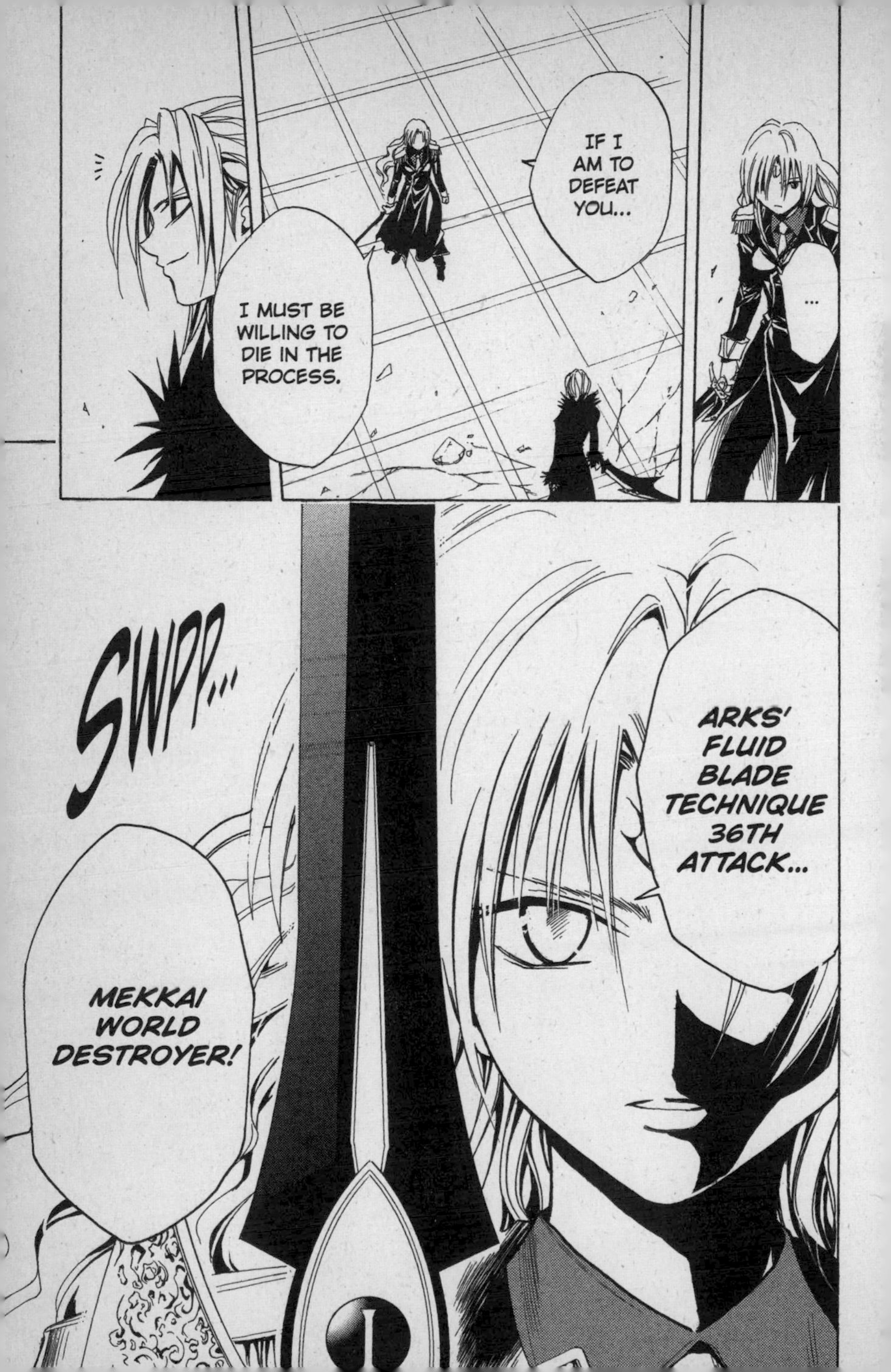
...
IF I AM TO DEFEAT YOU...
I MUST BE WILLING TO DIE IN THE PROCESS.
ARKS' FLUID BLADE TECHNIQUE 36TH ATTACK...
SWPP...
MEKKAI WORLD DESTROYER!

Chapter 170: Mekkai World Destroyer

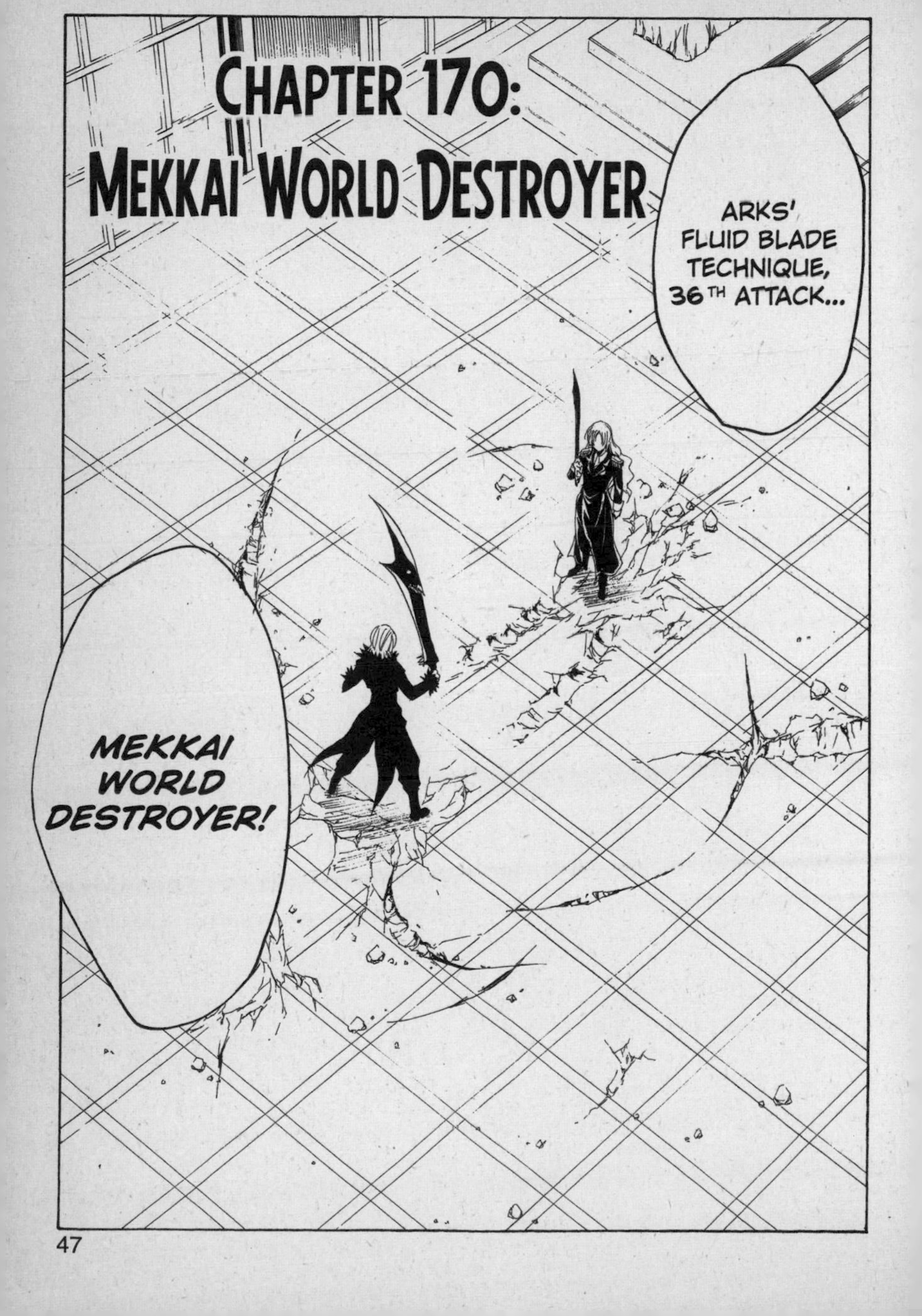
ARKS' FLUID BLADE TECHNIQUE, 36TH ATTACK...
MEKKAI WORLD DESTROYER!

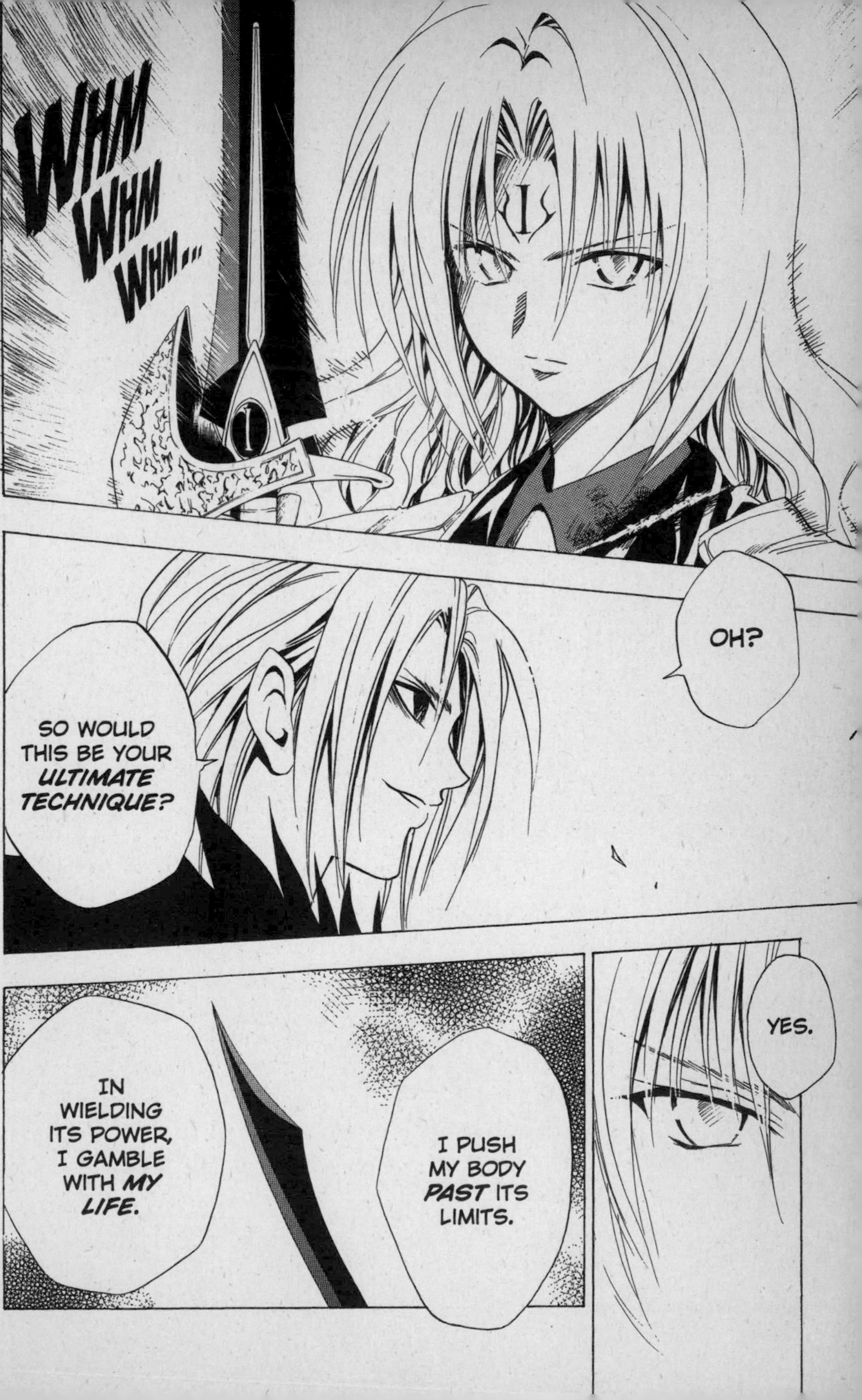
WHM WHM WHM...
OH?
SO WOULD THIS BE YOUR *ULTIMATE TECHNIQUE?*
YES.
I PUSH MY BODY *PAST* ITS LIMITS.
IN WIELDING ITS POWER, I GAMBLE WITH *MY LIFE.*

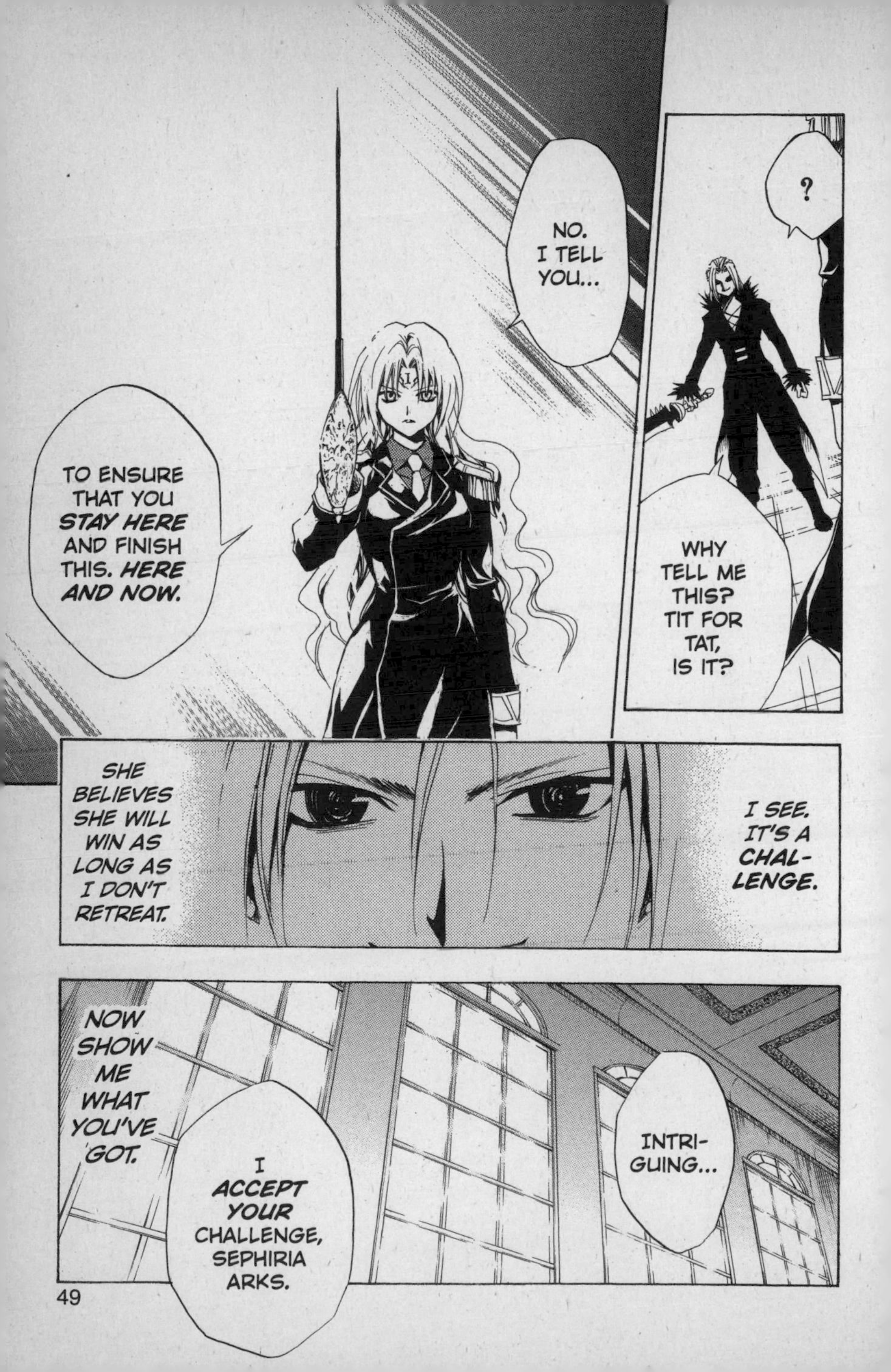
?
WHY TELL ME THIS? TIT FOR TAT, IS IT?
NO. I TELL YOU...
TO ENSURE THAT YOU *STAY HERE* AND FINISH THIS. *HERE AND NOW.*
I SEE. IT'S A **CHALLENGE.**
SHE BELIEVES SHE WILL WIN AS LONG AS I DON'T RETREAT.
INTRIGUING...
NOW SHOW ME WHAT YOU'VE GOT.
I *ACCEPT YOUR* CHALLENGE, SEPHIRIA ARKS.

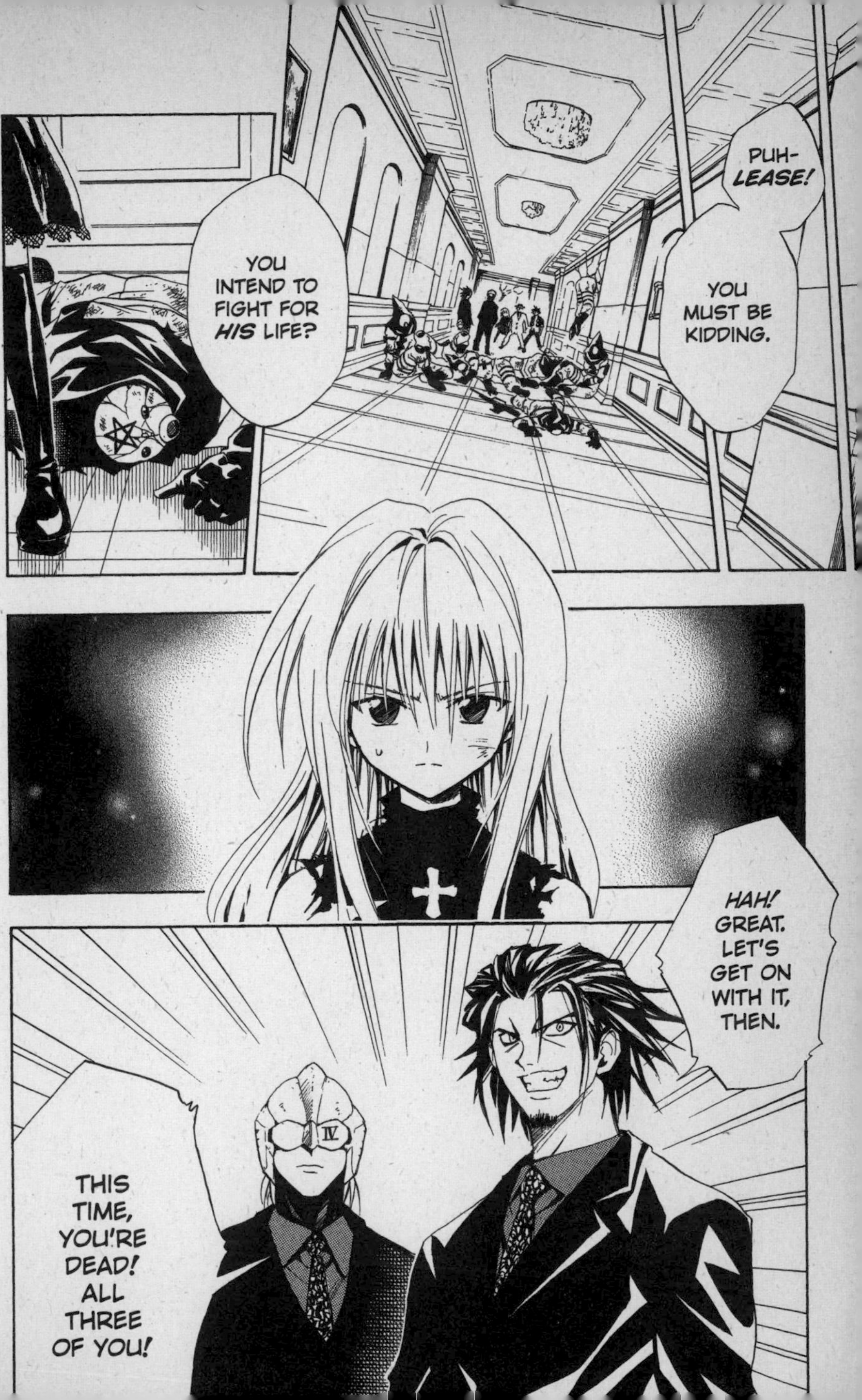
PUH-LEASE!
YOU MUST BE KIDDING.
YOU INTEND TO FIGHT FOR HIS LIFE?
HAH! GREAT. LET'S GET ON WITH IT, THEN.
THIS TIME, YOU'RE DEAD! ALL THREE OF YOU!

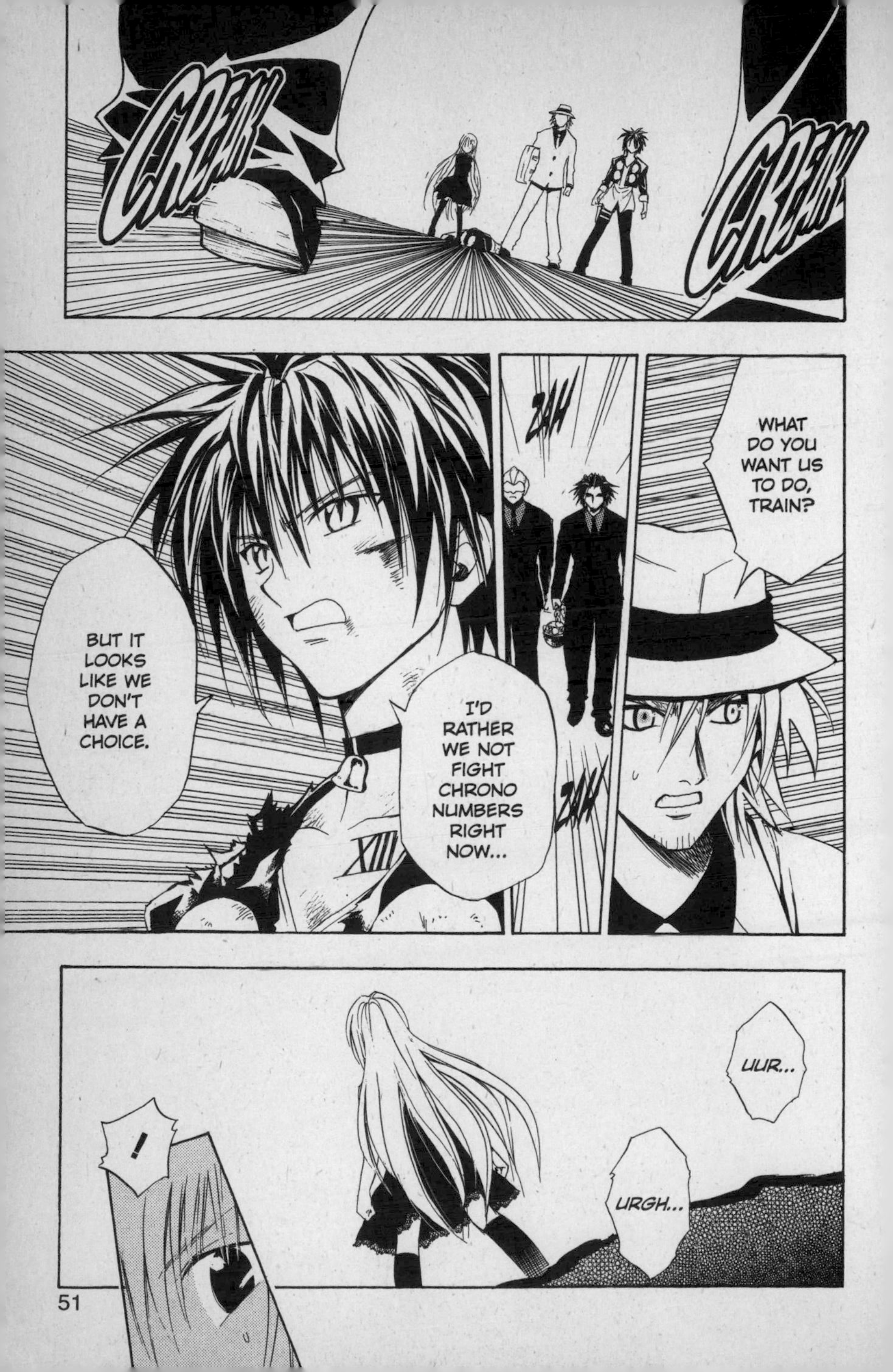
CREAK
CREAK
WHAT DO YOU WANT US TO DO, TRAIN?
ZAH
ZAH
I'D RATHER WE NOT FIGHT CHRONO NUMBERS RIGHT NOW...
BUT IT LOOKS LIKE WE DON'T HAVE A CHOICE.
UUR...
URGH...
!

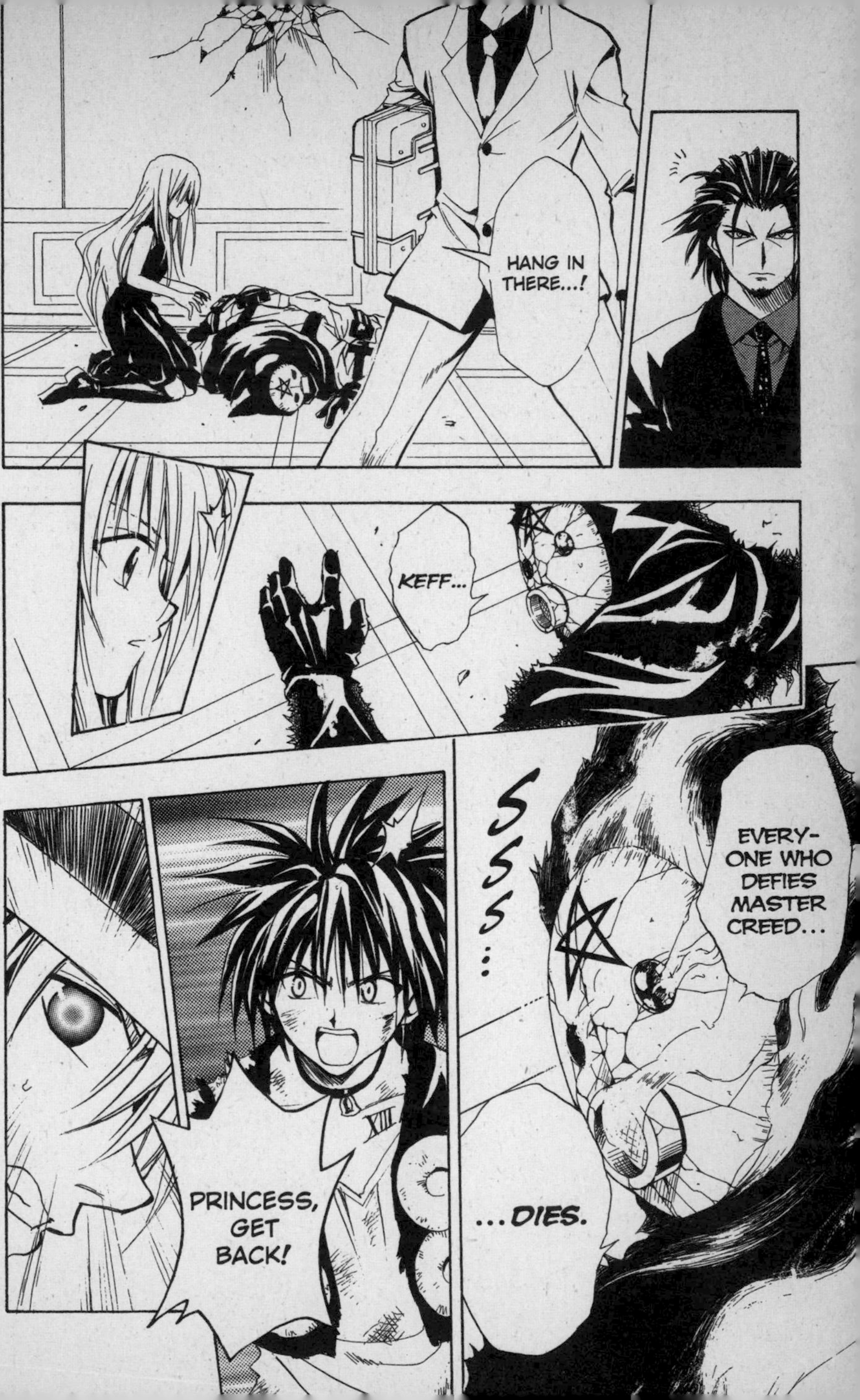
HANG IN THERE...!
KEFF...
EVERY-ONE WHO DEFIES MASTER CREED...
SSS...
...DIES.
PRINCESS, GET BACK!

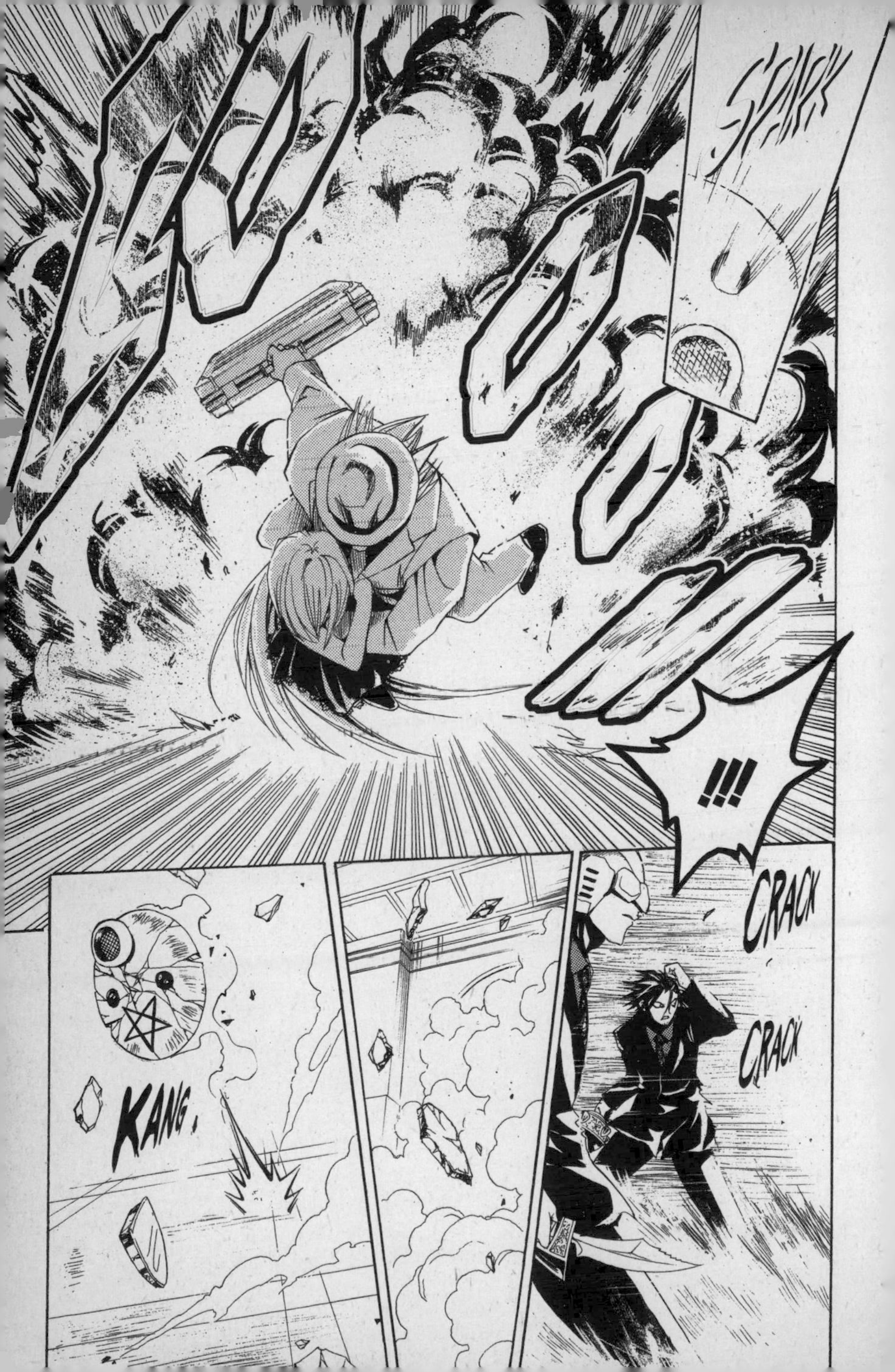

!!!
CRACK
CRACK
KANG

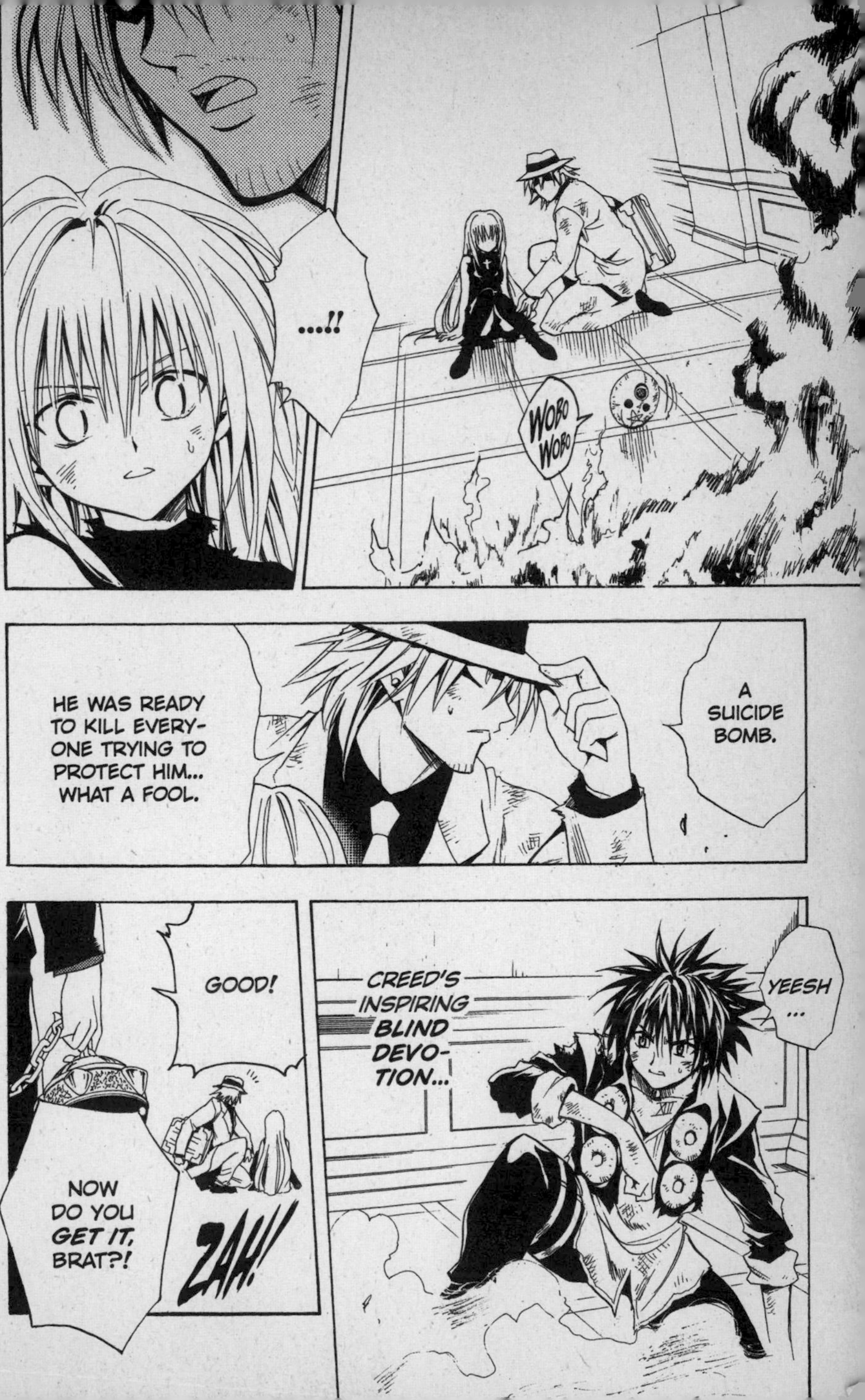

WOBO WOBO
...!!
A SUICIDE BOMB.
HE WAS READY TO KILL EVERY-ONE TRYING TO PROTECT HIM... WHAT A FOOL.
YEESH...
CREED'S INSPIRING BLIND DEVO-TION...
GOOD!
NOW DO YOU GET IT, BRAT?!
ZAH!

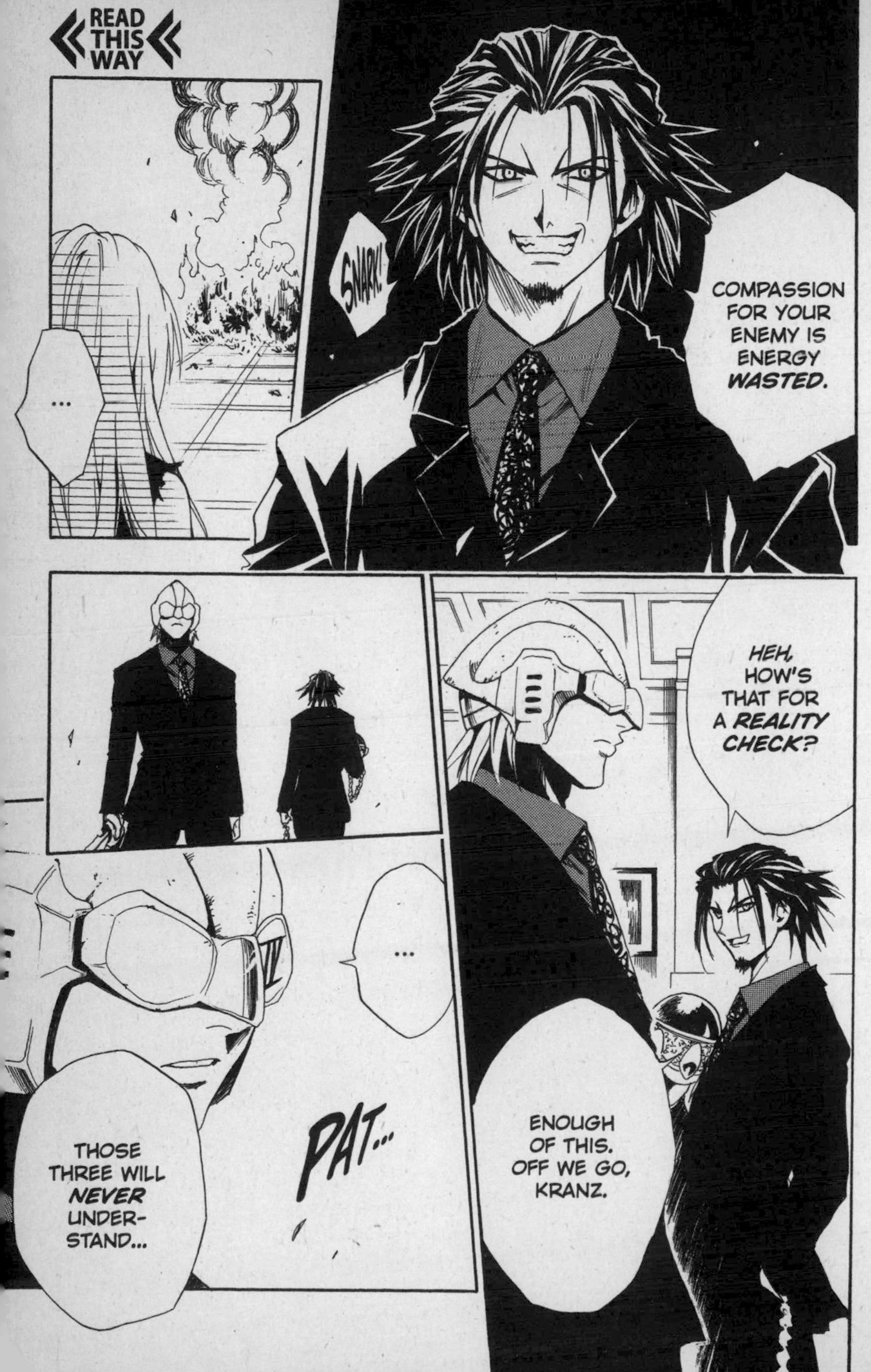
READ THIS WAY
SNARK!
COMPASSION FOR YOUR ENEMY IS ENERGY *WASTED.*
...
HEH, HOW'S THAT FOR A *REALITY CHECK?*
ENOUGH OF THIS. OFF WE GO, KRANZ.
...
PAT...
THOSE THREE WILL *NEVER* UNDER-STAND...

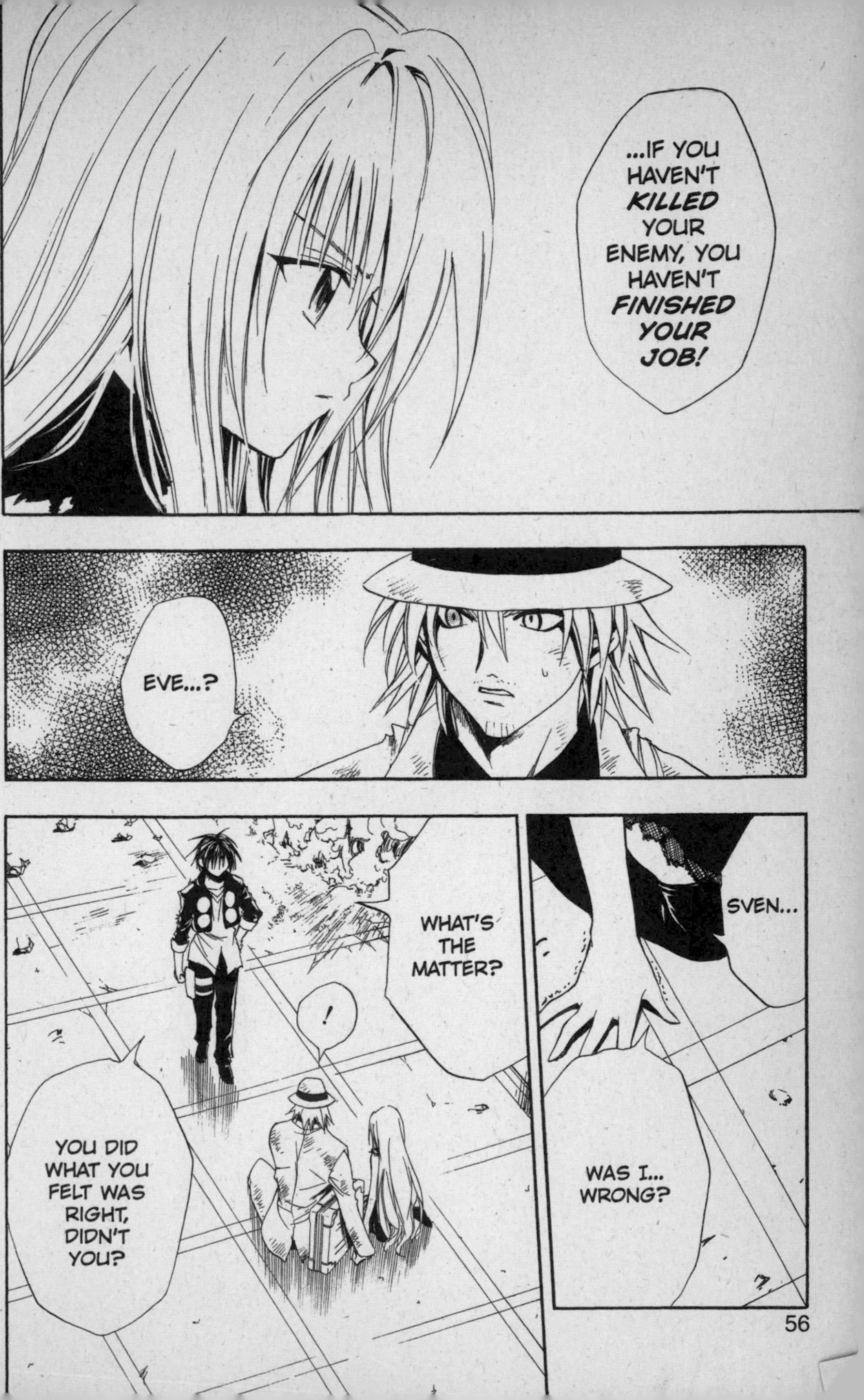
...IF YOU HAVEN'T KILLED YOUR ENEMY, YOU HAVEN'T FINISHED YOUR JOB!
EVE...?
SVEN...
WAS I... WRONG?
WHAT'S THE MATTER?
!
YOU DID WHAT YOU FELT WAS RIGHT, DIDN'T YOU?

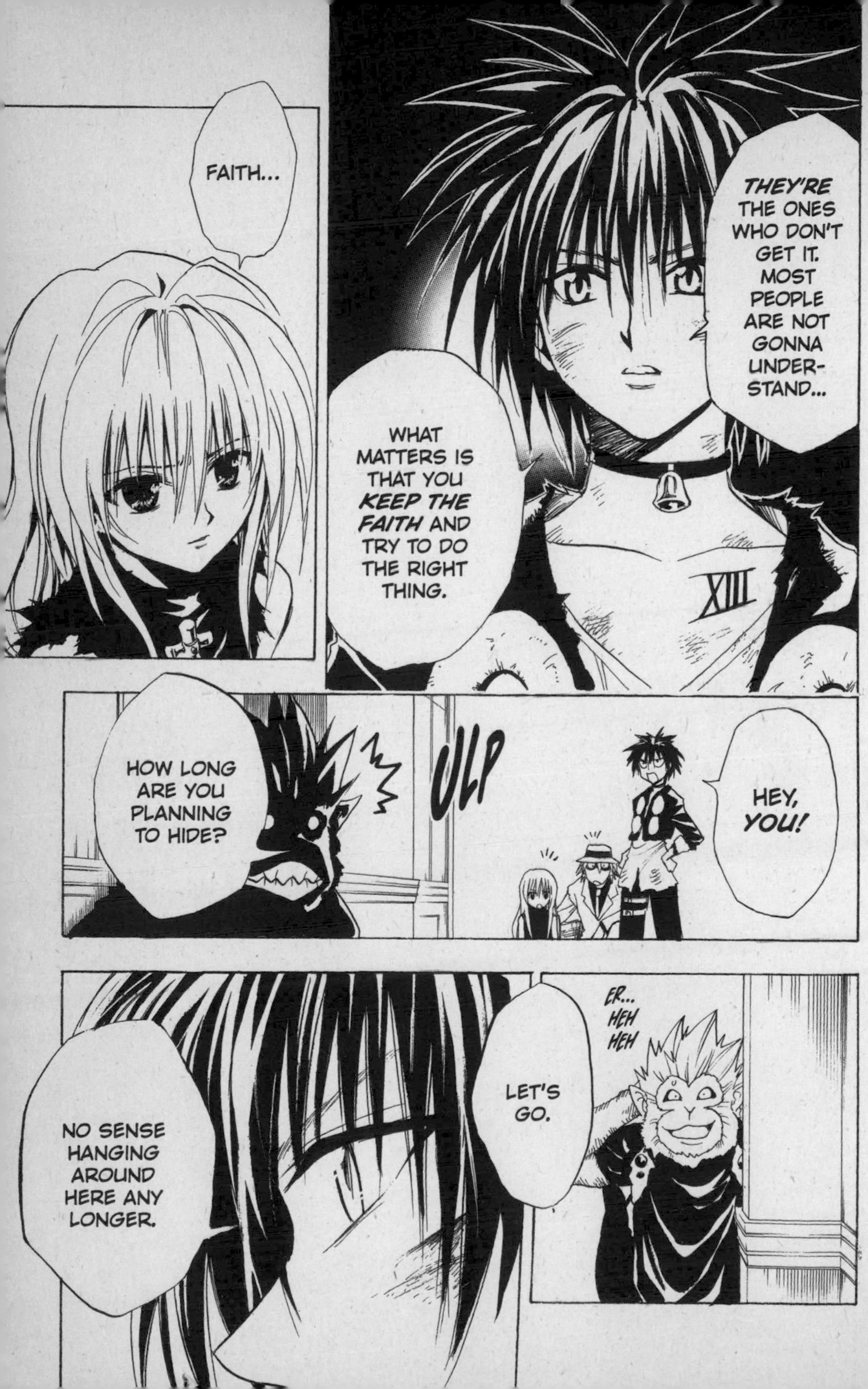
THEY'RE THE ONES WHO DON'T GET IT. MOST PEOPLE ARE NOT GONNA UNDER-STAND...
WHAT MATTERS IS THAT YOU KEEP THE FAITH AND TRY TO DO THE RIGHT THING.
FAITH...
HEY, YOU!
ULP
HOW LONG ARE YOU PLANNING TO HIDE?
ER... HEH HEH
LET'S GO.
NO SENSE HANGING AROUND HERE ANY LONGER.

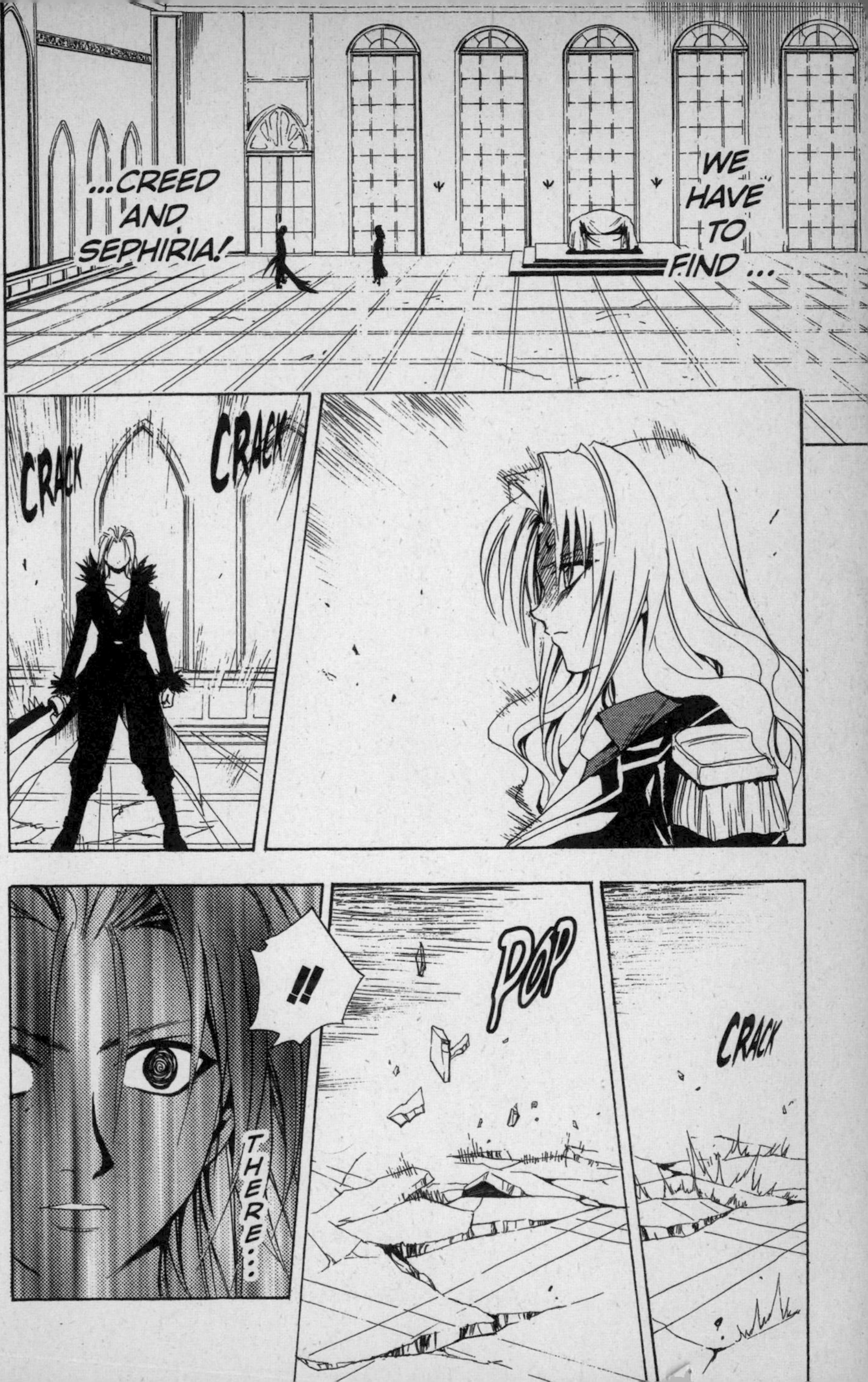
WE HAVE TO FIND ...
...CREED AND SEPHIRIA!
CRACK
CRACK
CRACK
POP
!!
THERE...

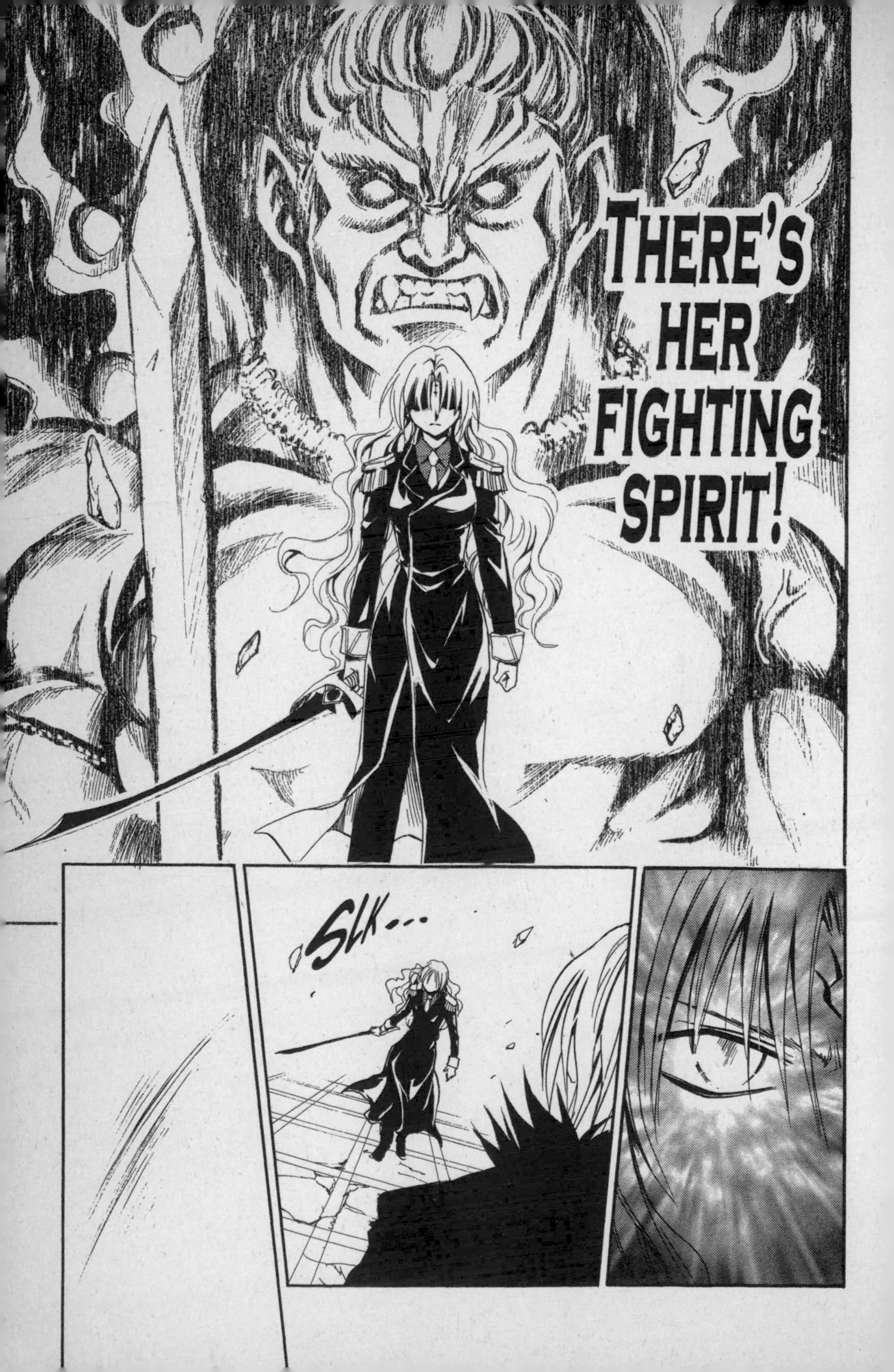
THERE'S HER FIGHTING SPIRIT!
SLK...

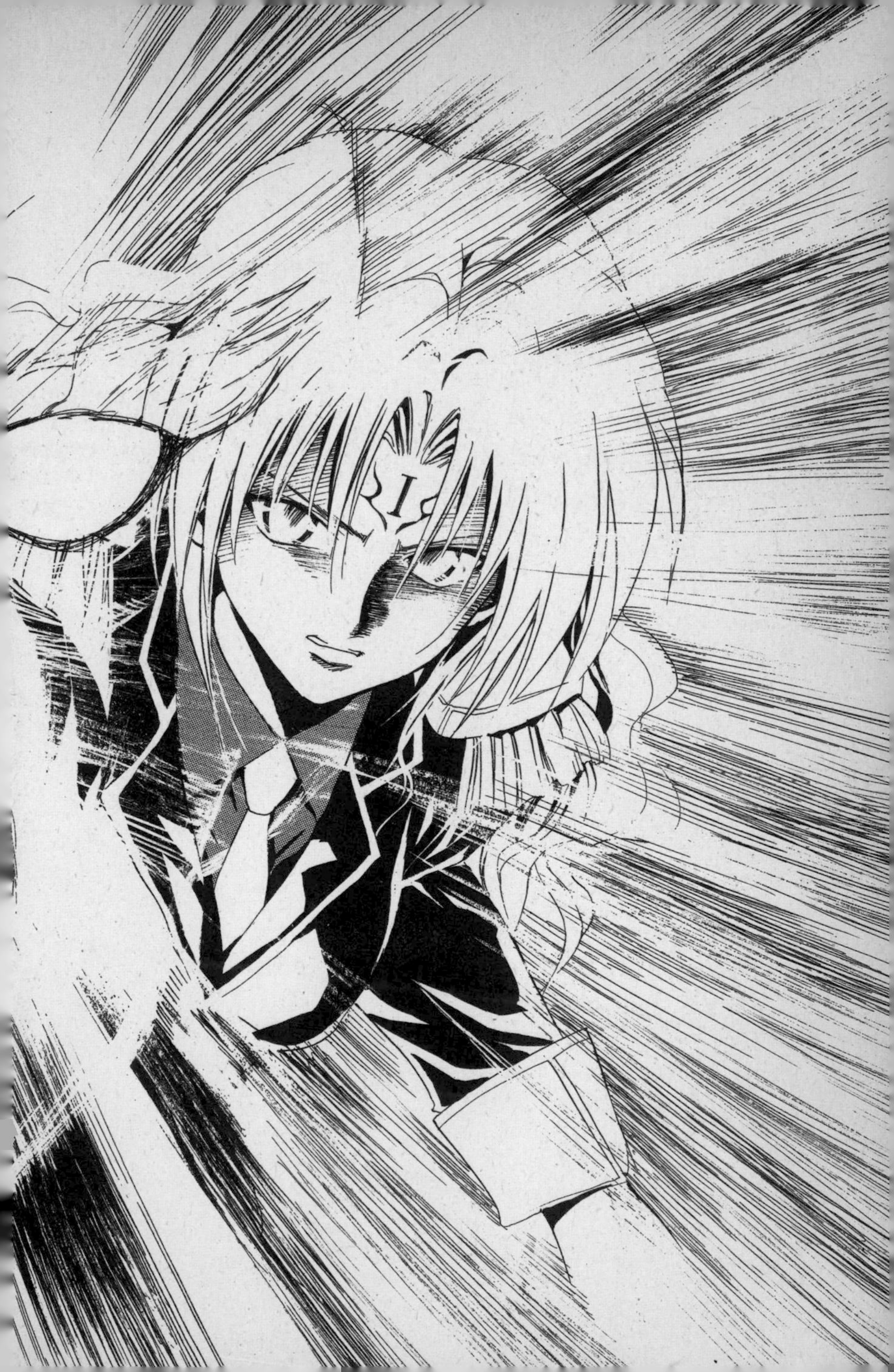

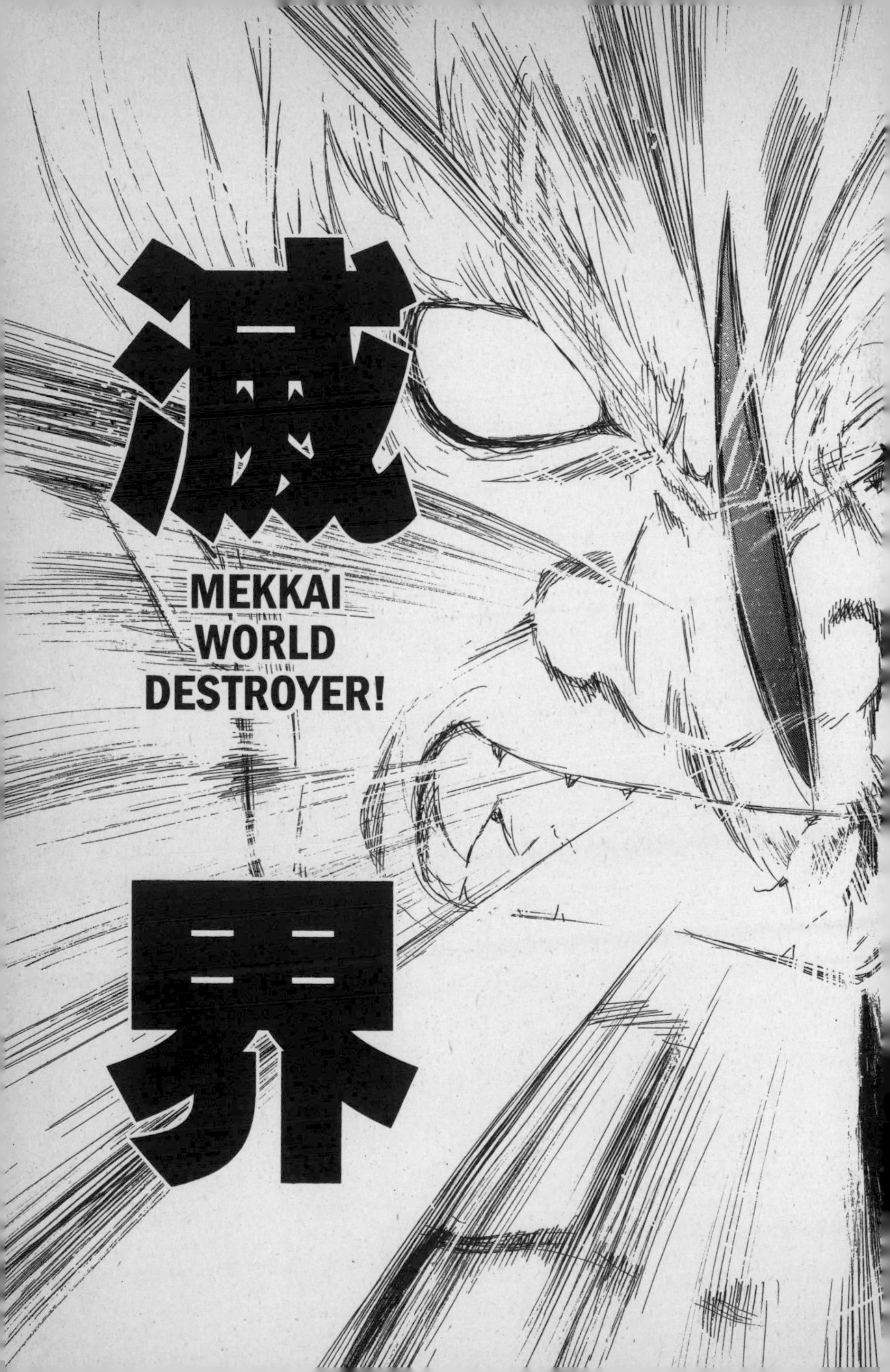

滅
MEKKAI
WORLD
DESTROYER!
界

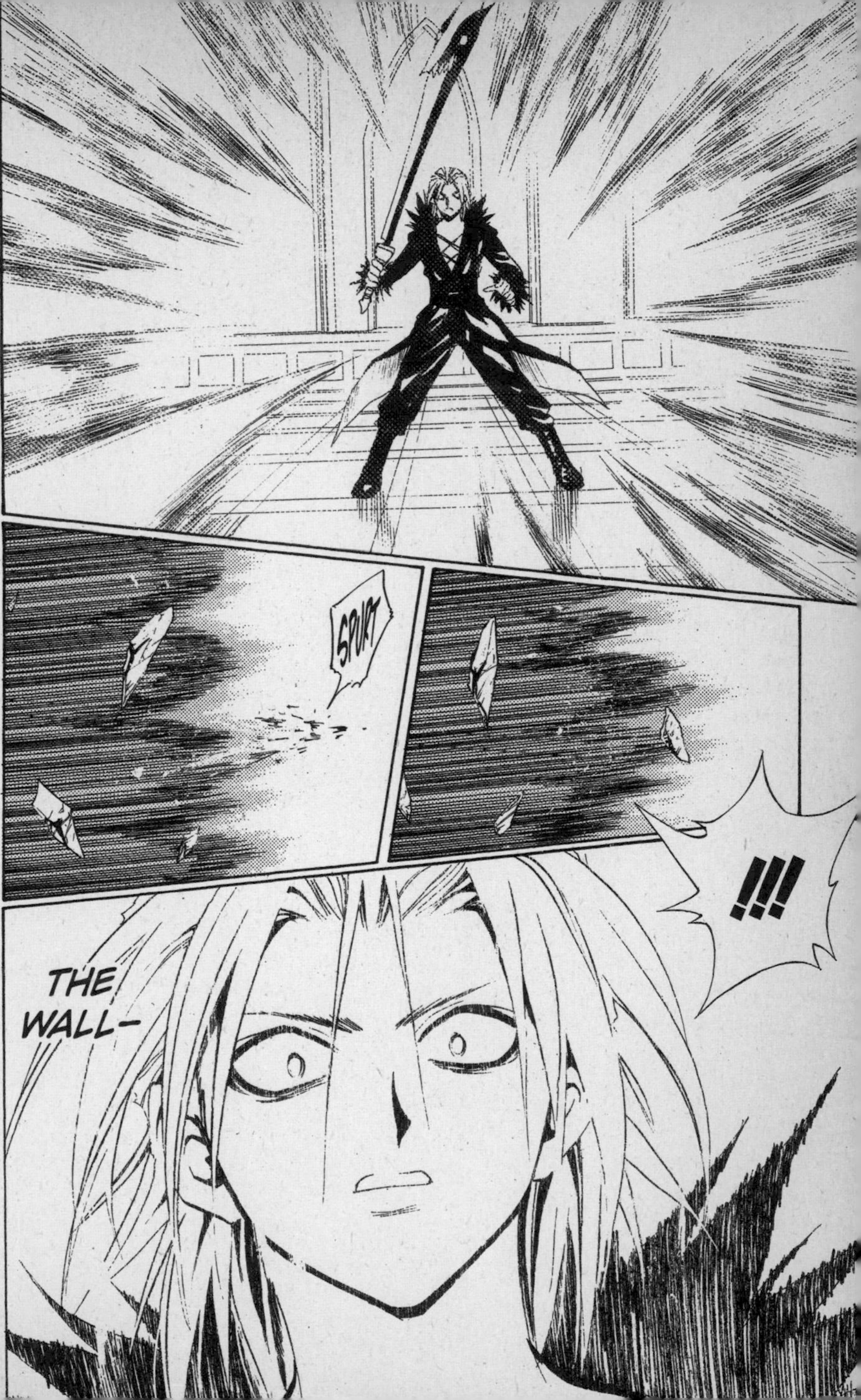
SPURT
!!!
THE WALL-

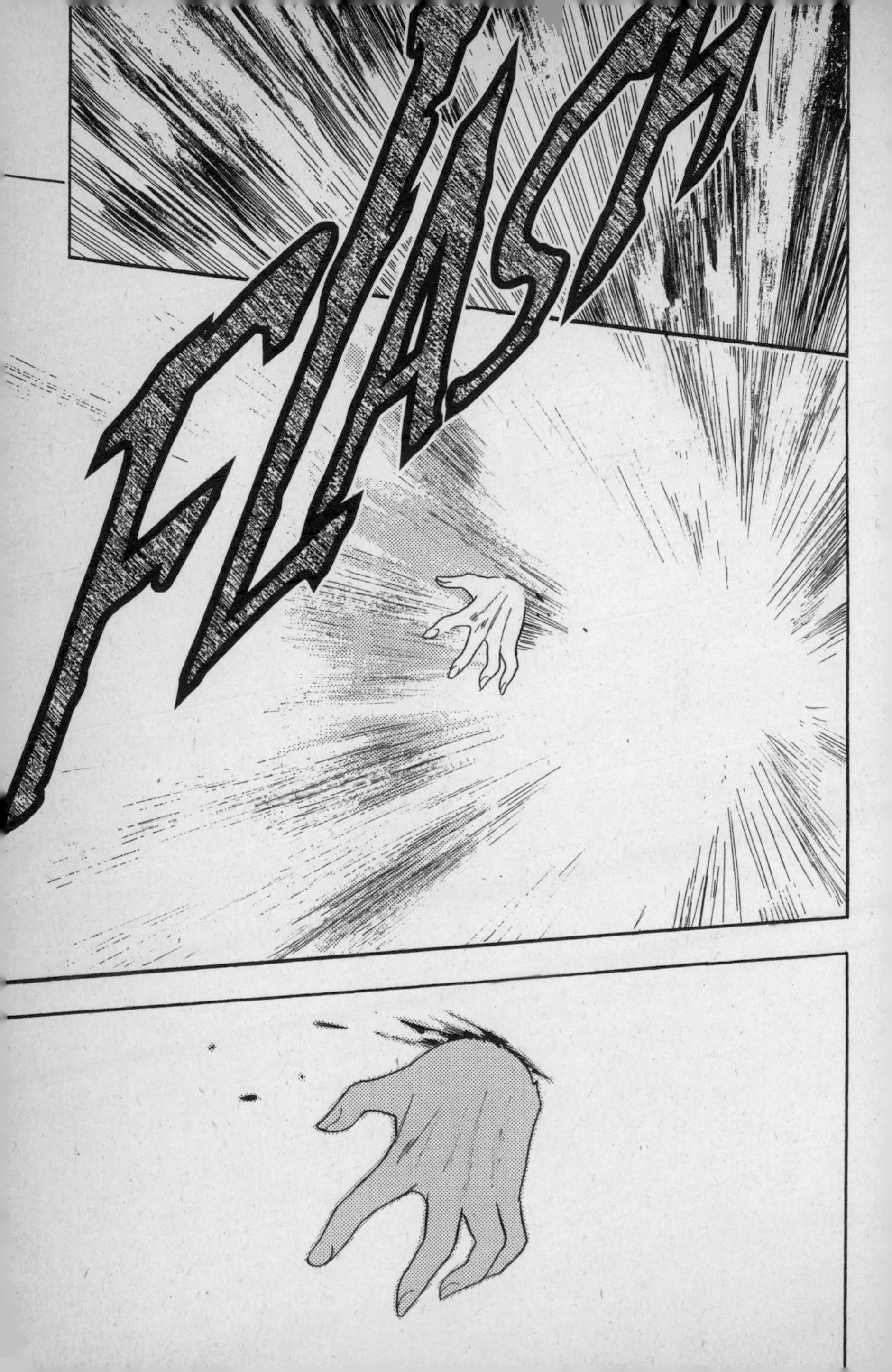
FLASH

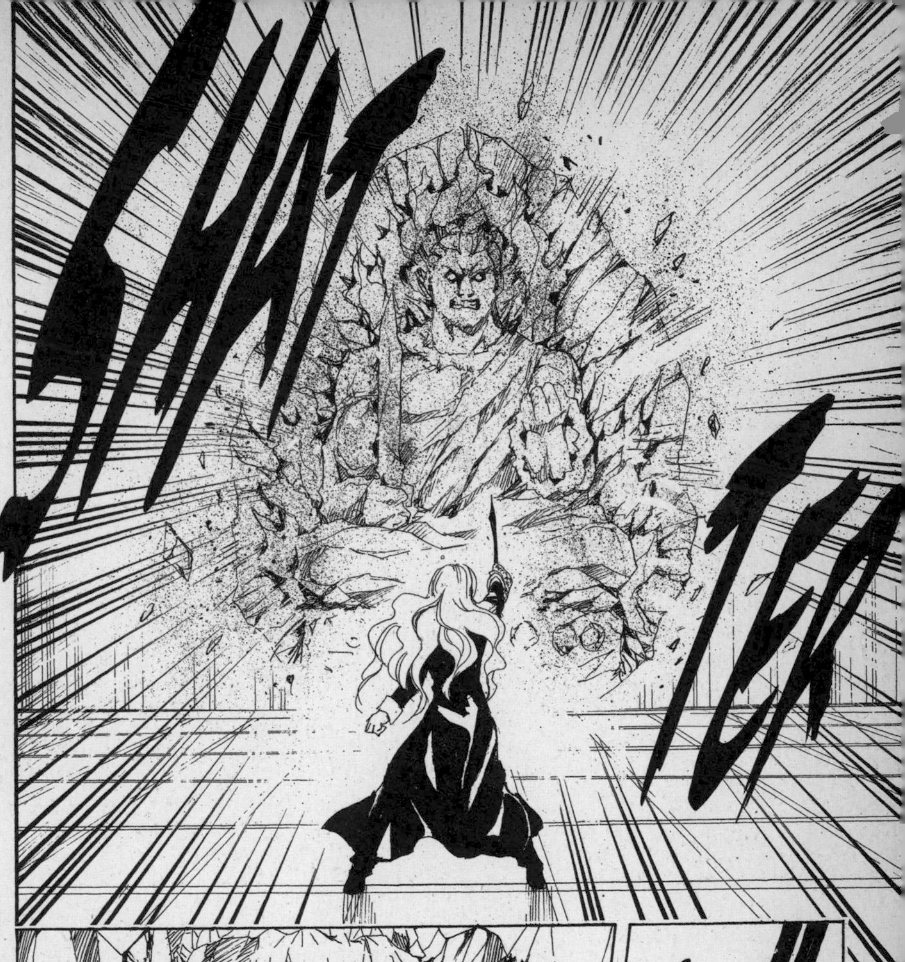
SHAT
TER
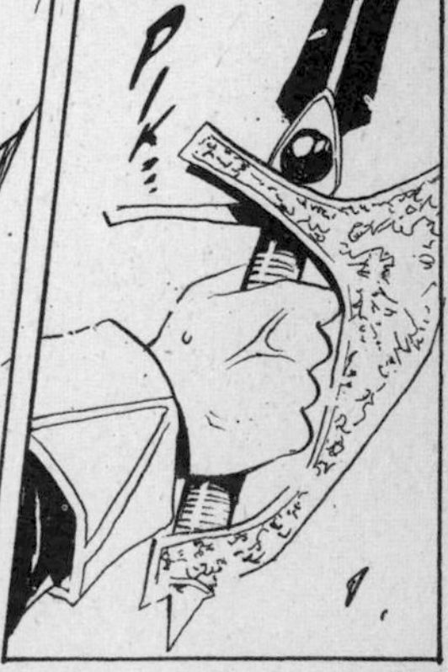
PIK...
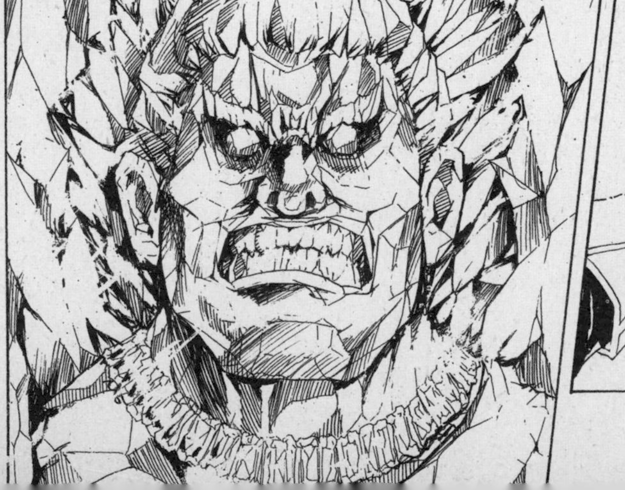

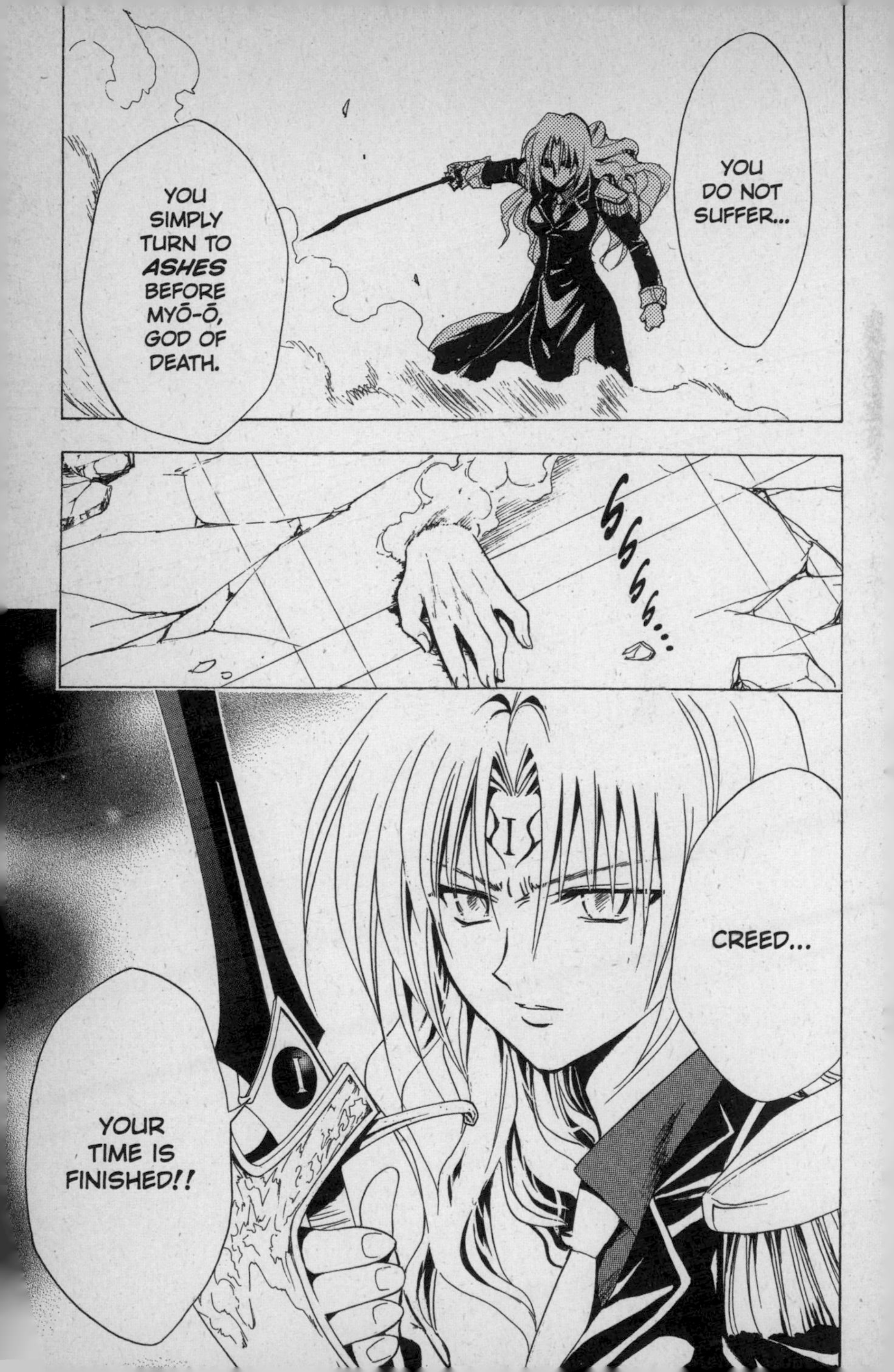
YOU DO NOT SUFFER...
YOU SIMPLY TURN TO ASHES BEFORE MYŌ-Ō, GOD OF DEATH.
SSSS...
CREED...
YOUR TIME IS FINISHED!!

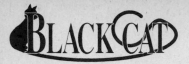

BLACK CAT FACTOID

MEKKAI WORLD DESTROYER

THE ULTIMATE OF THE 36 ATTACKS IN ARKS' FLUID BLADE TECHNIQUE. IT DEFIES THE LIMITS OF THE HUMAN BODY AND LANDS CONTINUOUS BLOWS AT SUPERSONIC SPEED. AT CLOSE RANGE, ENEMIES ARE PULVERIZED.

THIS ATTACK IS INITIATED BY WRITING THE CHARACTERS FOR FUDÔ MYŌ-Ō. THOSE WHO PERISH FROM IT ARE SAID TO HAVE SEEN THE FACE OF THAT GOD IN THEIR LAST MOMENTS.

USE OF THIS TECHNIQUE IS ONLY POSSIBLE BECAUSE OF SEPHIRIA'S SUPERHUMAN SPEED AND SWORDSMANSHIP. STILL, THE PRICE SHE PAYS IS GREAT.

MEKKAI WORLD DESTROYER!

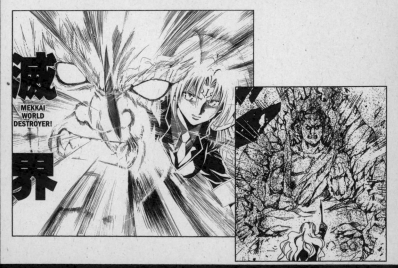

Chapter 171: A New Threat

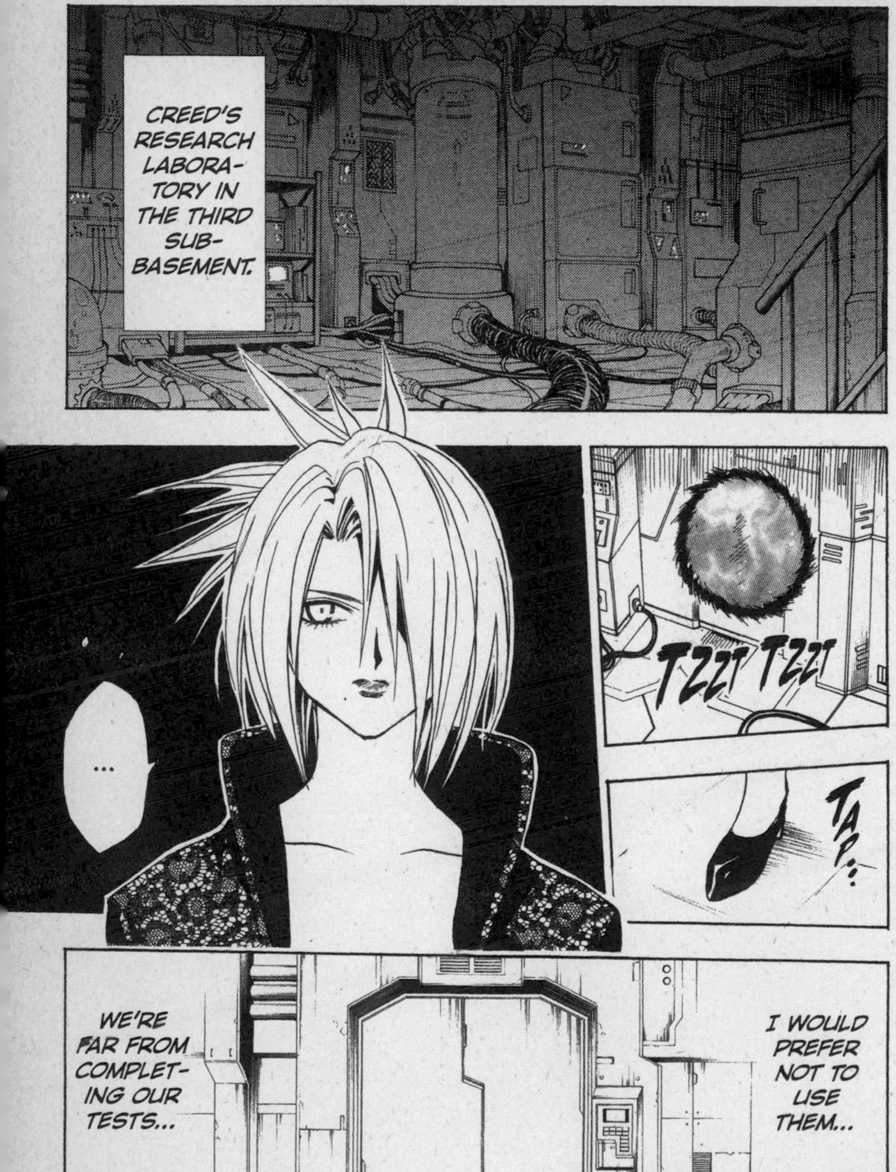

CREED'S RESEARCH LABORATORY IN THE THIRD SUB-BASEMENT.
TZZT TZZT
TAP...
...
I WOULD PREFER NOT TO USE THEM...
WE'RE FAR FROM COMPLETING OUR TESTS...

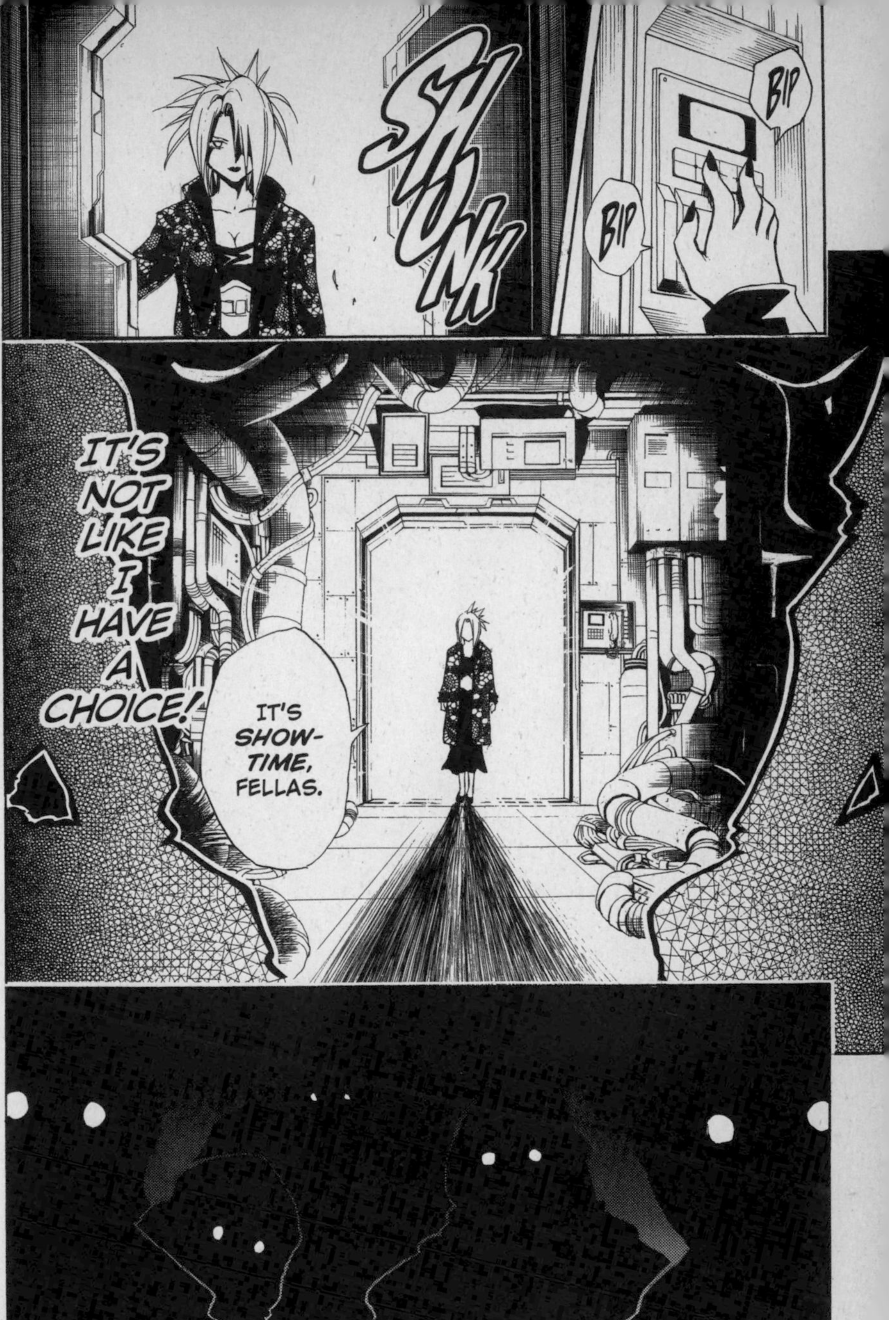
BIP
BIP
SHUNK
IT'S NOT LIKE I HAVE A CHOICE!
IT'S SHOW-TIME, FELLAS.

Chapter 171: A New Threat

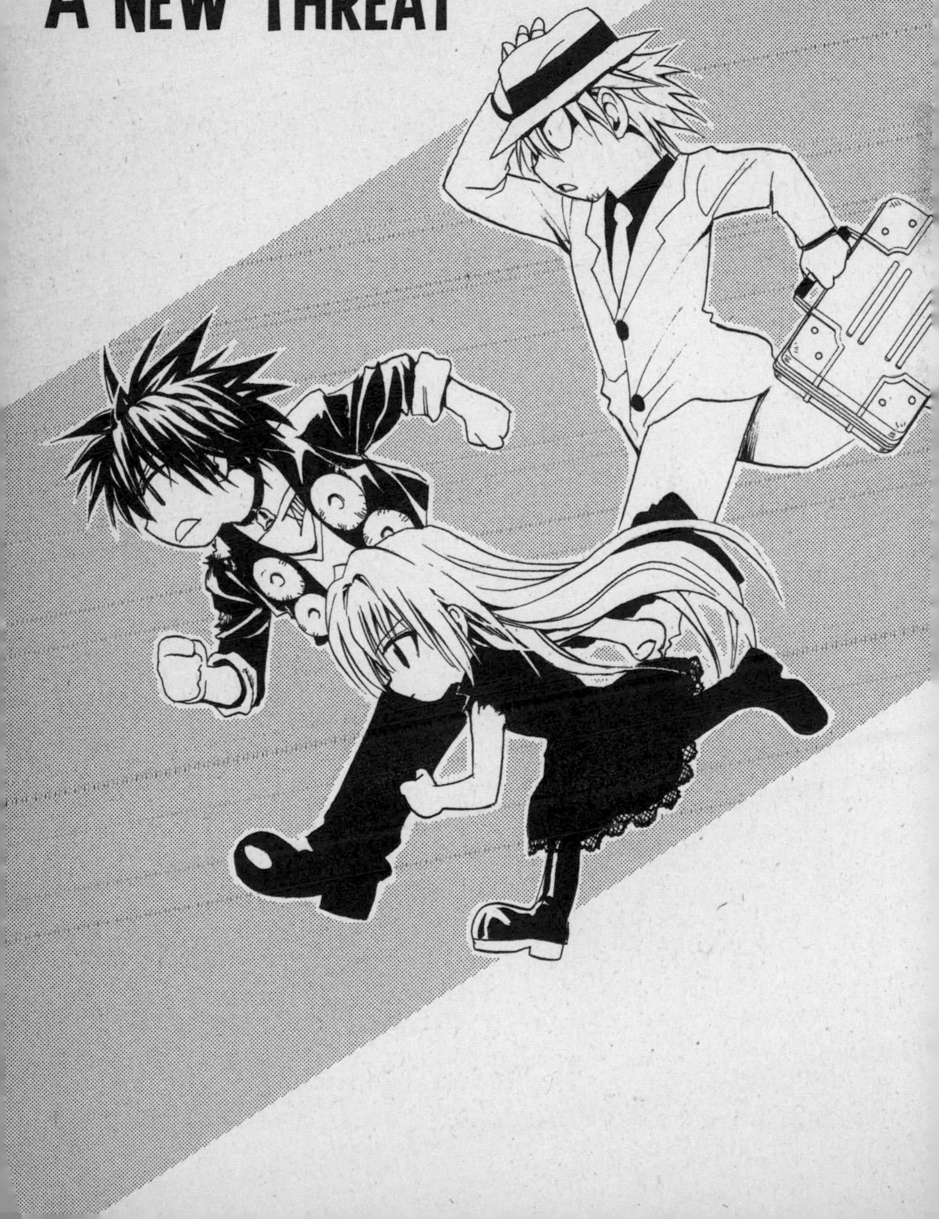

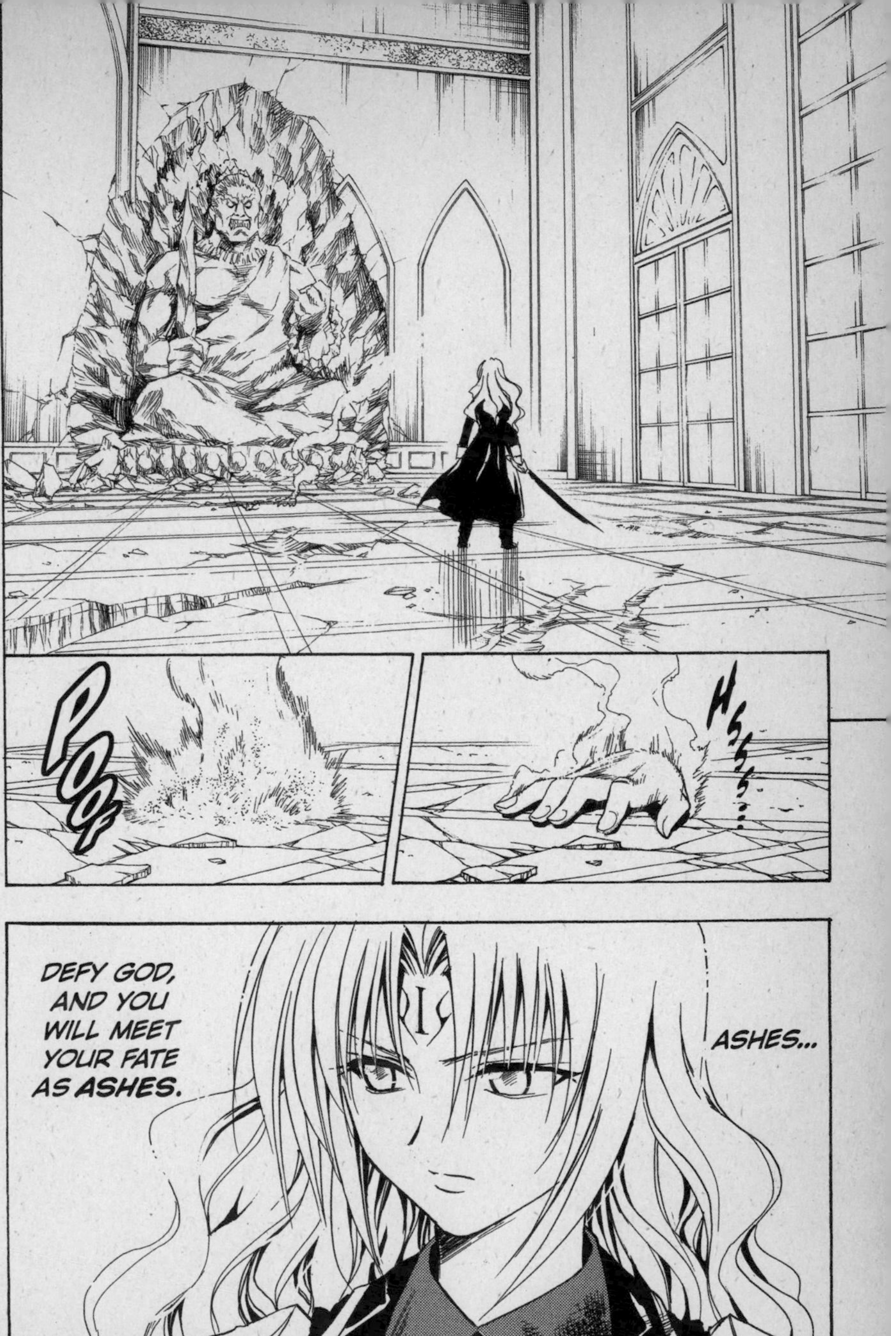
HSSSS...
POOF
DEFY GOD, AND YOU WILL MEET YOUR FATE AS ASHES.
ASHES...

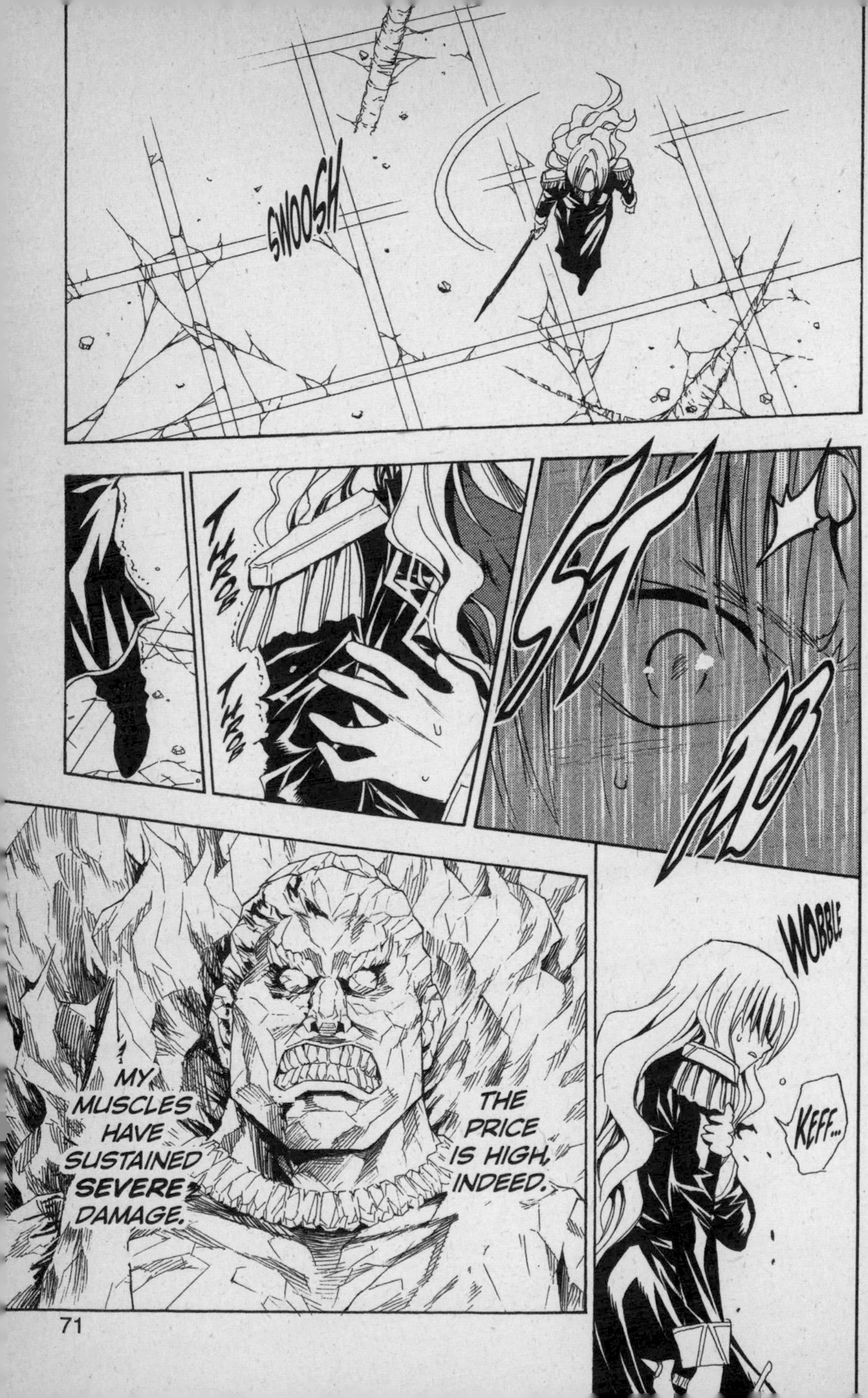
SWOOSH
THROB
THROB
WOBBLE
KEFF...
THE PRICE IS HIGH, INDEED.
MY MUSCLES HAVE SUSTAINED SEVERE DAMAGE.

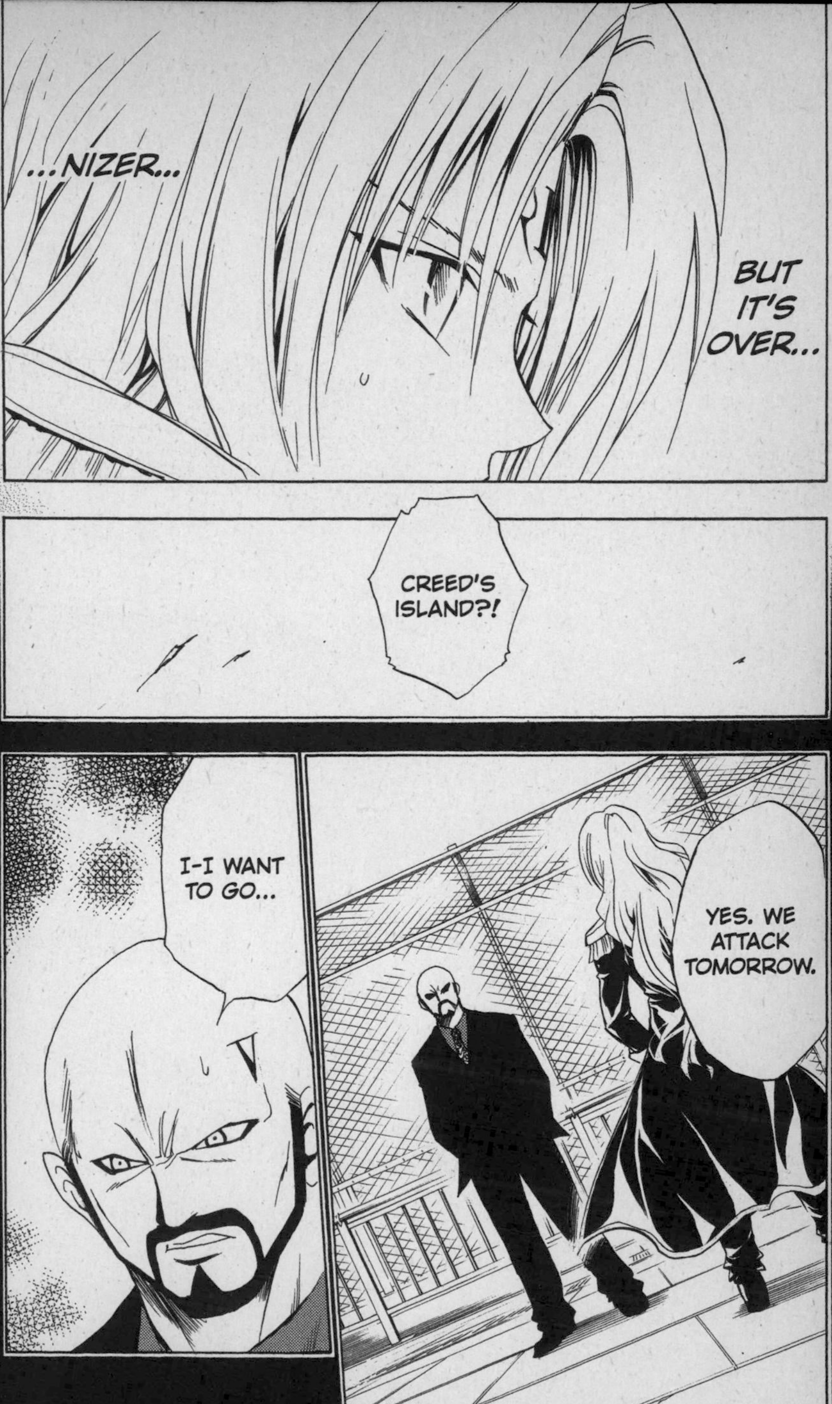
BUT IT'S OVER...
...NIZER...
CREED'S ISLAND?!
YES. WE ATTACK TOMORROW.
I-I WANT TO GO...

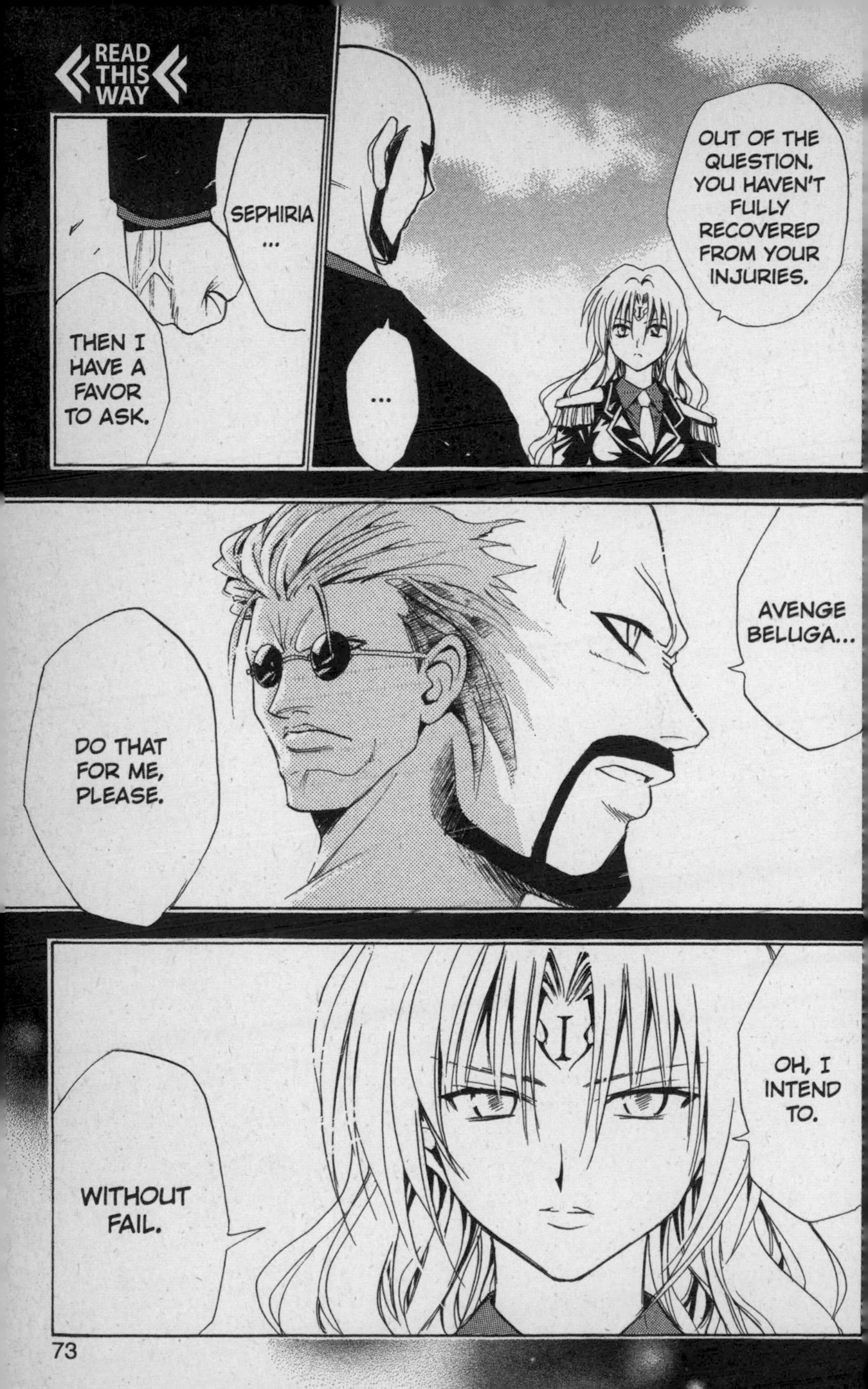
READ THIS WAY
OUT OF THE QUESTION. YOU HAVEN'T FULLY RECOVERED FROM YOUR INJURIES.
...
SEPHIRIA ...
THEN I HAVE A FAVOR TO ASK.
AVENGE BELUGA...
DO THAT FOR ME, PLEASE.
OH, I INTEND TO.
WITHOUT FAIL.

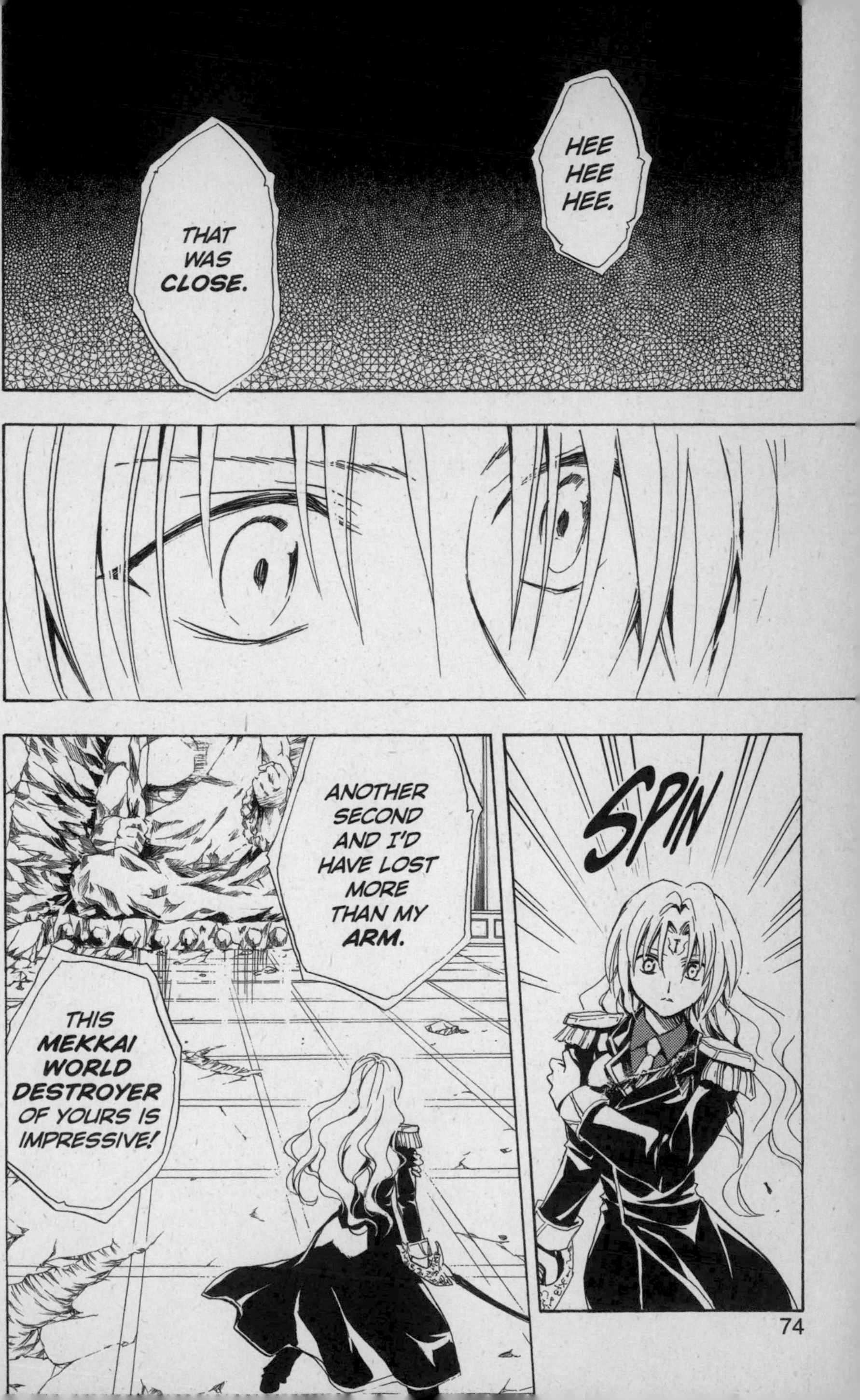
HEE HEE HEE.
THAT WAS CLOSE.
SPIN
ANOTHER SECOND AND I'D HAVE LOST MORE THAN MY ARM.
THIS MEKKAI WORLD DESTROYER OF YOURS IS IMPRESSIVE!

READ THIS WAY

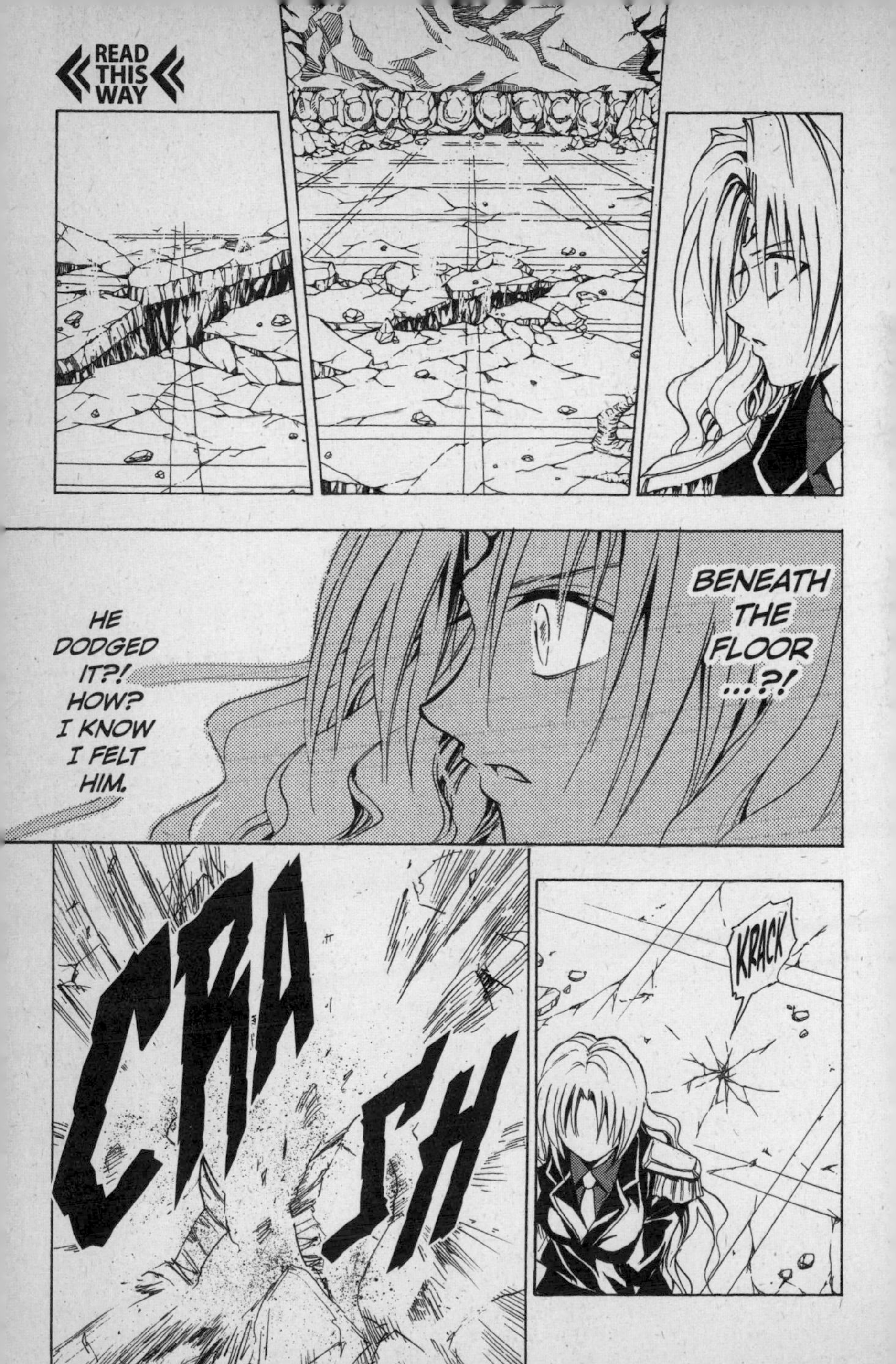
BENEATH THE FLOOR ...?!
HE DODGED IT?! HOW? I KNOW I FELT HIM.
KRACK
CRASH

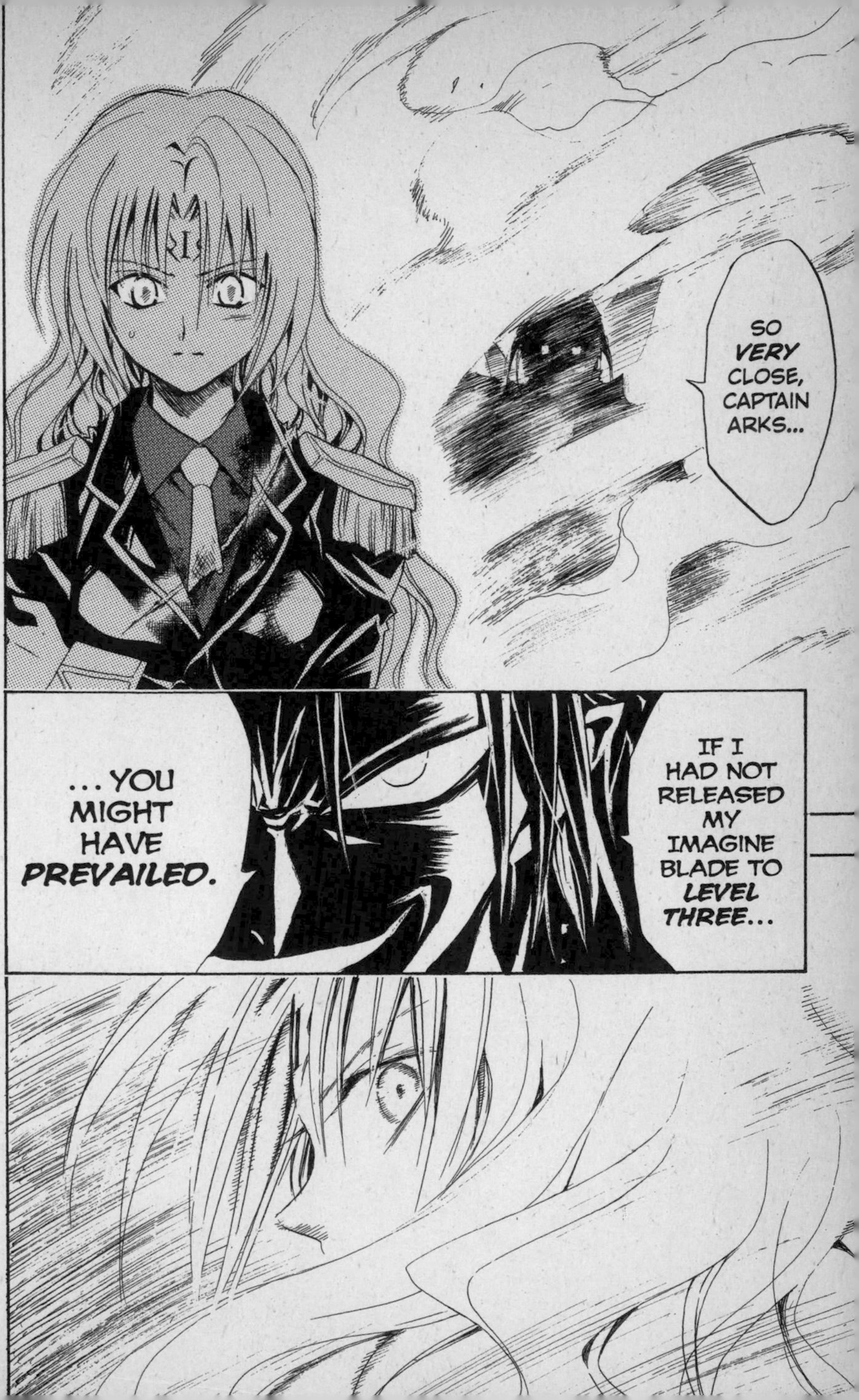
SO VERY CLOSE, CAPTAIN ARKS...
IF I HAD NOT RELEASED MY IMAGINE BLADE TO LEVEL THREE...
... YOU MIGHT HAVE PREVAILED.

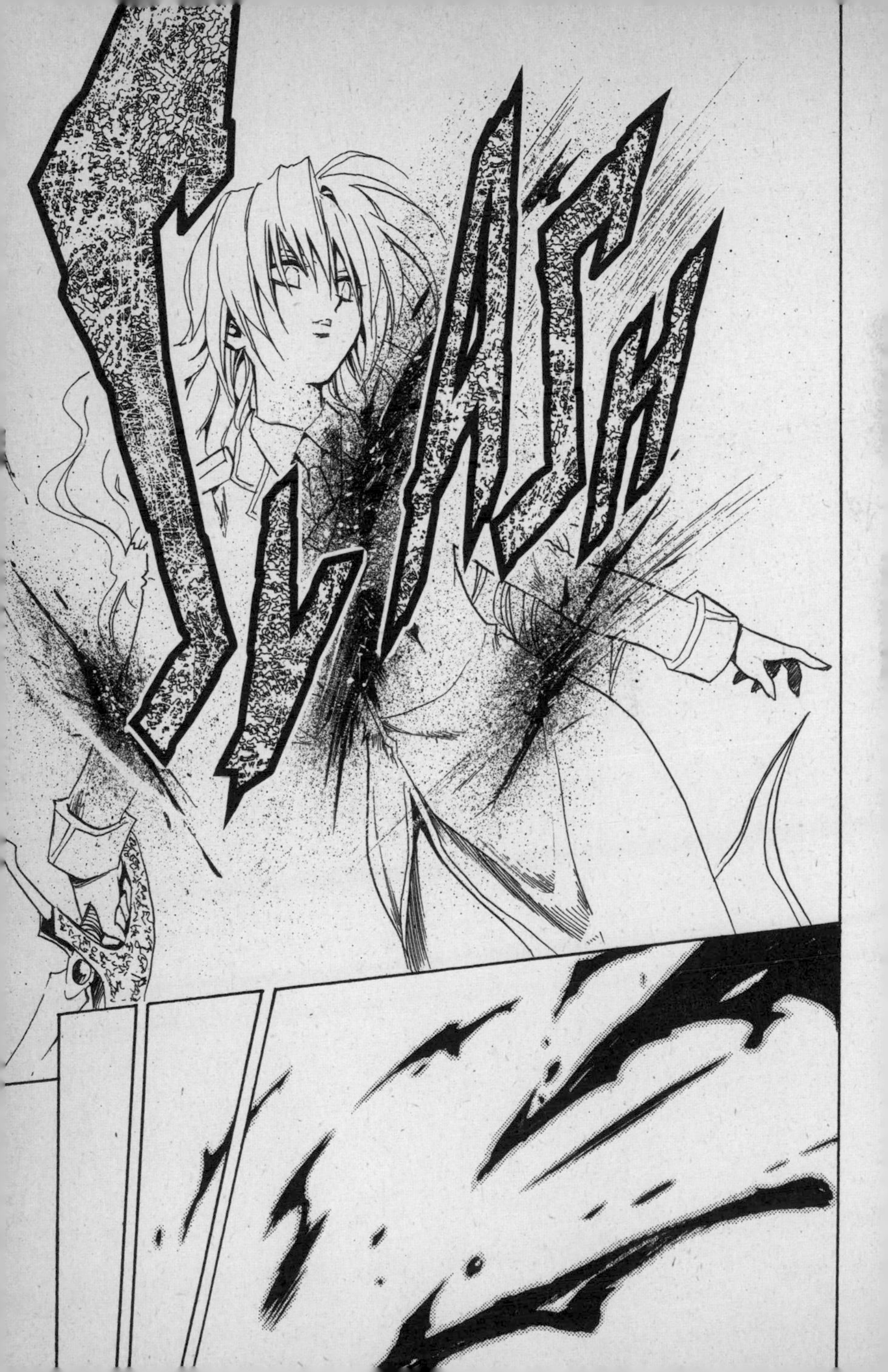
SLASH

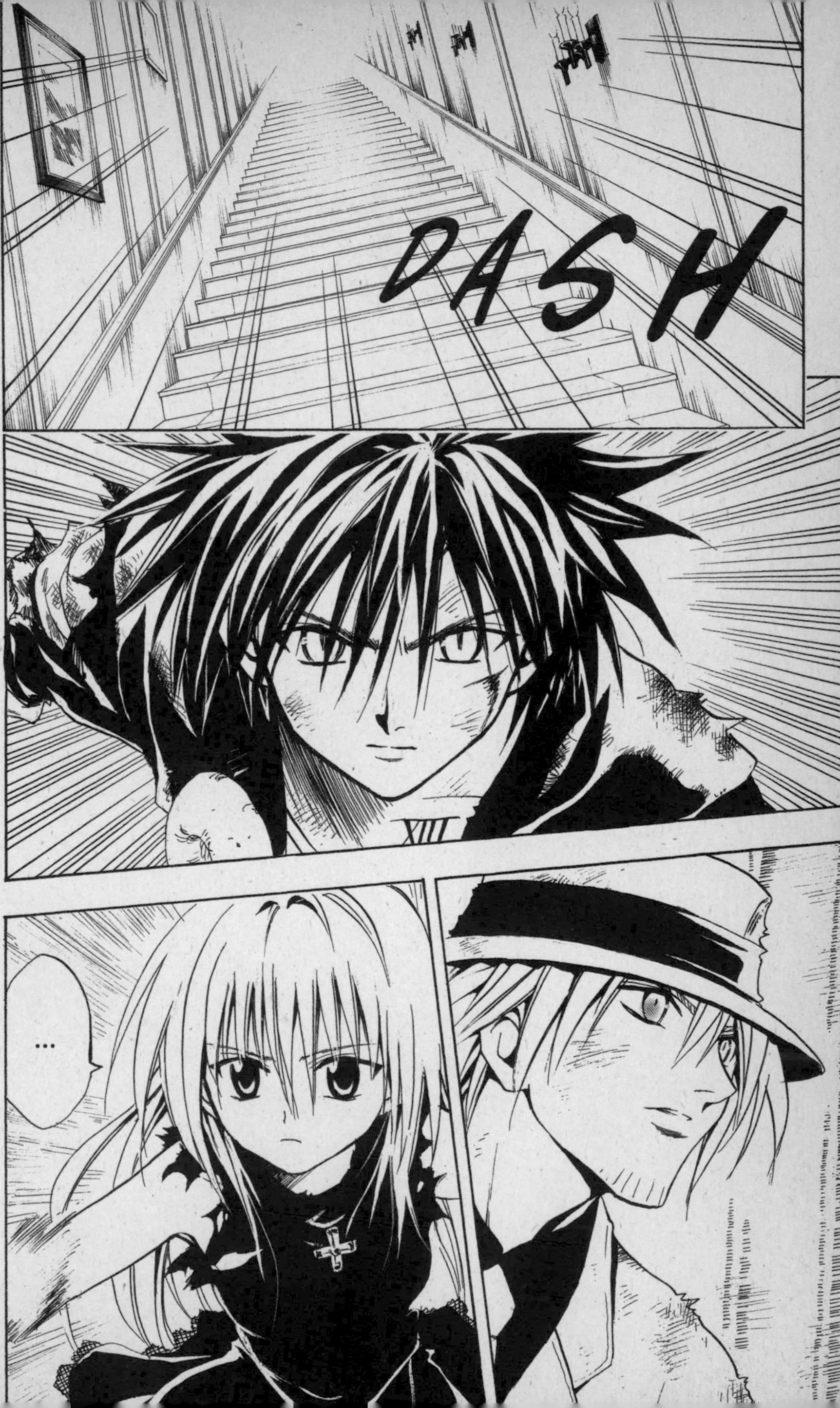
DASH
XIII
...

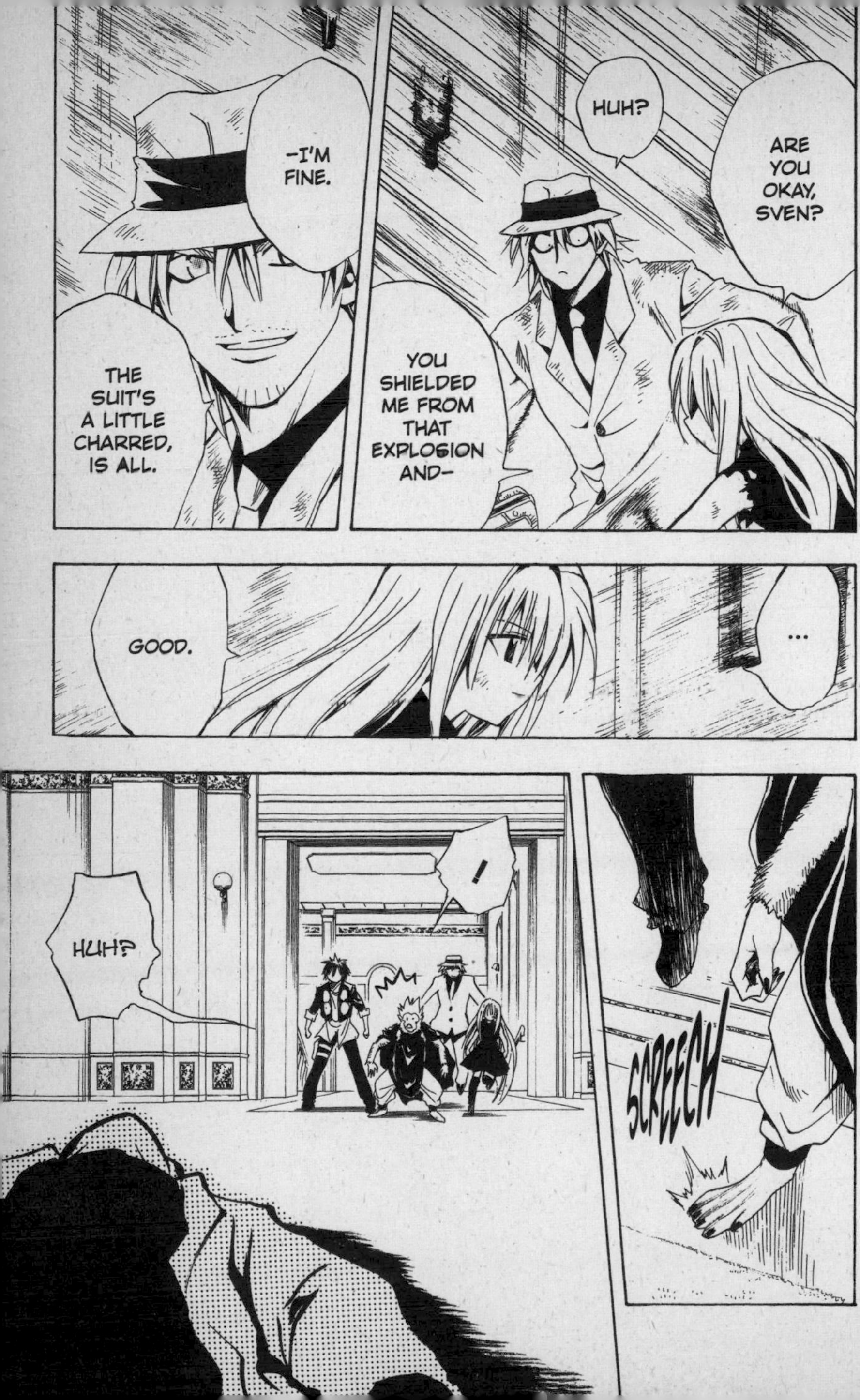
ARE YOU OKAY, SVEN?
HUH?
YOU SHIELDED ME FROM THAT EXPLOSION AND-
-I'M FINE.
THE SUIT'S A LITTLE CHARRED, IS ALL.
...
GOOD.
SCREECH
!
HUH?

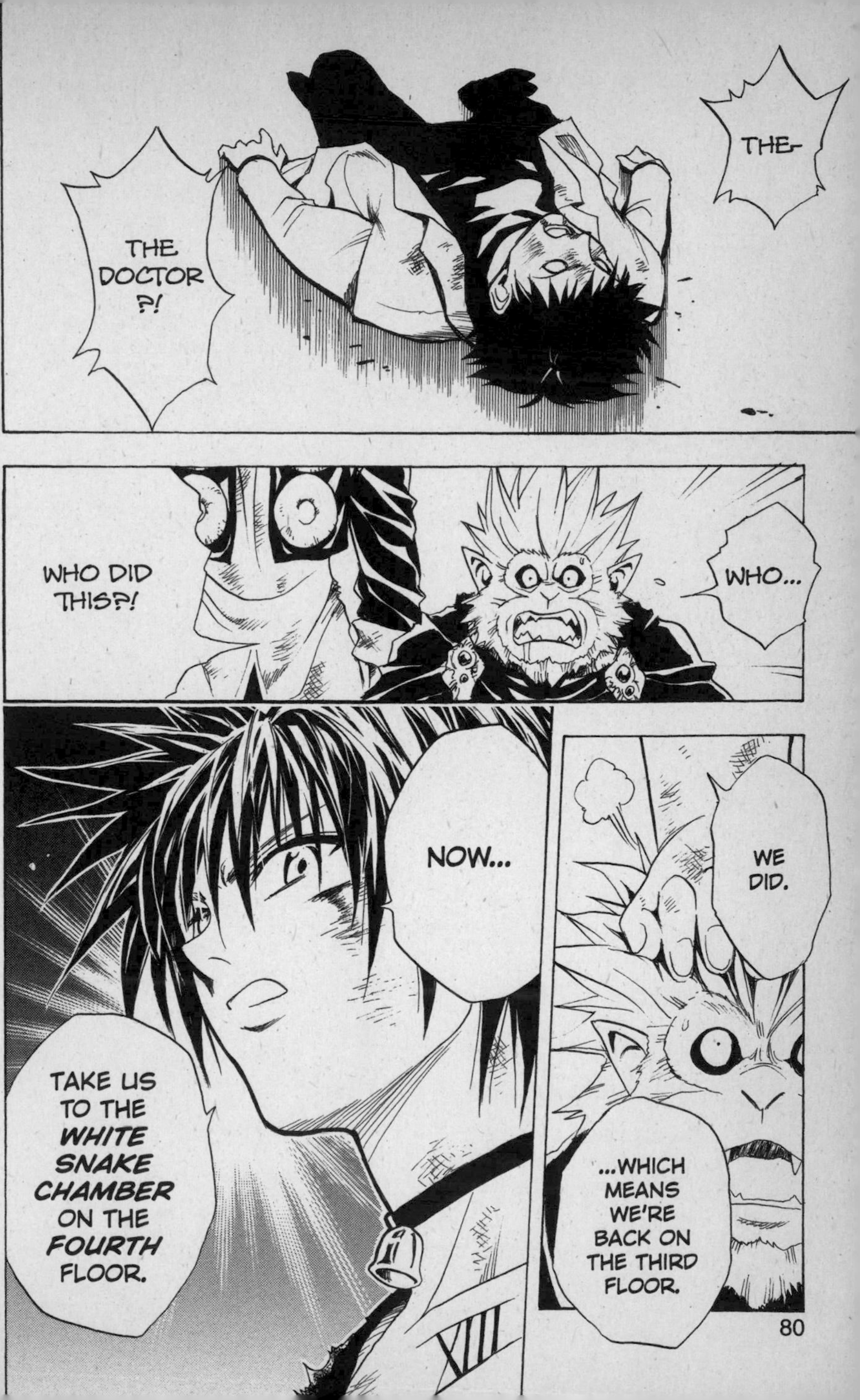
THE-
THE DOCTOR ?!
WHO...
WHO DID THIS?!
WE DID.
...WHICH MEANS WE'RE BACK ON THE THIRD FLOOR.
NOW...
TAKE US TO THE *WHITE SNAKE CHAMBER* ON THE *FOURTH* FLOOR.

READ THIS WAY

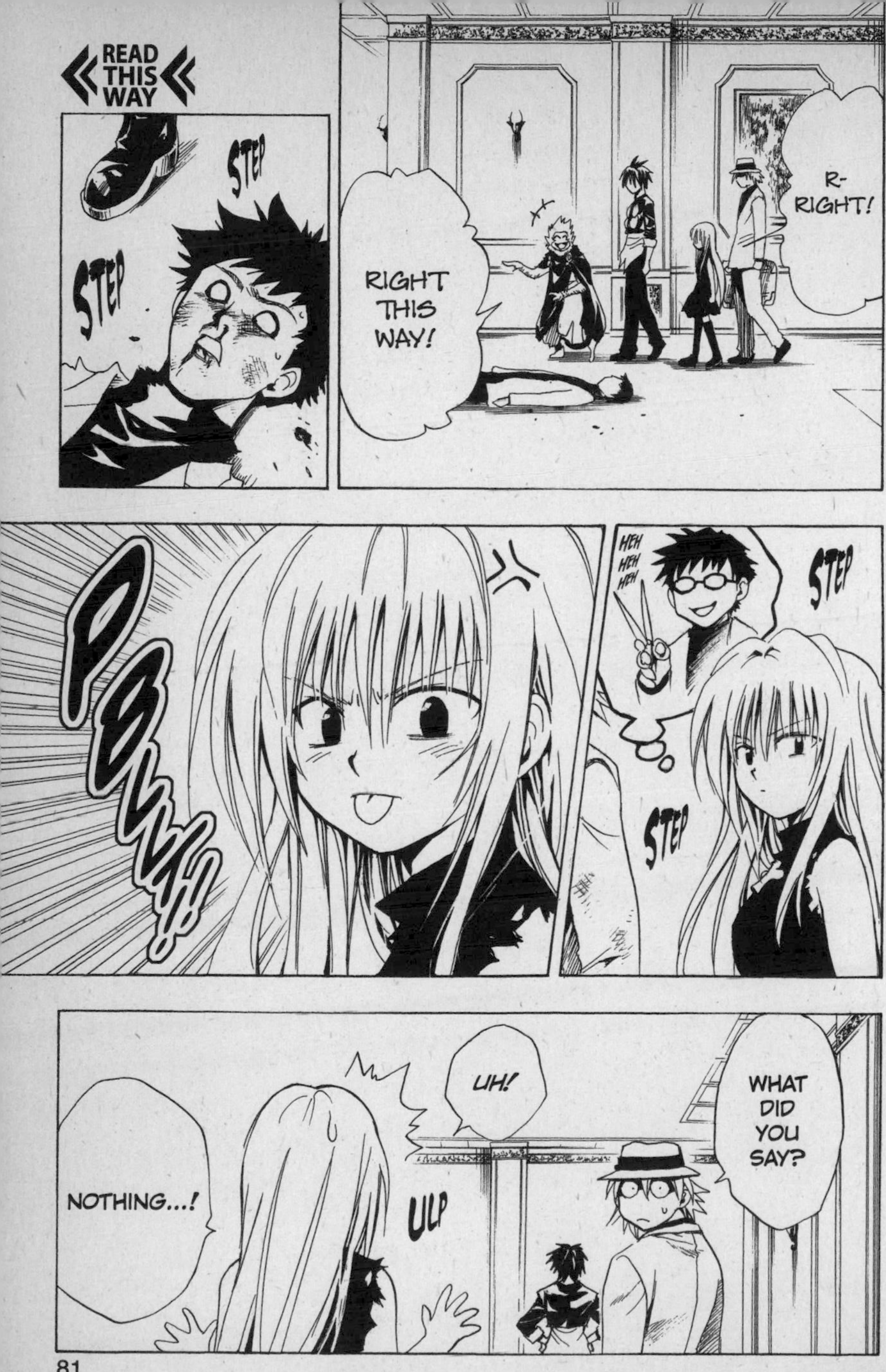
R-
RIGHT!
RIGHT THIS WAY!
STEP
STEP
HEH HEH HEH
STEP
STEP
WHAT DID YOU SAY?
UH!
ULP
NOTHING...!

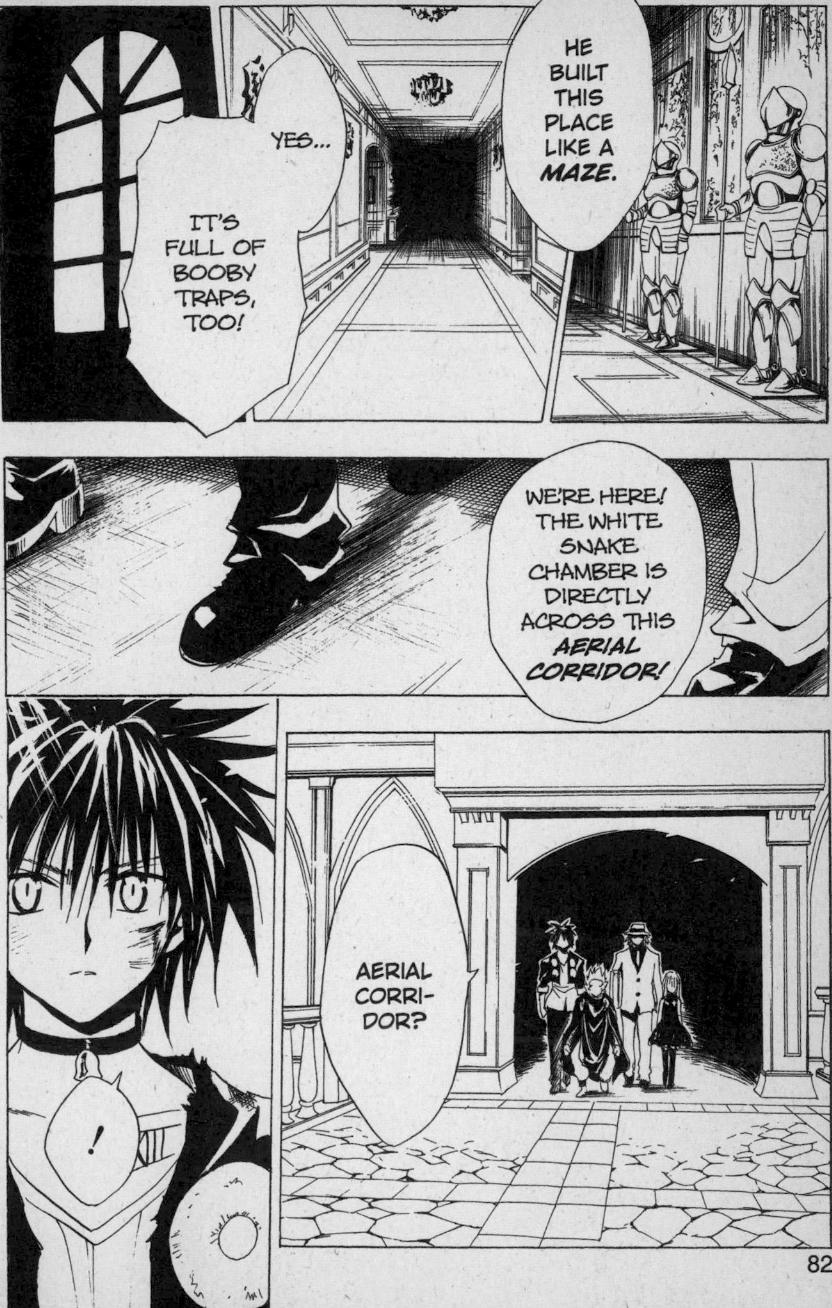
HE BUILT THIS PLACE LIKE A *MAZE.*
YES...
IT'S FULL OF BOOBY TRAPS, TOO!
WE'RE HERE! THE WHITE SNAKE CHAMBER IS DIRECTLY ACROSS THIS *AERIAL CORRIDOR!*
AERIAL CORRI-DOR?
!

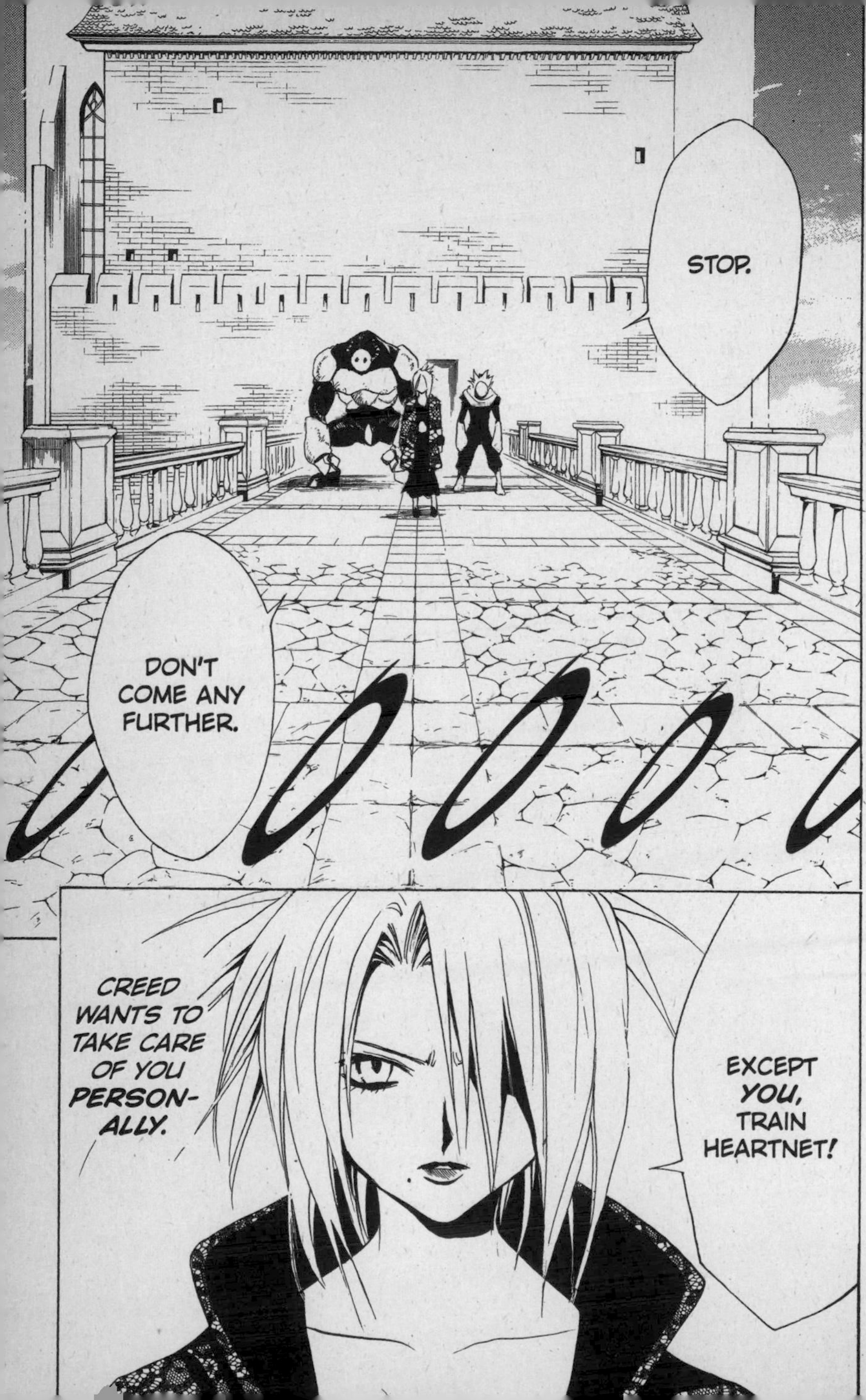
STOP.
DON'T COME ANY FURTHER.
EXCEPT YOU, TRAIN HEARTNET!
CREED WANTS TO TAKE CARE OF YOU PERSON-ALLY.

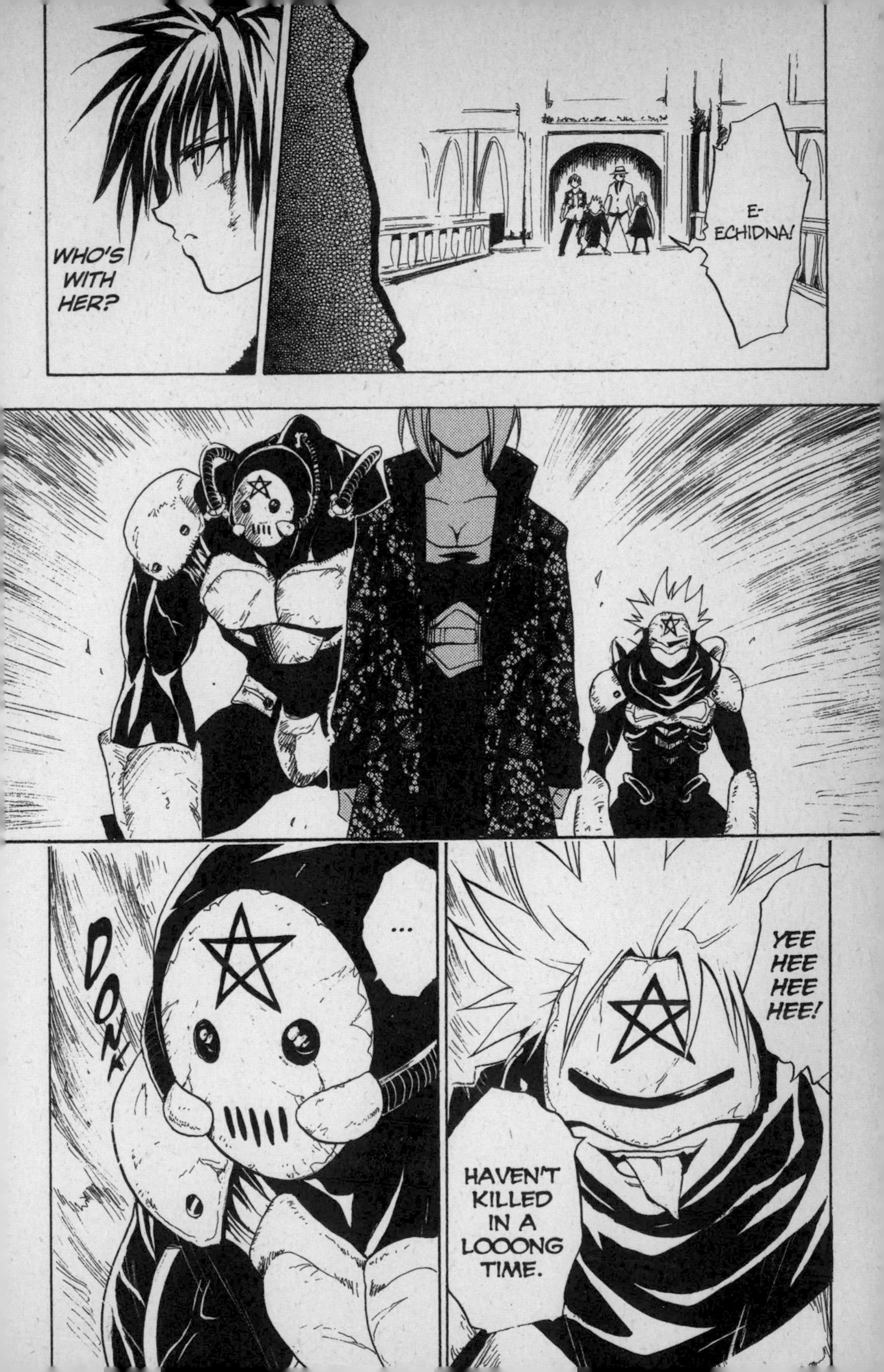
E-ECHIDNA!
WHO'S WITH HER?
YEE HEE HEE HEE!
HAVEN'T KILLED IN A LOOOONG TIME.
...
DONK

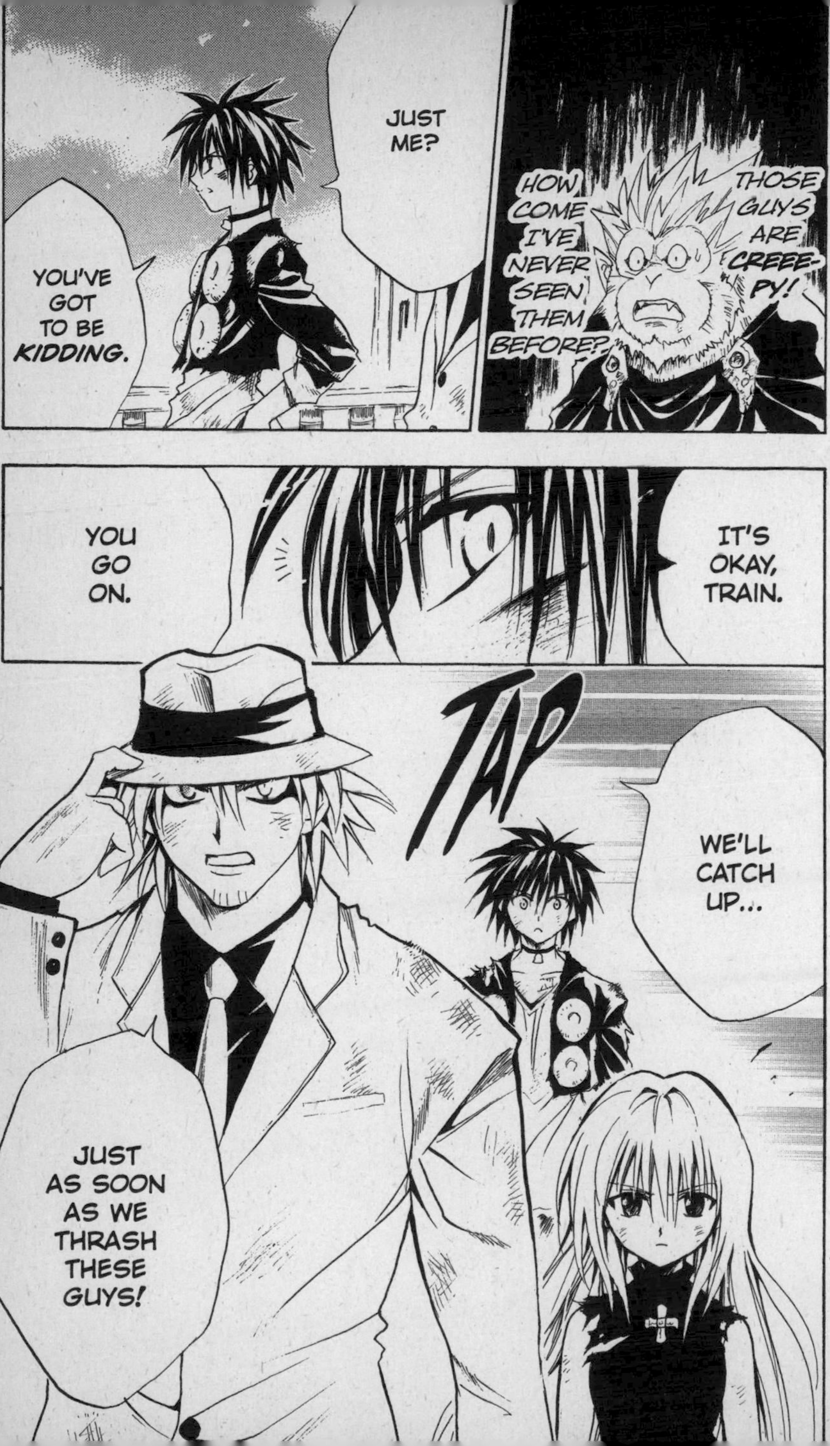
THOSE GUYS ARE CREEEPY!
HOW COME I'VE NEVER SEEN THEM BEFORE?
JUST ME?
YOU'VE GOT TO BE KIDDING.
IT'S OKAY, TRAIN.
YOU GO ON.
TAP
WE'LL CATCH UP...
JUST AS SOON AS WE THRASH THESE GUYS!

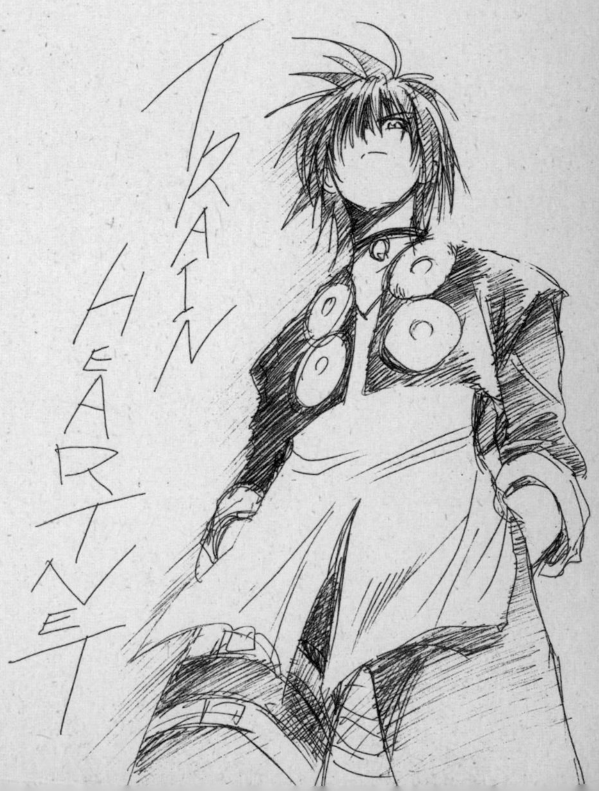
TRAIN
HEARTNET

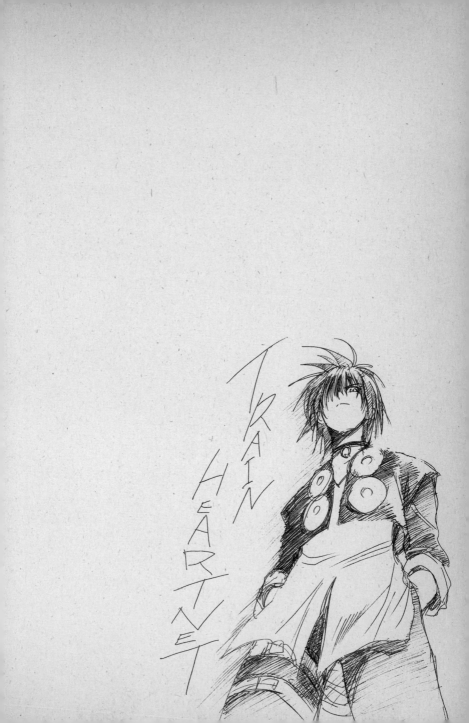

Chapter 172: Kiseitai

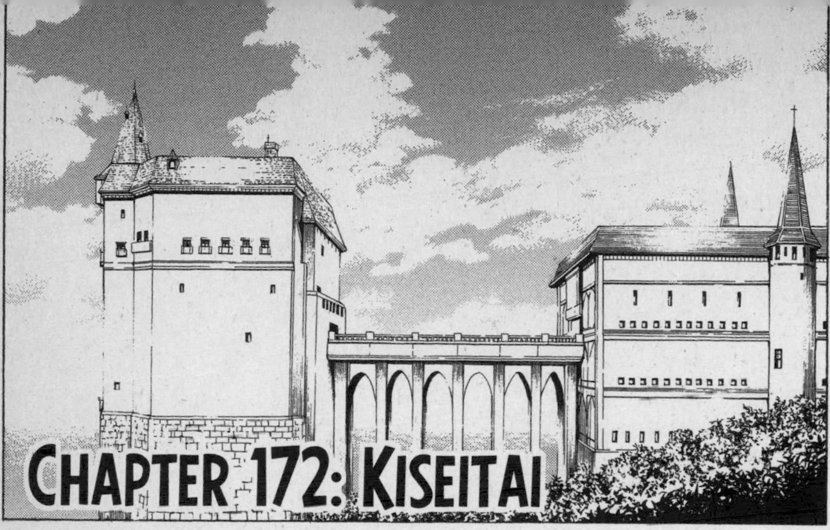

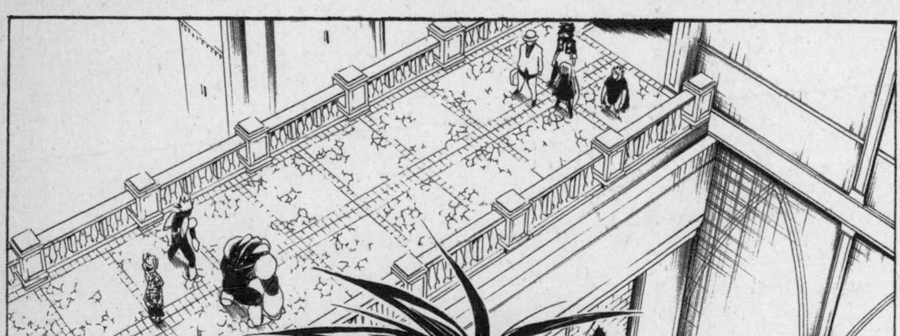

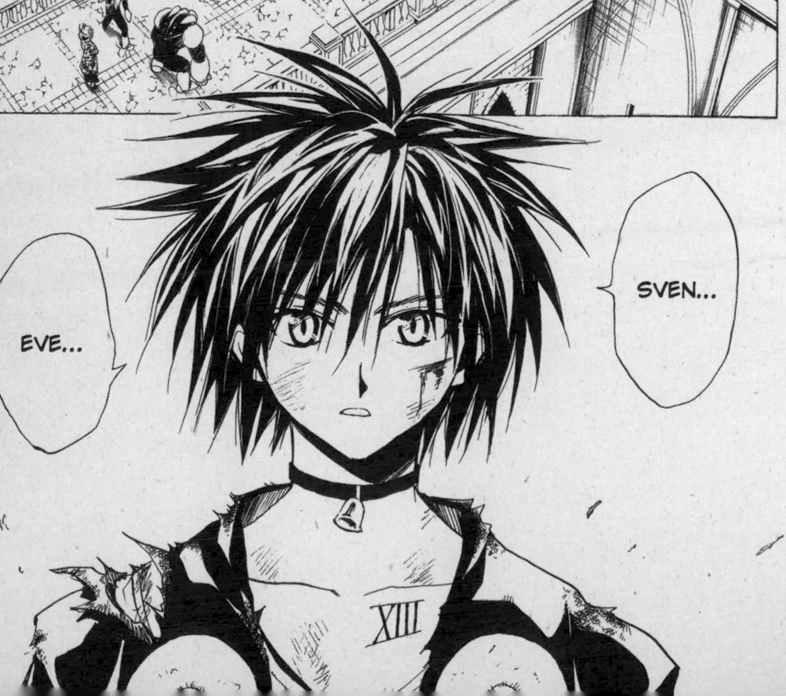
SVEN...
EVE...

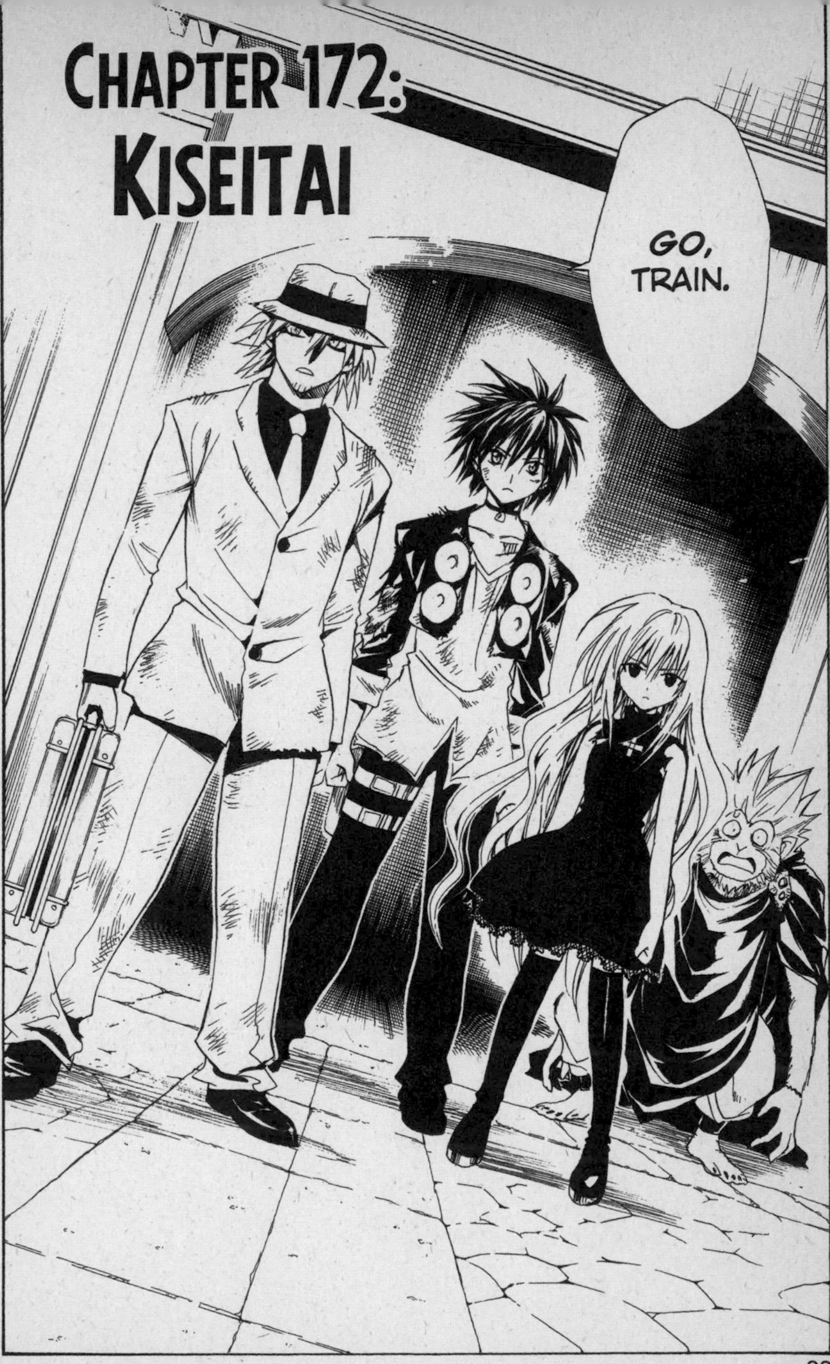
CHAPTER 172:
KISEITAI
GO, TRAIN.

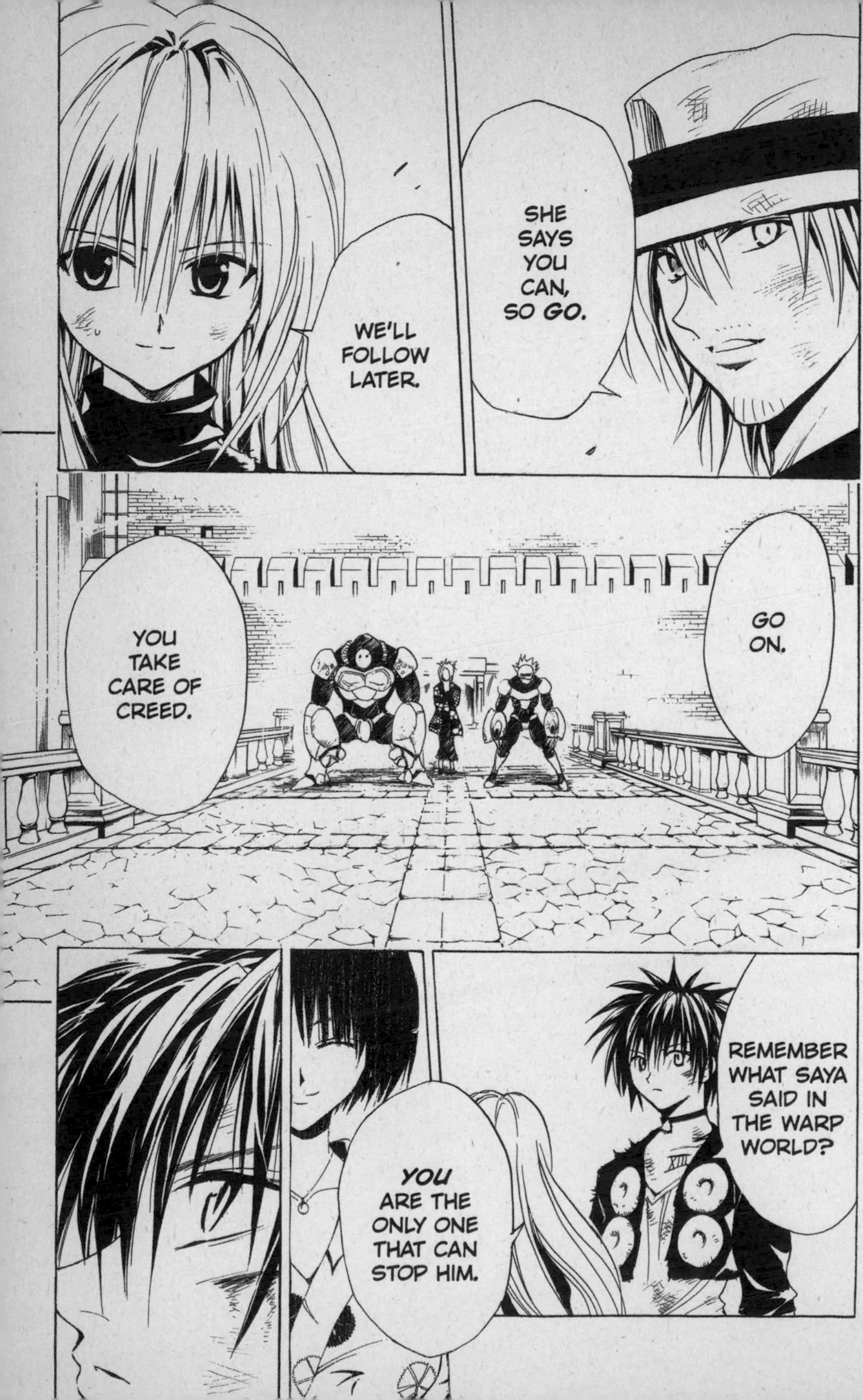
SHE SAYS YOU CAN, SO GO.
WE'LL FOLLOW LATER.
GO ON.
YOU TAKE CARE OF CREED.
REMEMBER WHAT SAYA SAID IN THE WARP WORLD?
YOU ARE THE ONLY ONE THAT CAN STOP HIM.

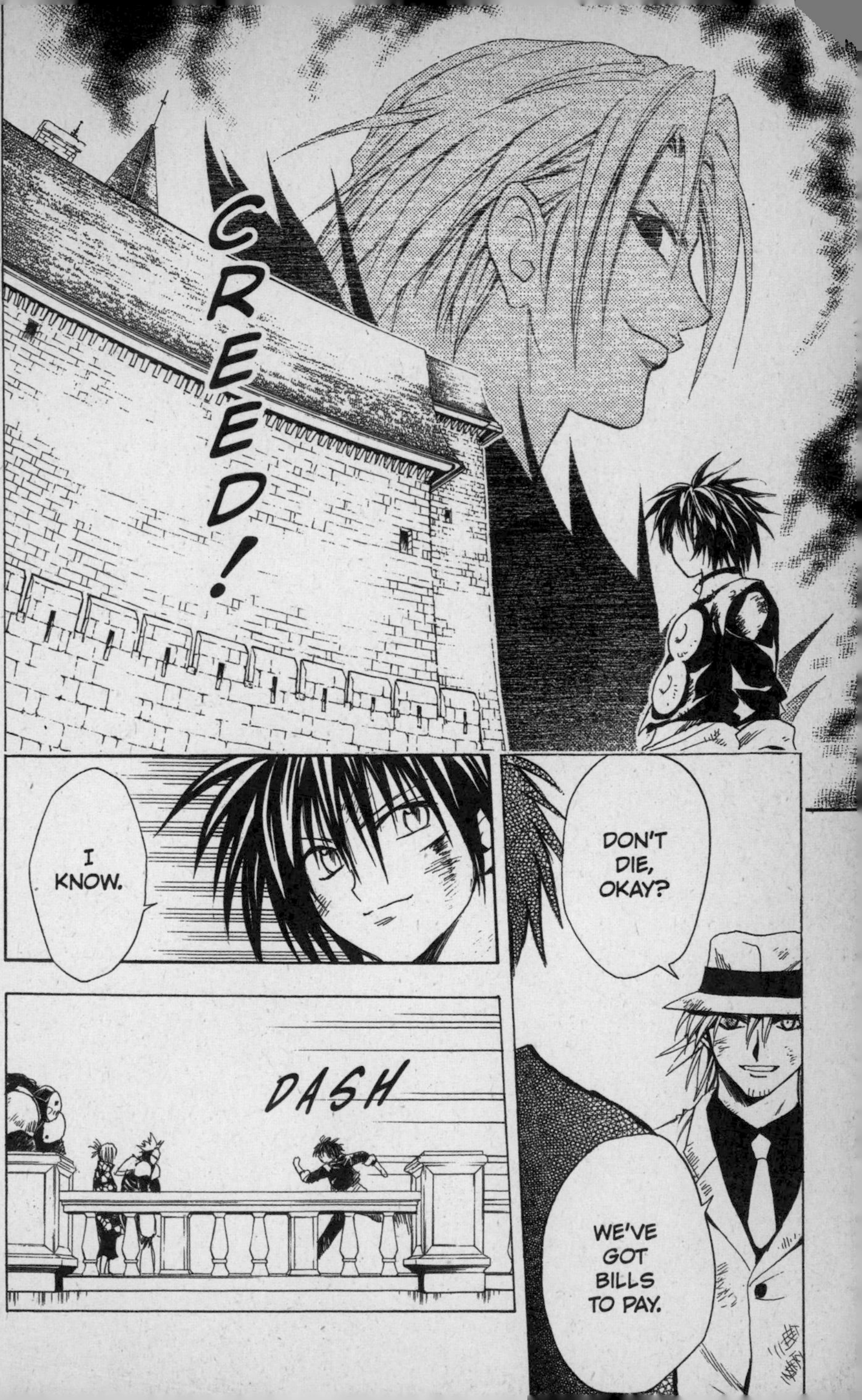
CREED!
DON'T DIE, OKAY?
WE'VE GOT BILLS TO PAY.
I KNOW.
DASH

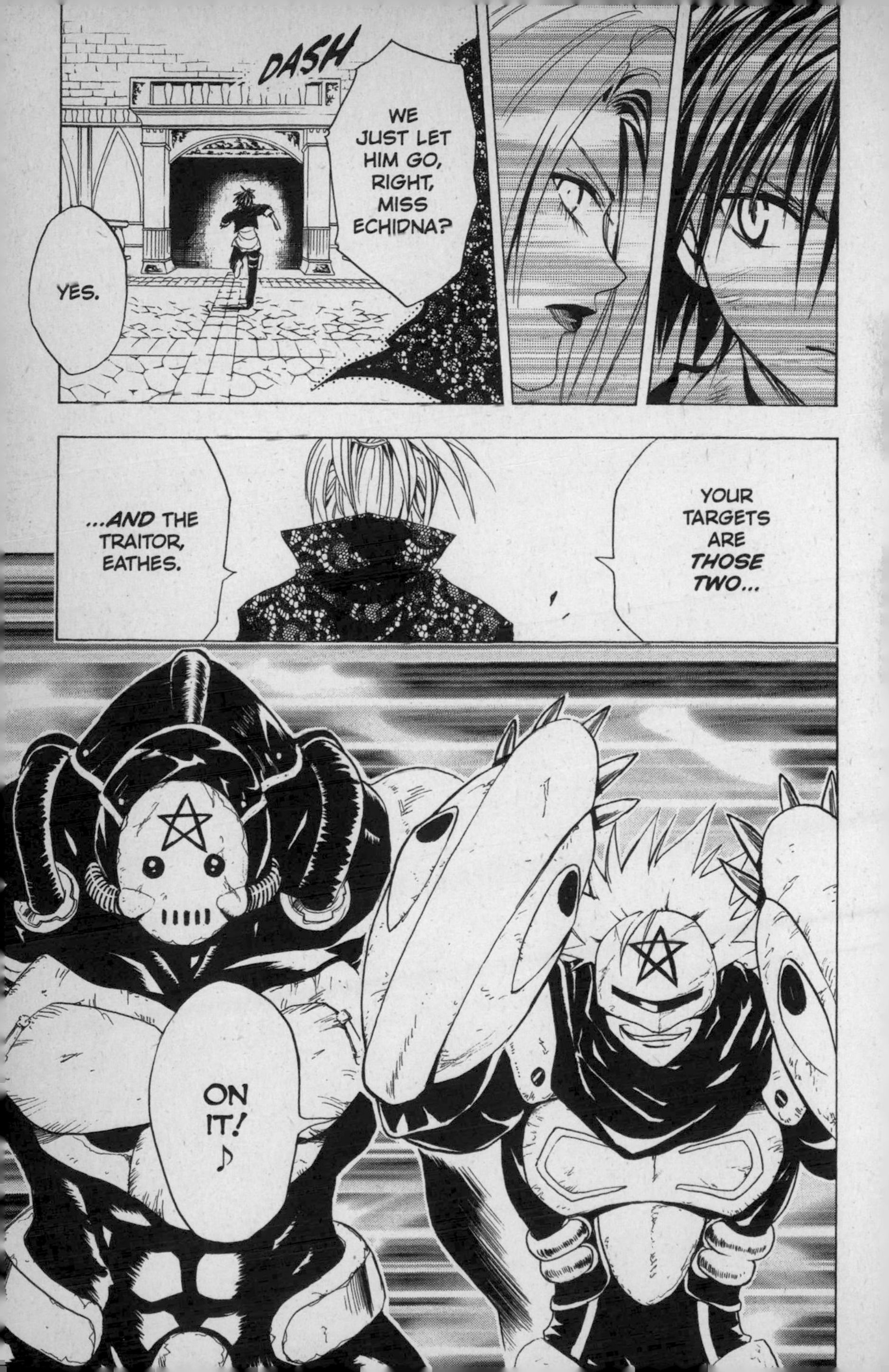
DASH
WE JUST LET HIM GO, RIGHT, MISS ECHIDNA?
YES.
YOUR TARGETS ARE *THOSE TWO*...
...*AND* THE TRAITOR, EATHES.
ON IT! ♪

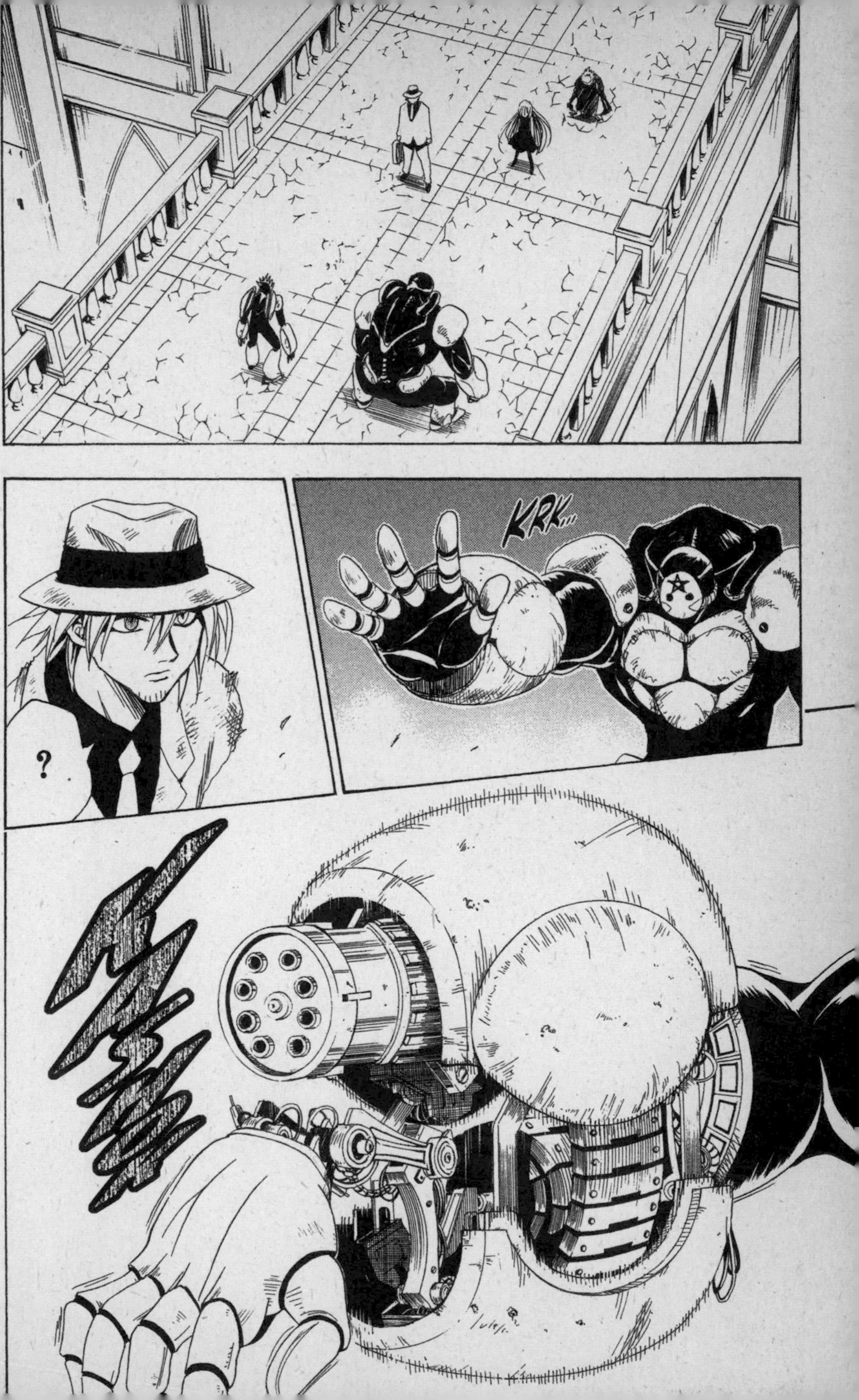
KRK...
?

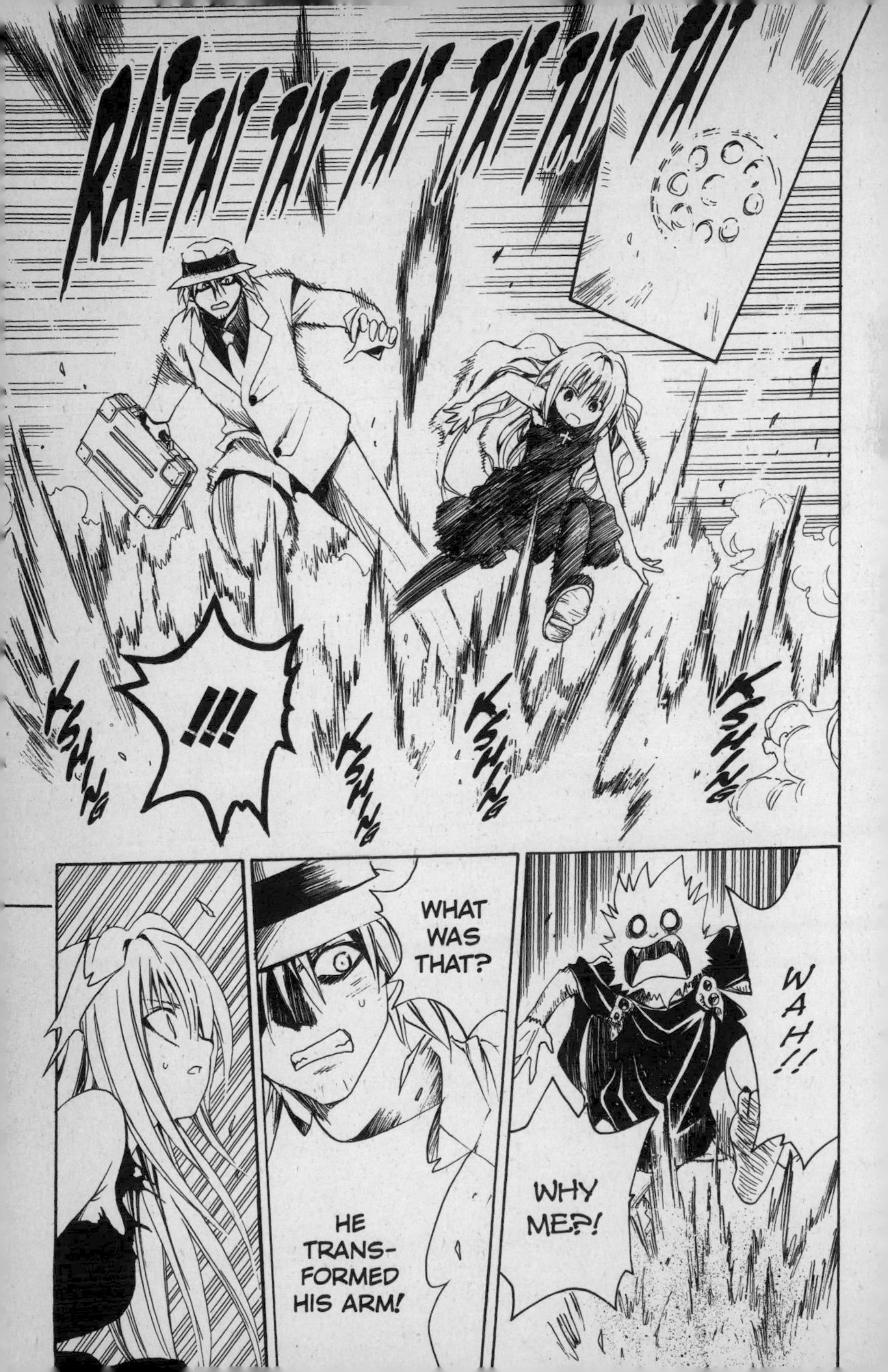
RATATATATATATATATA
KSHING
KSHING
KSHING
!!!
KSHING
WAH!!
WHY ME?!
WHAT WAS THAT?
HE TRANS-FORMED HIS ARM!

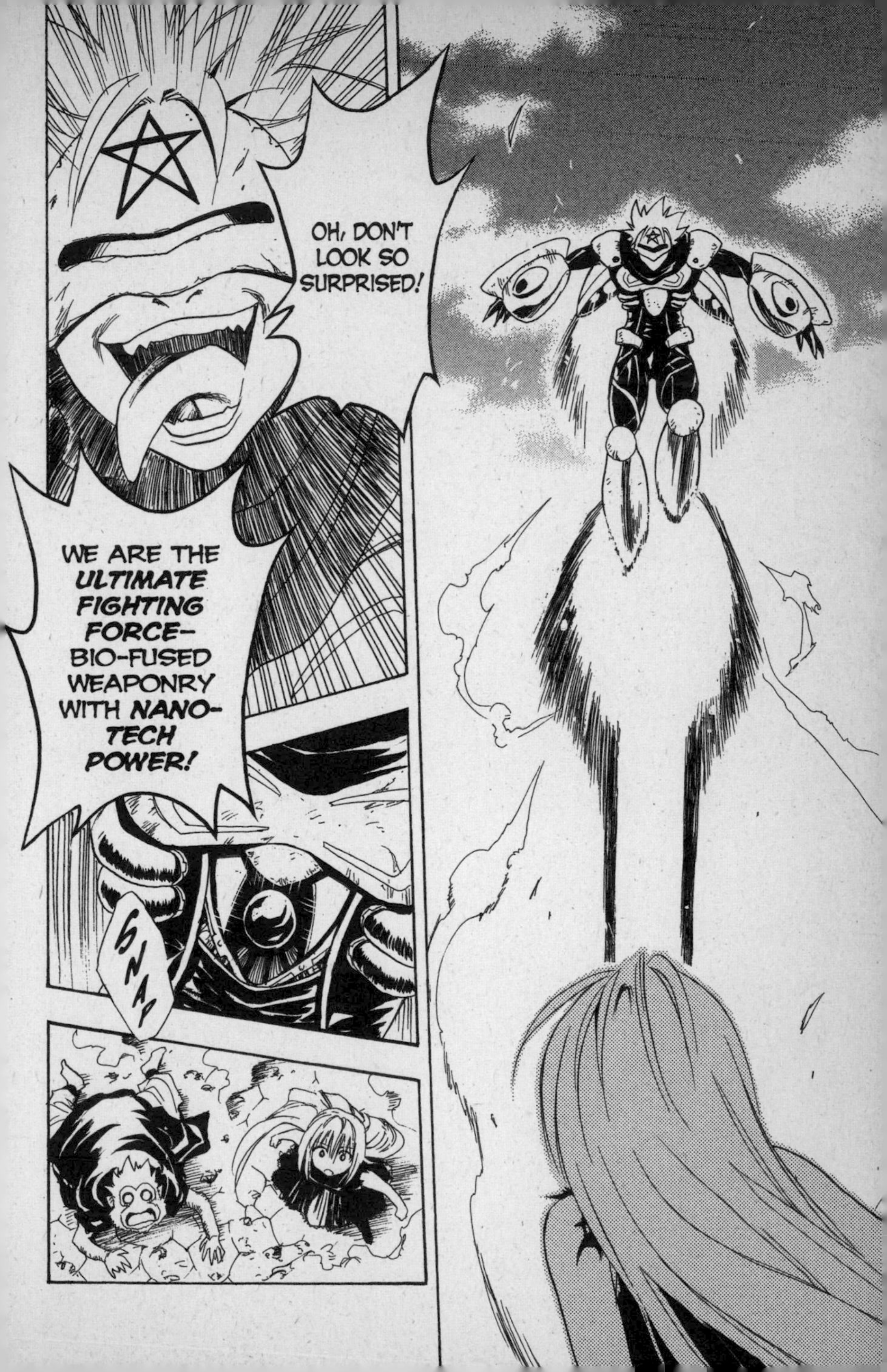
OH, DON'T LOOK SO SURPRISED!
WE ARE THE ULTIMATE FIGHTING FORCE- BIO-FUSED WEAPONRY WITH NANO-TECH POWER!
SNAP

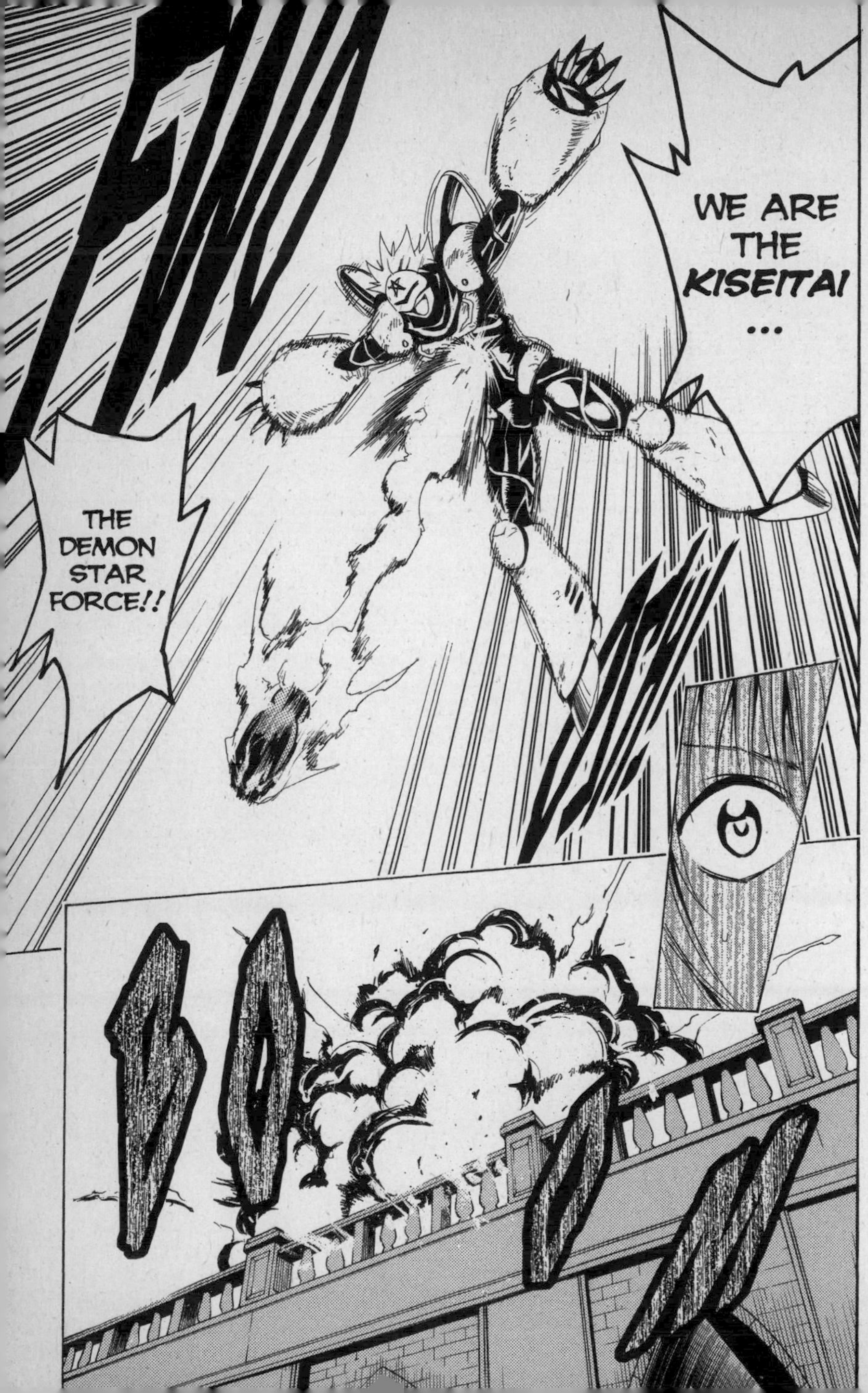
WE ARE THE KISEITAI ...
THE DEMON STAR FORCE!!

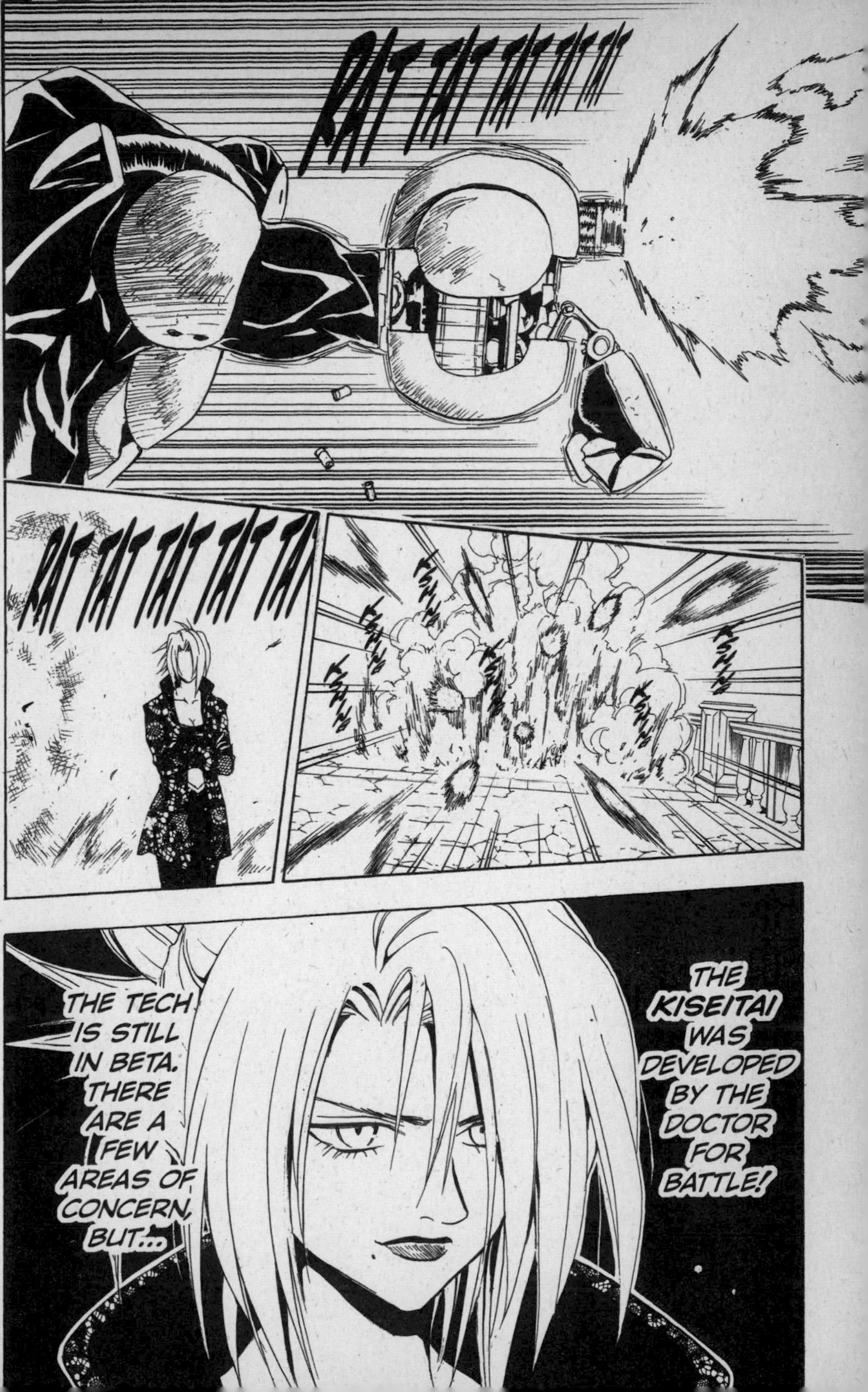
RAT TAT TAT TAT TAT
RAT TAT TAT TAT TAT
THE KISEITAI WAS DEVELOPED BY THE DOCTOR FOR BATTLE!
THE TECH IS STILL IN BETA. THERE ARE A FEW AREAS OF CONCERN, BUT...

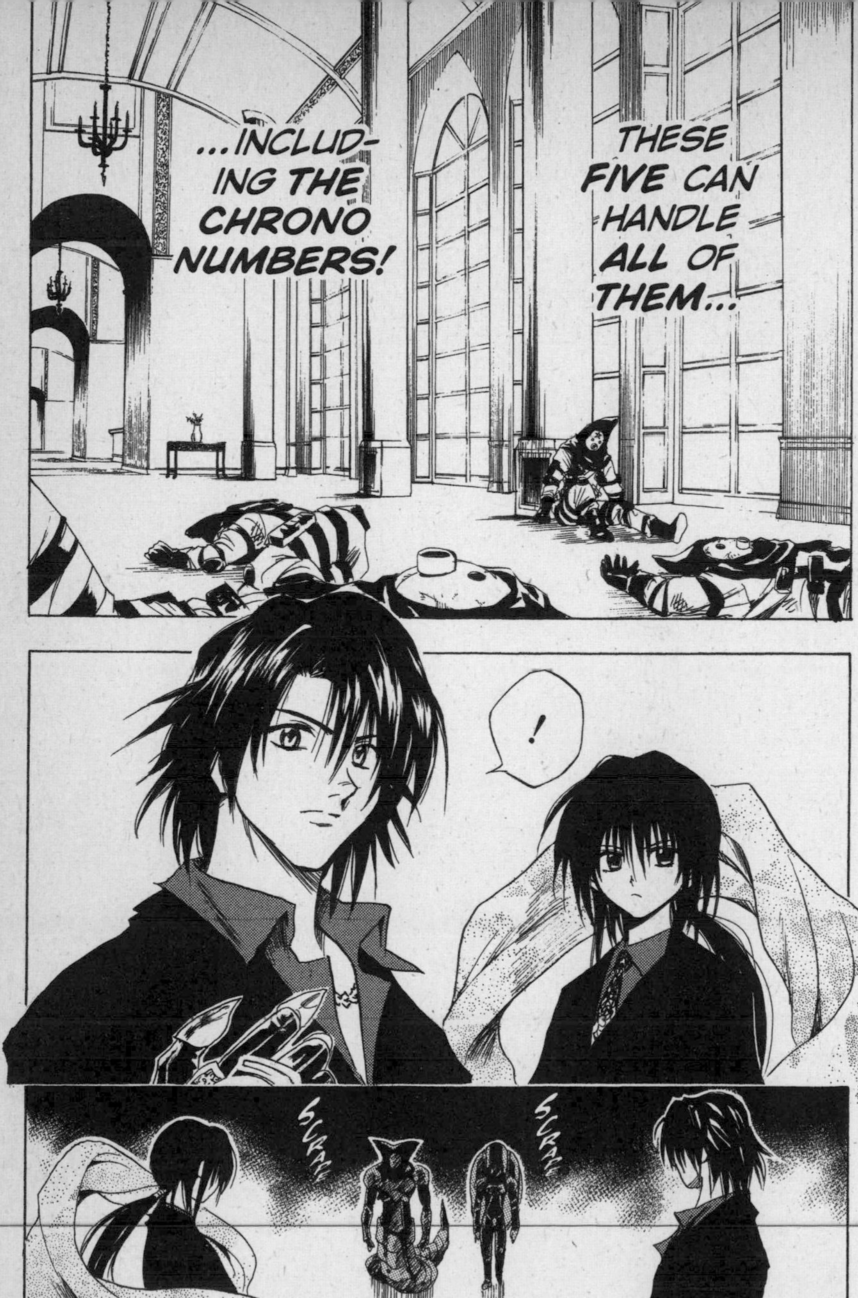
THESE FIVE CAN HANDLE ALL OF THEM...
...INCLUDING THE CHRONO NUMBERS!
!

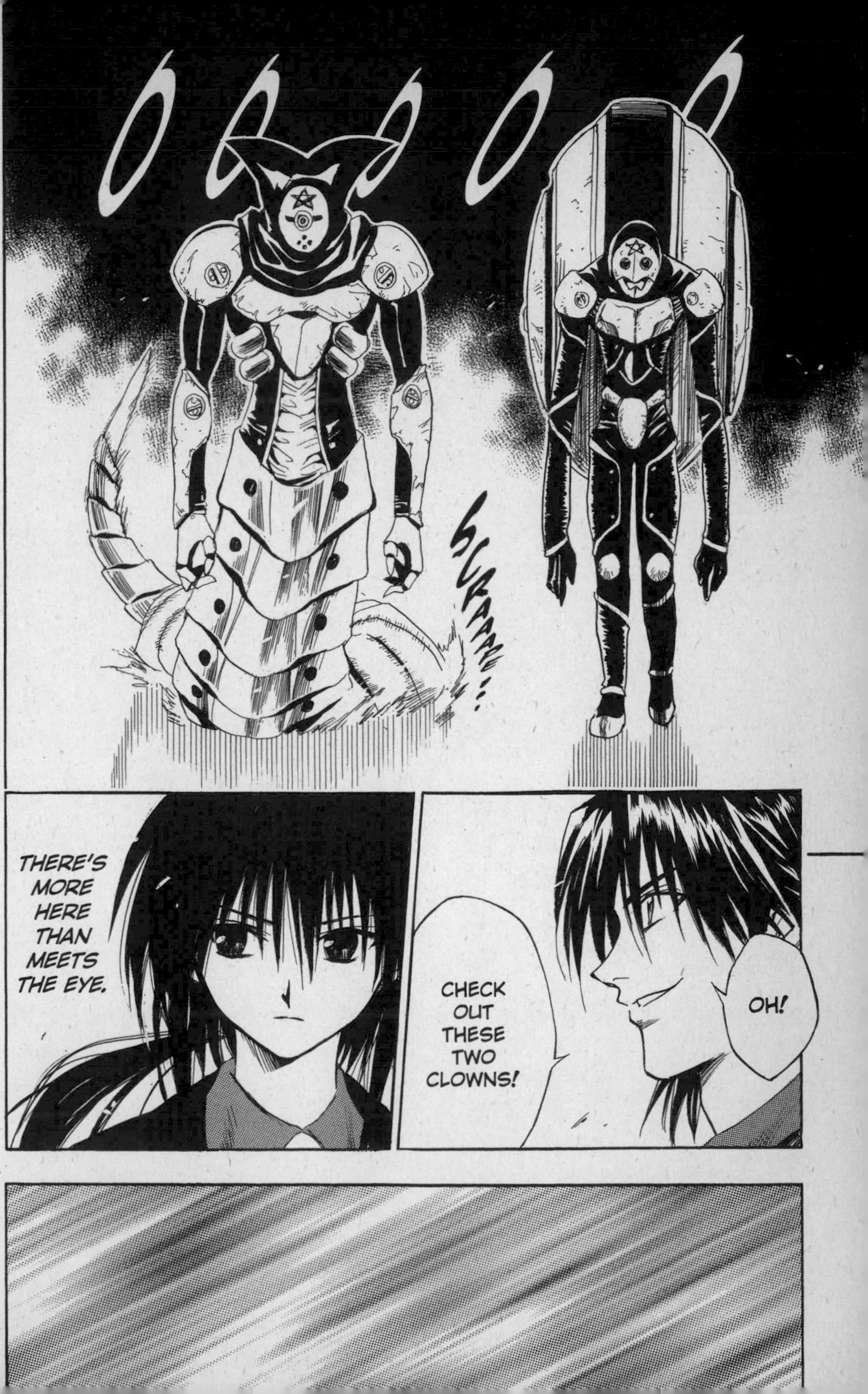
SCRAAAPE!!
OH!
CHECK OUT THESE TWO CLOWNS!
THERE'S MORE HERE THAN MEETS THE EYE.

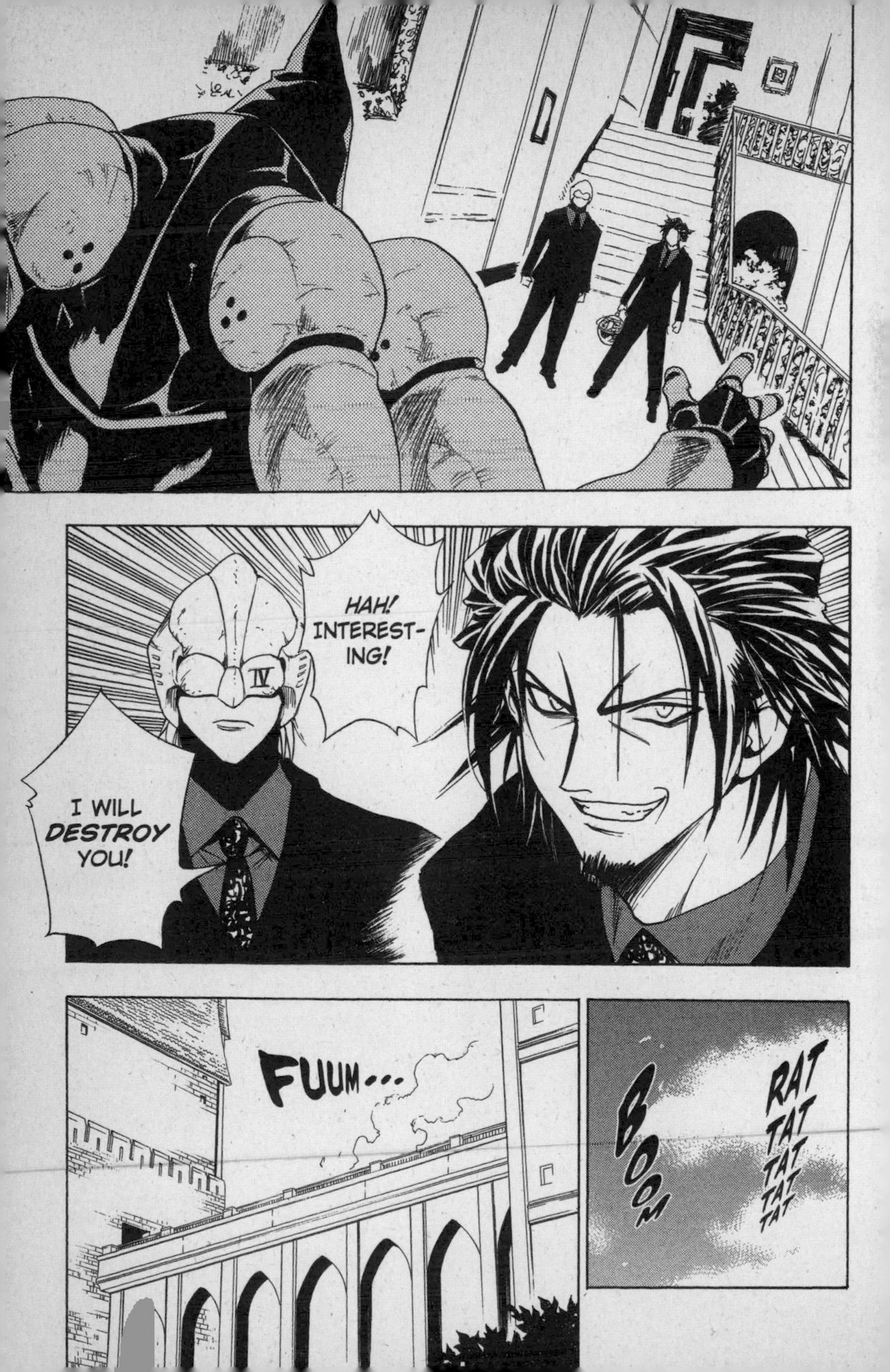
HAH! INTERESTING!
I WILL DESTROY YOU!
BOOM
RAT TAT TAT TAT TAT
FUUM...

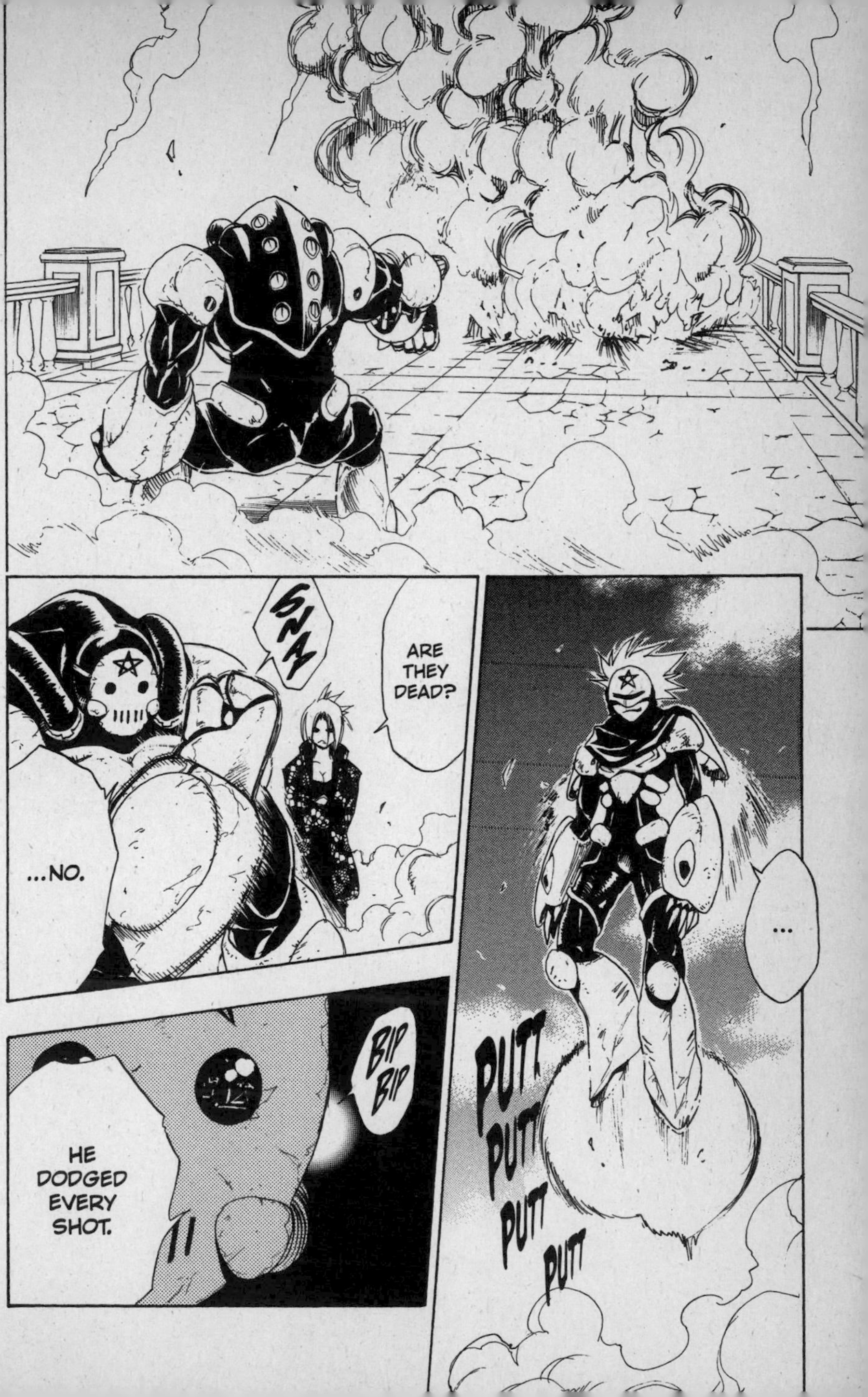
...
PUTT PUTT PUTT PUTT
SNM
ARE THEY DEAD?
...NO.
BIP BIP
HE DODGED EVERY SHOT.

READ THIS WAY

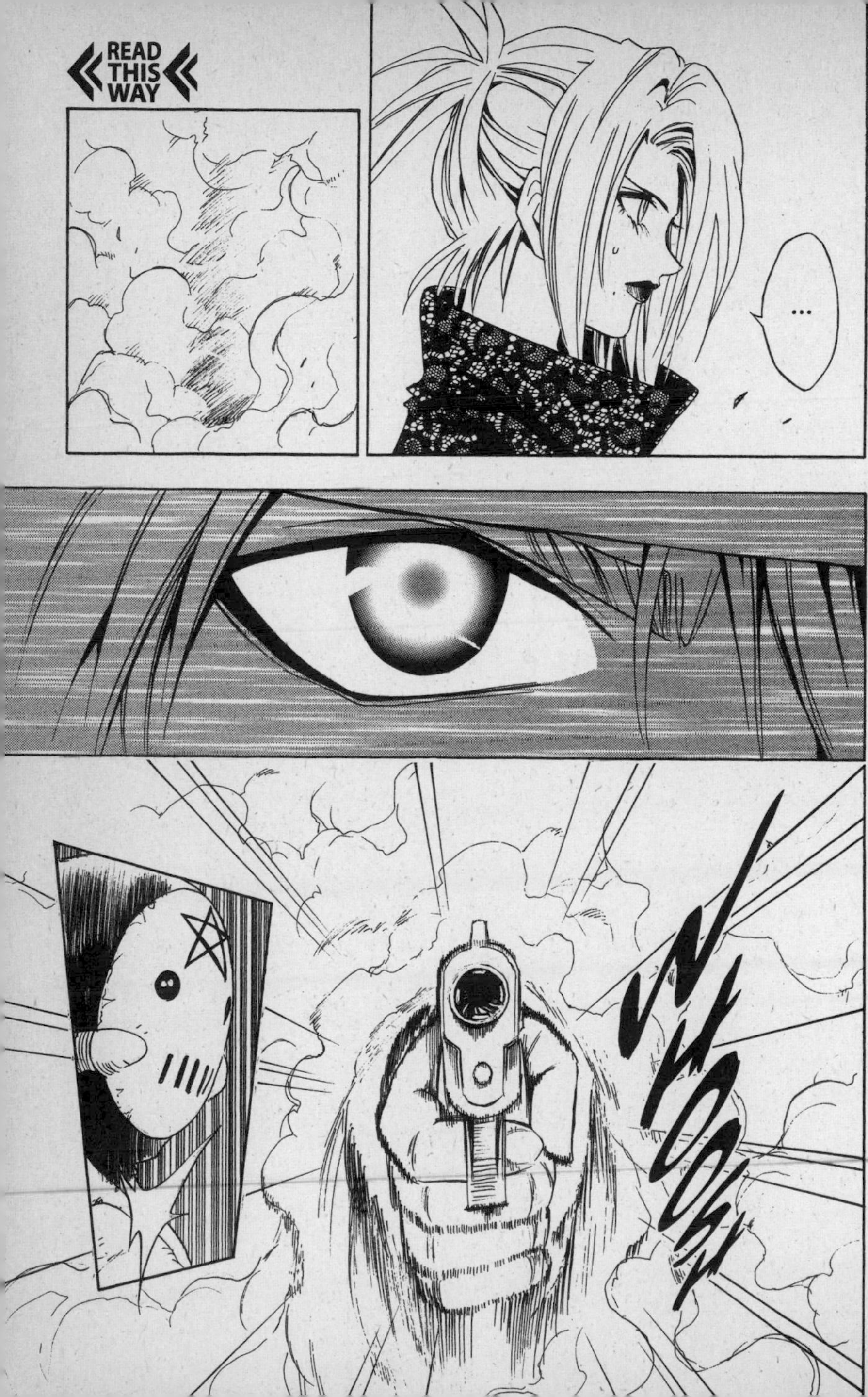
...

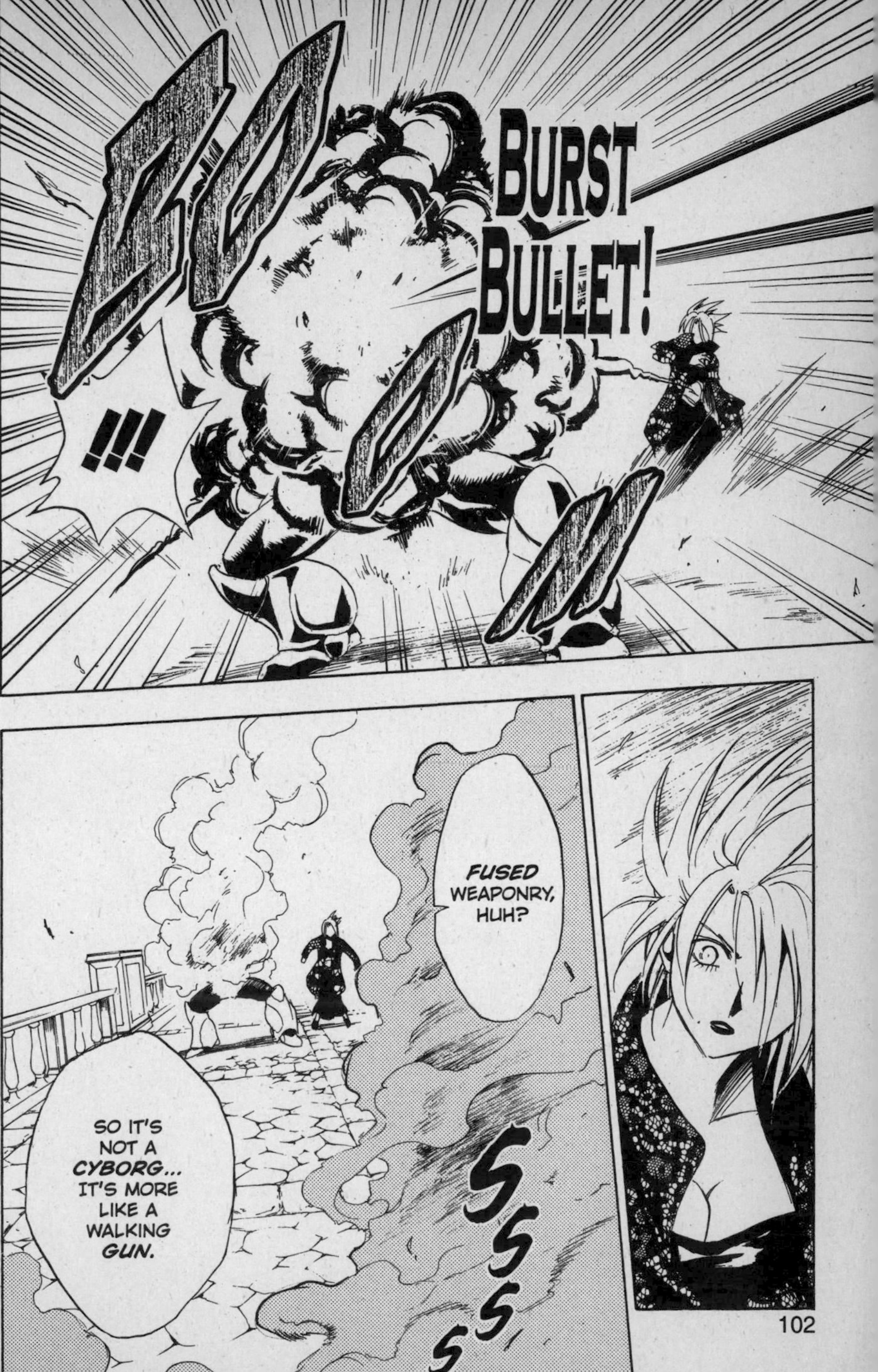
BURST BULLET!
ZOOM
!!!
FUSED WEAPONRY, HUH?
SO IT'S NOT A CYBORG... IT'S MORE LIKE A WALKING GUN.
SSSSS

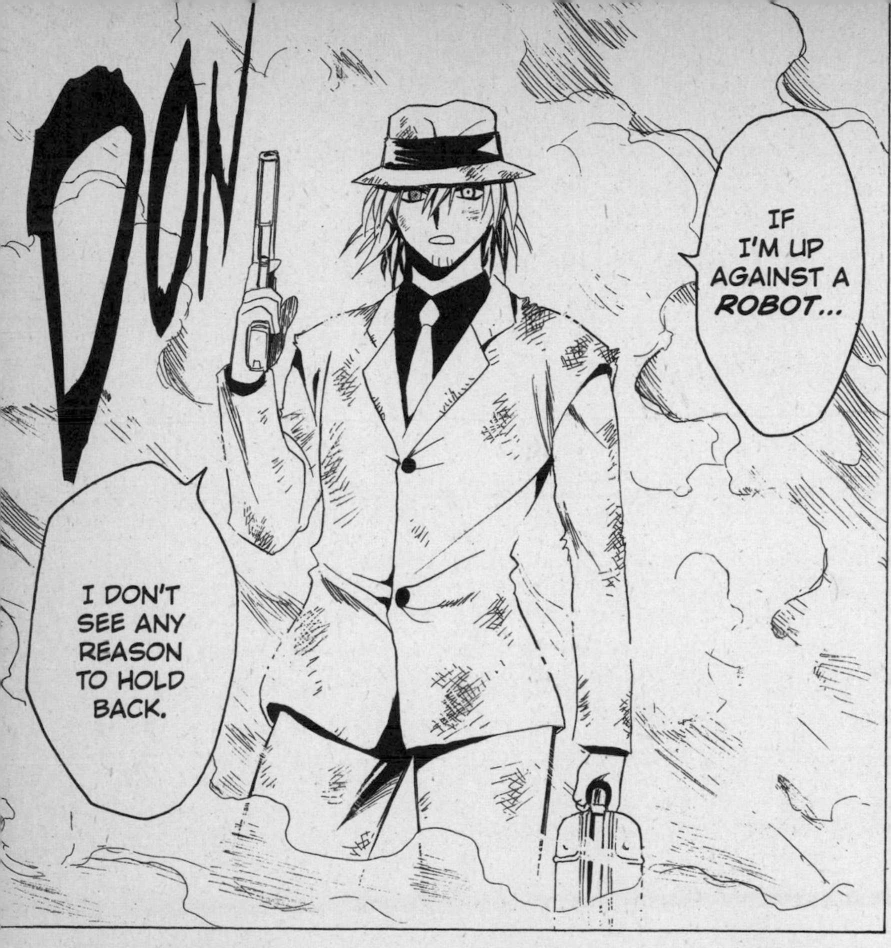
IF I'M UP AGAINST A *ROBOT...*
DON
I DON'T SEE ANY REASON TO HOLD BACK.
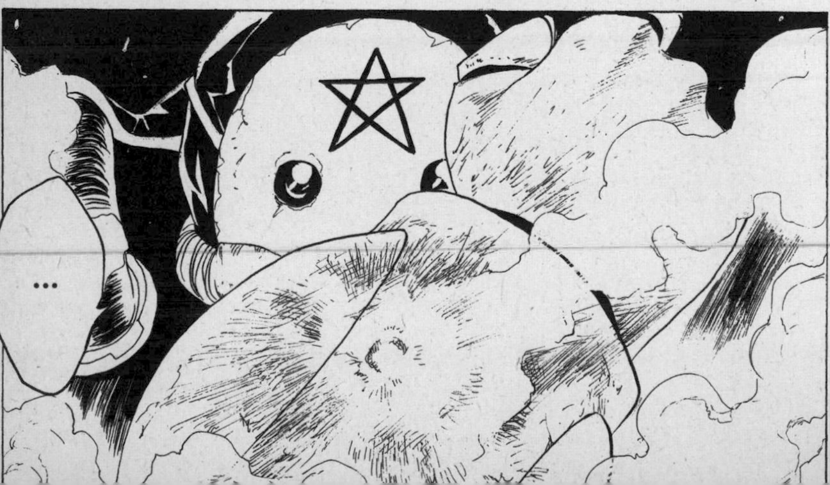
...

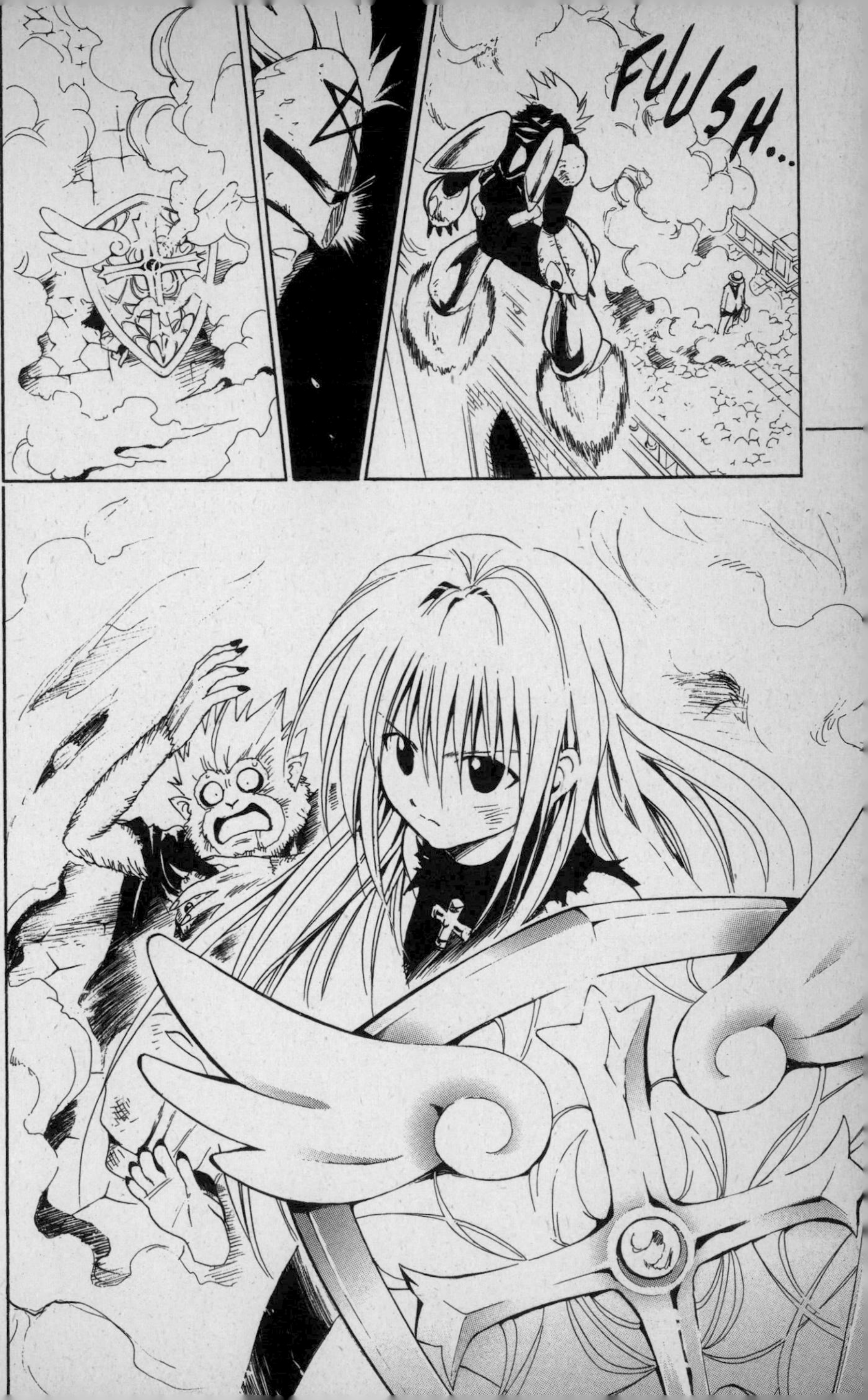
FUUSH...

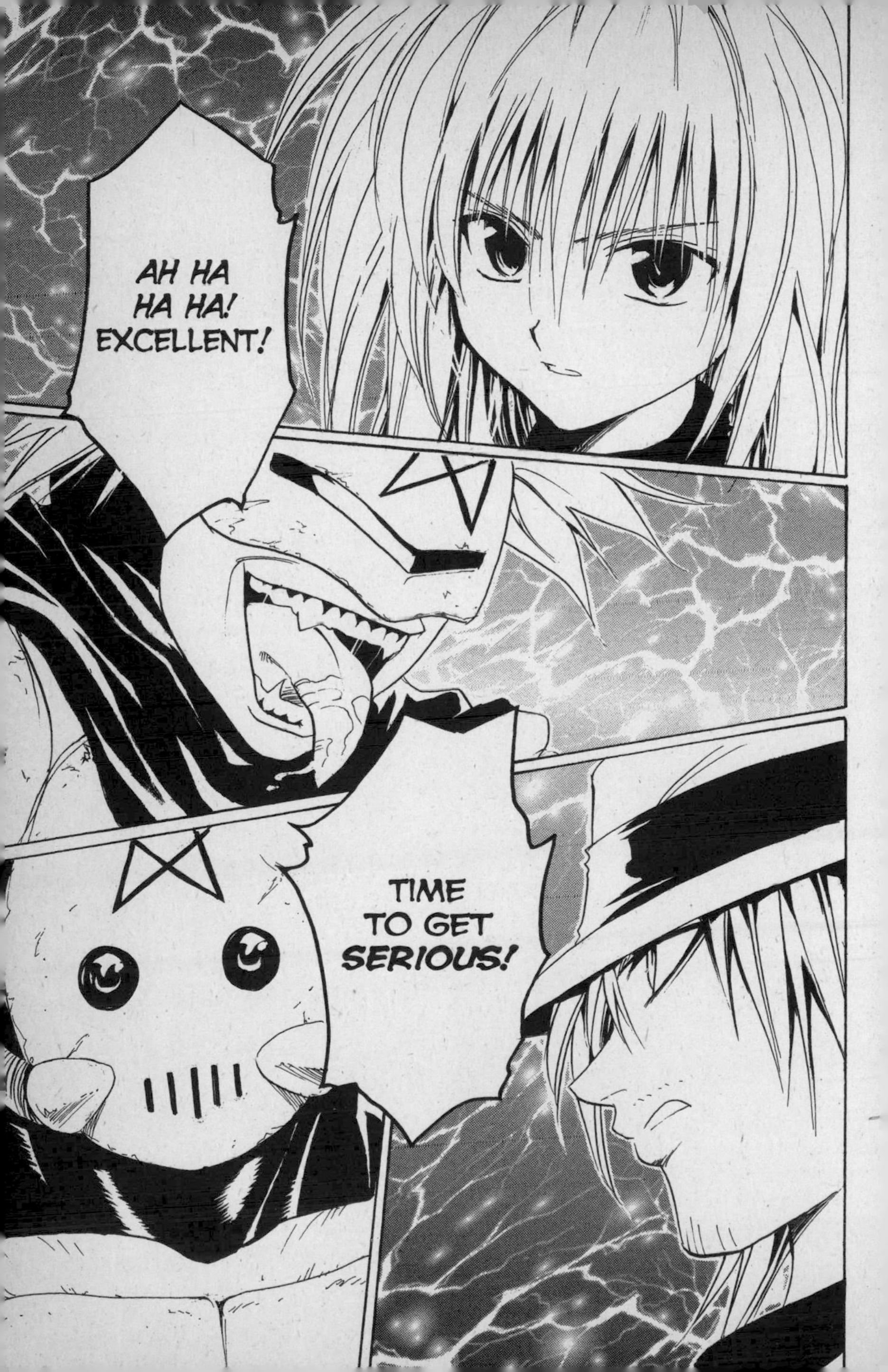
AH HA HA HA! EXCELLENT!
TIME TO GET SERIOUS!

BLACK CAT

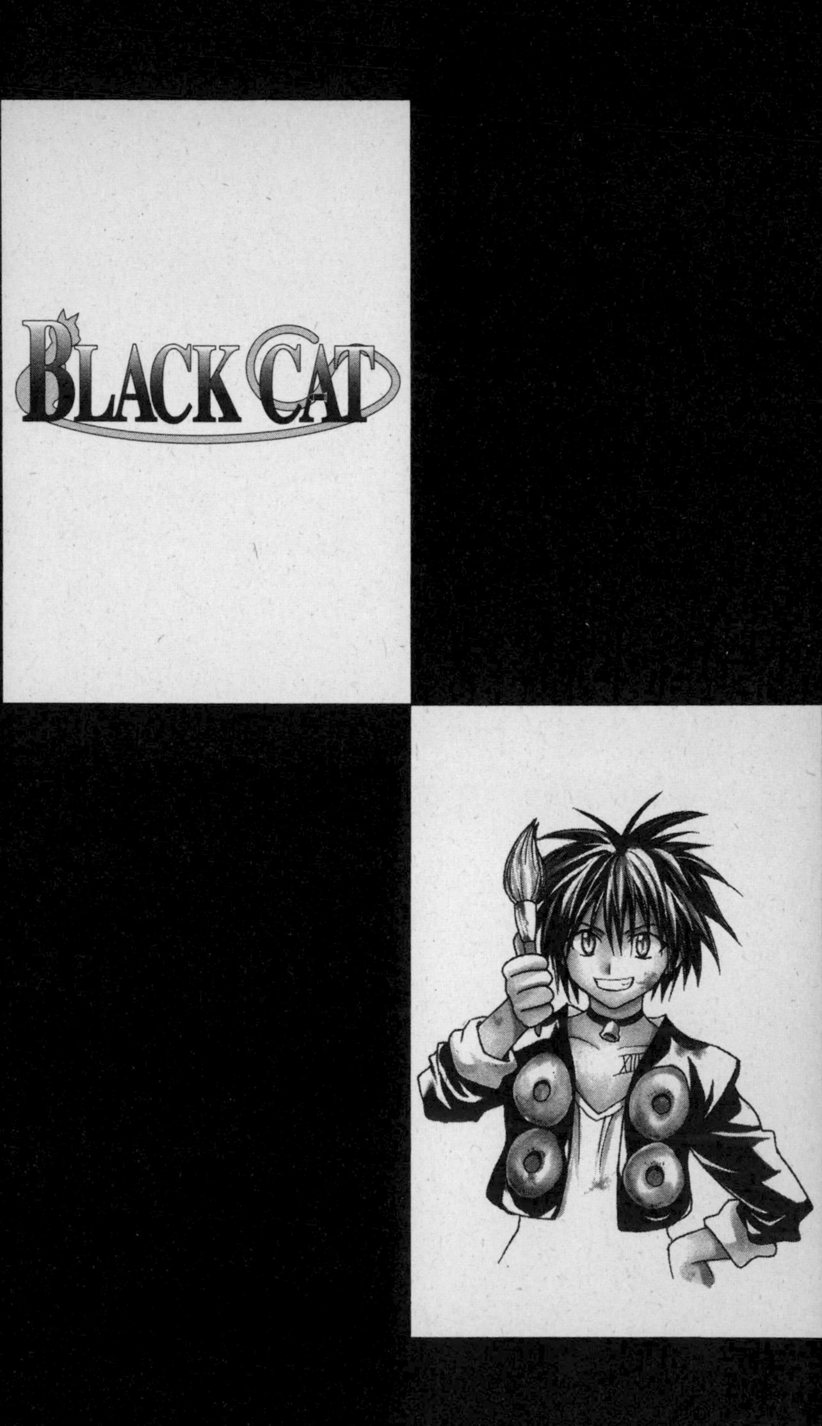

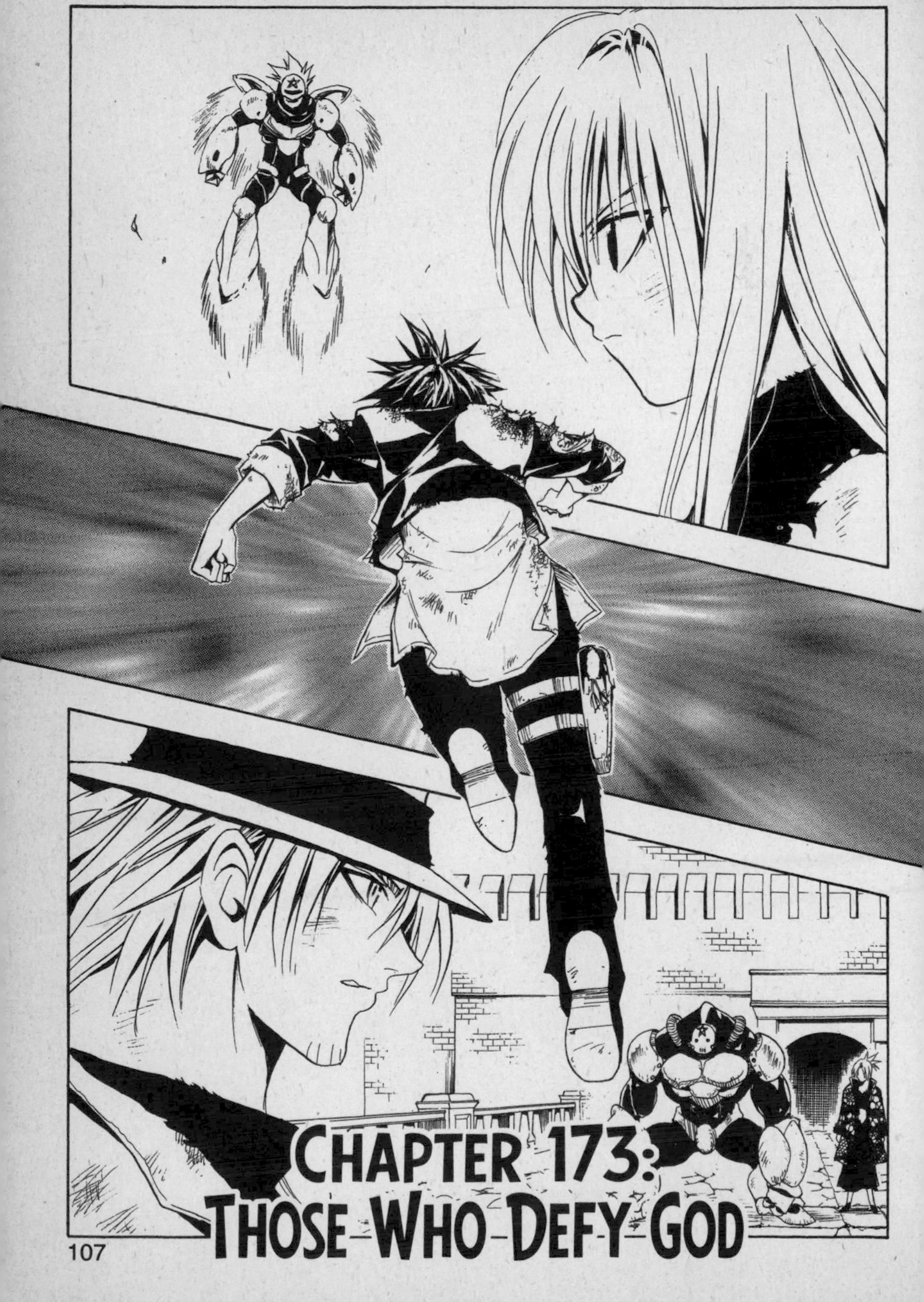
CHAPTER 173:
THOSE WHO DEFY GOD

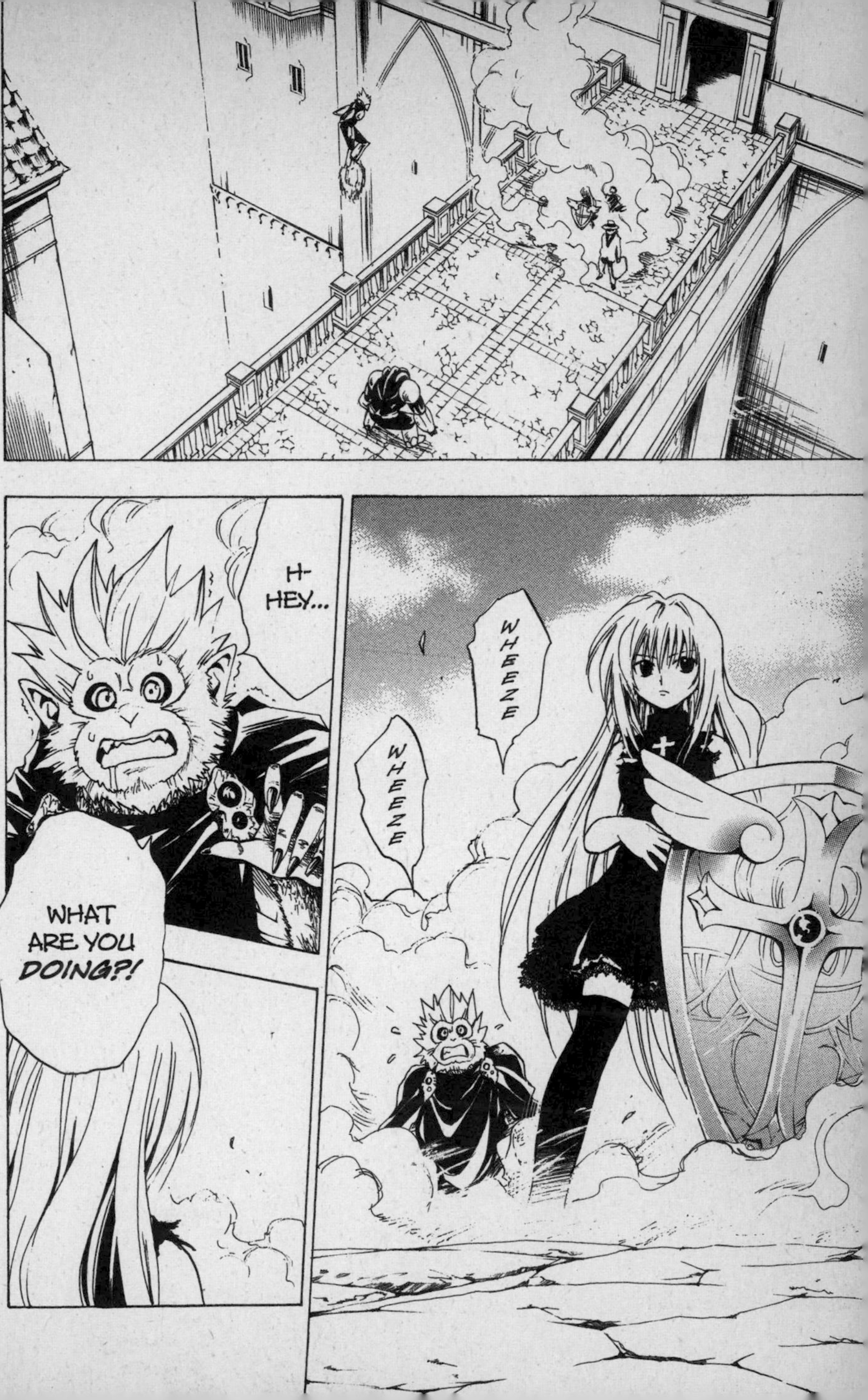
WHEEZE
WHEEZE
H- HEY...
WHAT ARE YOU DOING?!

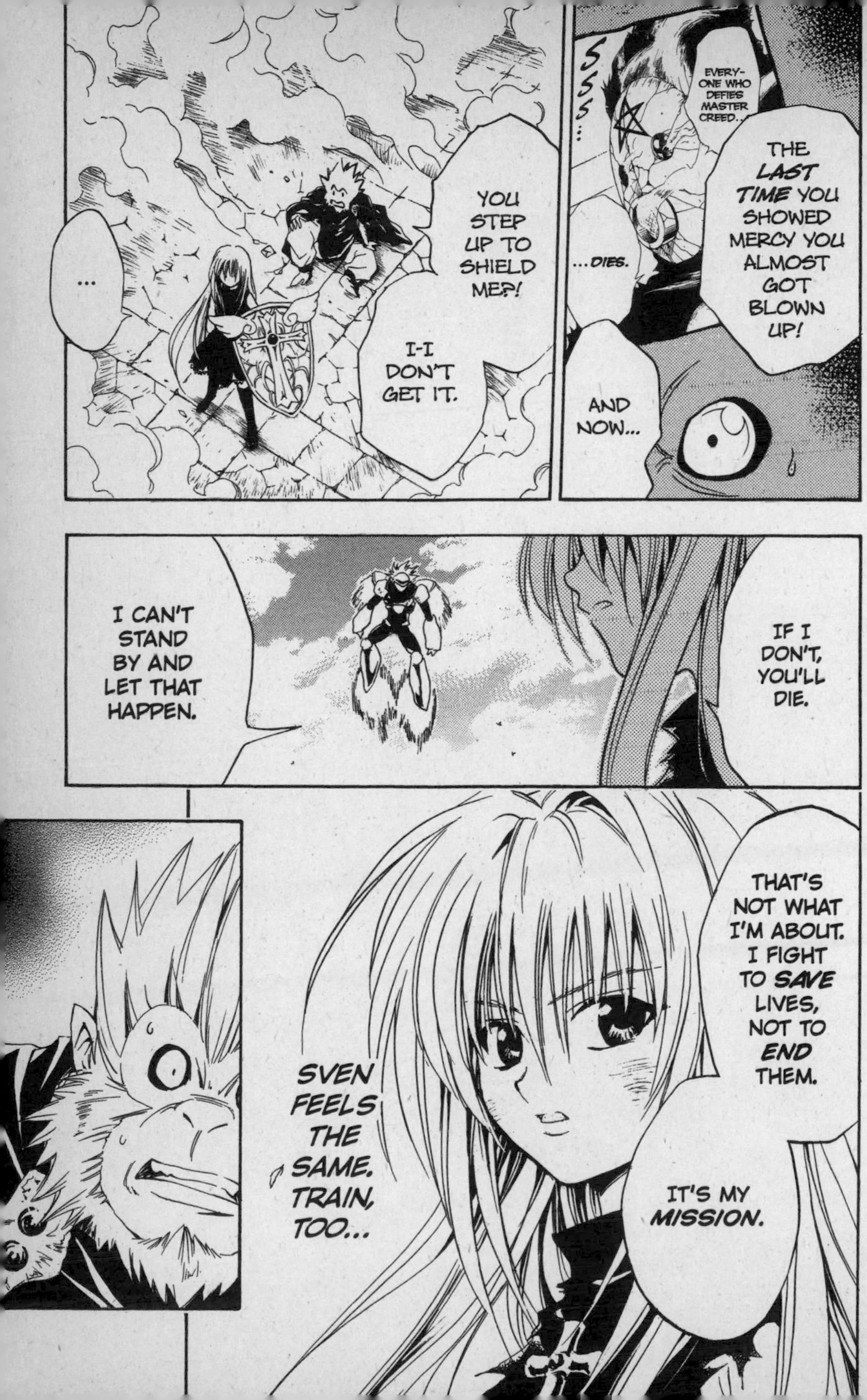
SSS...
EVERY-ONE WHO DEFIES MASTER CREED...
...DIES.
THE LAST TIME YOU SHOWED MERCY YOU ALMOST GOT BLOWN UP!
AND NOW...
YOU STEP UP TO SHIELD ME?!
I-I DON'T GET IT.
...
IF I DON'T, YOU'LL DIE.
I CAN'T STAND BY AND LET THAT HAPPEN.
THAT'S NOT WHAT I'M ABOUT. I FIGHT TO SAVE LIVES, NOT TO END THEM.
IT'S MY MISSION.
SVEN FEELS THE SAME. TRAIN, TOO...

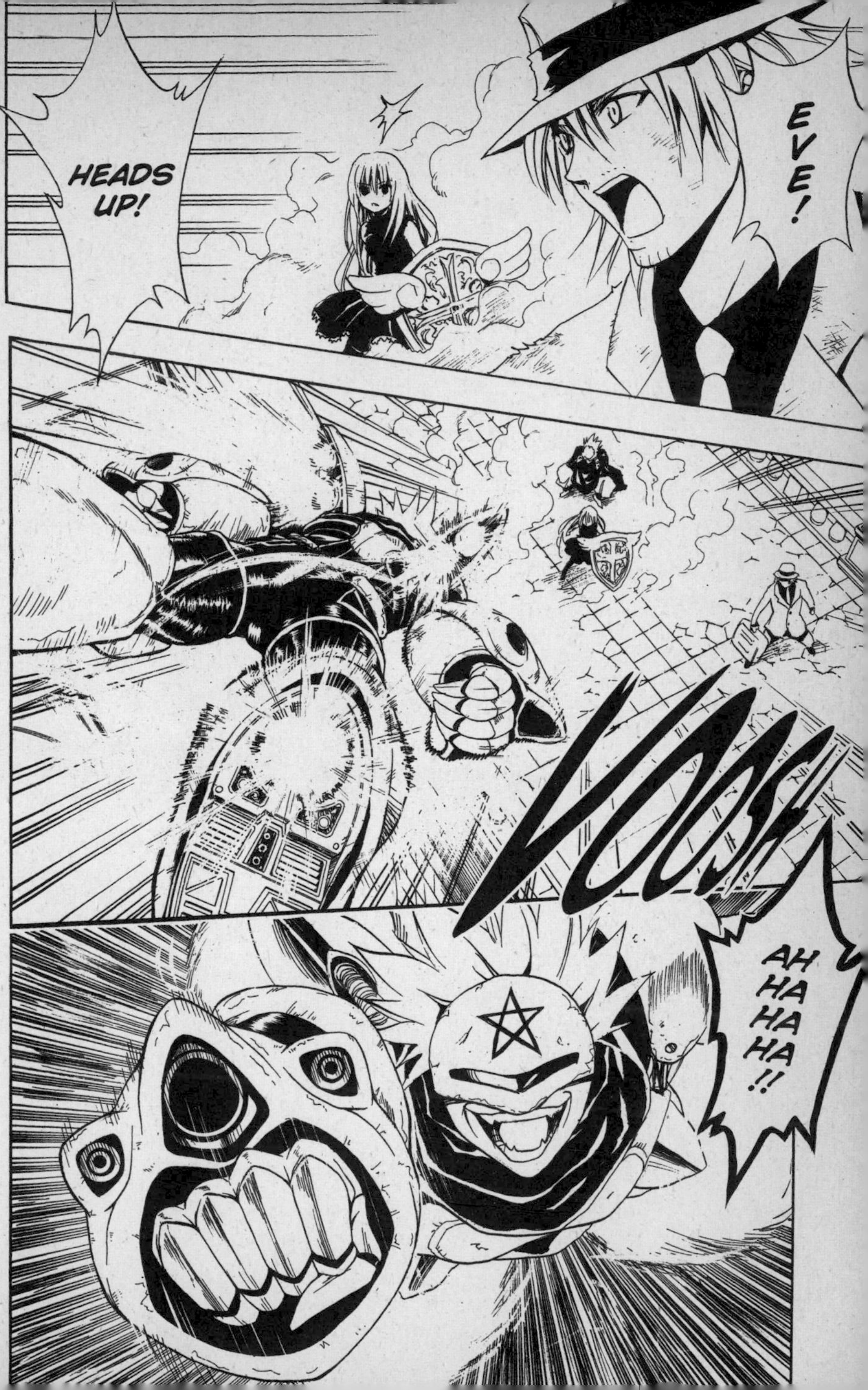
EVE!
HEADS UP!
VOOSH
AH HA HA HA!!

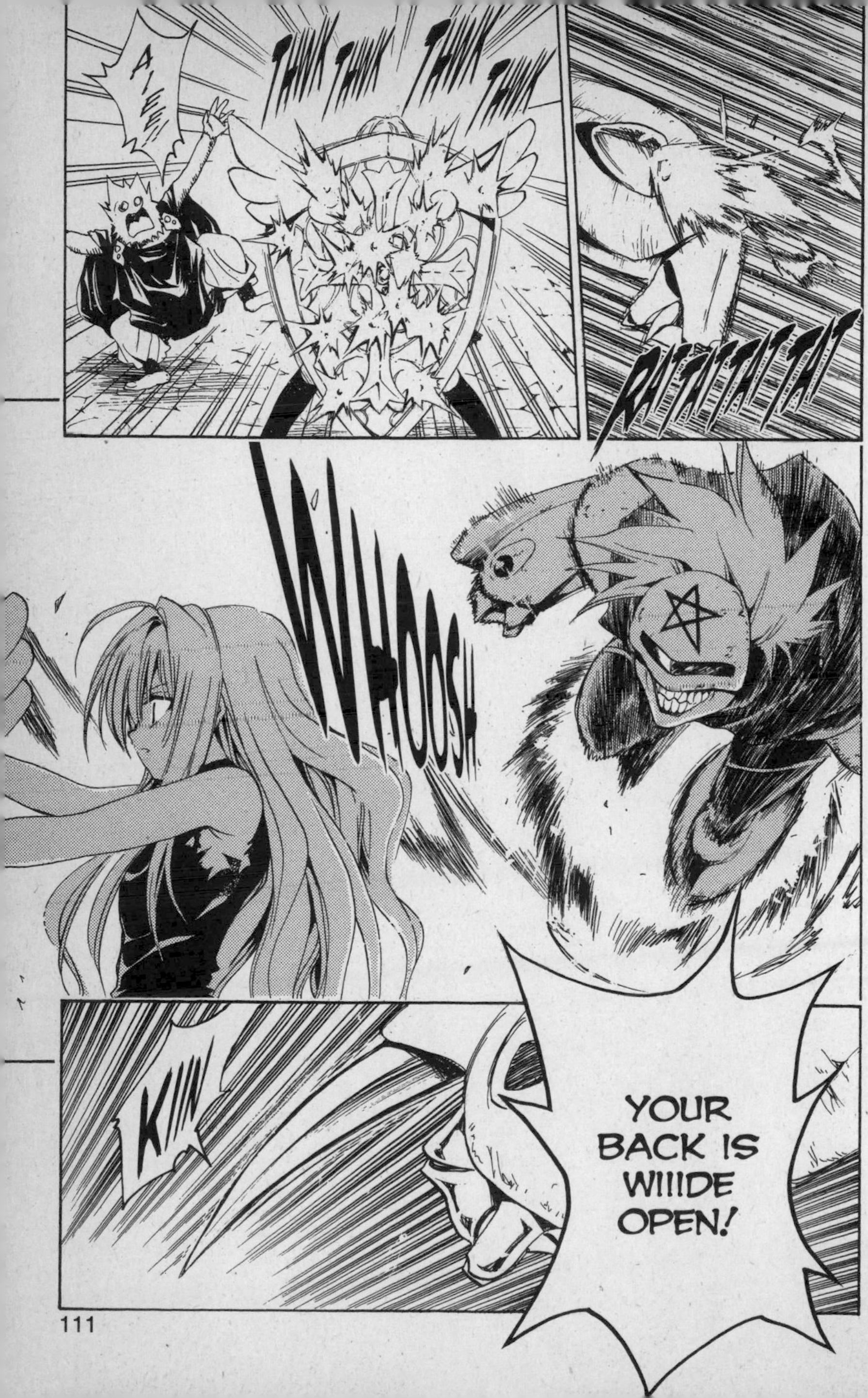
RATATATATAT
THNK THNK THNK THNK
AIEE!
WHOOSH
YOUR BACK IS WIIIDE OPEN!
KIIN

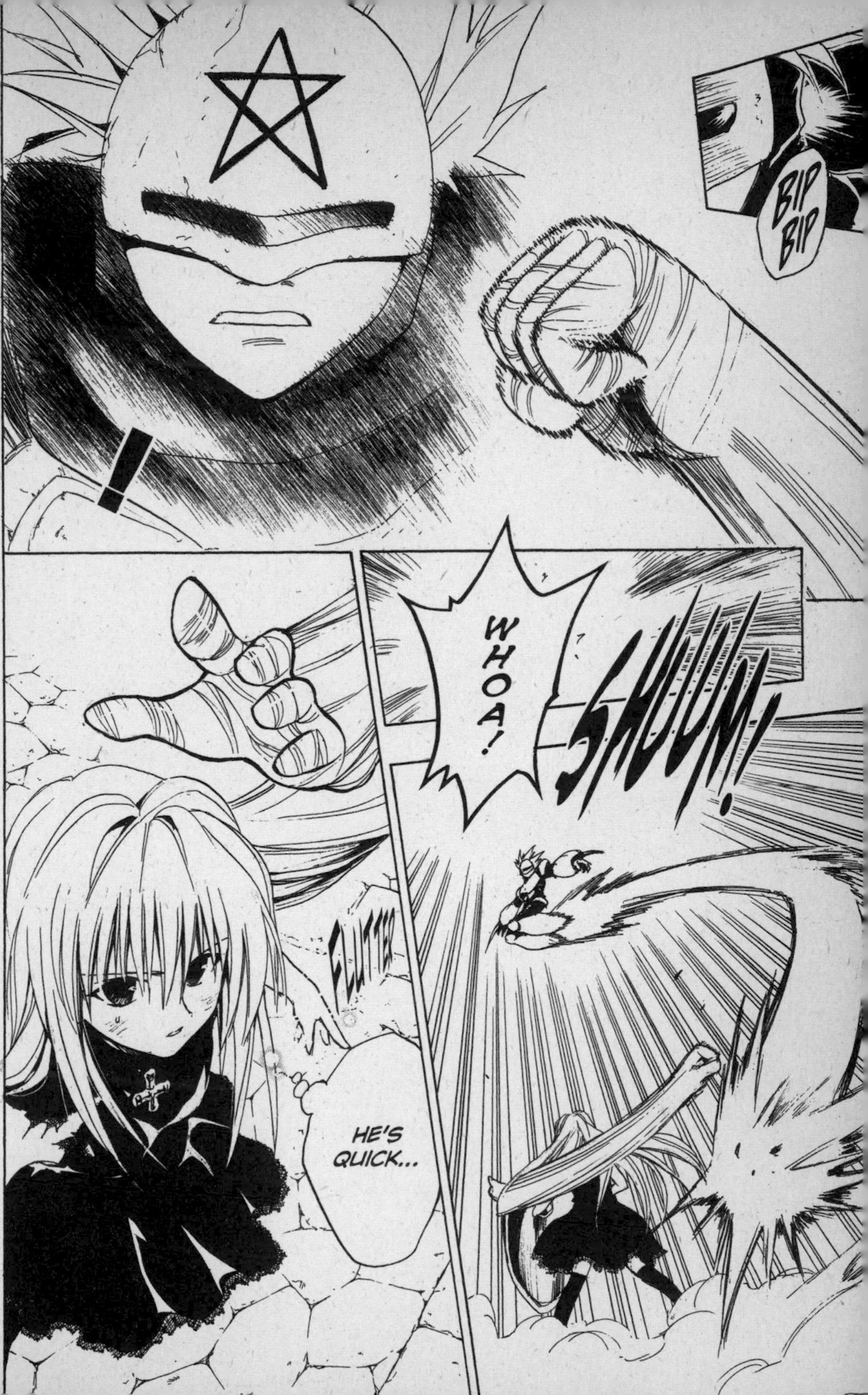
BIP BIP
!
WHOA!
SHUUN!
FLUTTER
HE'S QUICK...

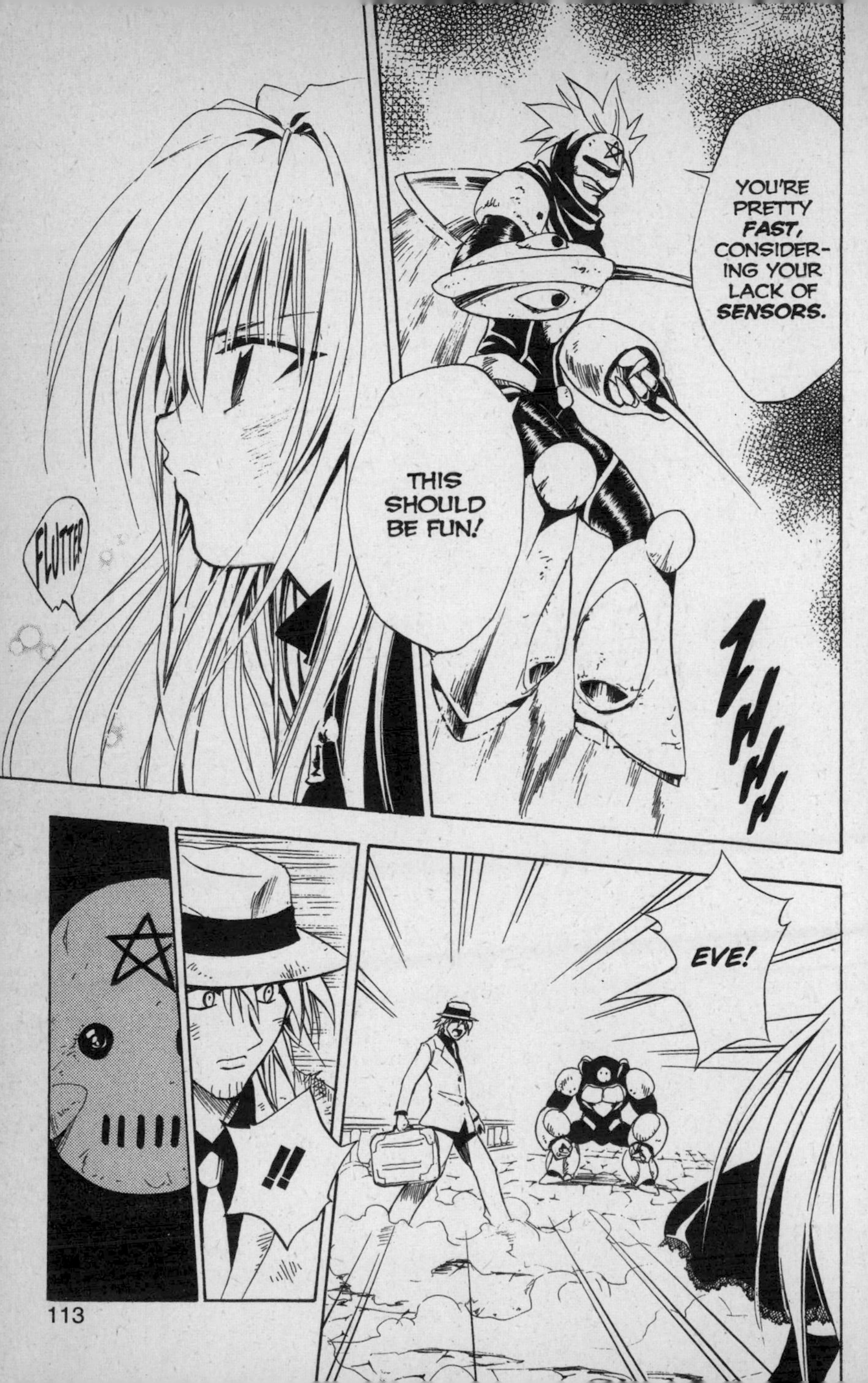
YOU'RE PRETTY FAST, CONSIDER-ING YOUR LACK OF SENSORS.
THIS SHOULD BE FUN!
ZHHH
FLUTTER
EVE!
!!

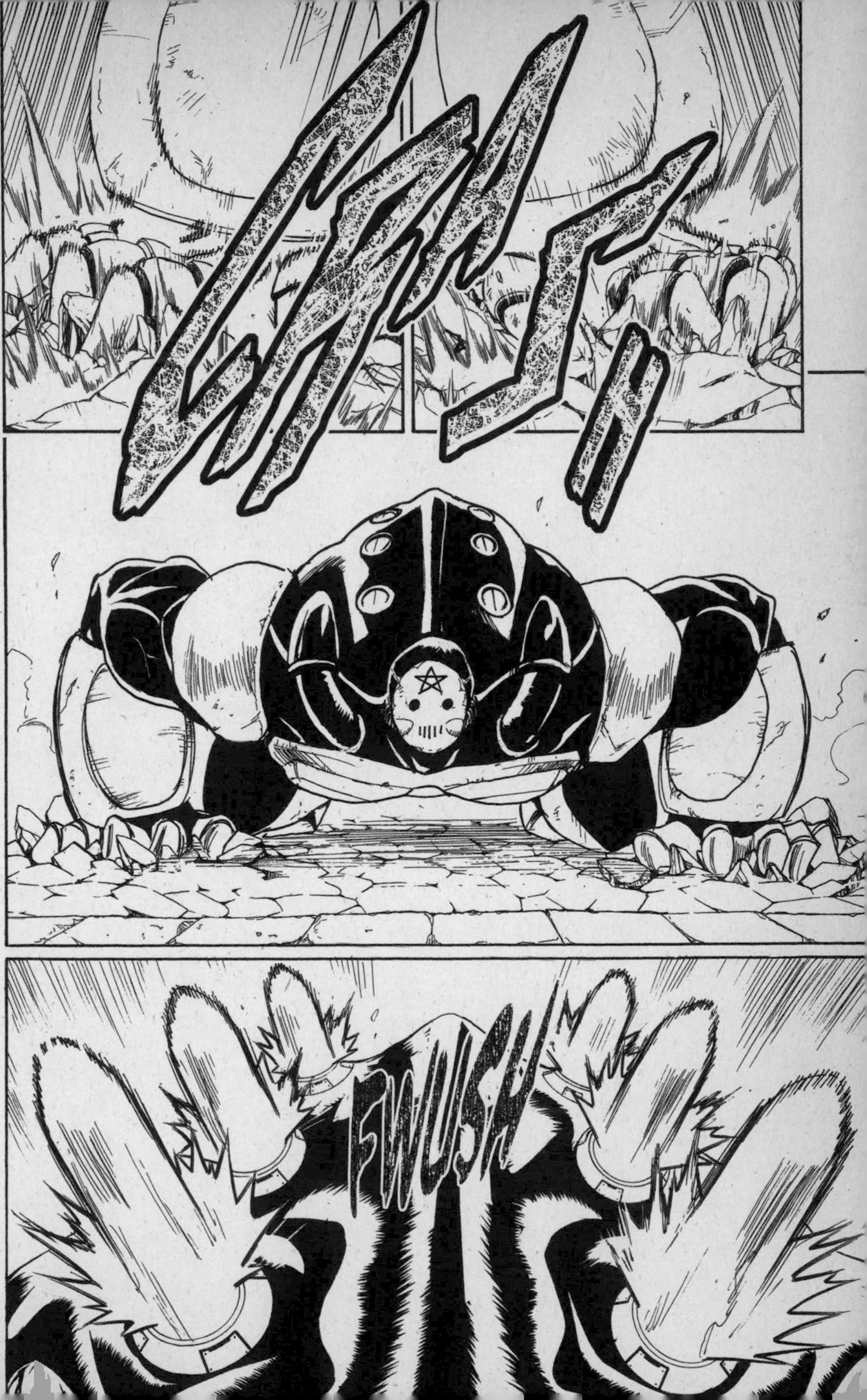
FWUSH

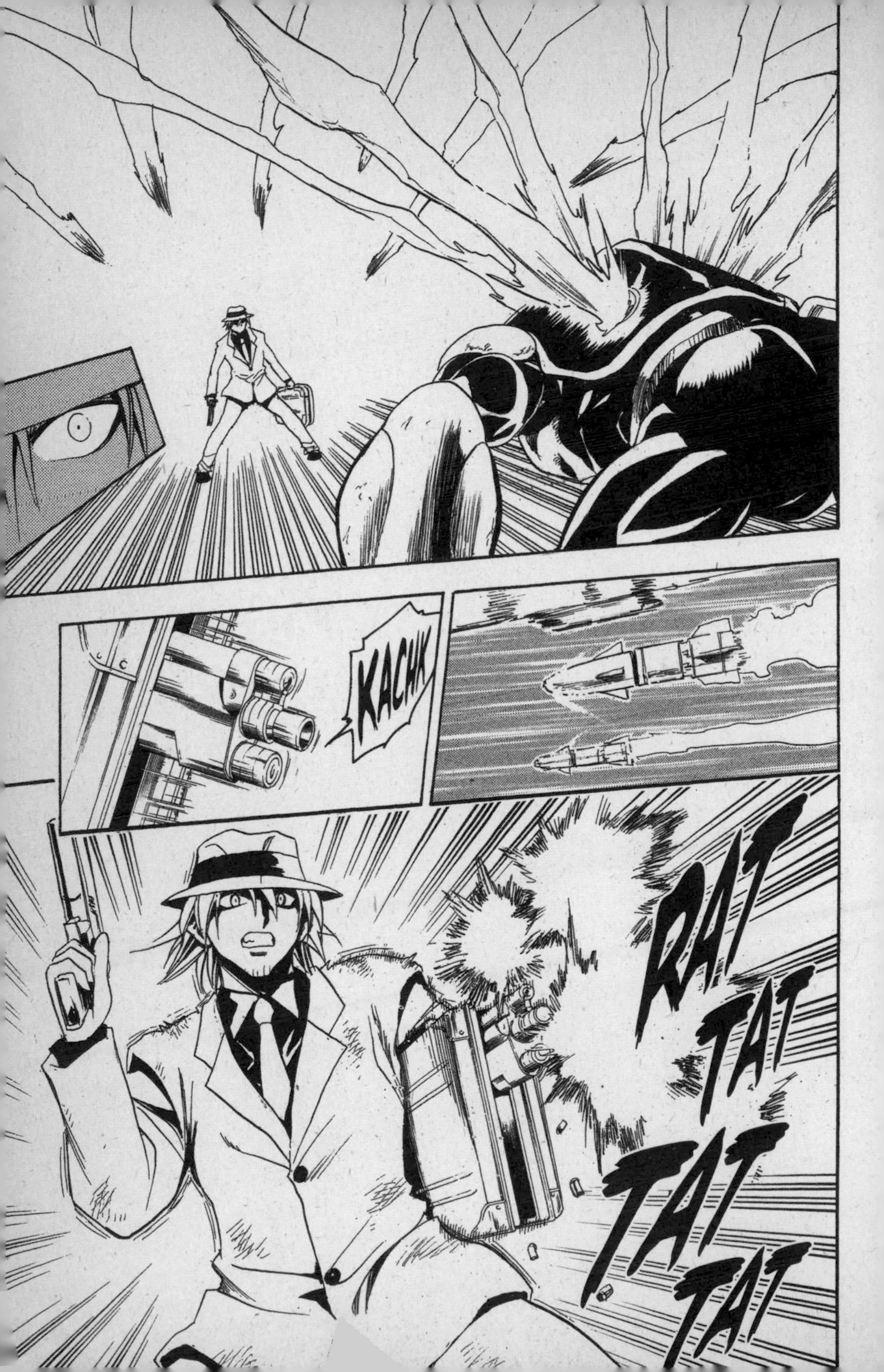
KACHK
RAT TAT TAT TAT

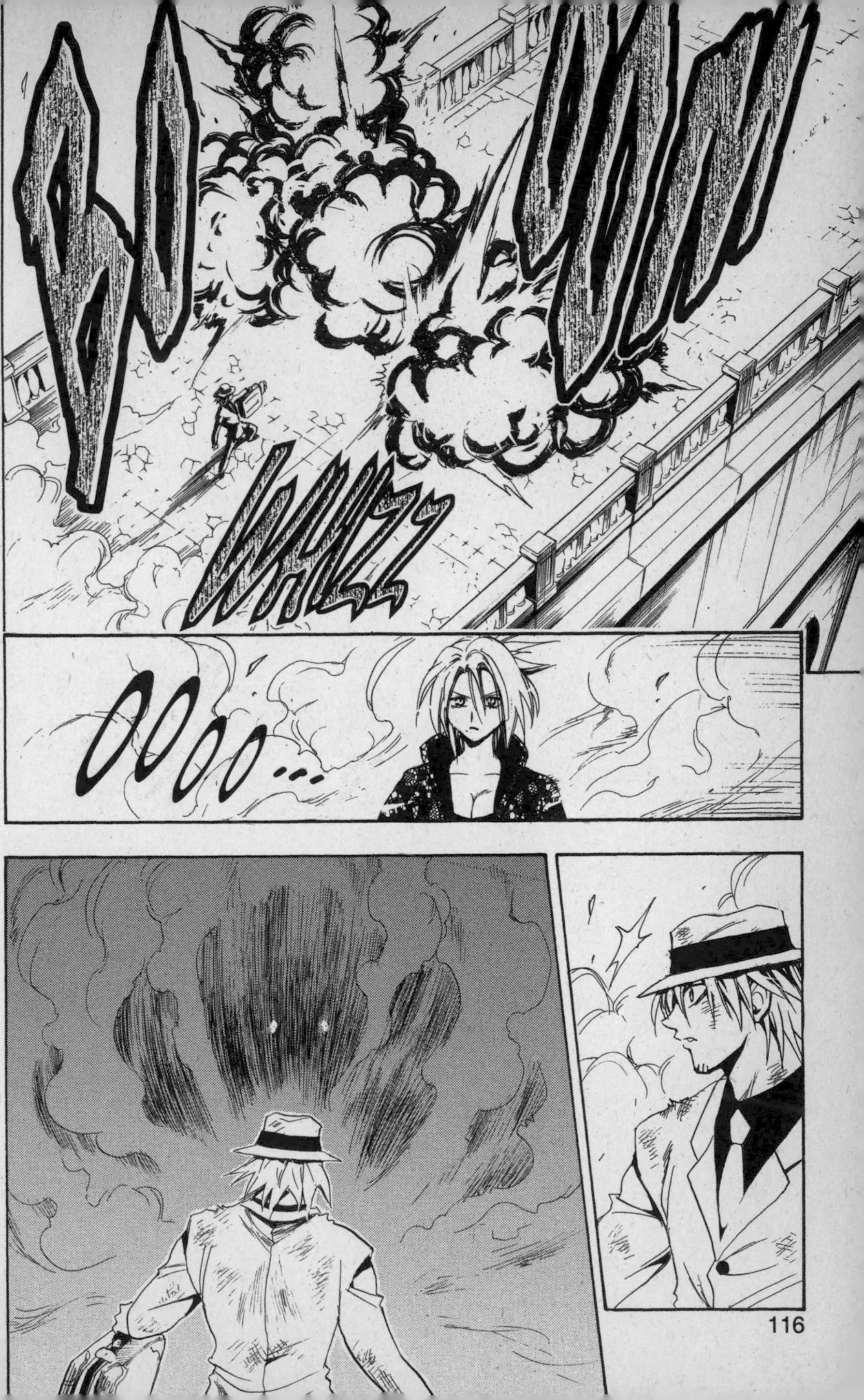

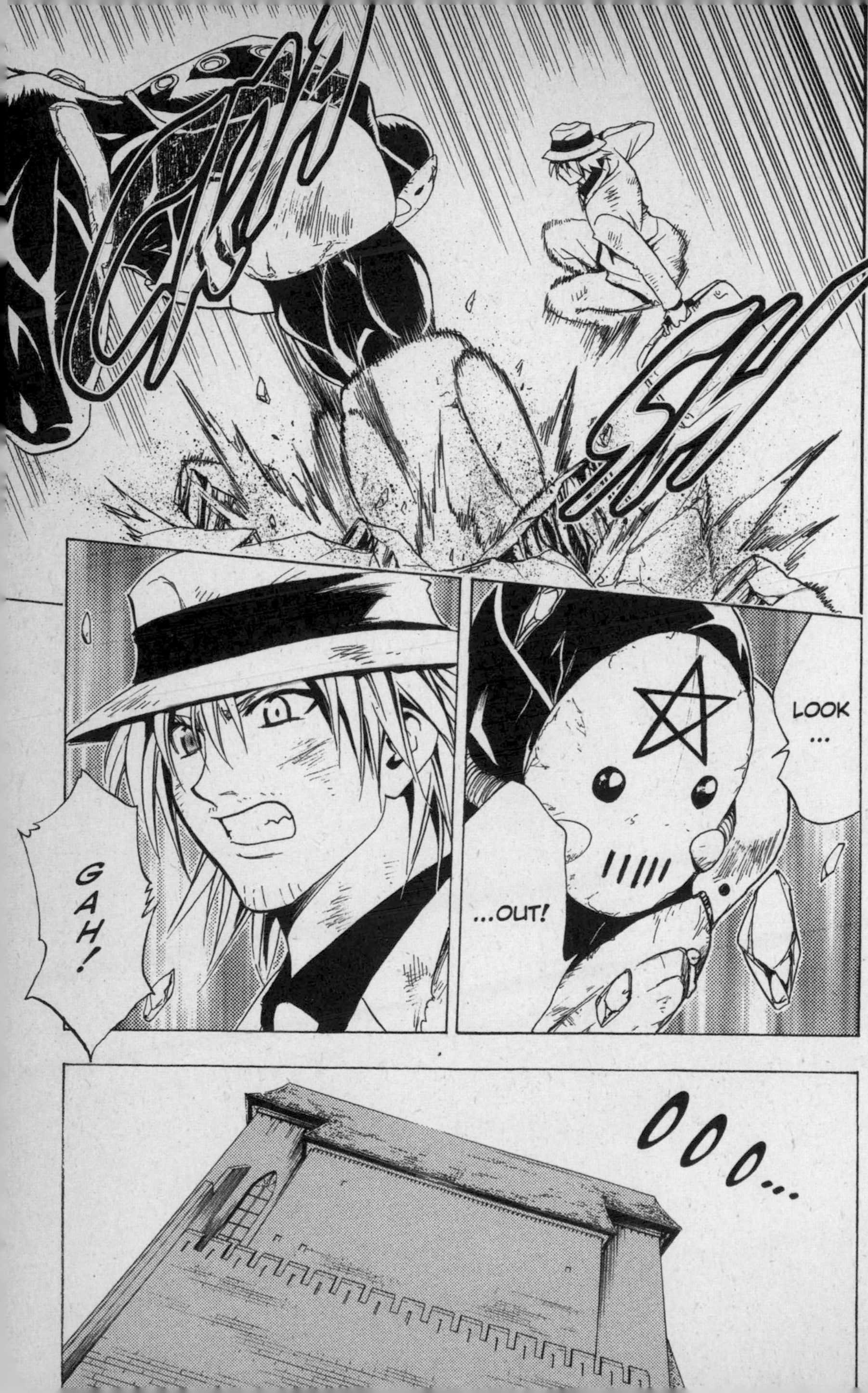
LOOK ...
...OUT!
GAH!
OOO...

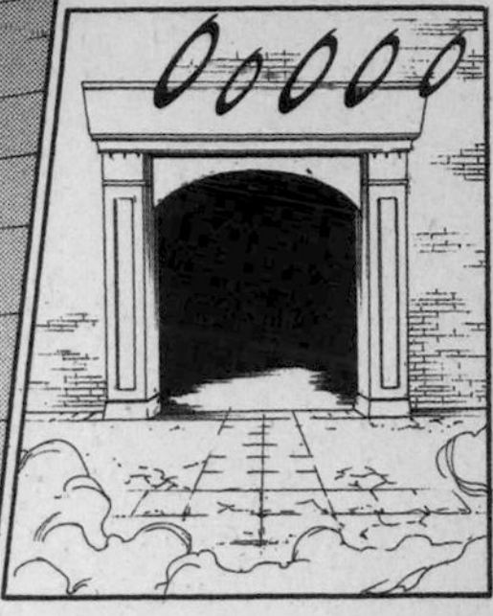
OOOOO
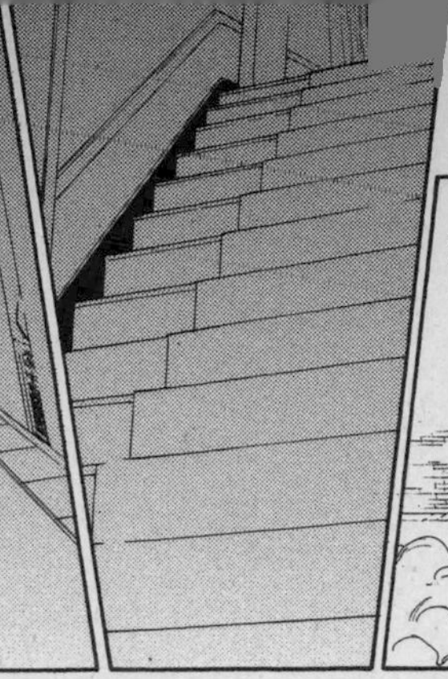
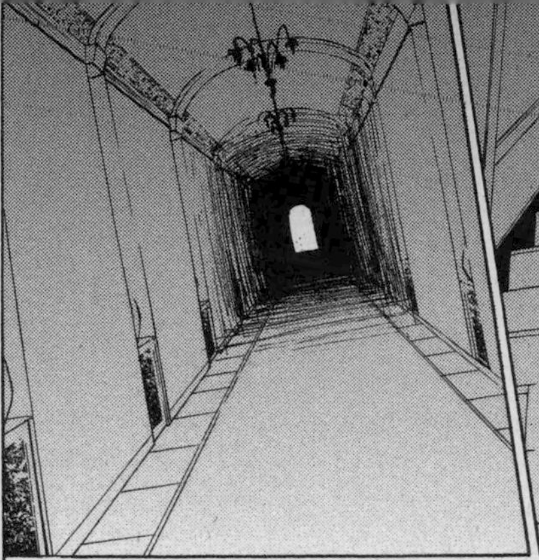
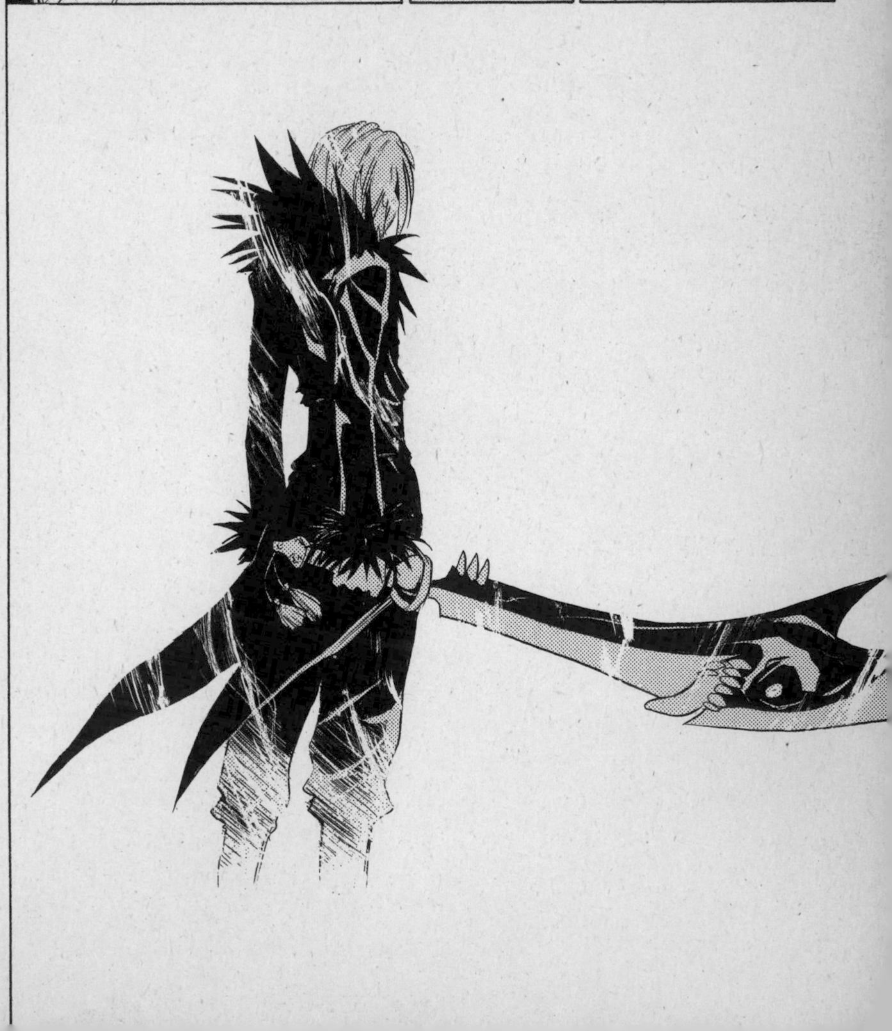

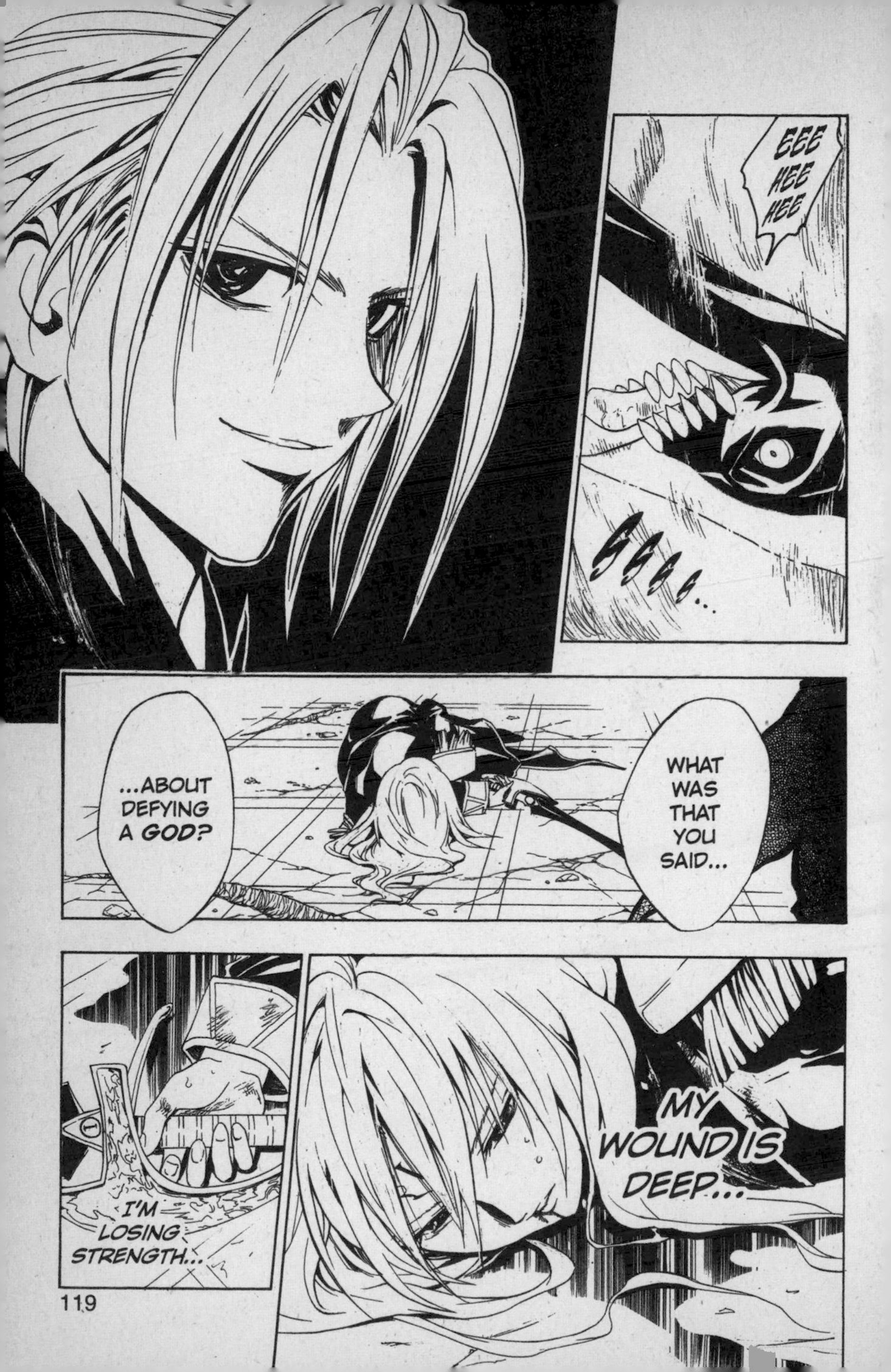
EEE HEE HEE
SSSS...
WHAT WAS THAT YOU SAID...
...ABOUT DEFYING A GOD?
MY WOUND IS DEEP...
I'M LOSING STRENGTH...

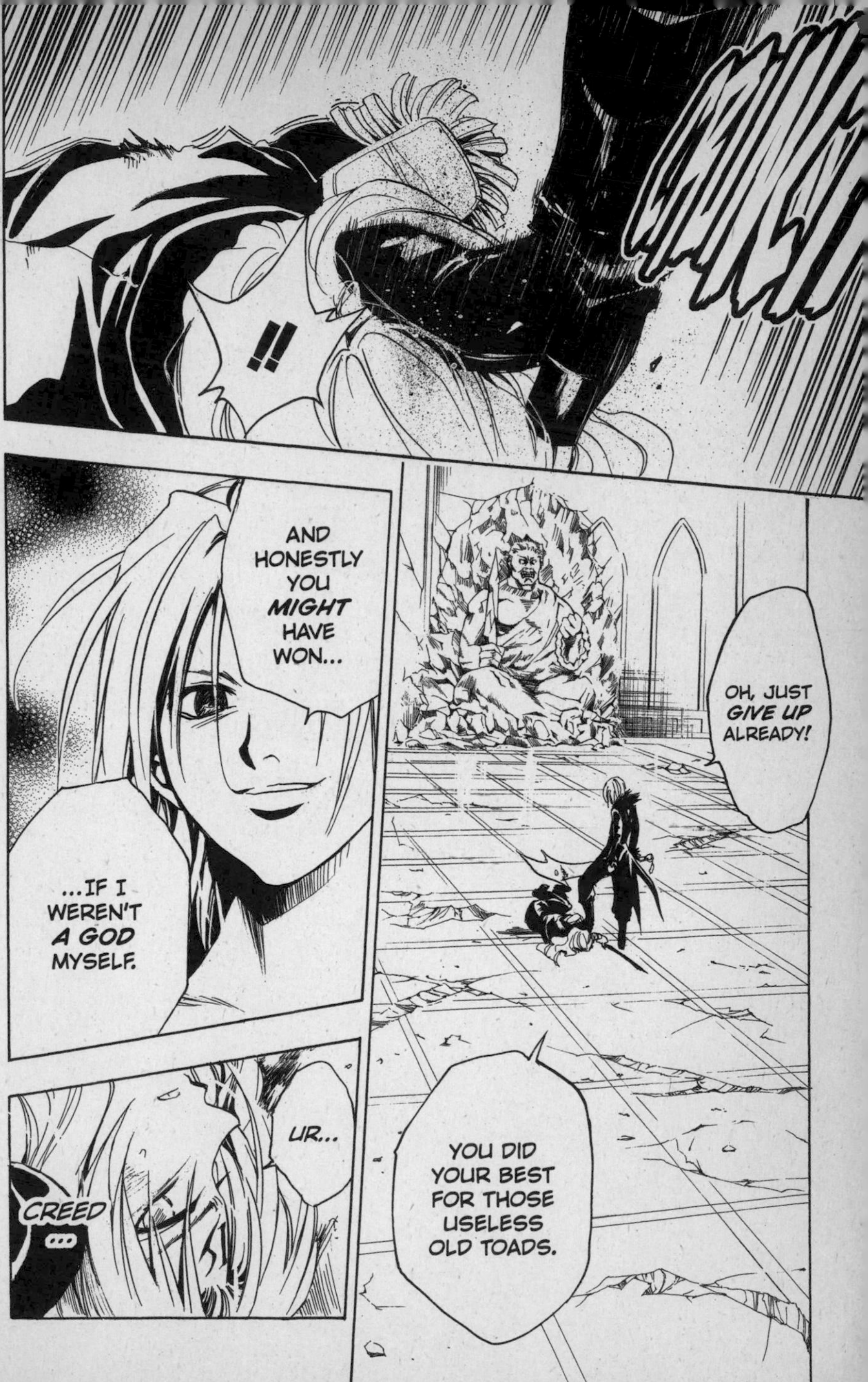
!!
OH, JUST GIVE UP ALREADY!
YOU DID YOUR BEST FOR THOSE USELESS OLD TOADS.
AND HONESTLY YOU MIGHT HAVE WON...
...IF I WEREN'T A GOD MYSELF.
UR...
CREED ...

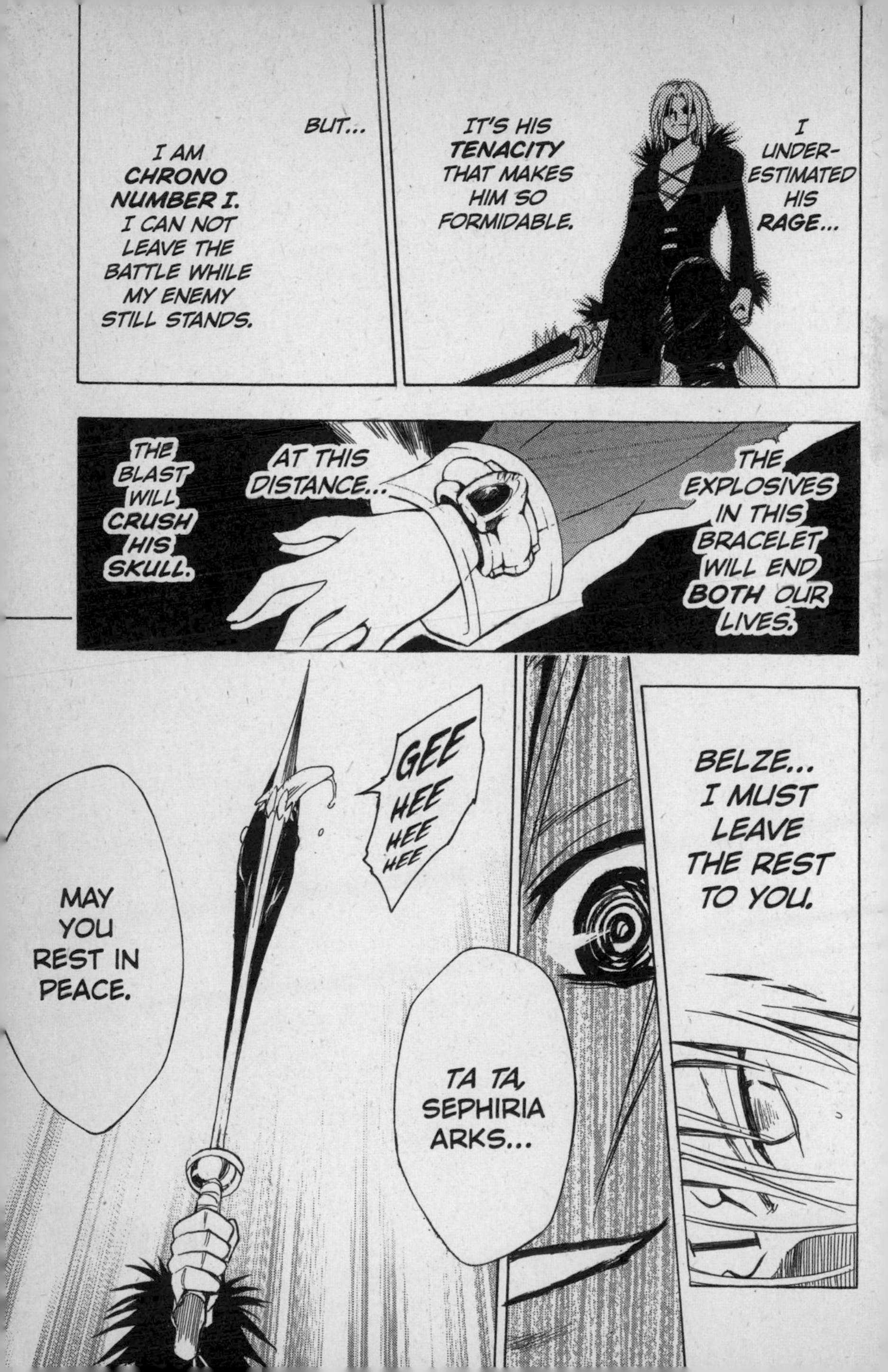
I UNDER-ESTIMATED HIS RAGE...
IT'S HIS TENACITY THAT MAKES HIM SO FORMIDABLE.
BUT...
I AM CHRONO NUMBER I. I CAN NOT LEAVE THE BATTLE WHILE MY ENEMY STILL STANDS.
THE EXPLOSIVES IN THIS BRACELET WILL END BOTH OUR LIVES.
AT THIS DISTANCE...
THE BLAST WILL CRUSH HIS SKULL.
BELZE... I MUST LEAVE THE REST TO YOU.
TA TA, SEPHIRIA ARKS...
GEE HEE HEE HEE
MAY YOU REST IN PEACE.

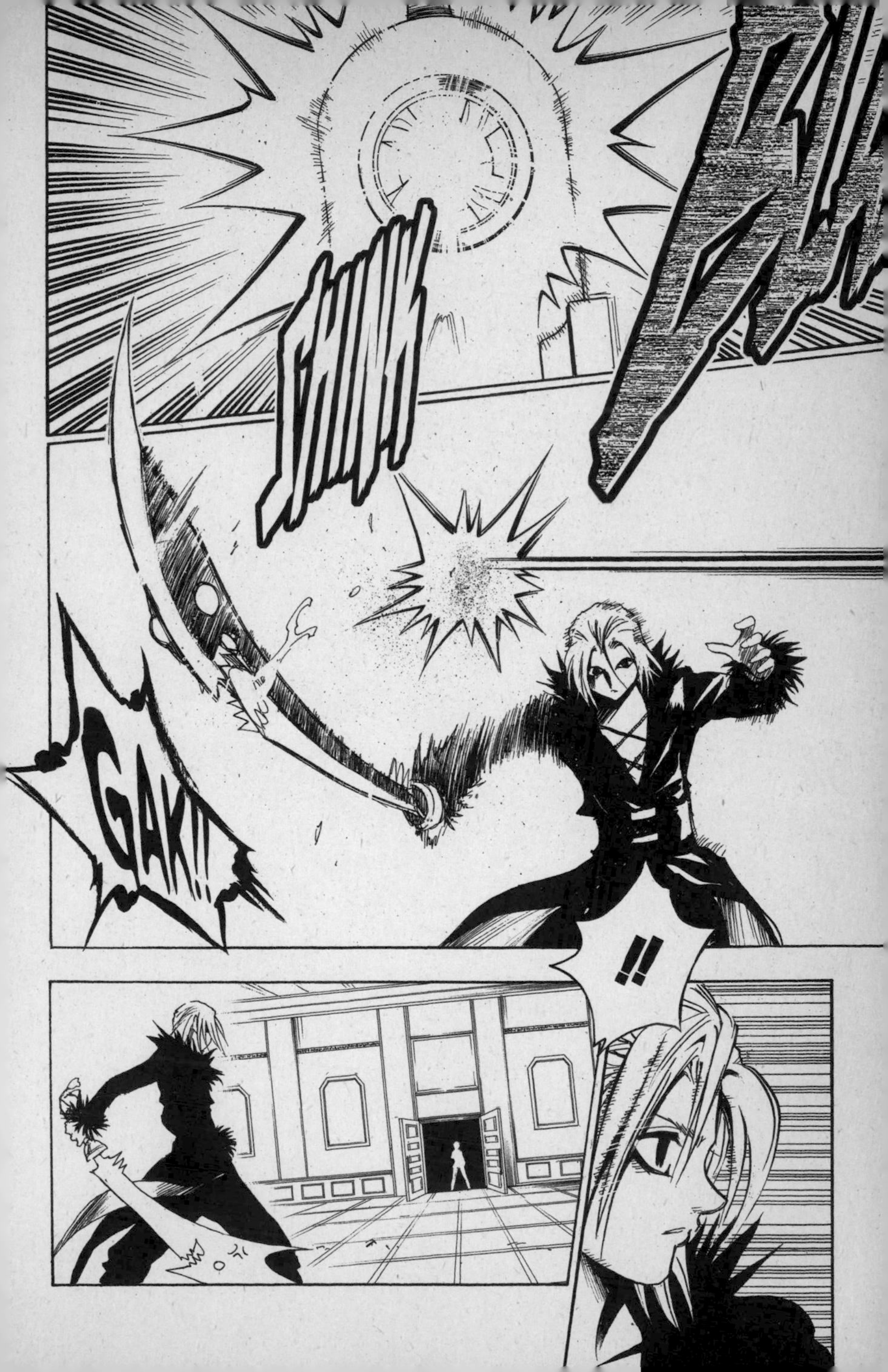
CHINK
GAK!!
!!

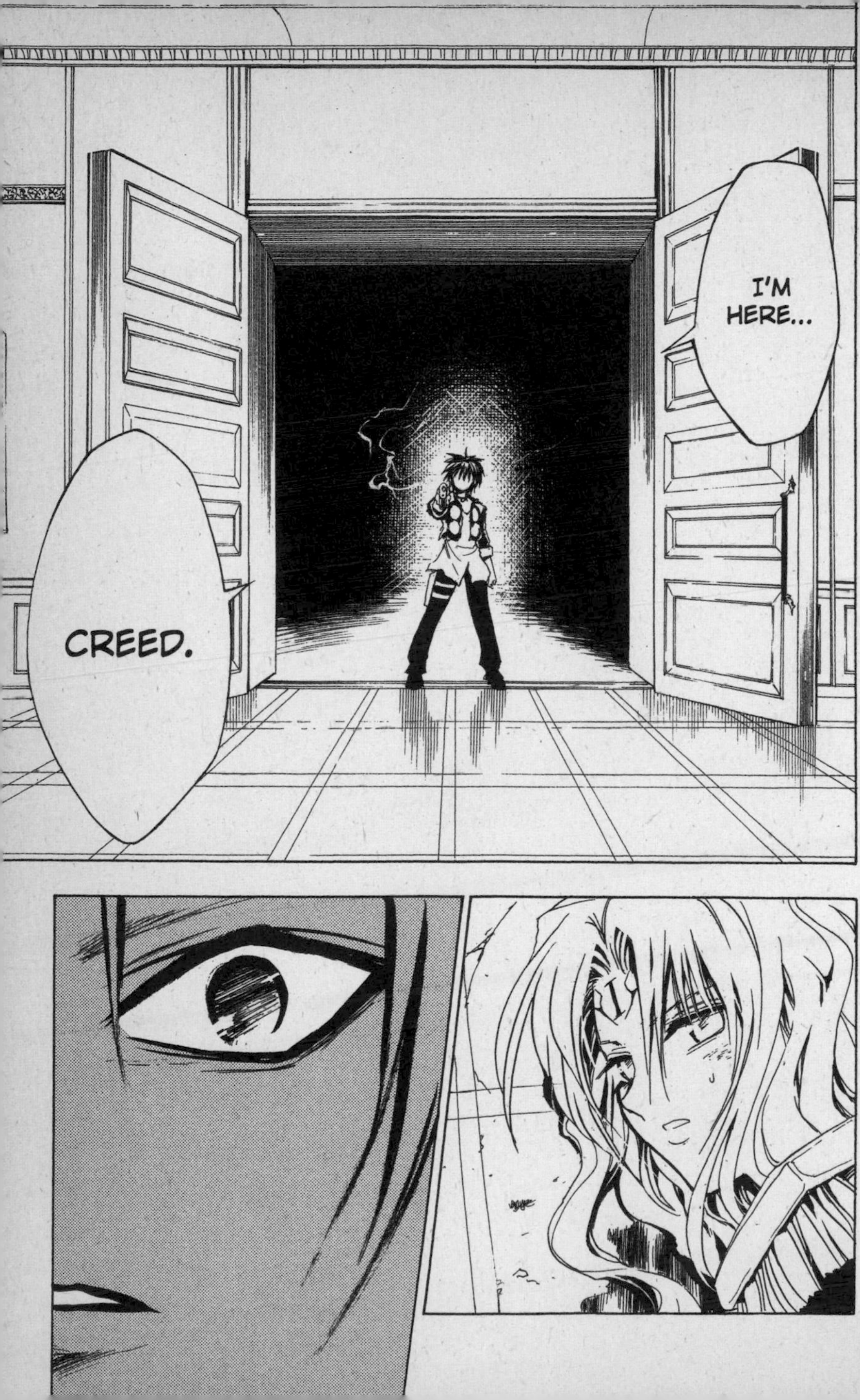
I'M HERE...
CREED.

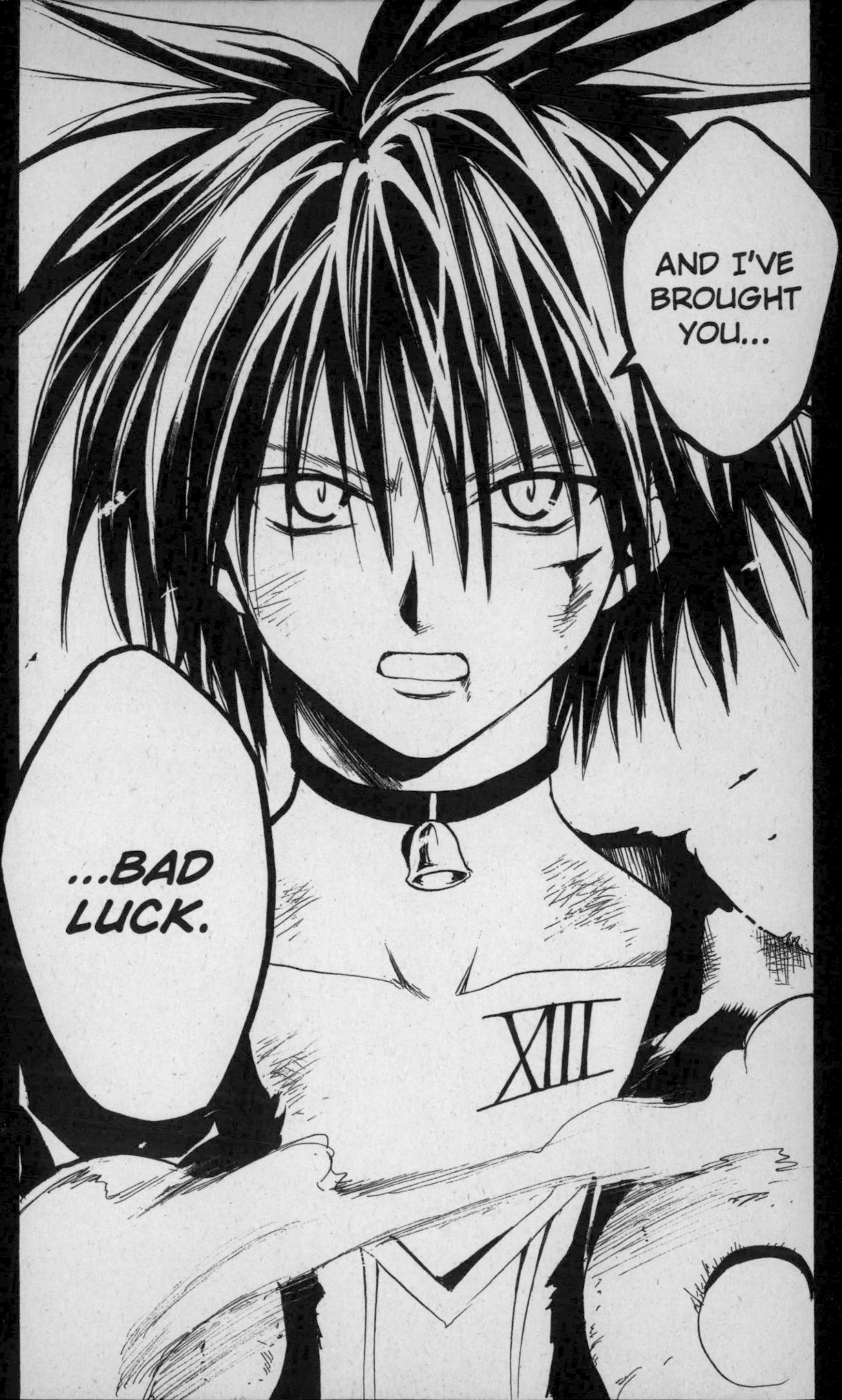

AND I'VE BROUGHT YOU...
...BAD LUCK.
XIII

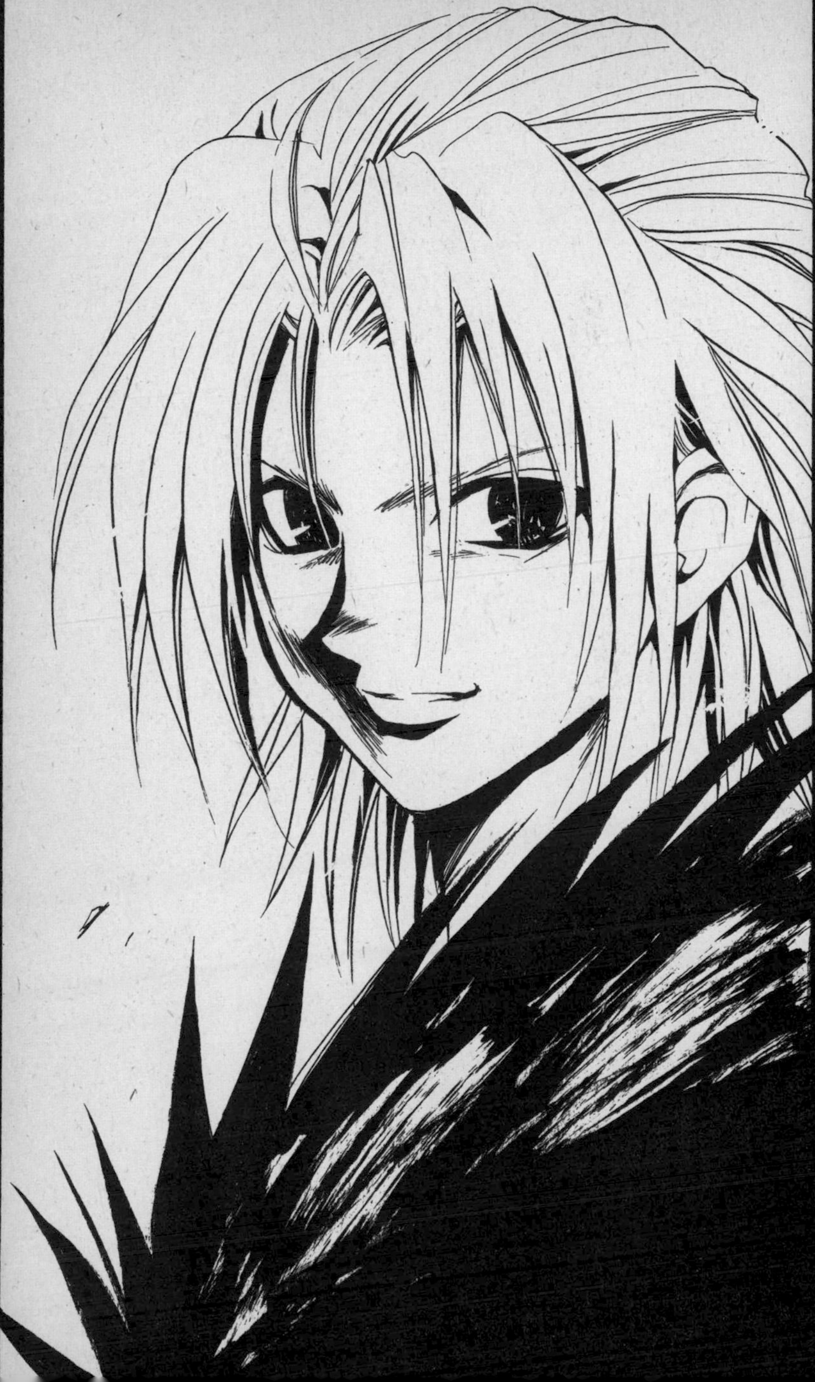

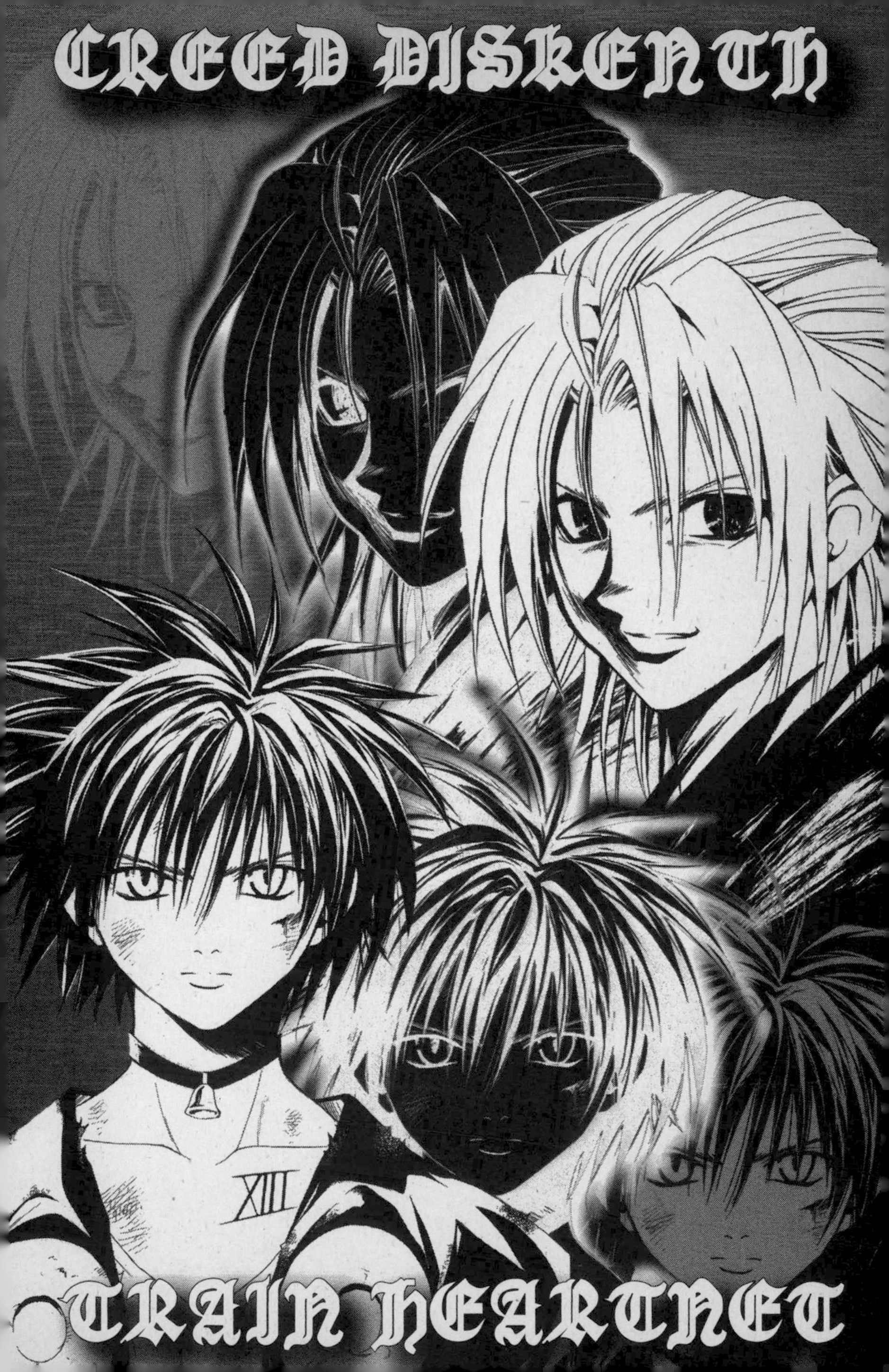
CREED DISKENTH
XIII
TRAIN HEARTNET

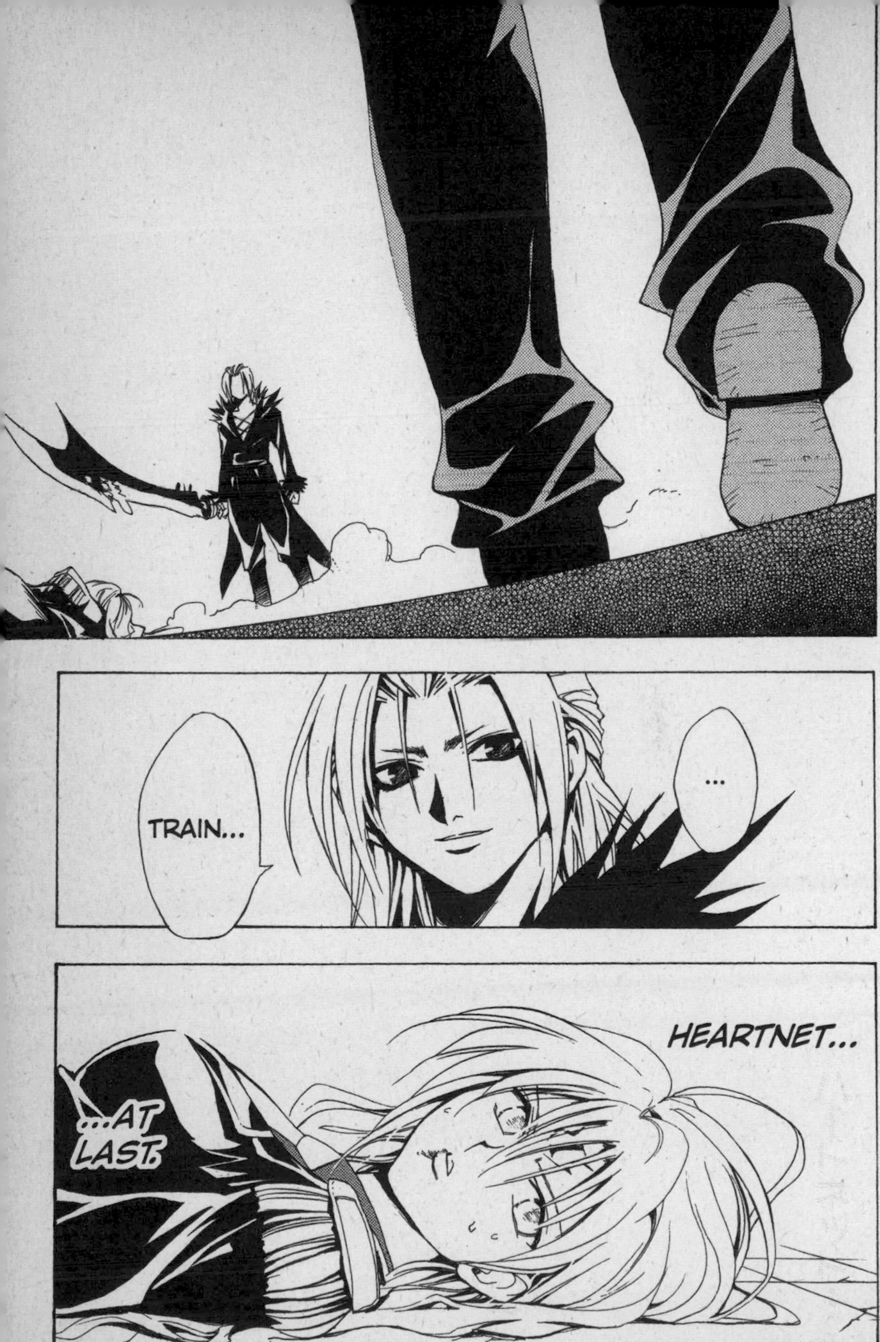
...
TRAIN...
HEARTNET...
...AT LAST.

Chapter 174: As a Sweeper

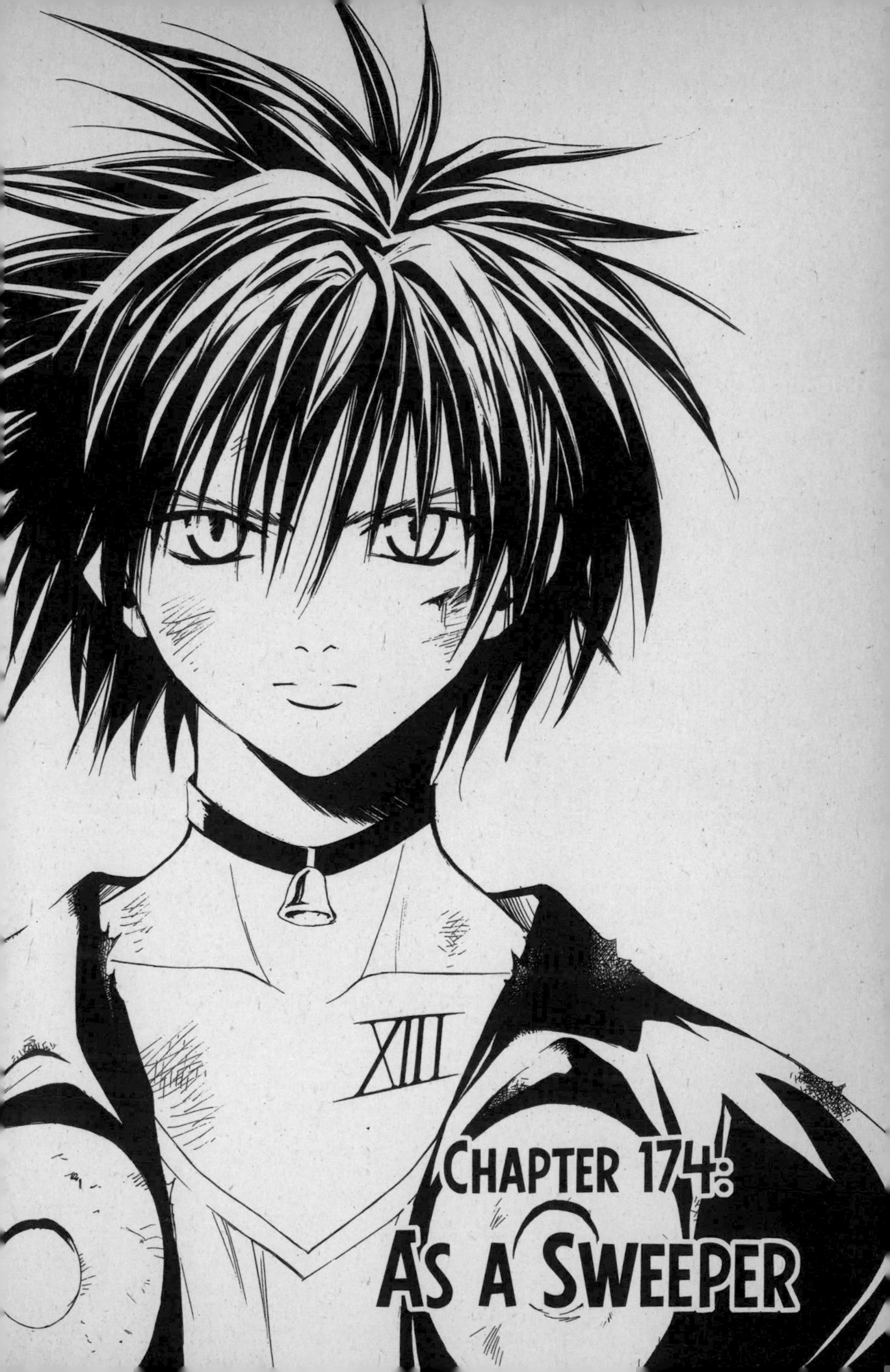
XIII
Chapter 174:
As a Sweeper

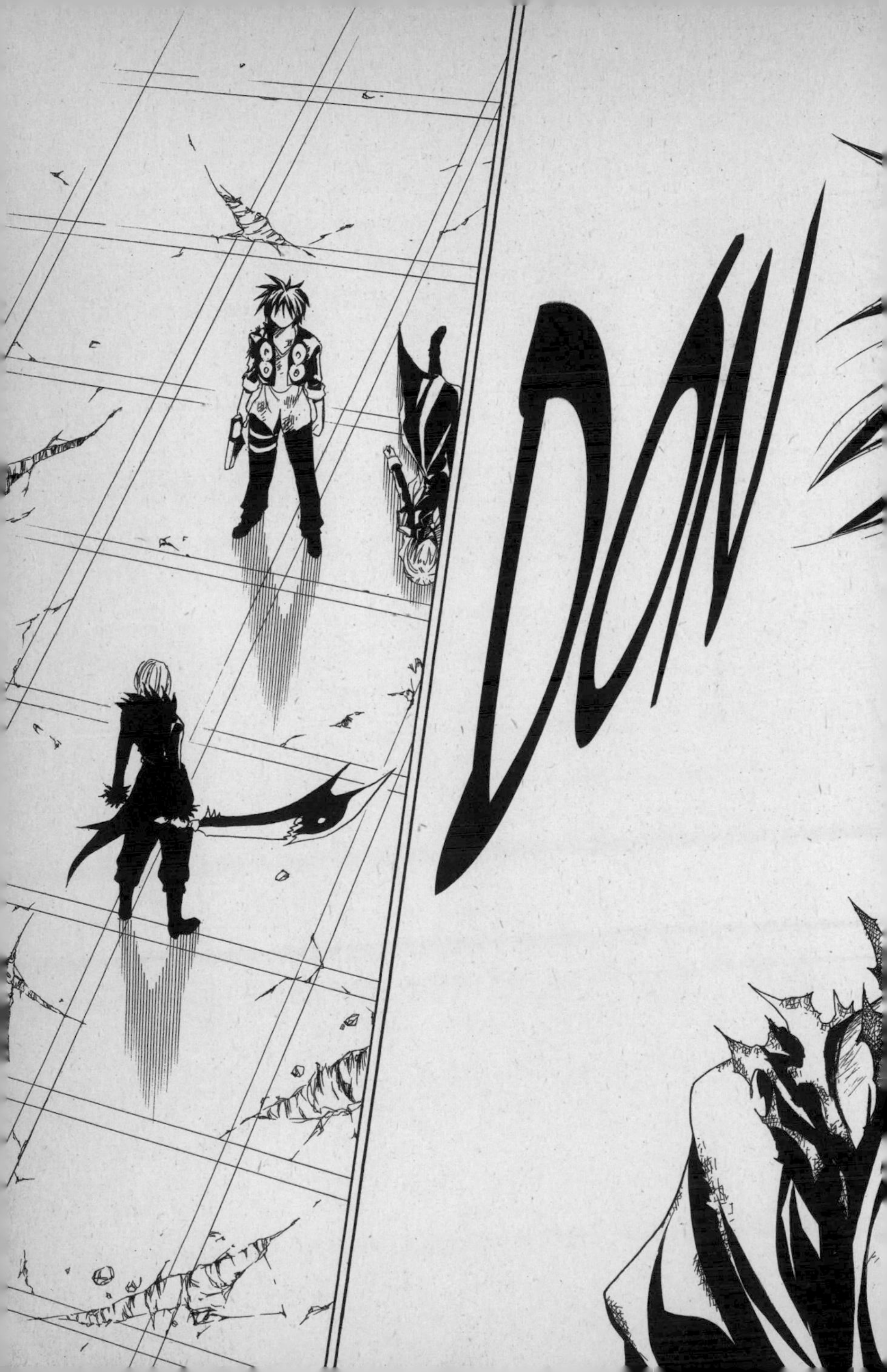
DON

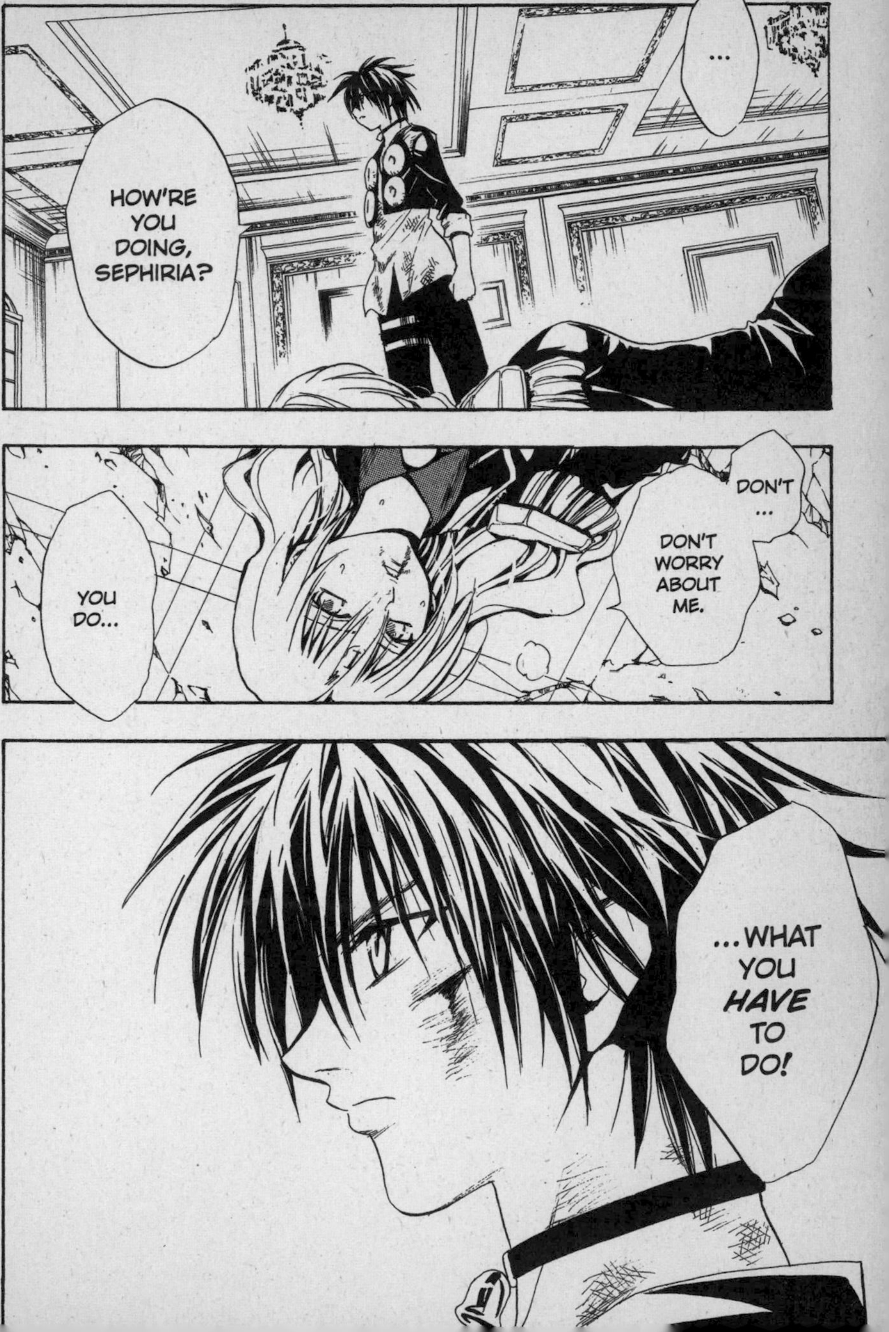
...
HOW'RE YOU DOING, SEPHIRIA?
DON'T ...
DON'T WORRY ABOUT ME.
YOU DO...
...WHAT YOU *HAVE* TO DO!

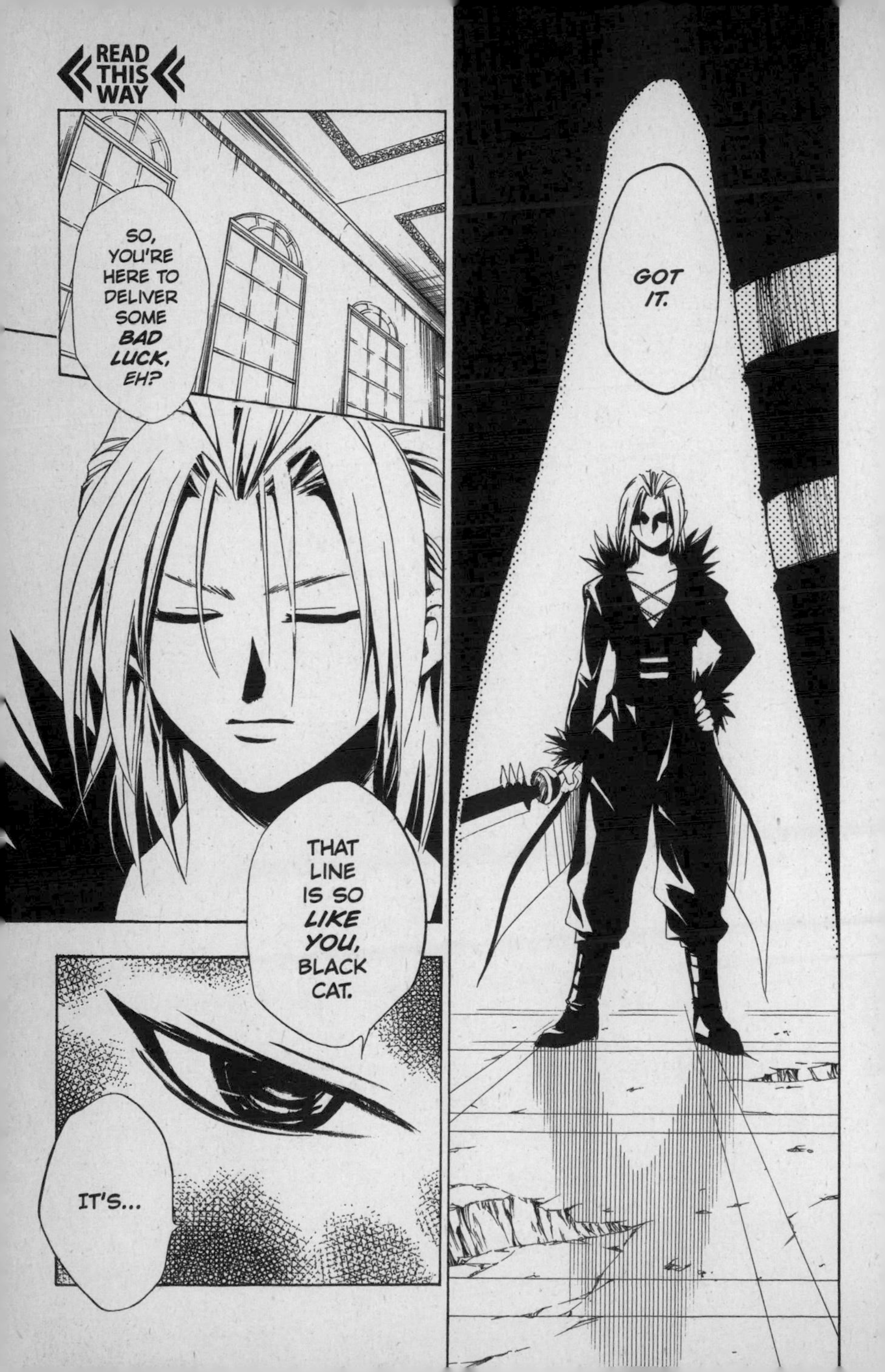
READ THIS WAY
GOT IT.
SO, YOU'RE HERE TO DELIVER SOME BAD LUCK, EH?
THAT LINE IS SO LIKE YOU, BLACK CAT.
IT'S...

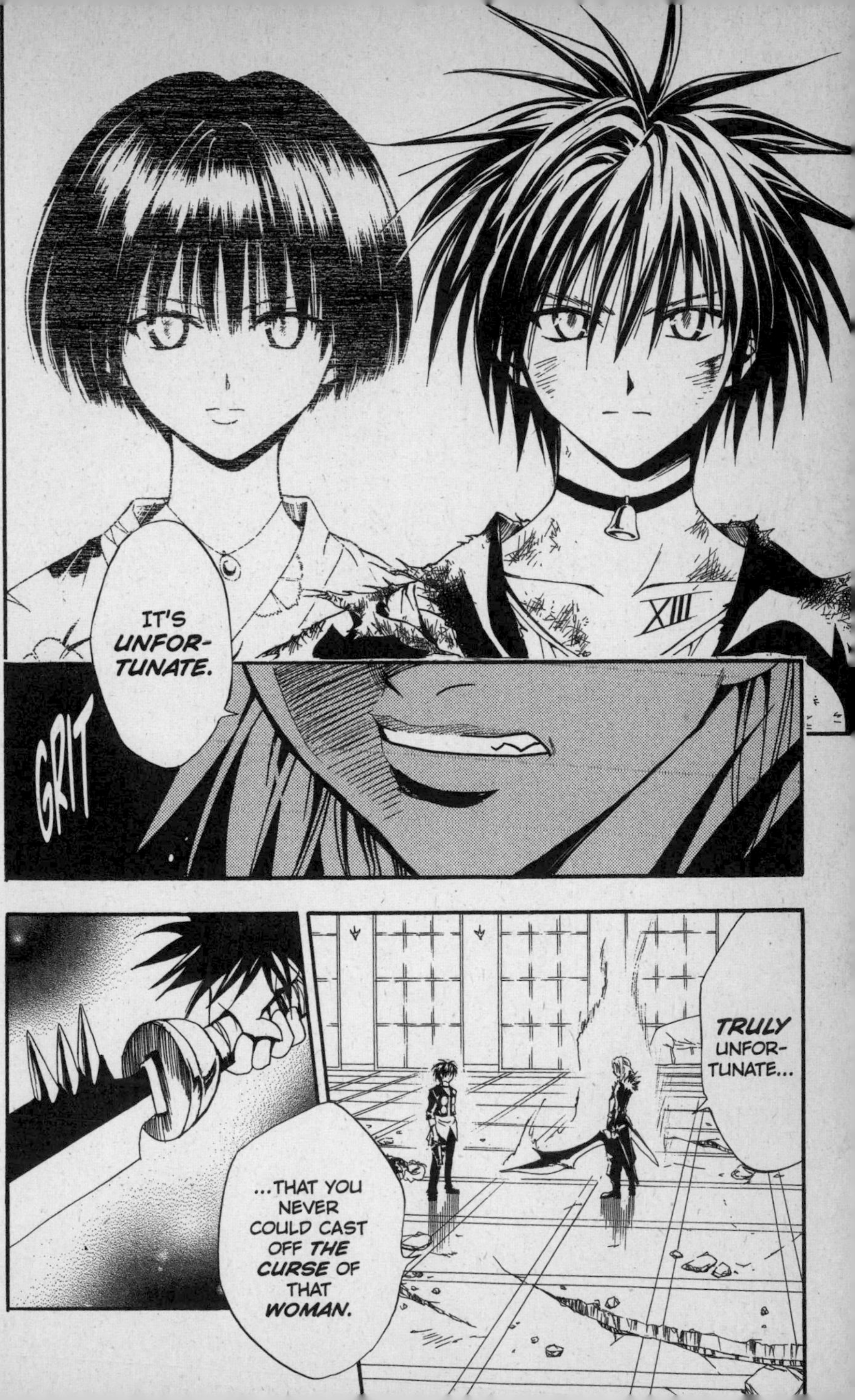
IT'S UNFOR-TUNATE.
GRIT
TRULY UNFOR-TUNATE...
...THAT YOU NEVER COULD CAST OFF THE CURSE OF THAT WOMAN.

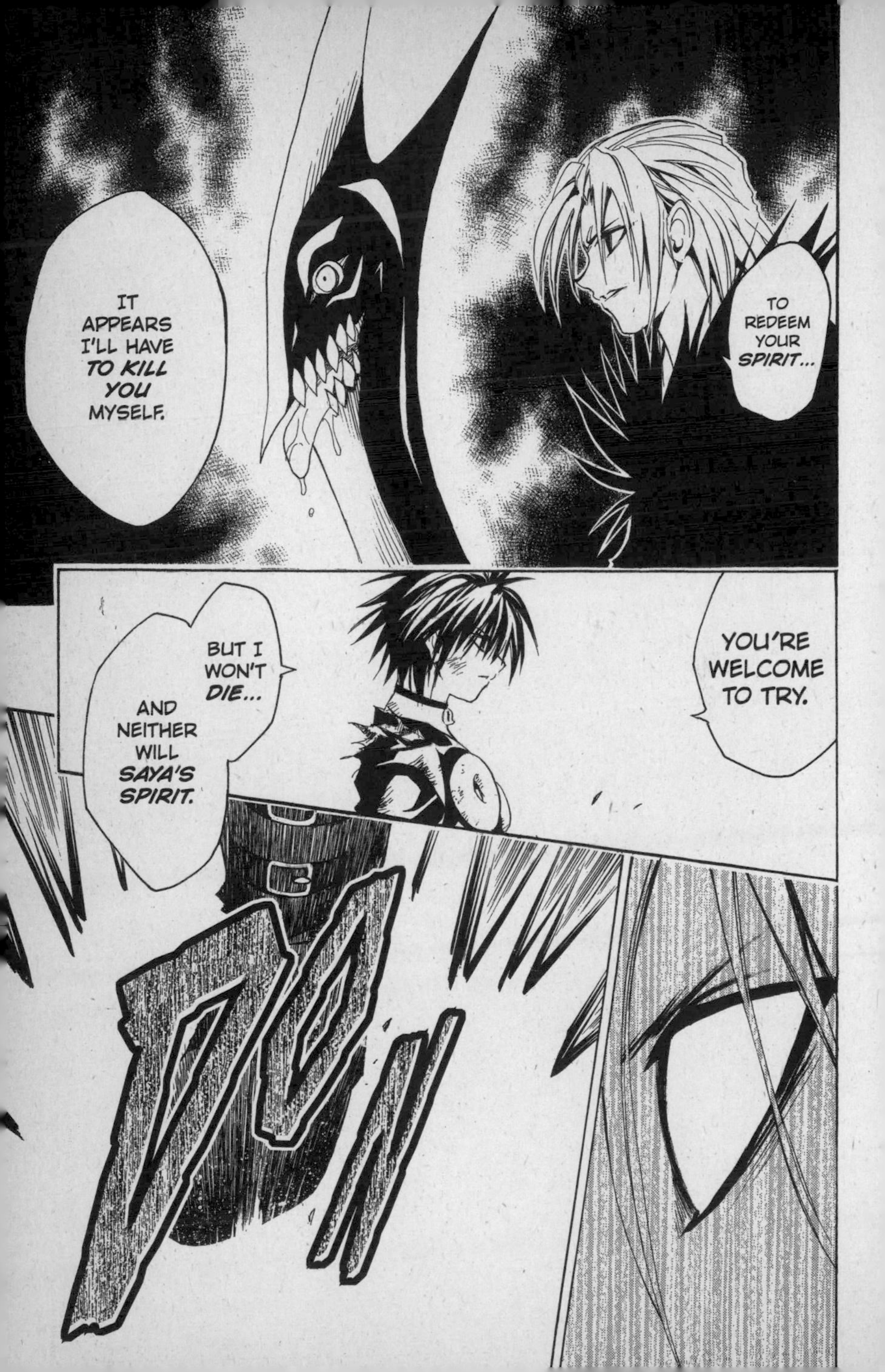
TO REDEEM YOUR SPIRIT...
IT APPEARS I'LL HAVE TO KILL YOU MYSELF.
YOU'RE WELCOME TO TRY.
BUT I WON'T DIE...
AND NEITHER WILL SAYA'S SPIRIT.

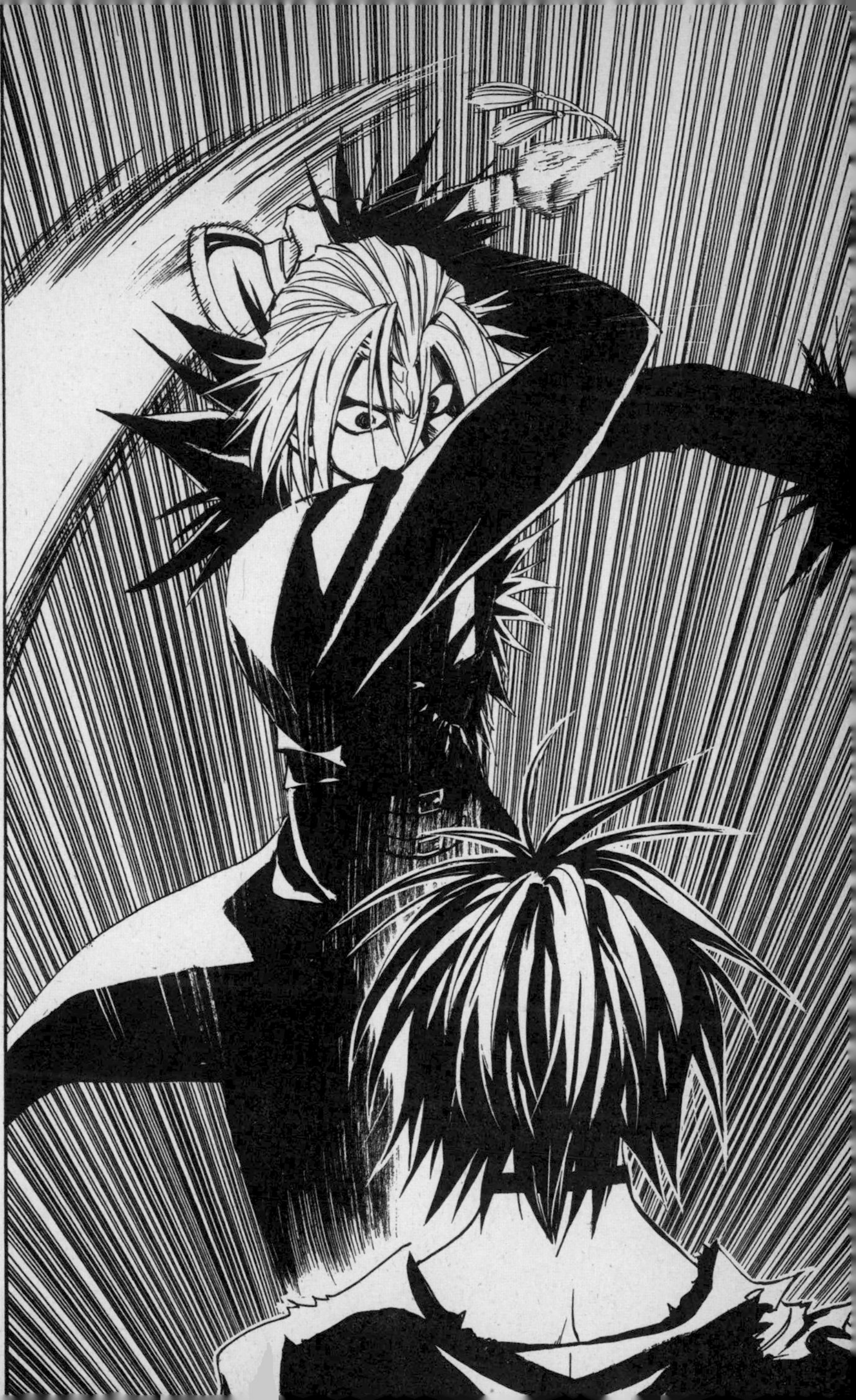

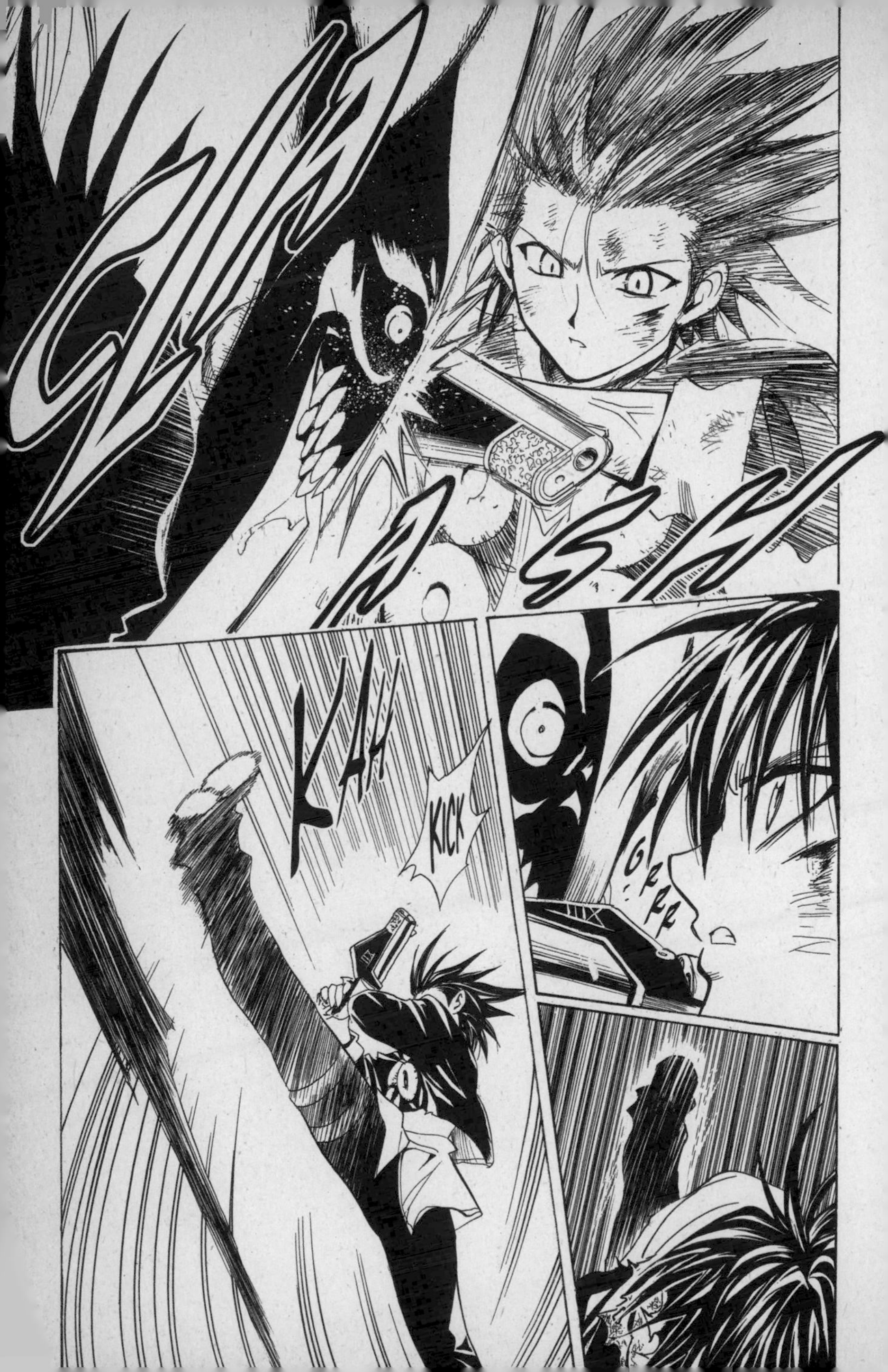
GRRR
KAH
KICK

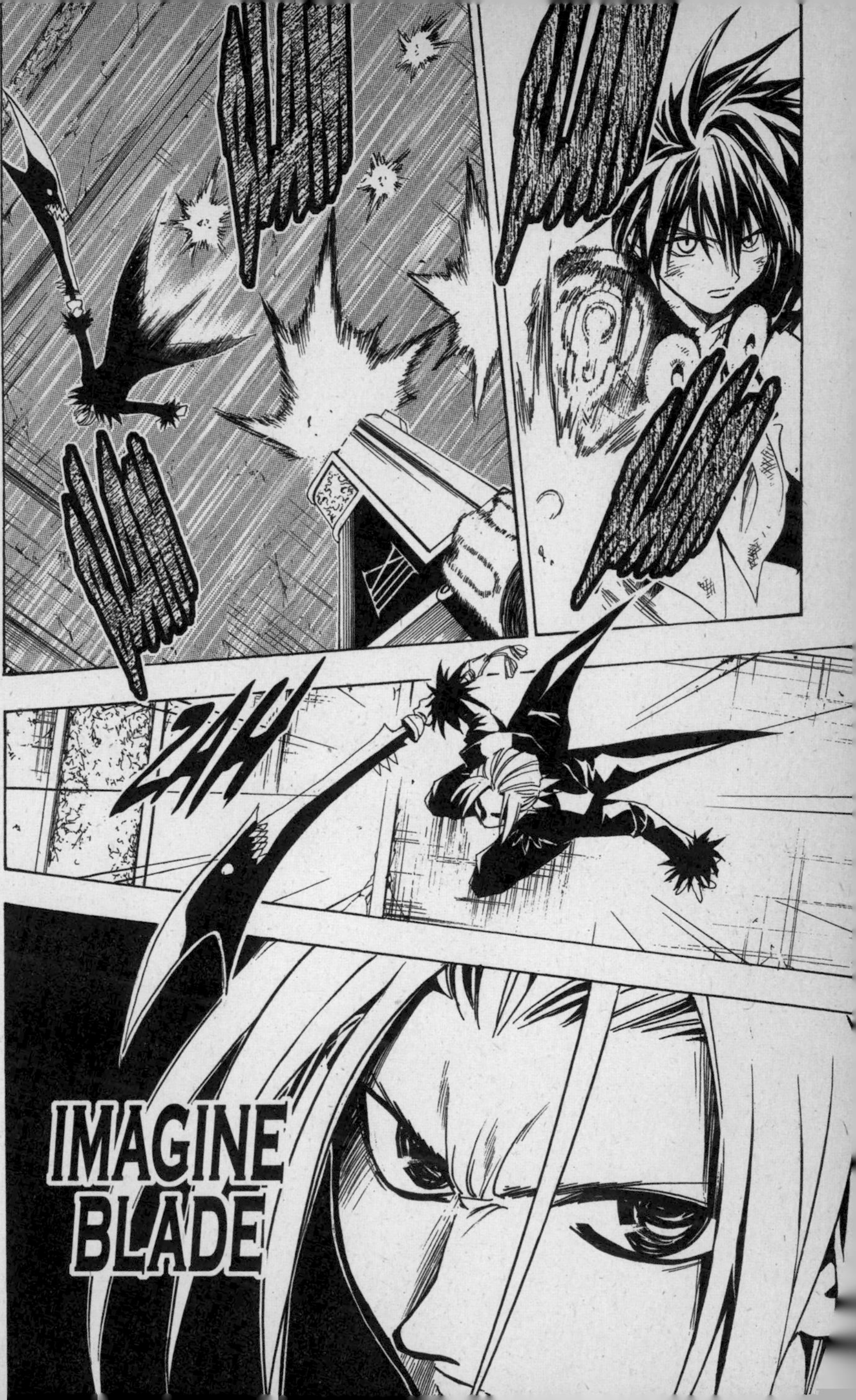
ZAH
IMAGINE BLADE

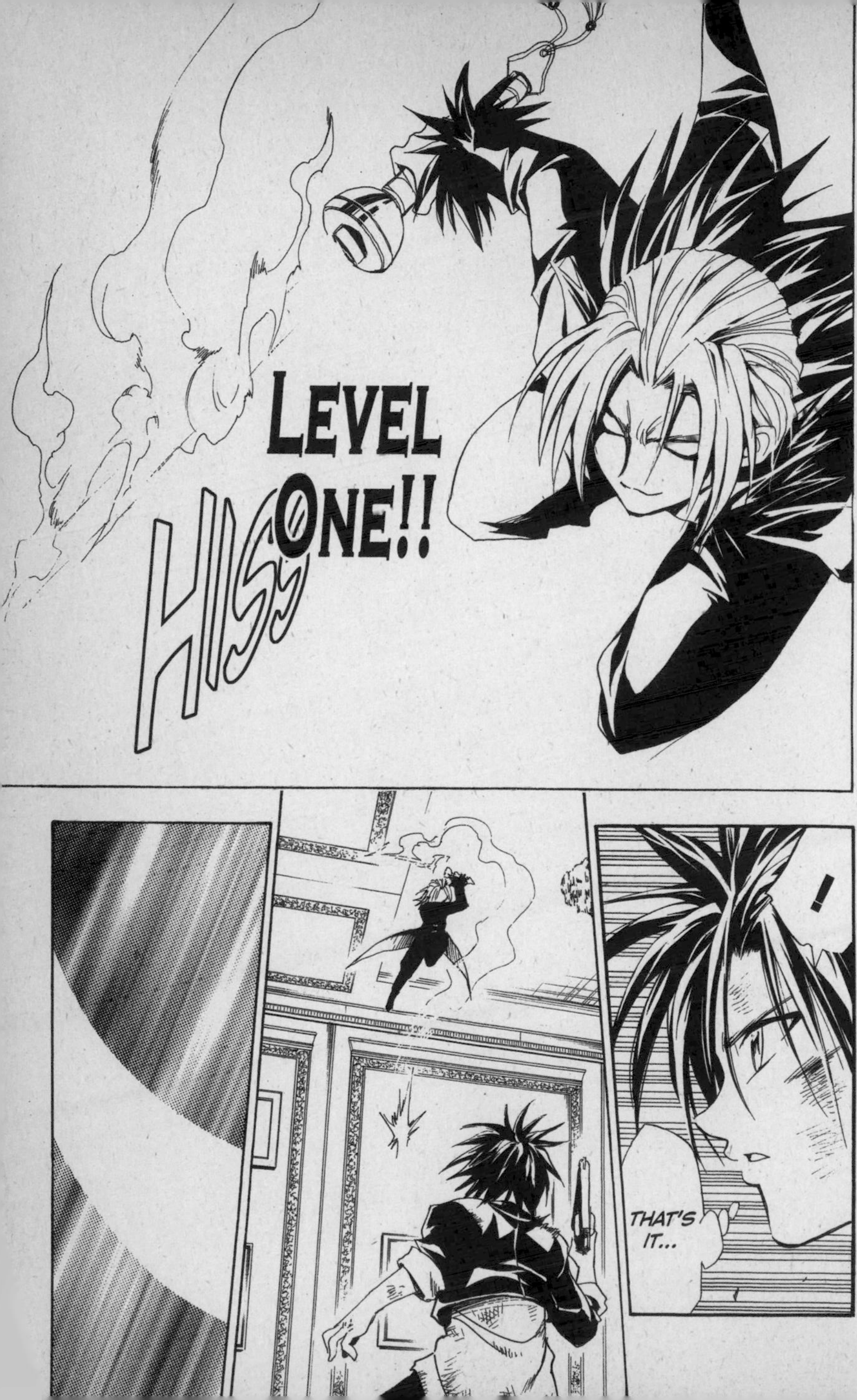
LEVEL ONE!!
HISS
!
THAT'S IT...

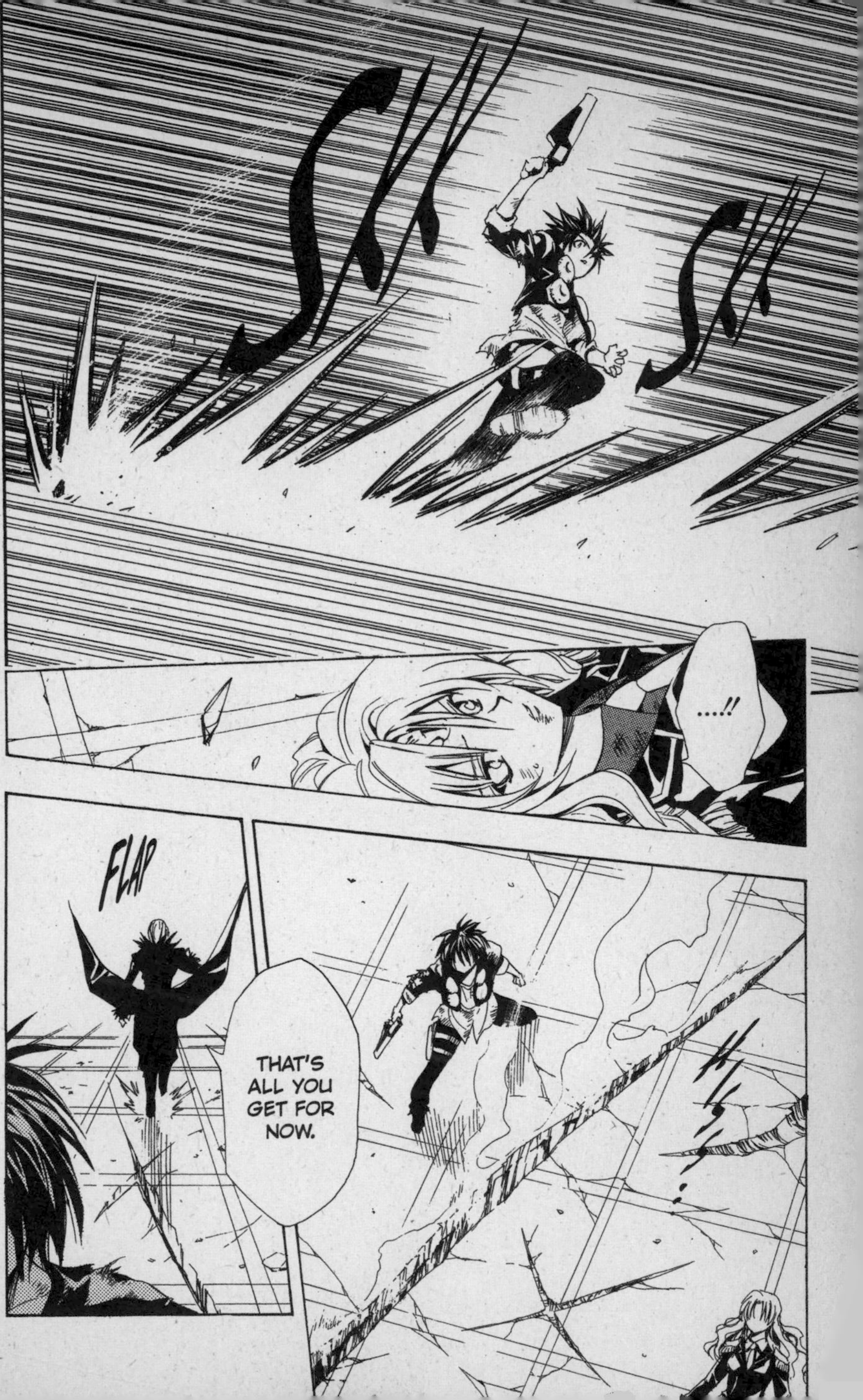
....!!
THAT'S ALL YOU GET FOR NOW.
FLAP

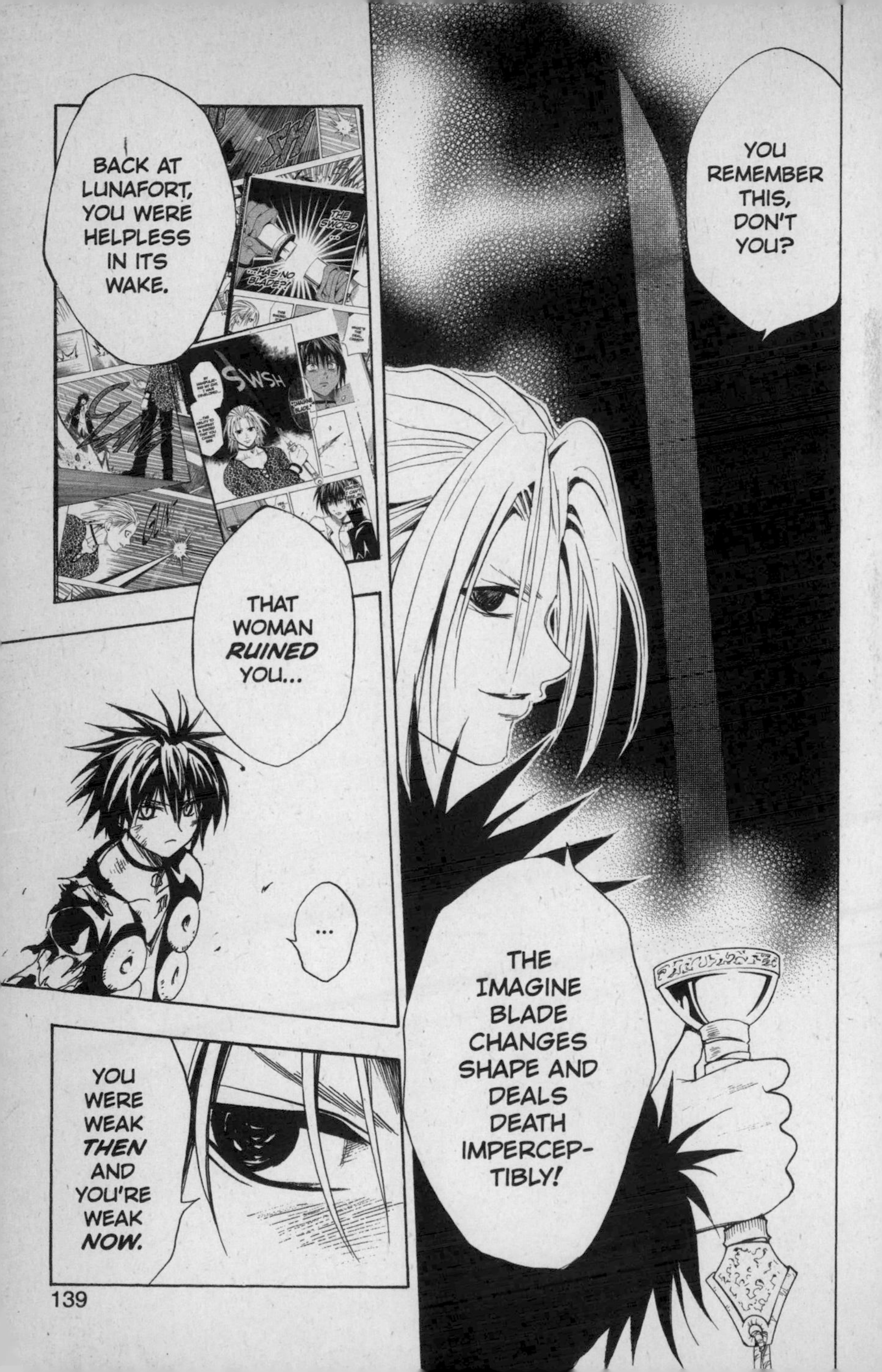
YOU REMEMBER THIS, DON'T YOU?
THE IMAGINE BLADE CHANGES SHAPE AND DEALS DEATH IMPERCEP-TIBLY!
BACK AT LUNAFORT, YOU WERE HELPLESS IN ITS WAKE.
THE SWORD...
...HAS NO BLADE?!
SWSH
THAT WOMAN *RUINED* YOU...
...
YOU WERE WEAK *THEN* AND YOU'RE WEAK *NOW*.

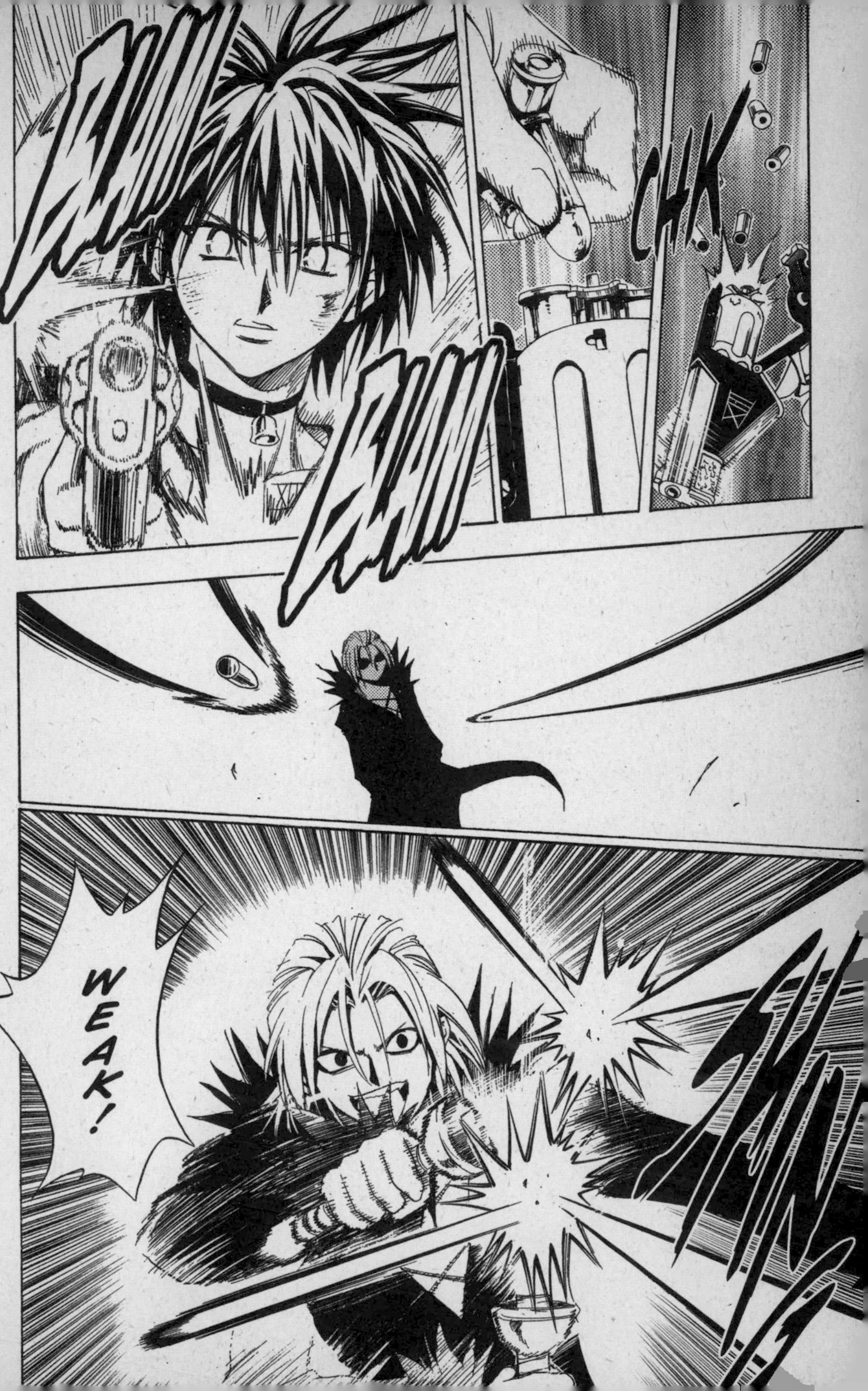
CHK
WEAK!

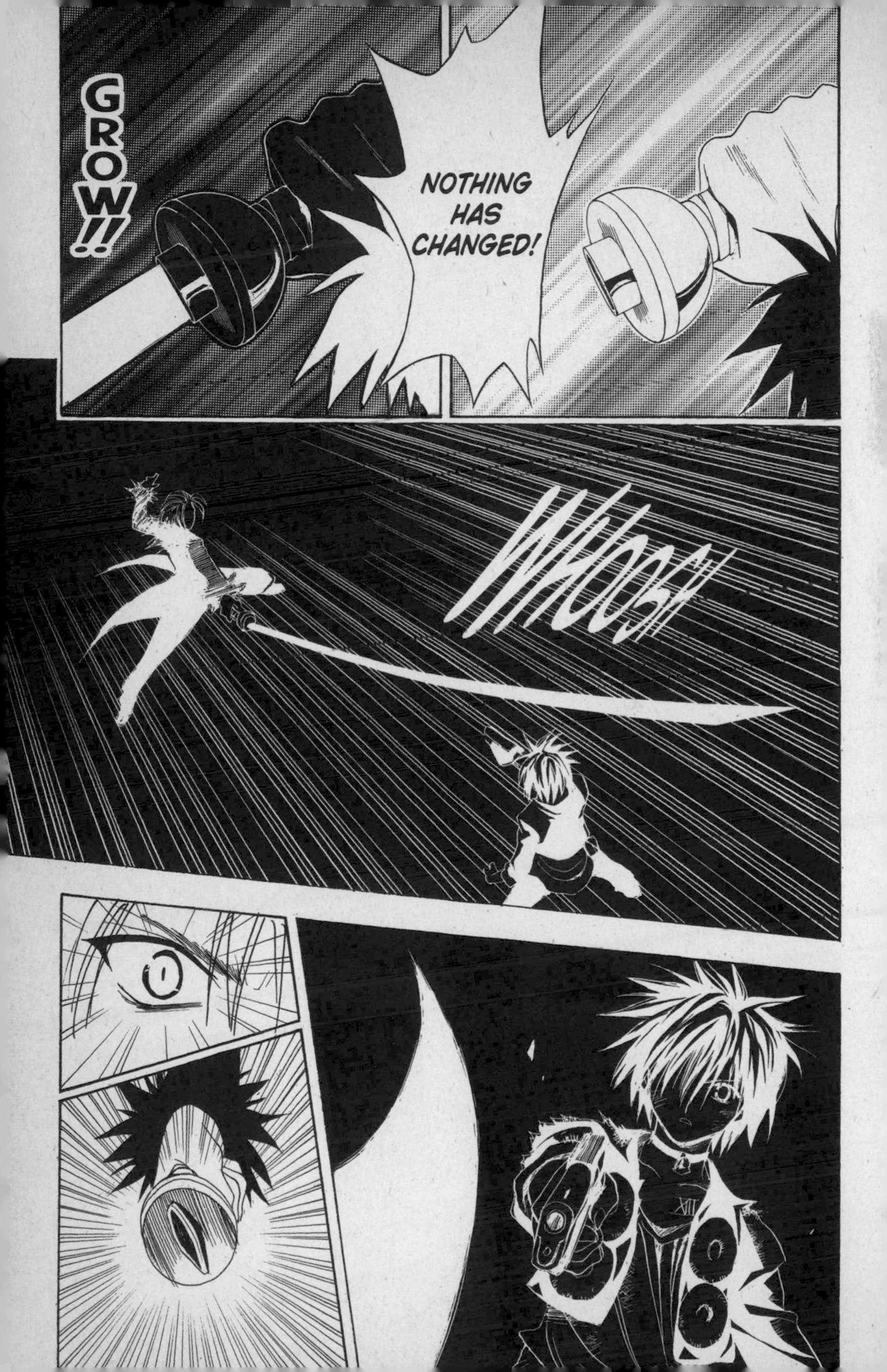
NOTHING HAS CHANGED!
GROW!!
WHOOSH

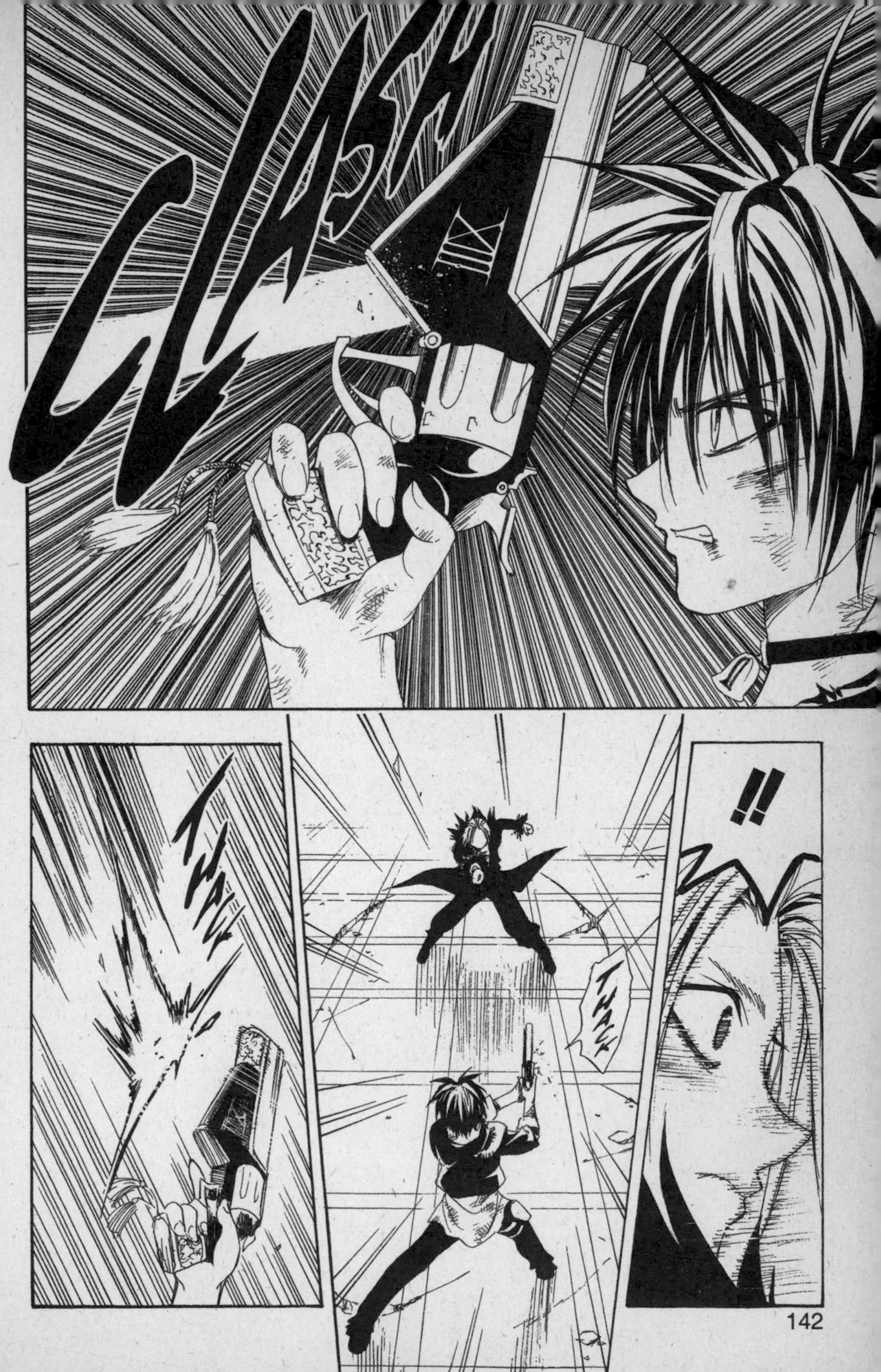
CLASH
!!
THACK
THAK

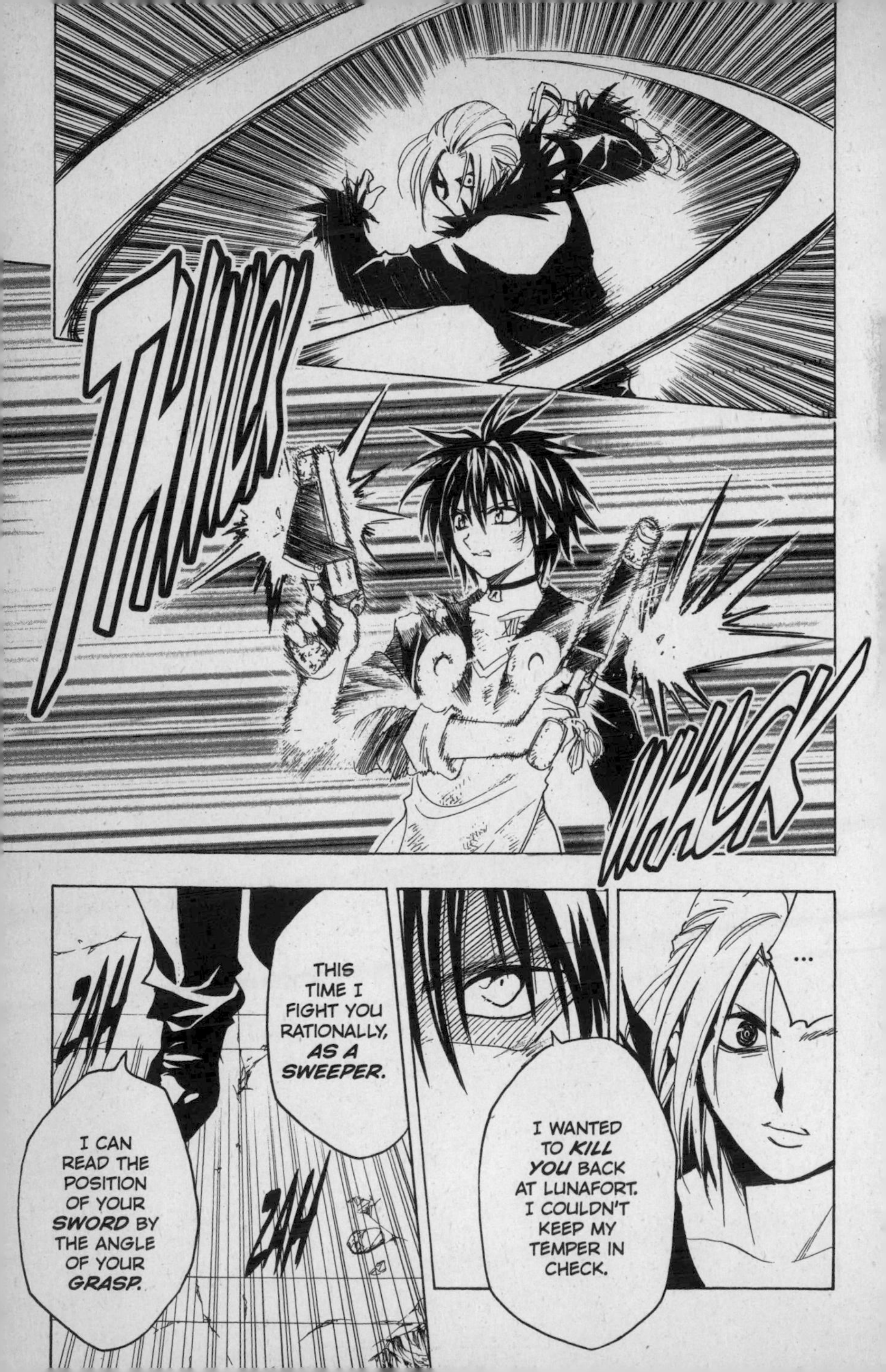
...
I WANTED TO **KILL YOU** BACK AT LUNAFORT. I COULDN'T KEEP MY TEMPER IN CHECK.
THIS TIME I FIGHT YOU RATIONALLY, **AS A SWEEPER.**
ZAH
ZAH
I CAN READ THE POSITION OF YOUR **SWORD** BY THE ANGLE OF YOUR **GRASP.**

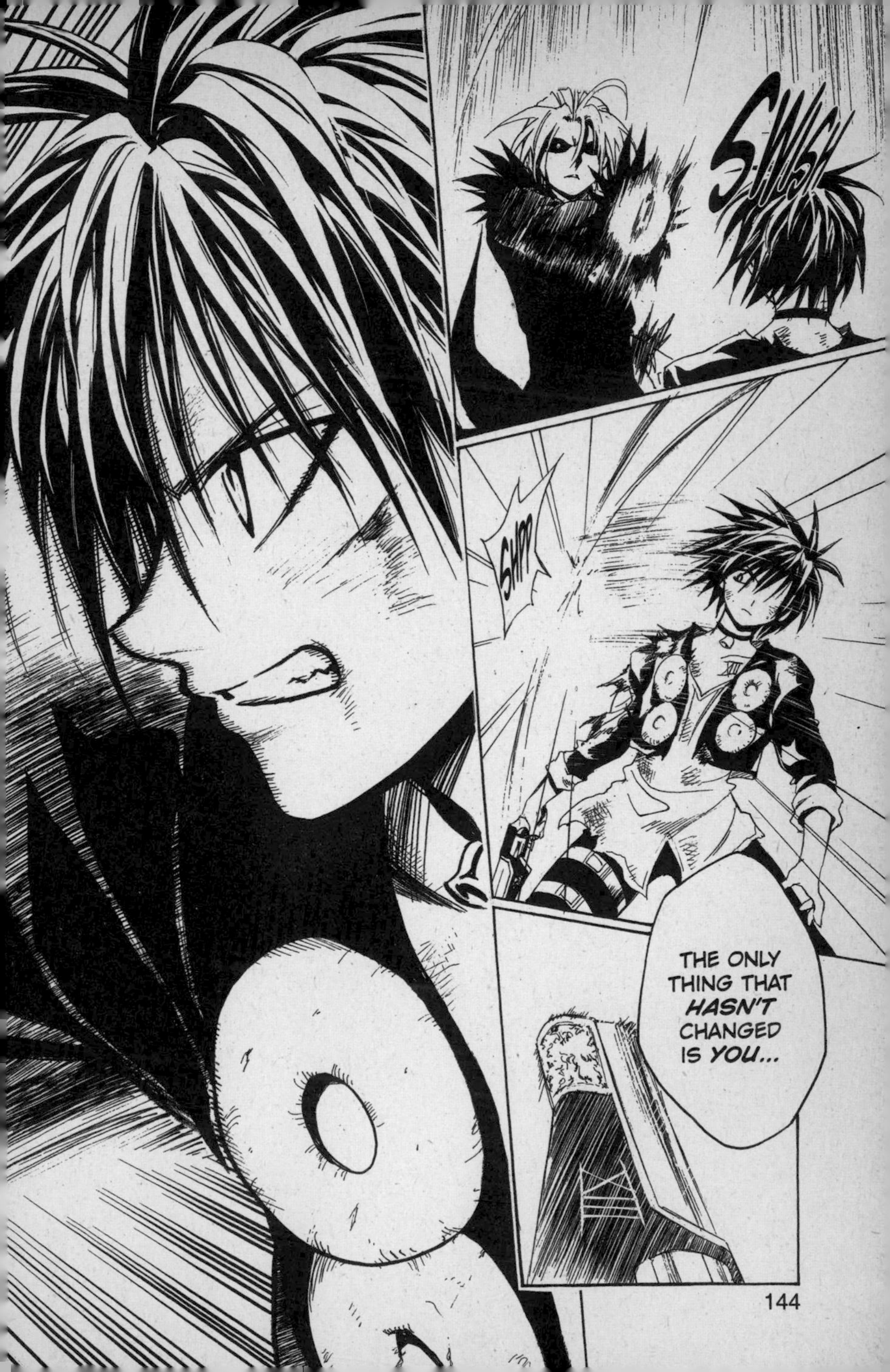
SWISH
SHPP
THE ONLY THING THAT *HASN'T* CHANGED IS *YOU*...

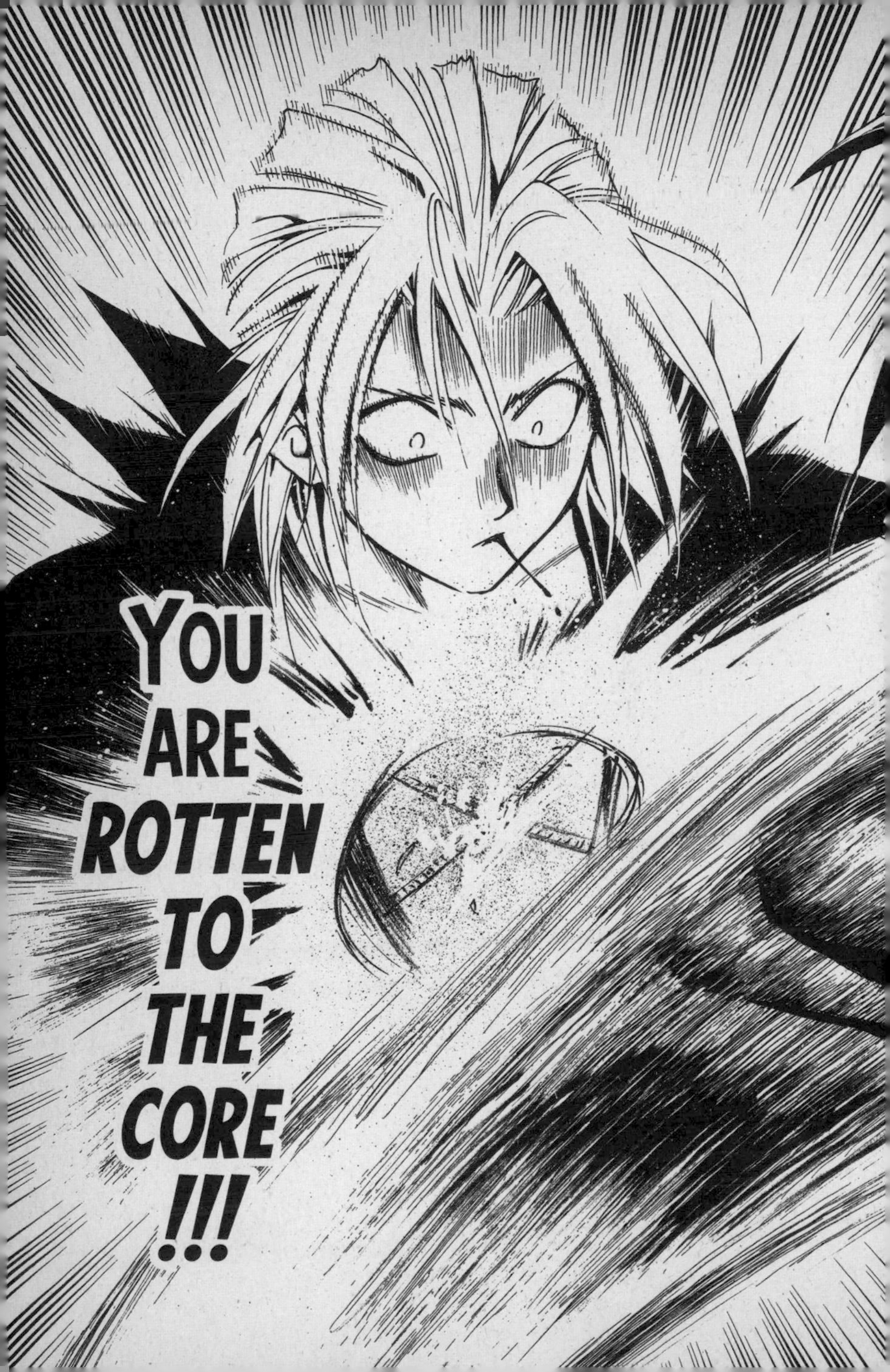
YOU ARE ROTTEN TO THE CORE!!!

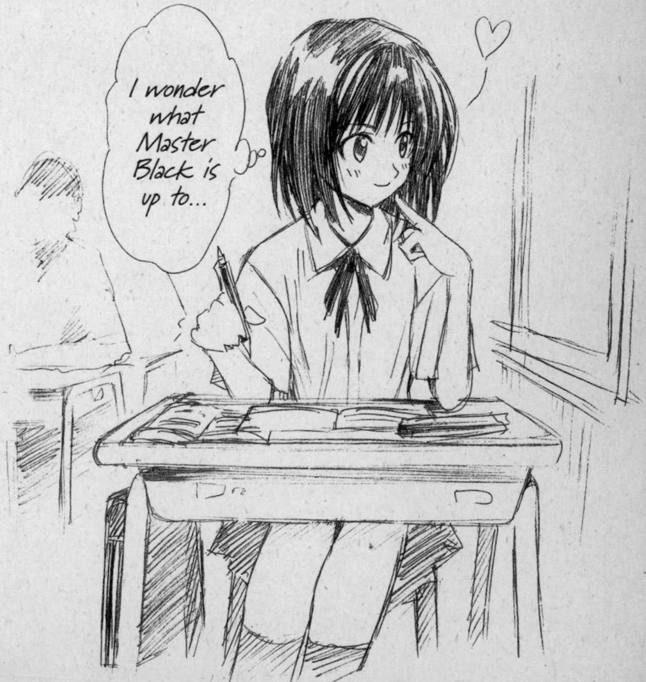
I wonder what Master Black is up to...

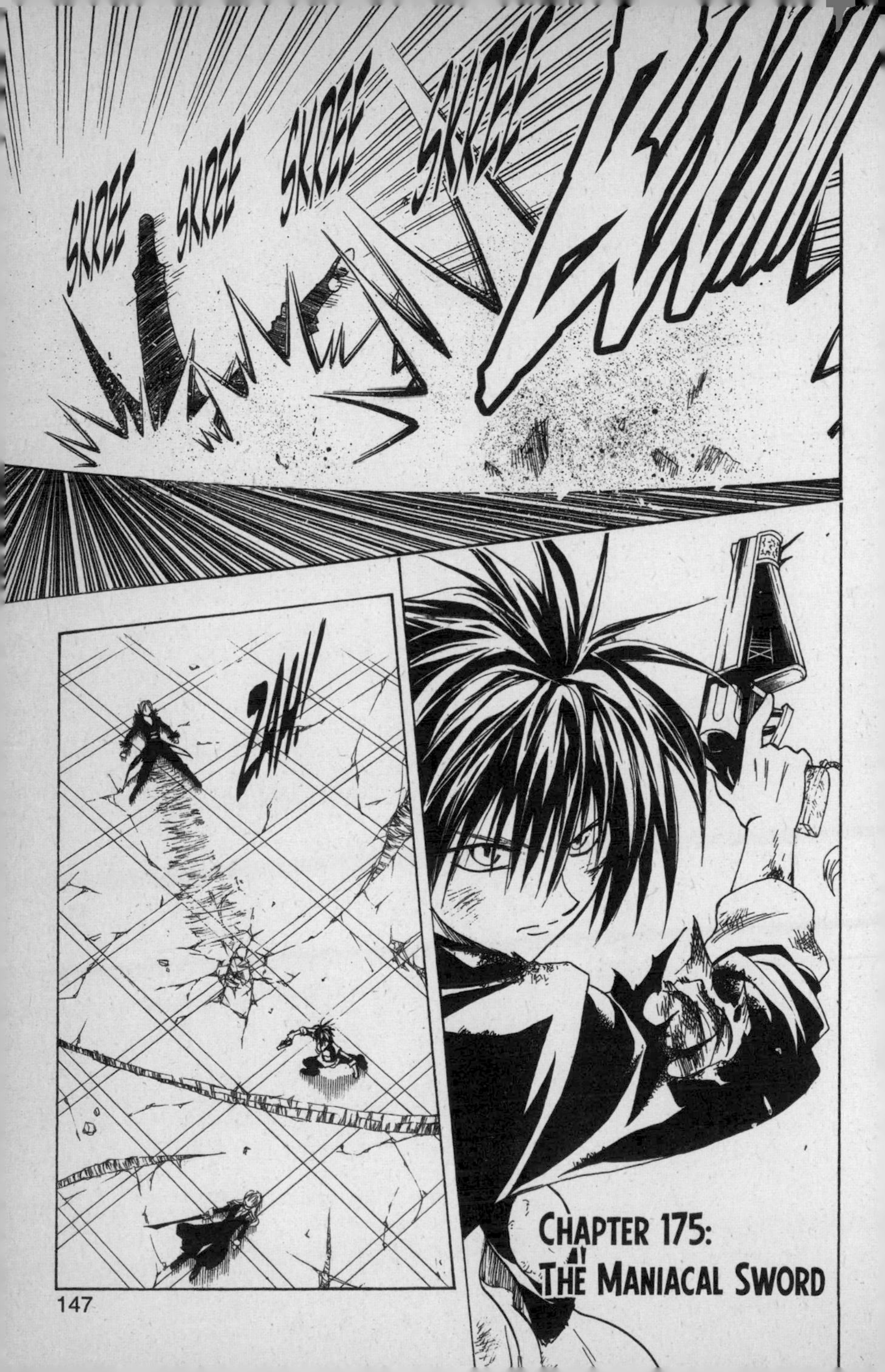
SKREE
SKREE
SKREE
SKREE
Chapter 175:
The Maniacal Sword
ZAH!

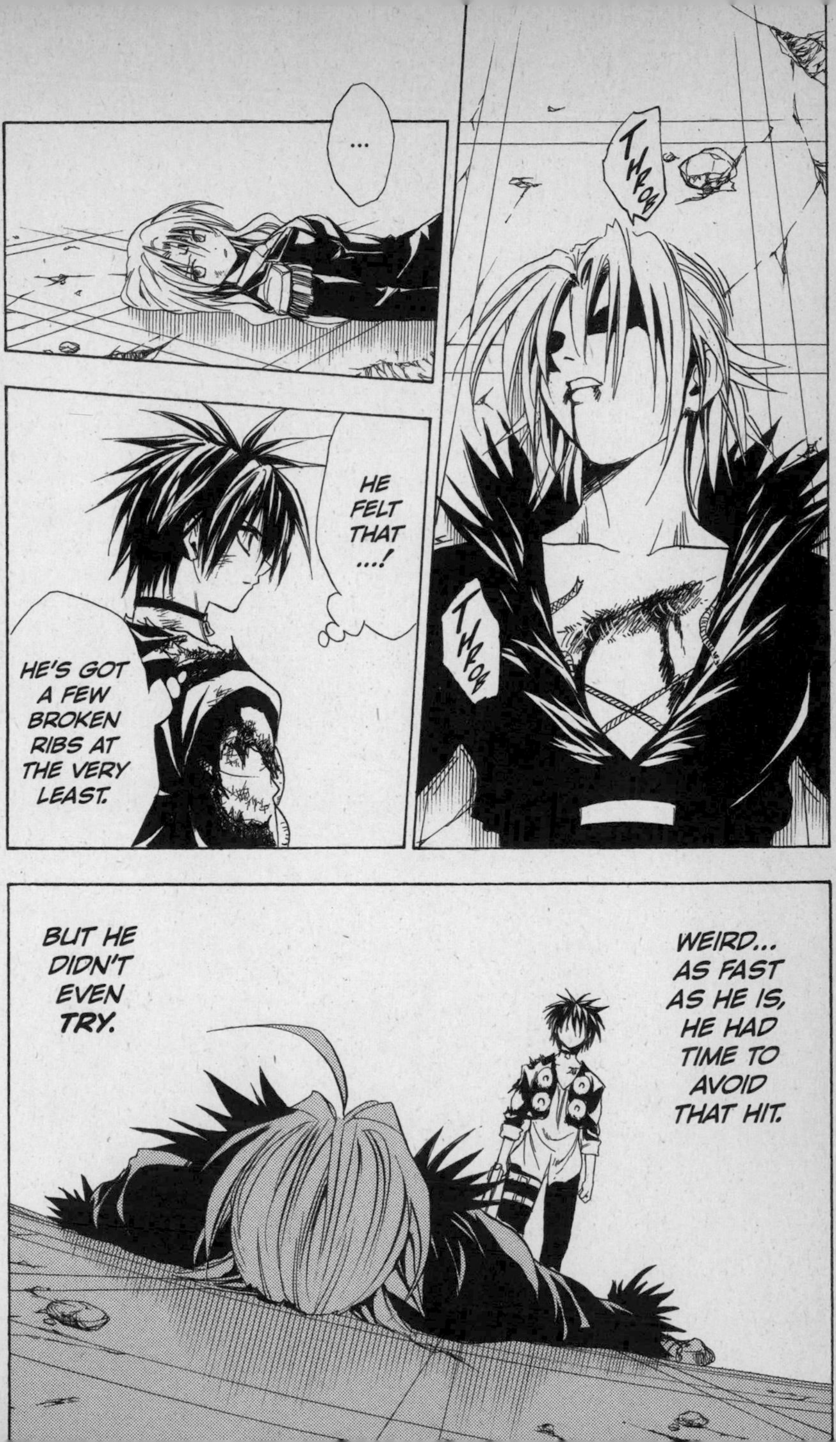
THROB
THROB
...
HE FELT THAT....!
HE'S GOT A FEW BROKEN RIBS AT THE VERY LEAST.
WEIRD... AS FAST AS HE IS, HE HAD TIME TO AVOID THAT HIT.
BUT HE DIDN'T EVEN TRY.

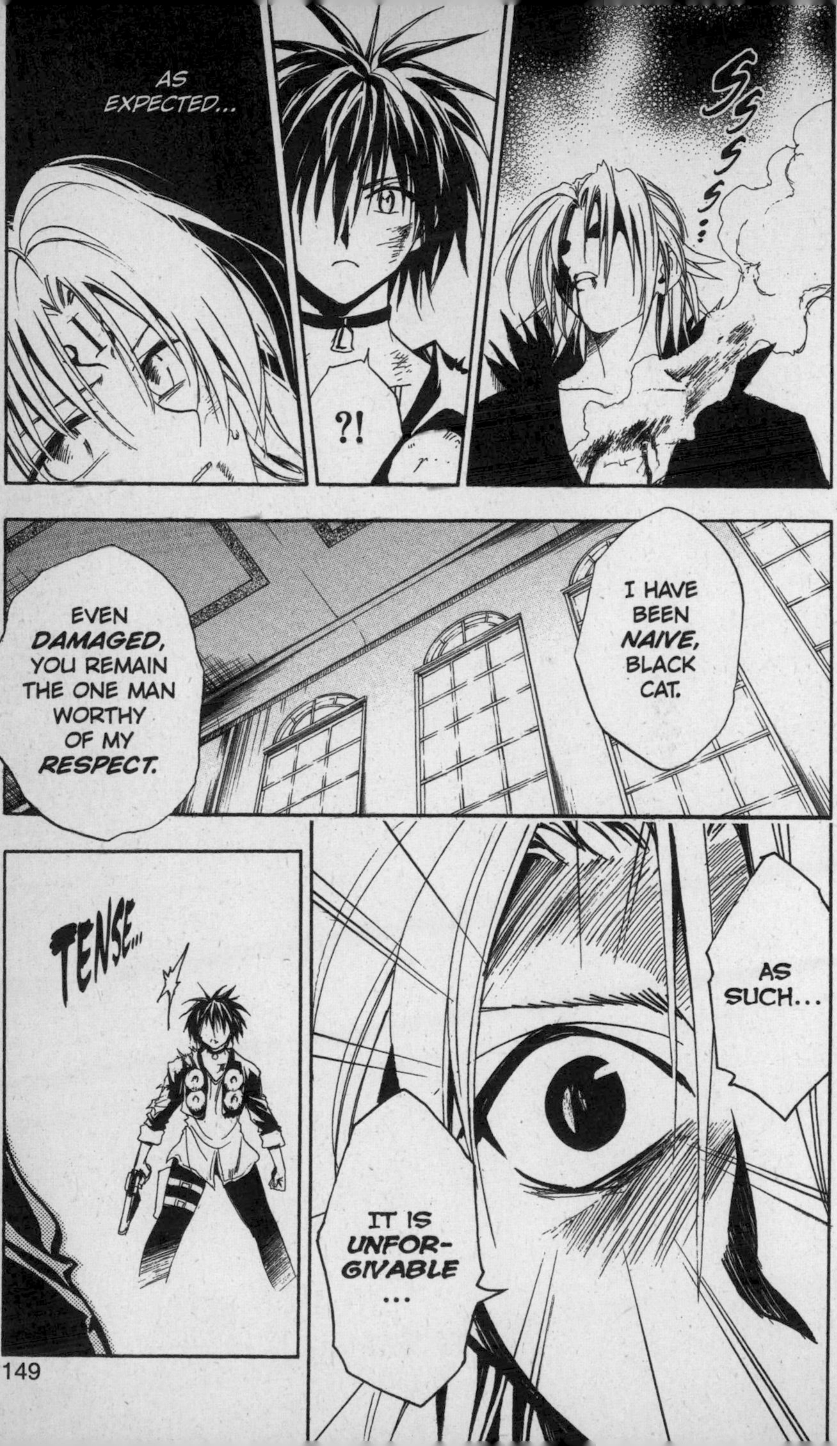
SSSS...
?!
AS EXPECTED...
I HAVE BEEN NAIVE, BLACK CAT.
EVEN DAMAGED, YOU REMAIN THE ONE MAN WORTHY OF MY RESPECT.
AS SUCH...
IT IS UNFORGIVABLE...
TENSE...

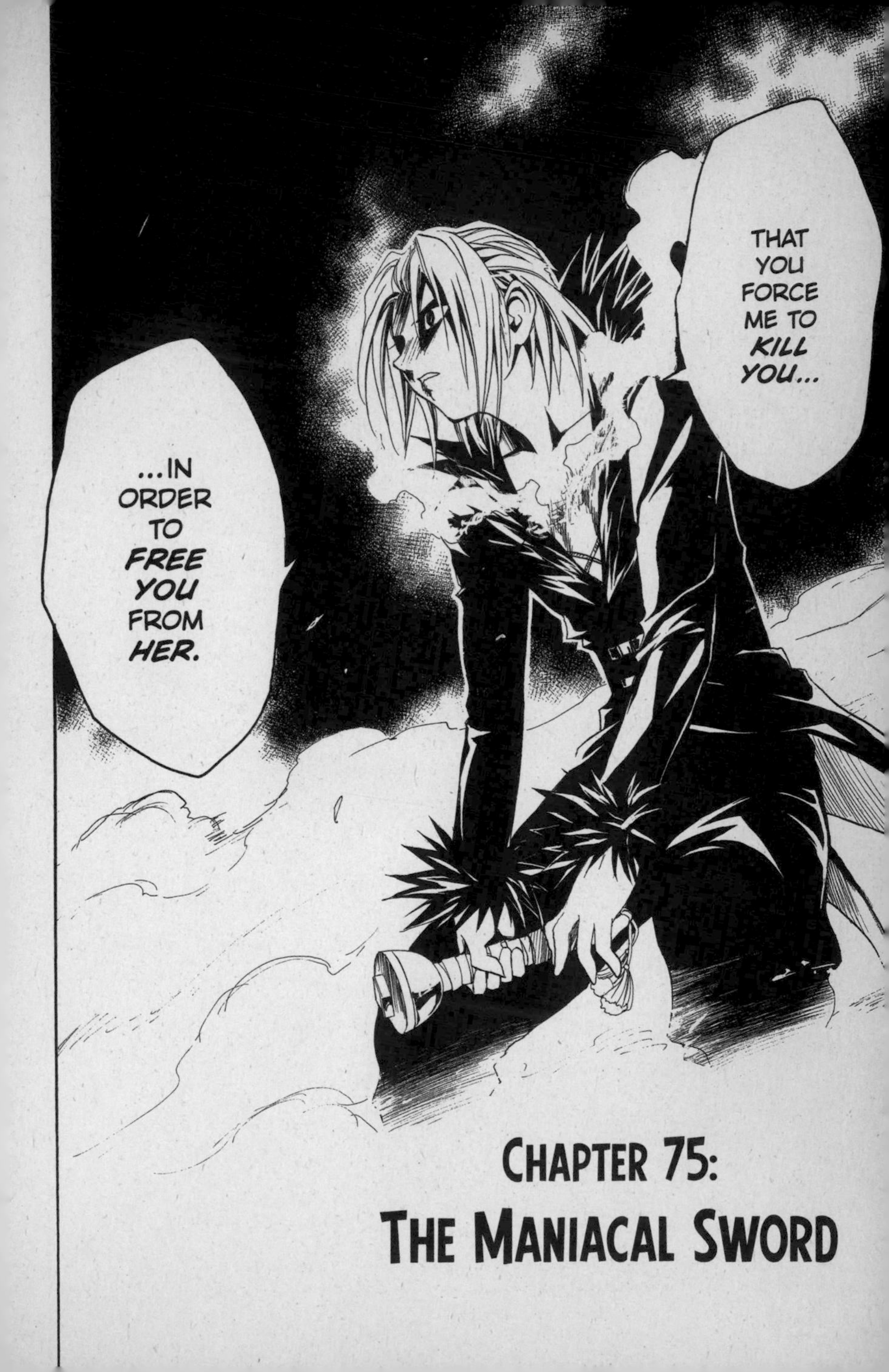
THAT YOU FORCE ME TO *KILL YOU...*
...IN ORDER TO *FREE YOU* FROM *HER.*

Chapter 75: The Maniacal Sword

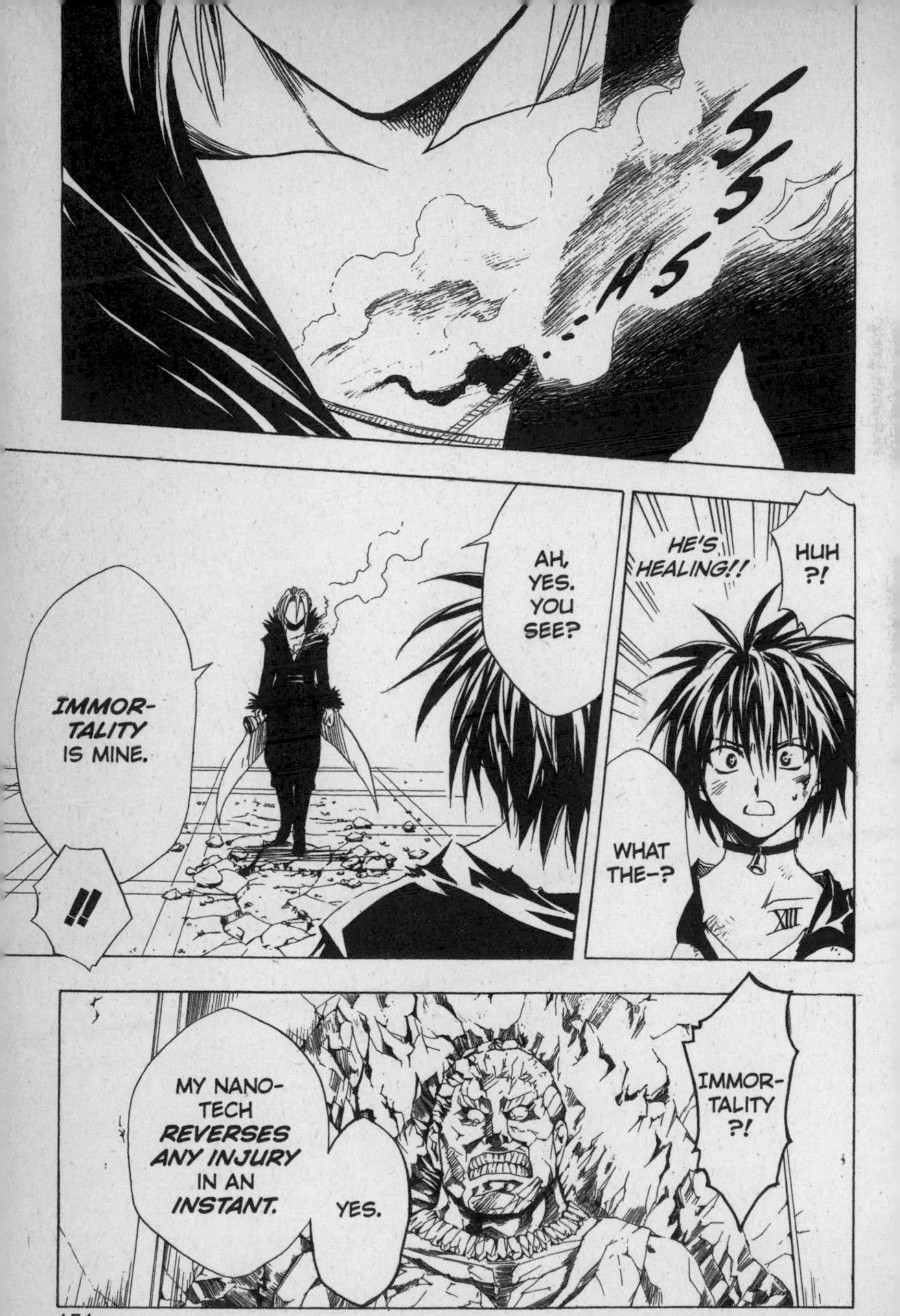
HUH ?!
HE'S HEALING!!
WHAT THE–?
AH, YES. YOU SEE?
IMMORTALITY IS MINE.
!!
IMMORTALITY ?!
YES.
MY NANOTECH REVERSES ANY INJURY IN AN INSTANT.

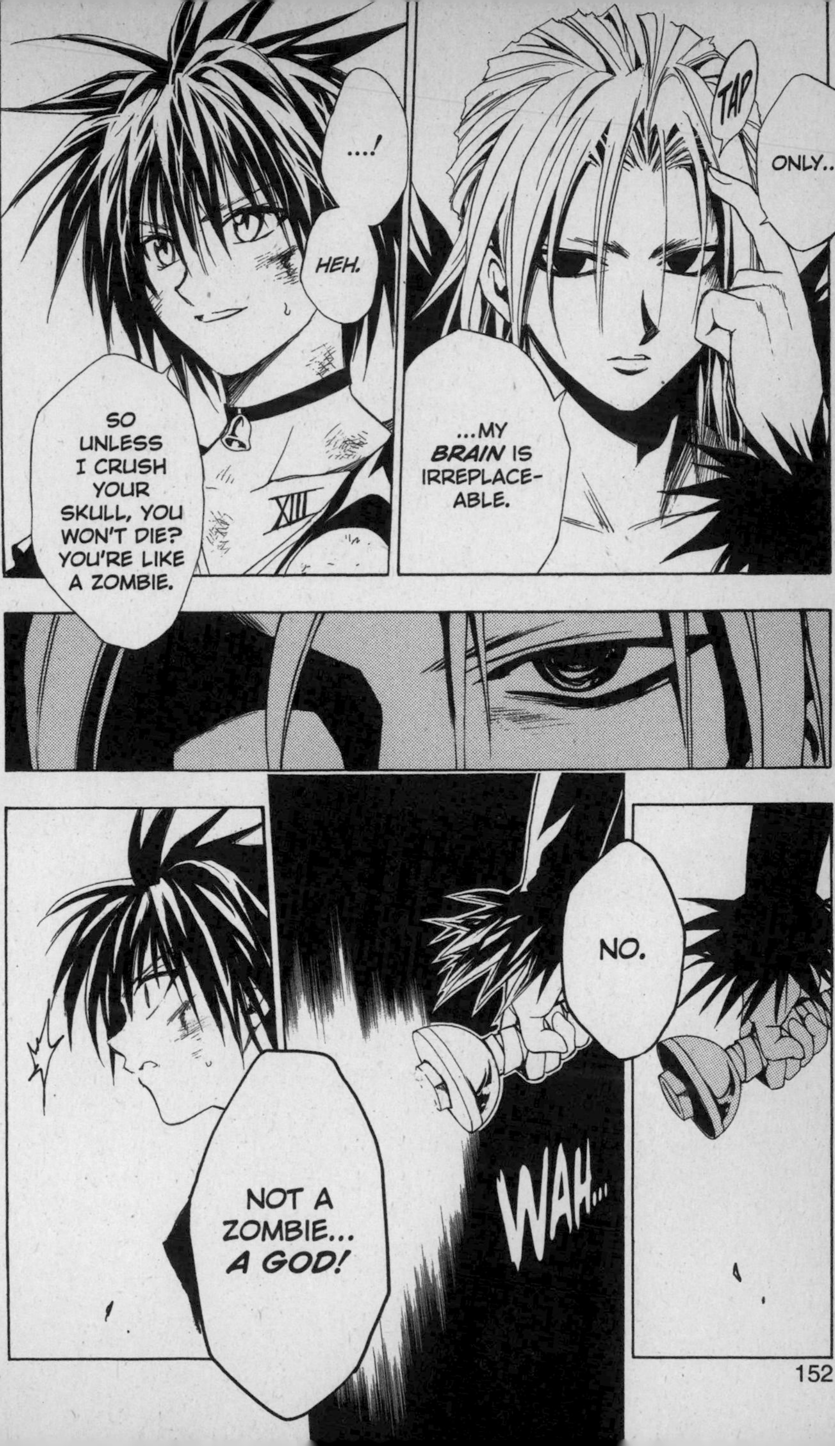
TAP
ONLY...
...MY *BRAIN* IS IRREPLACE-ABLE.
...!
HEH.
SO UNLESS I CRUSH YOUR SKULL, YOU WON'T DIE? YOU'RE LIKE A ZOMBIE.
NO.
WAH...
NOT A ZOMBIE... *A GOD!*

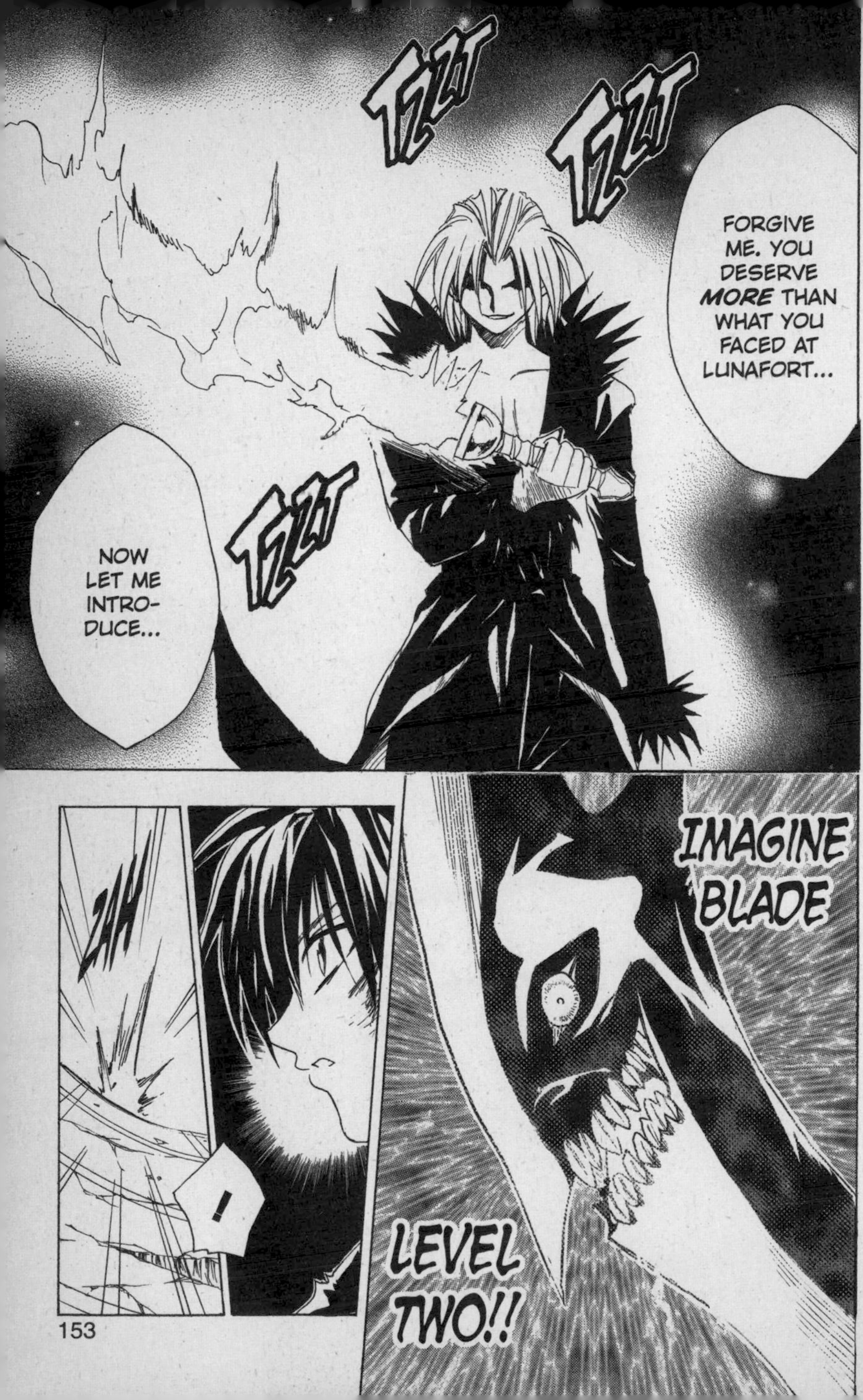
FORGIVE ME. YOU DESERVE *MORE* THAN WHAT YOU FACED AT LUNAFORT...
TZZT
TZZT
TZZT
NOW LET ME INTRO-DUCE...
IMAGINE BLADE
LEVEL TWO!!
!
ZAAH

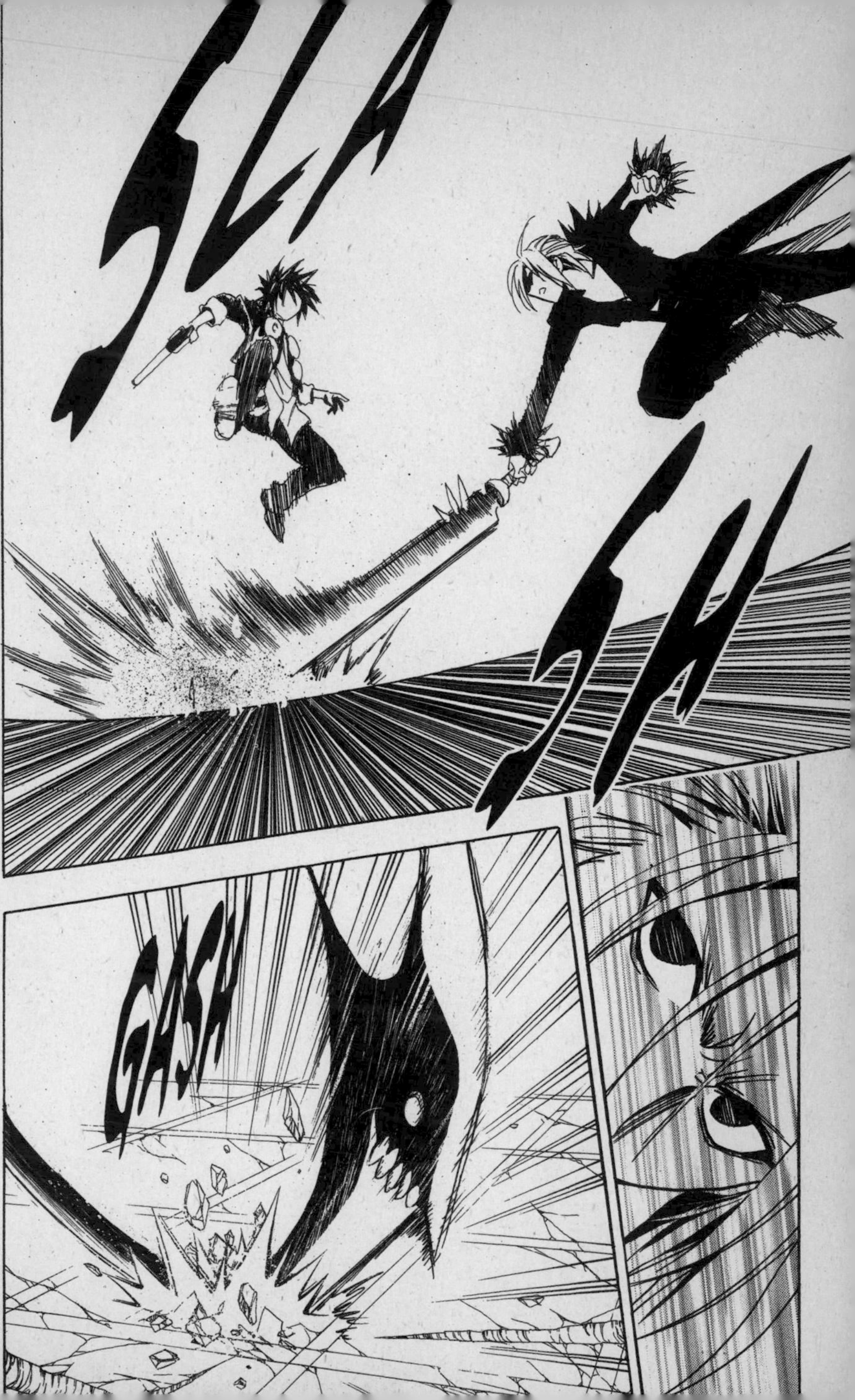
SLA
SH
GASH

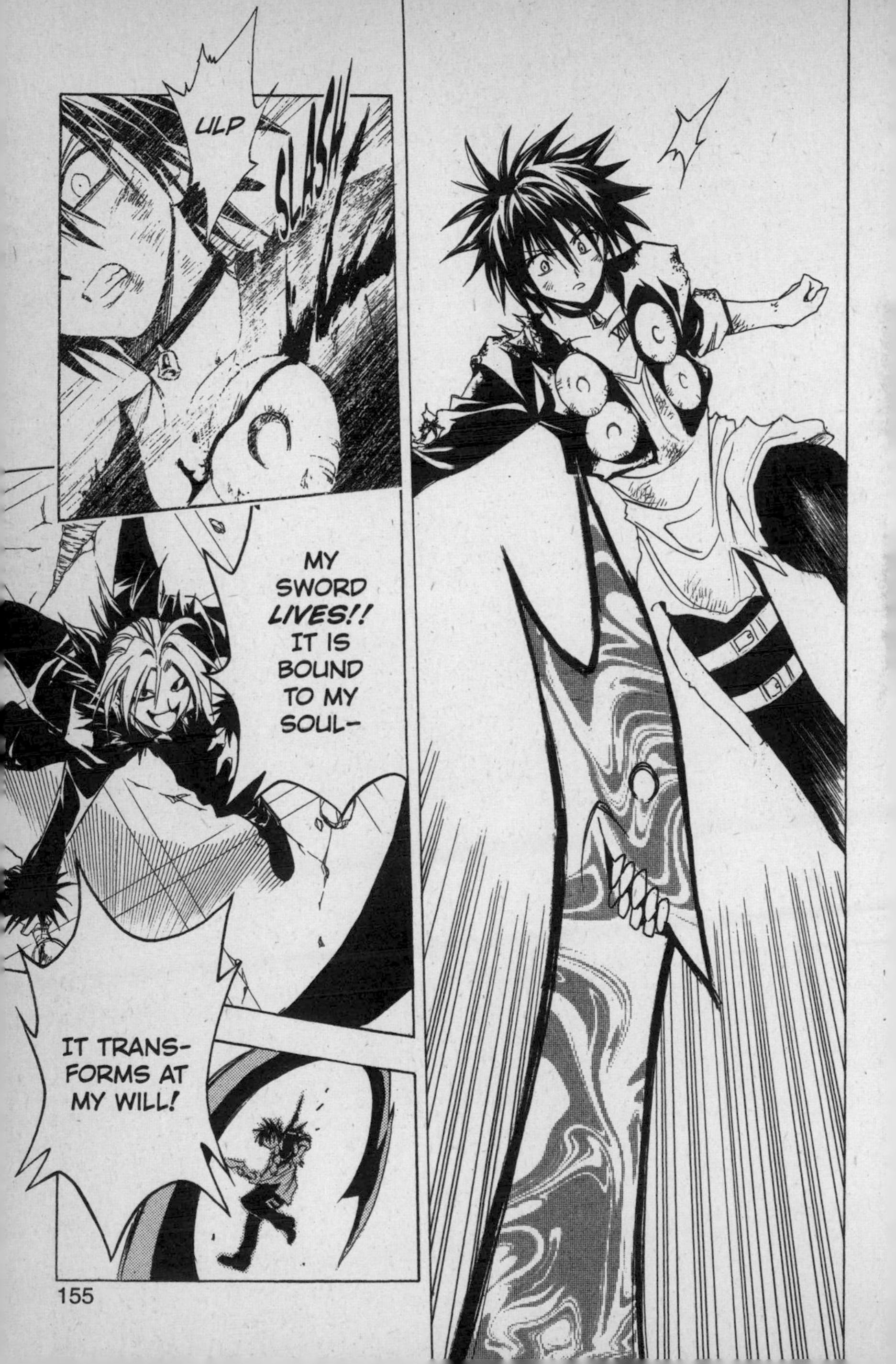
ULP
SLASH
MY SWORD *LIVES!!* IT IS BOUND TO MY SOUL-
IT TRANS-FORMS AT MY WILL!

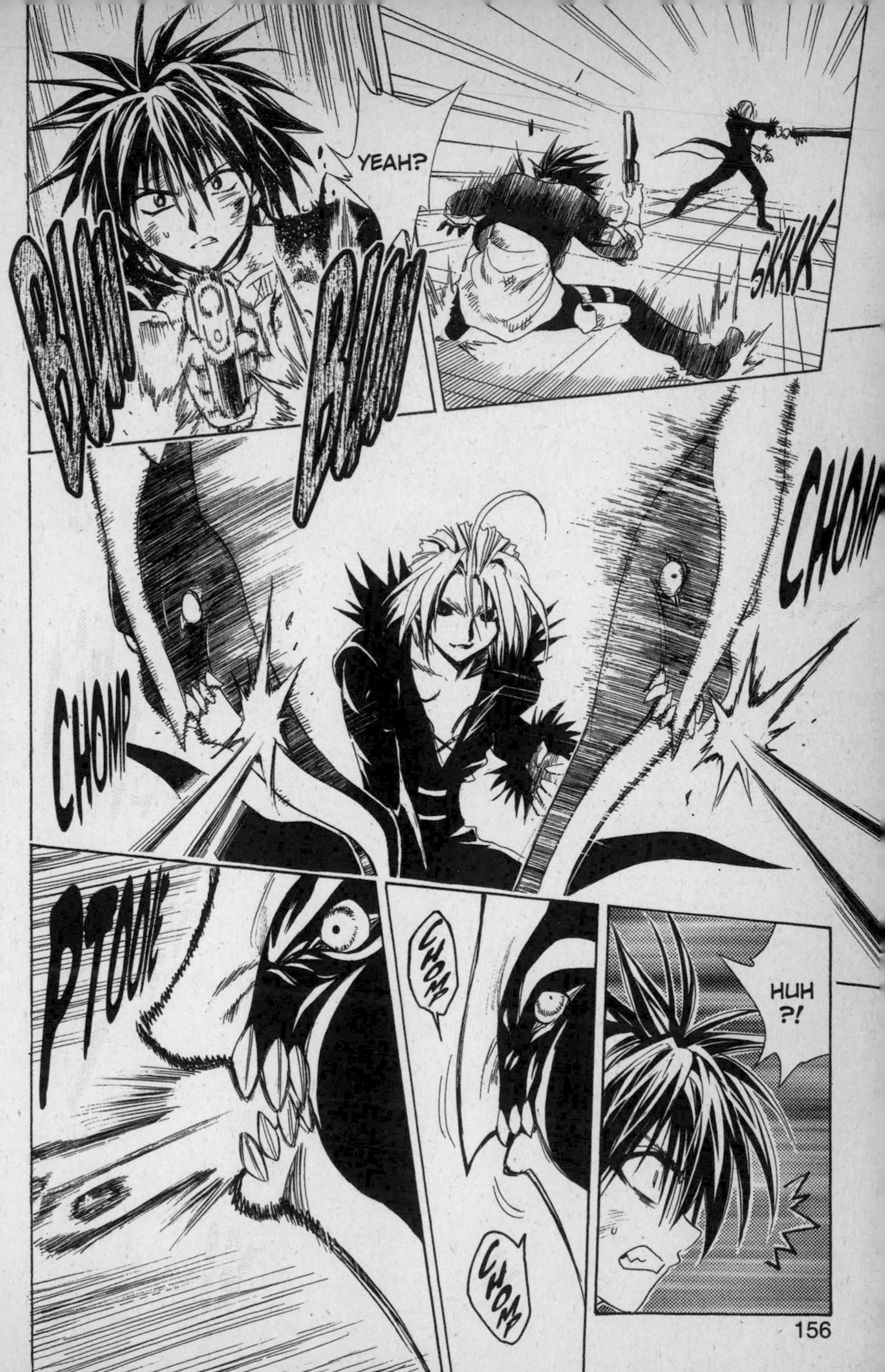
SKKK
YEAH?
BLAM
BLAM
CHOMP
CHOMP
HUH ?!
CHOMP
CHOMP
PTOOIE

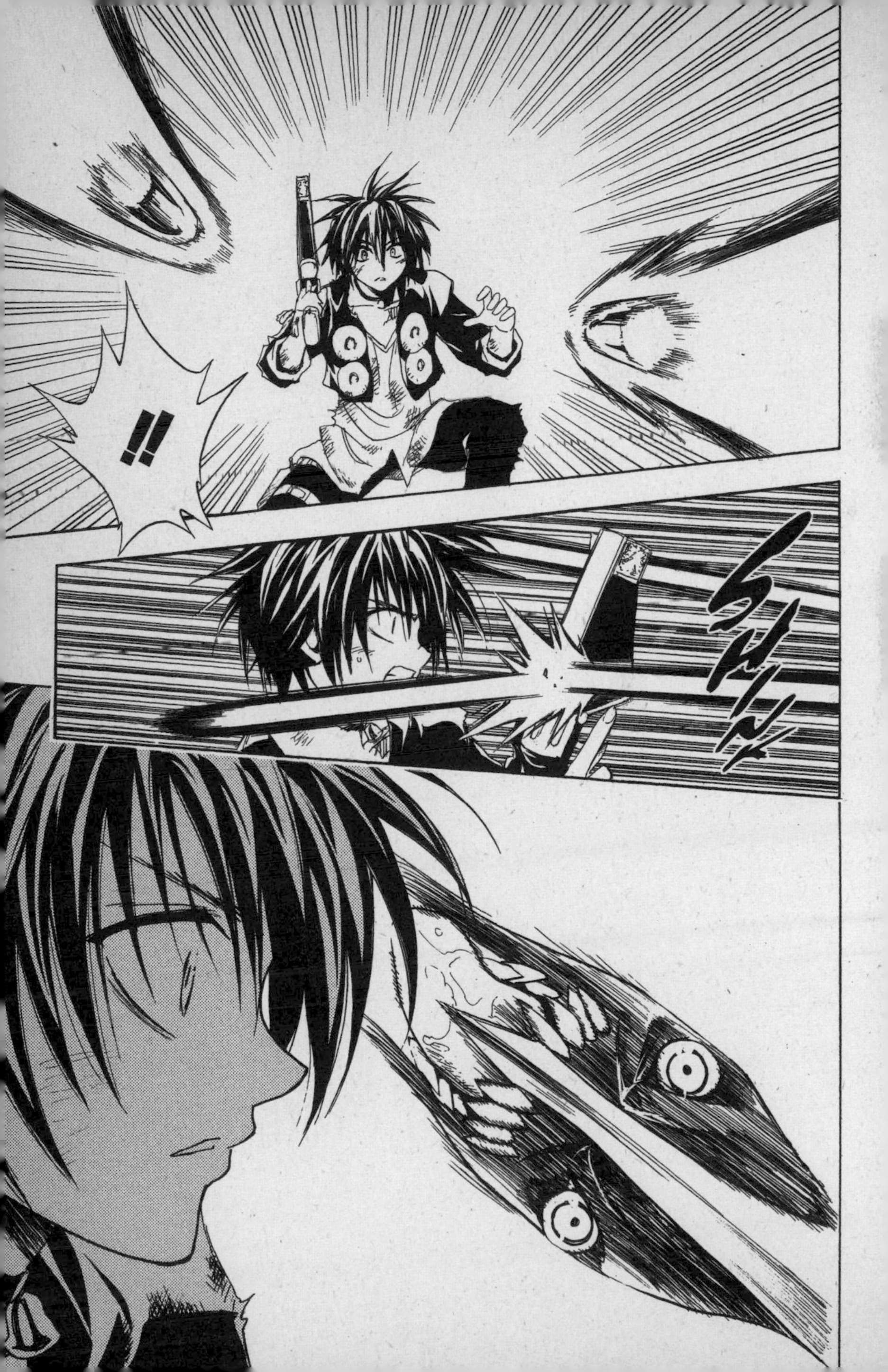
!!
SHUNK

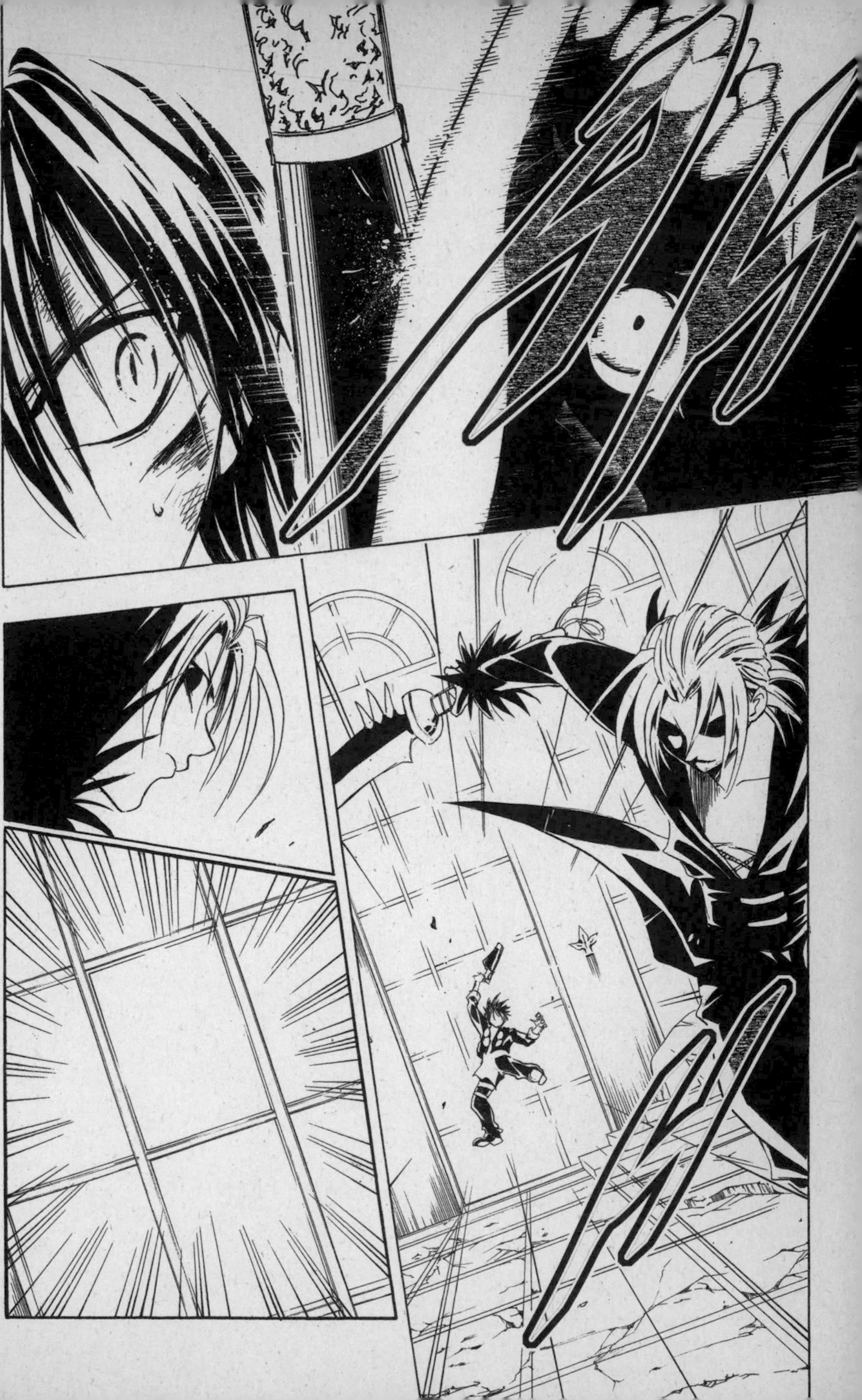

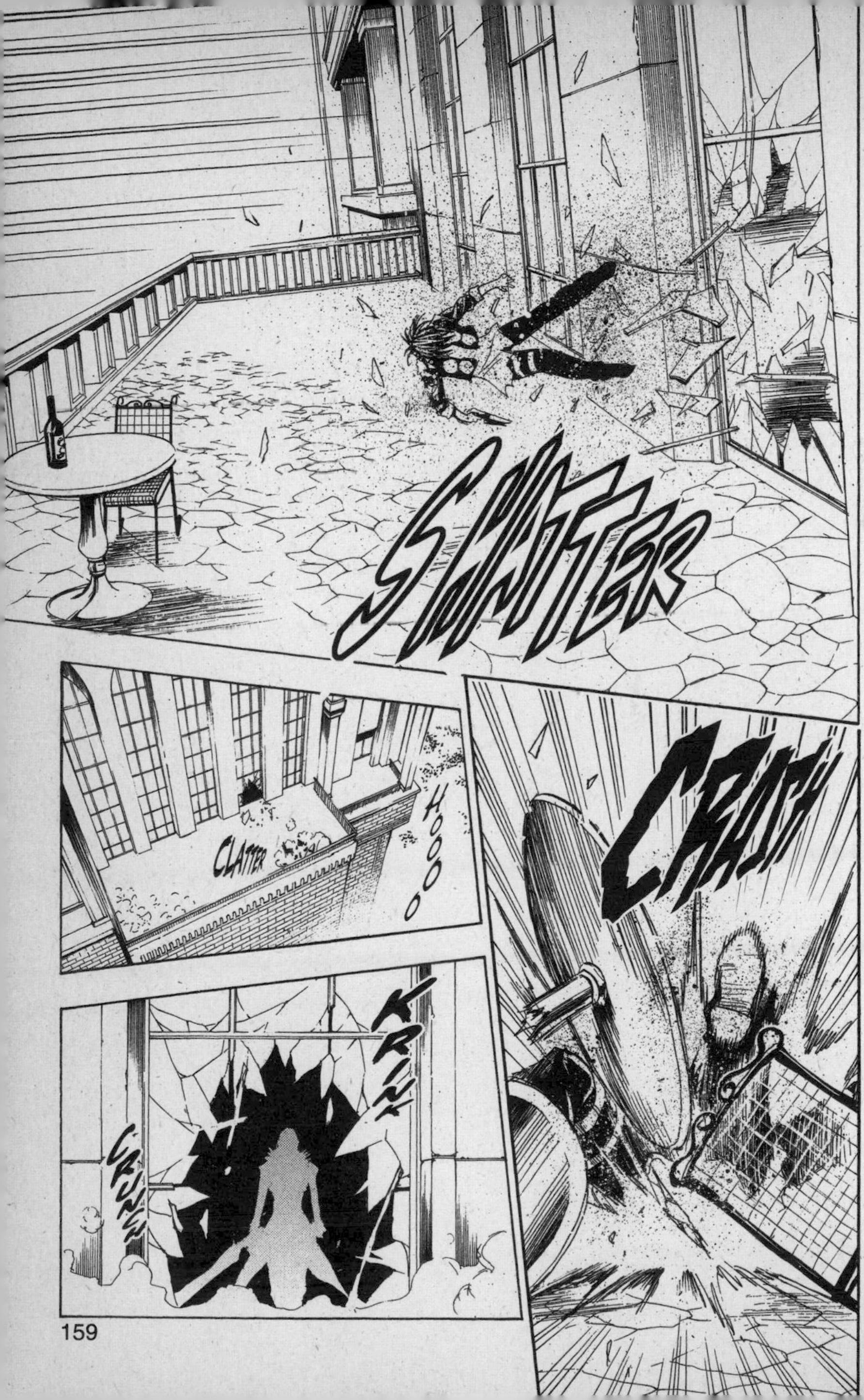
SPLATTER
CRASH
CLATTER
HOOOO
KRINK
CRUNCH

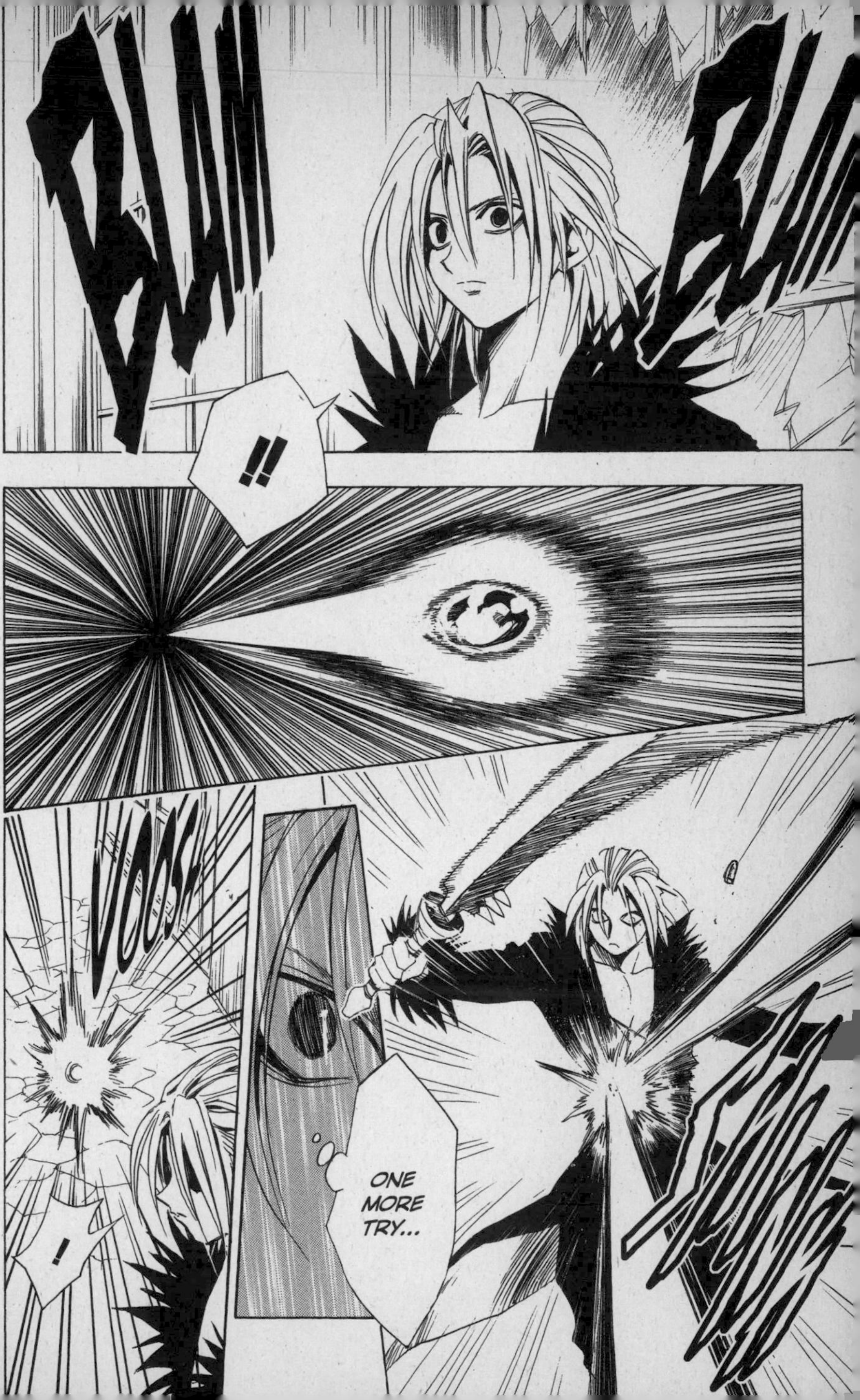
BLAM
BLAM
!!
ONE MORE TRY...
VOOSH
!

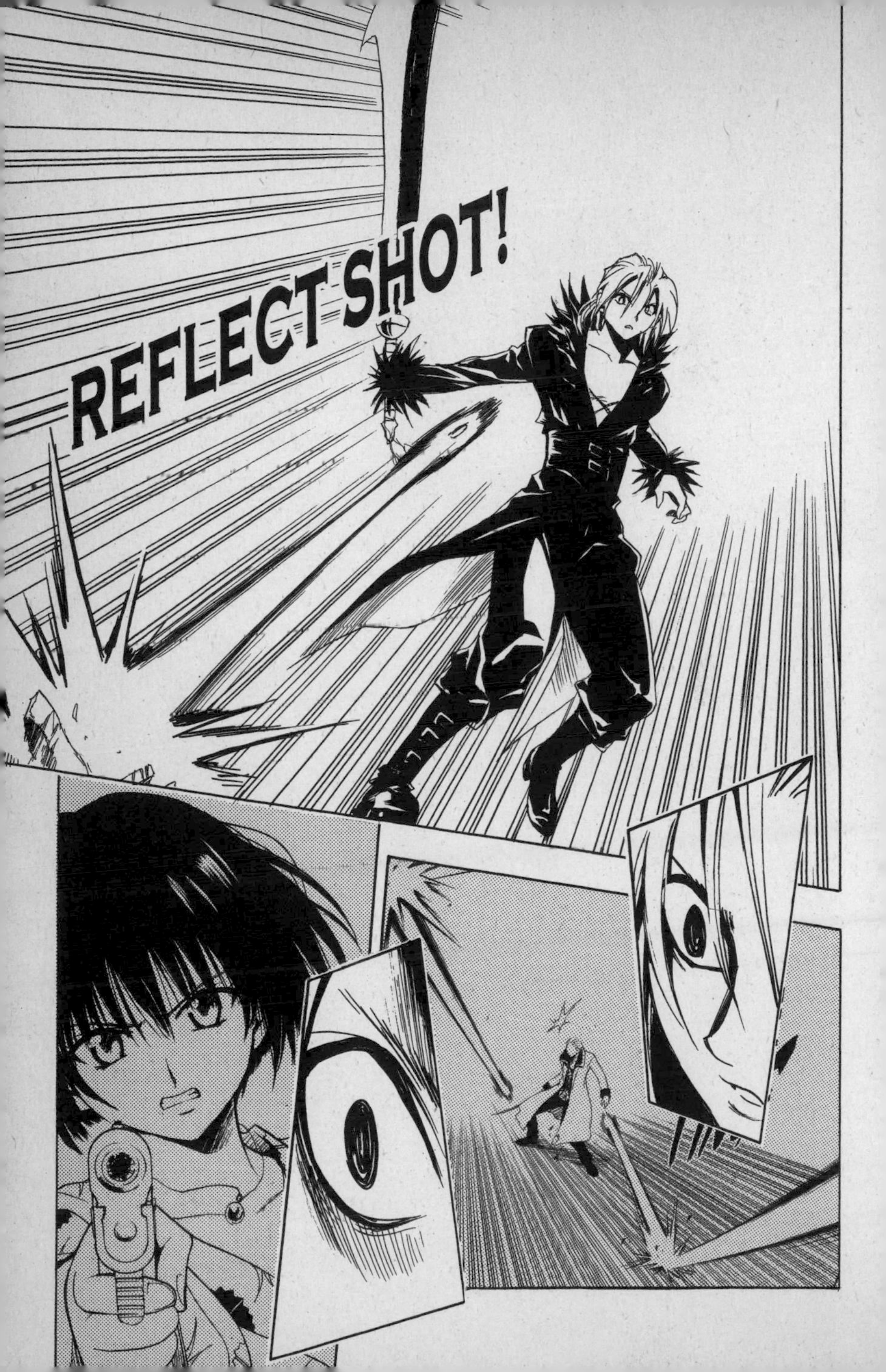
REFLECT SHOT!

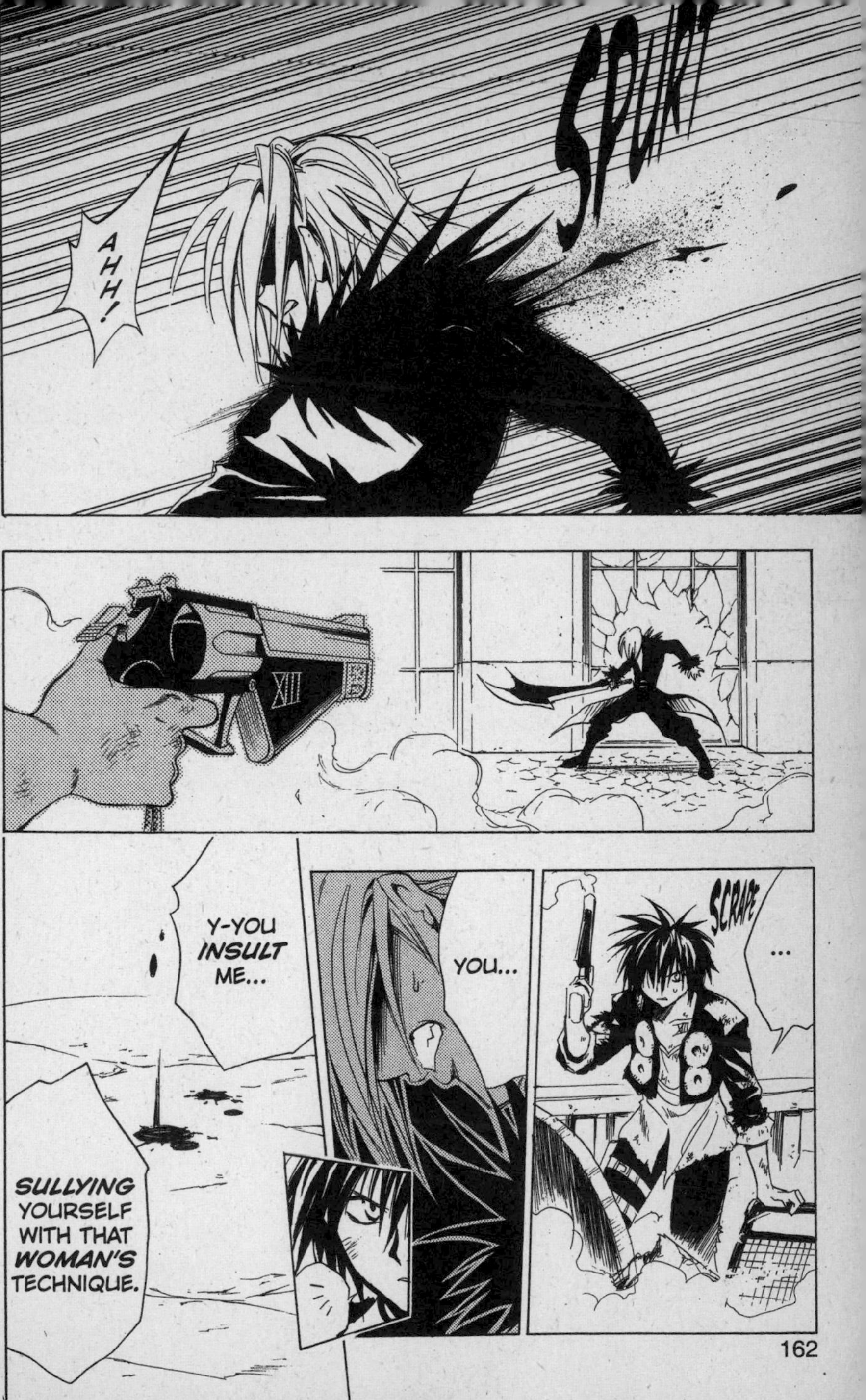
SPURT
AHH!
SCRAPE
...
YOU...
Y-YOU INSULT ME...
SULLYING YOURSELF WITH THAT WOMAN'S TECHNIQUE.

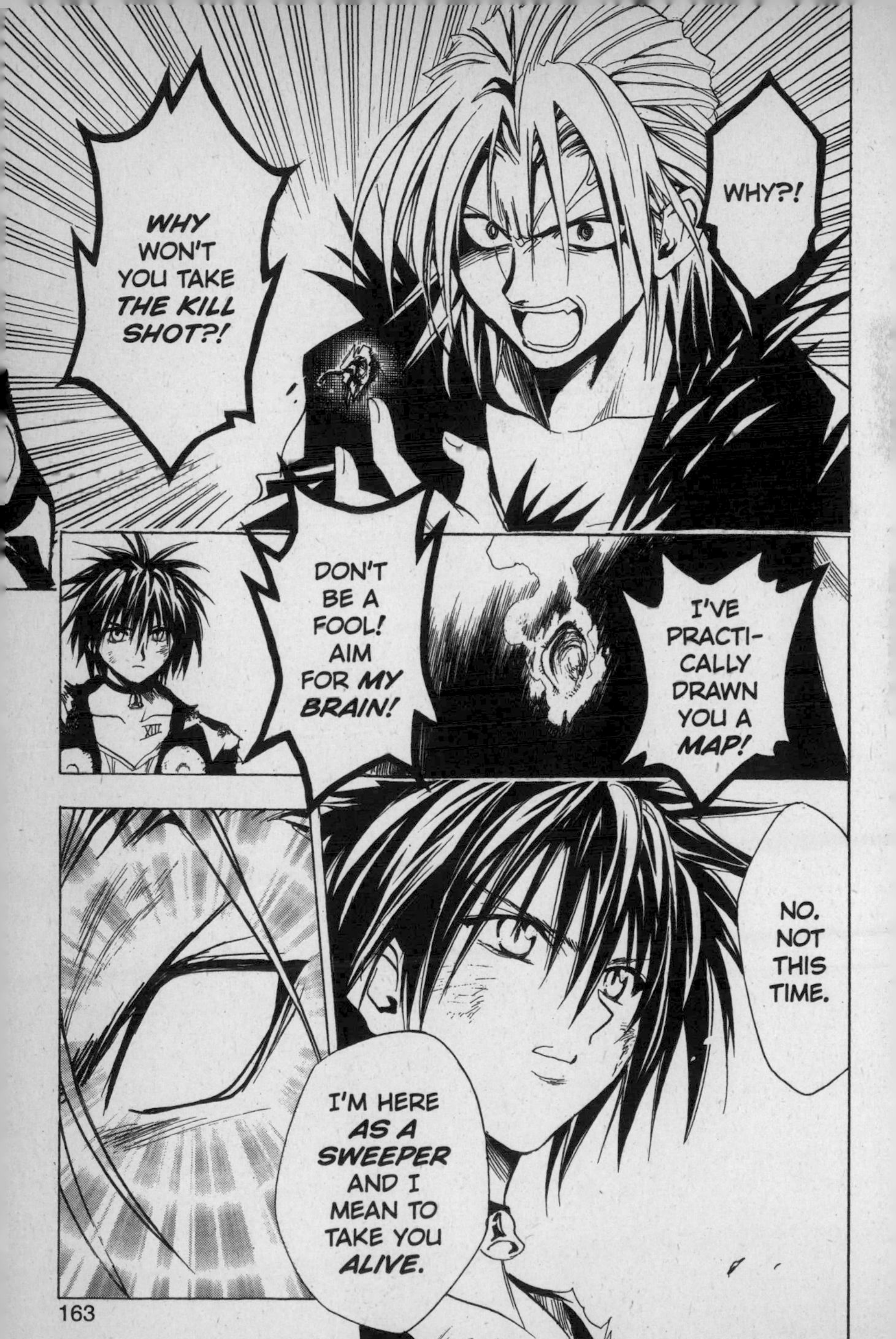
WHY?!
WHY WON'T YOU TAKE THE KILL SHOT?!
I'VE PRACTICALLY DRAWN YOU A MAP!
DON'T BE A FOOL! AIM FOR MY BRAIN!
NO. NOT THIS TIME.
I'M HERE AS A SWEEPER AND I MEAN TO TAKE YOU ALIVE.

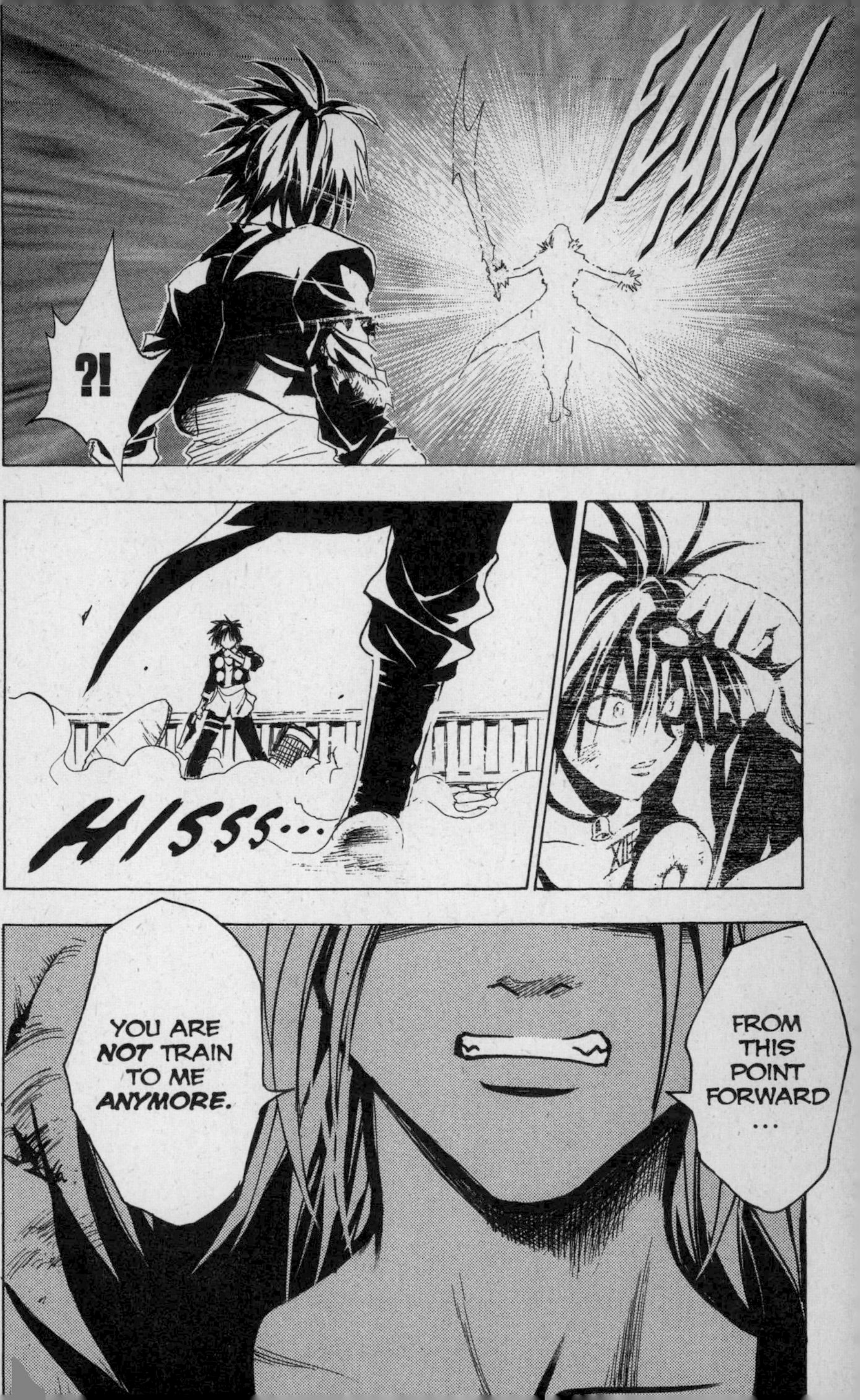
FLASH
?!
HISSS...
FROM THIS POINT FORWARD...
YOU ARE *NOT* TRAIN TO ME *ANYMORE.*

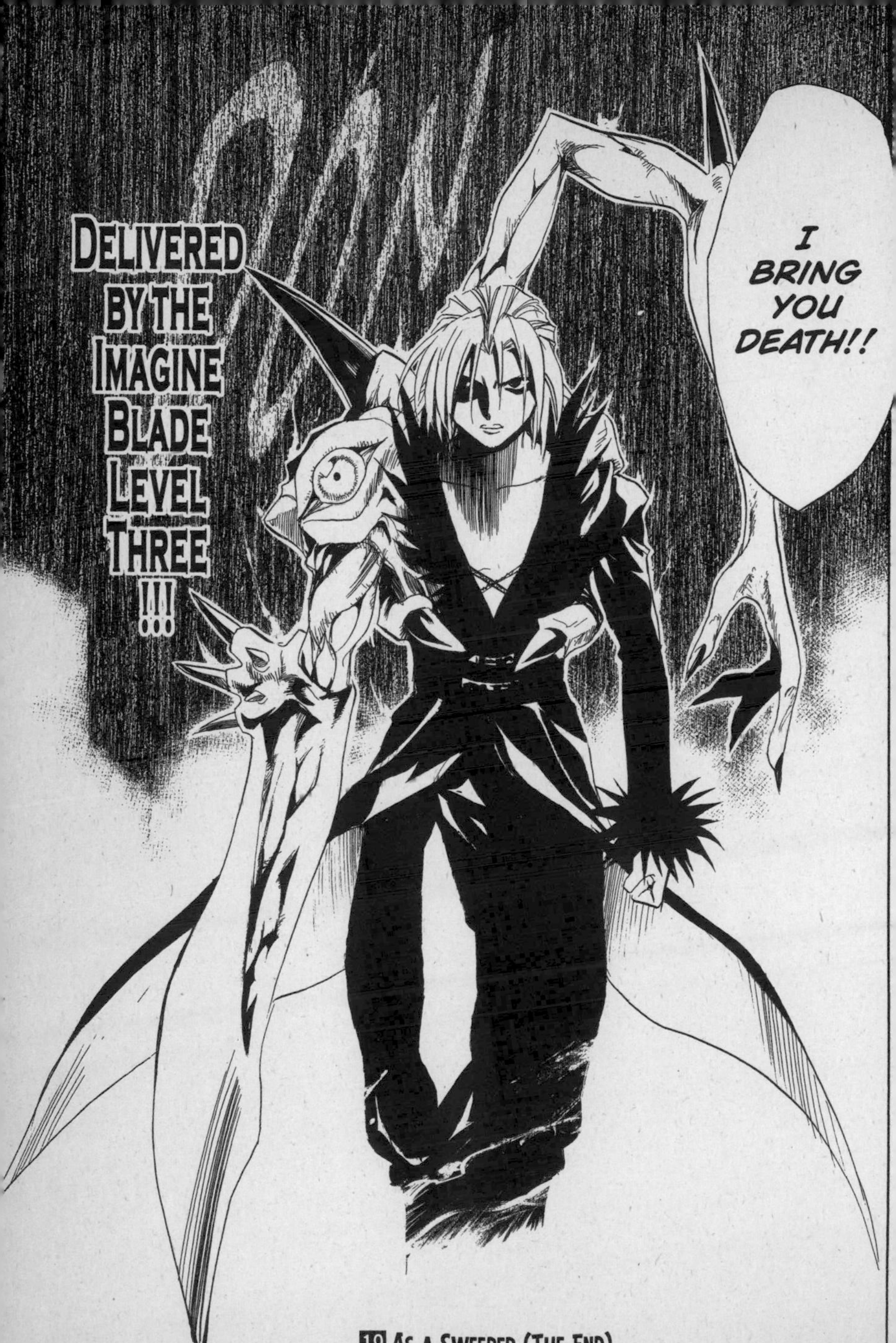
I BRING YOU DEATH!!
DELIVERED BY THE IMAGINE BLADE LEVEL THREE!!!

19 As a Sweeper (The End)

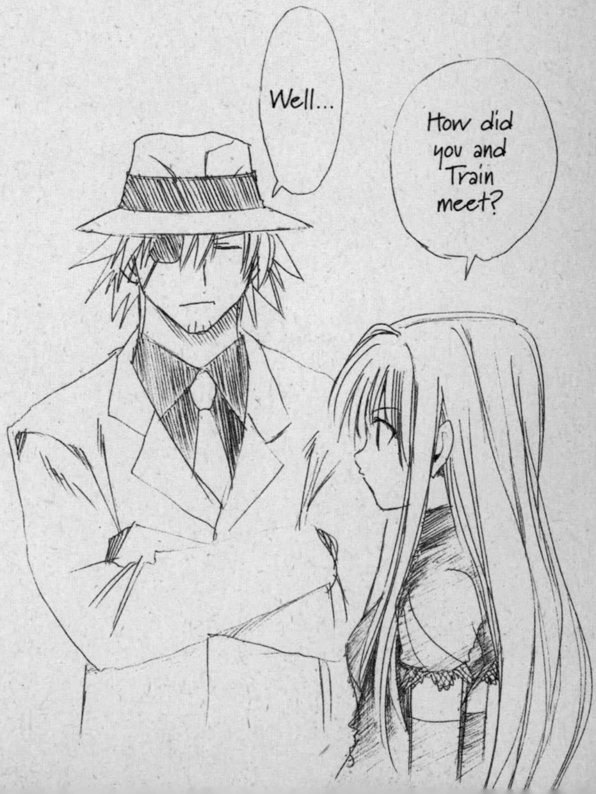
How did you and Train meet?
Well...

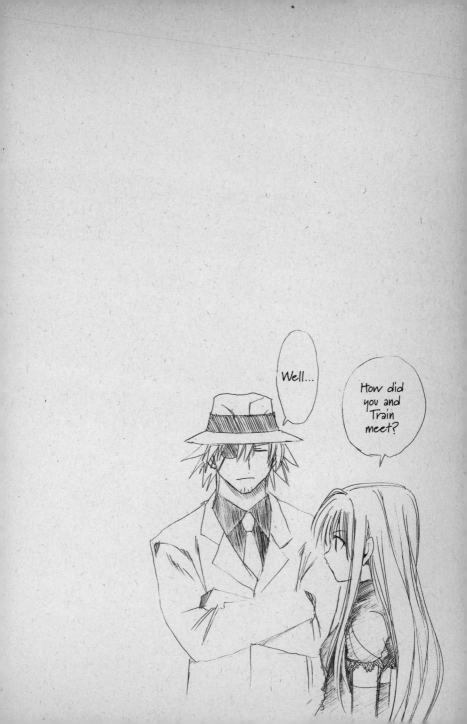

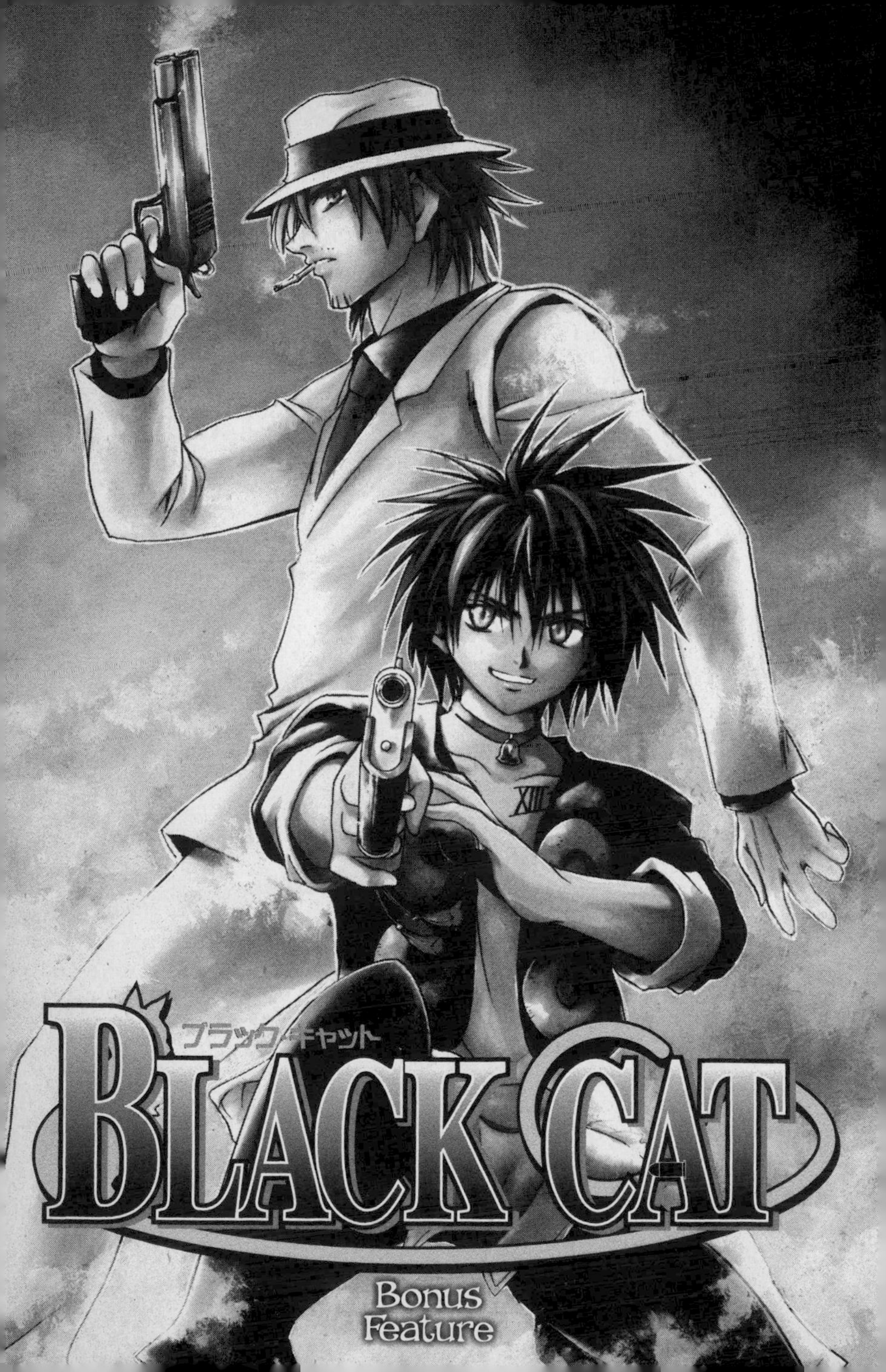
BLACK CAT
ブラック・キャット
Bonus
Feature

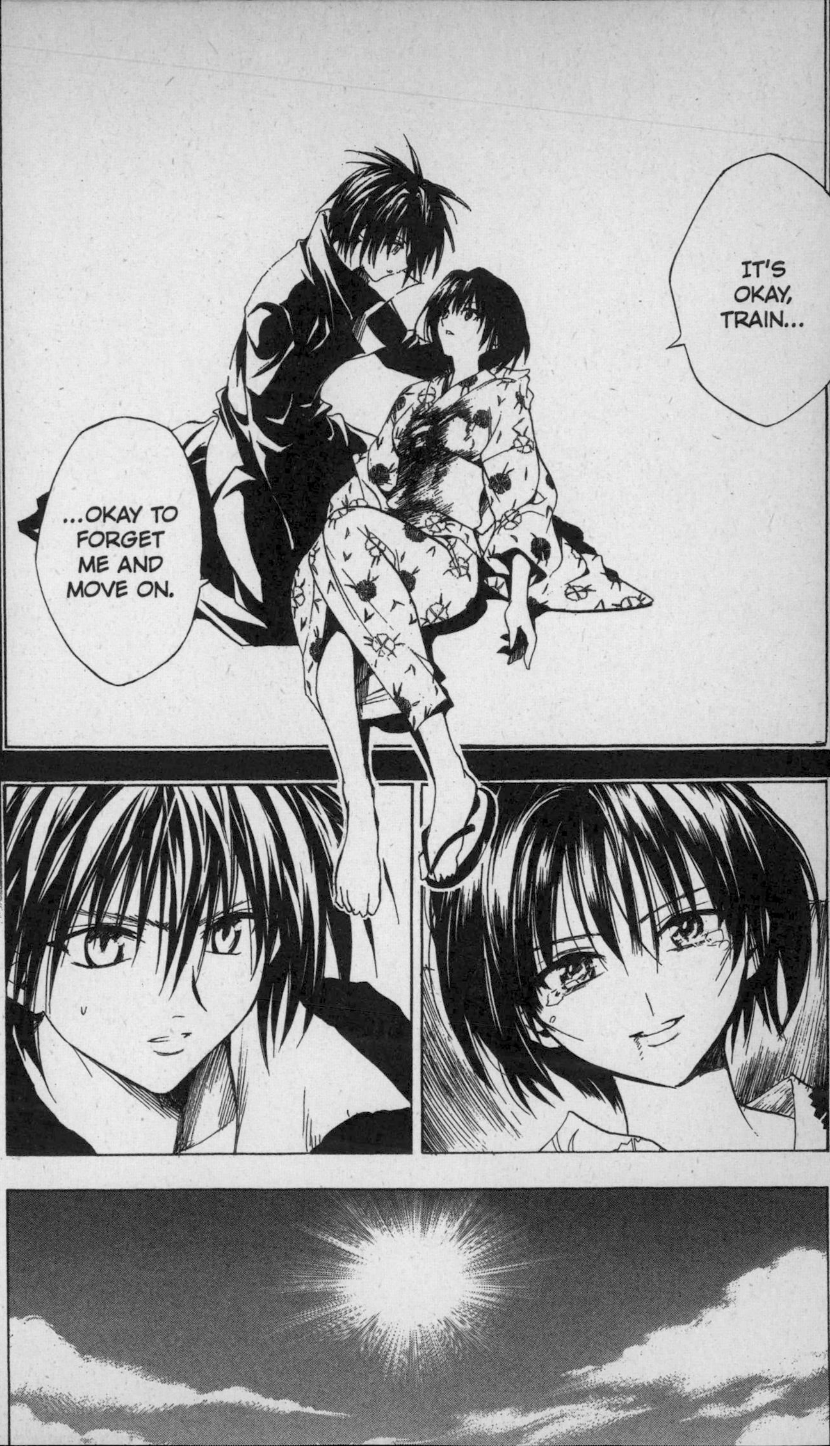
IT'S OKAY, TRAIN...
...OKAY TO FORGET ME AND MOVE ON.

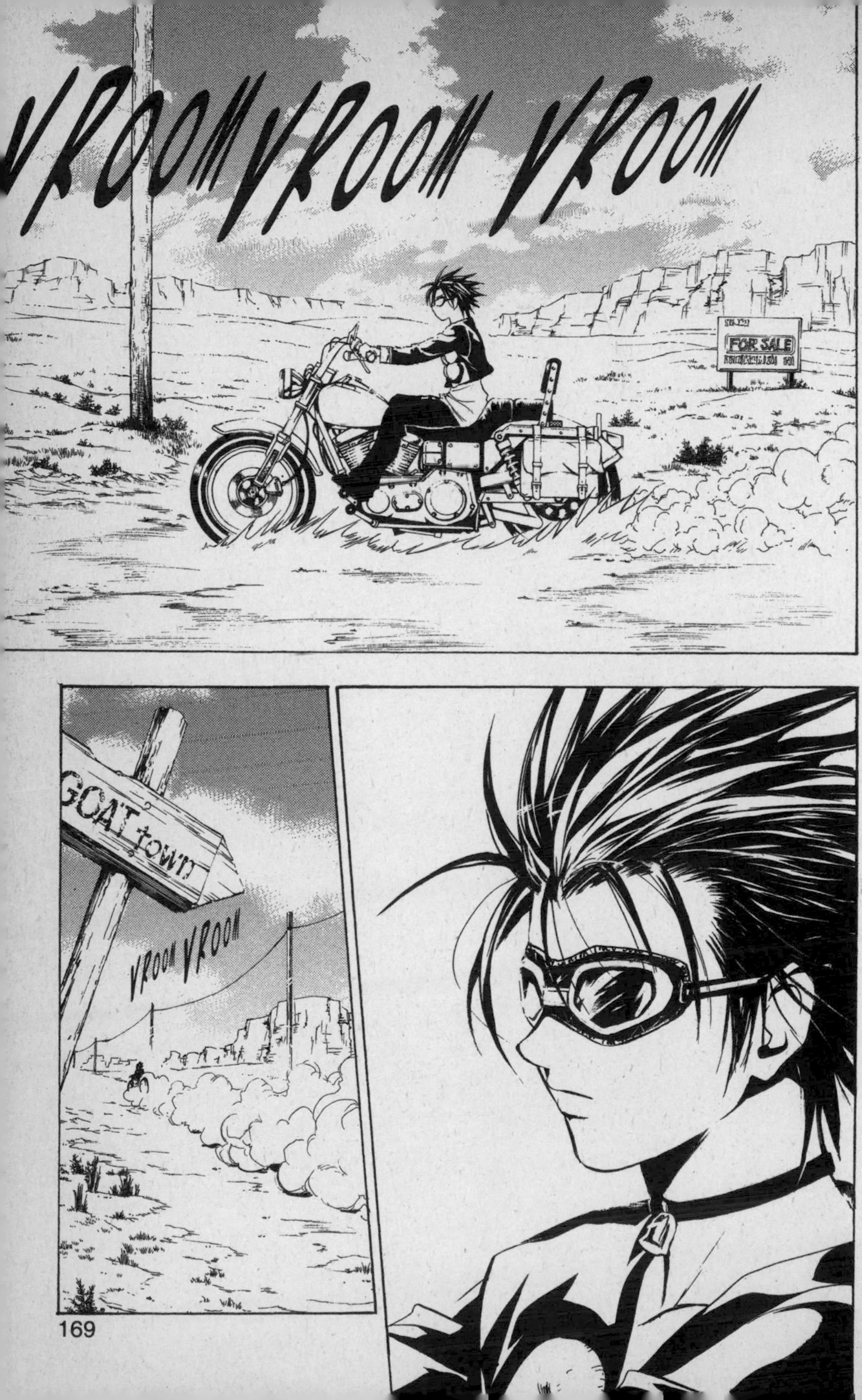
VROOM VROOM VROOM
FOR SALE
GOAT town
VROOM VROOM

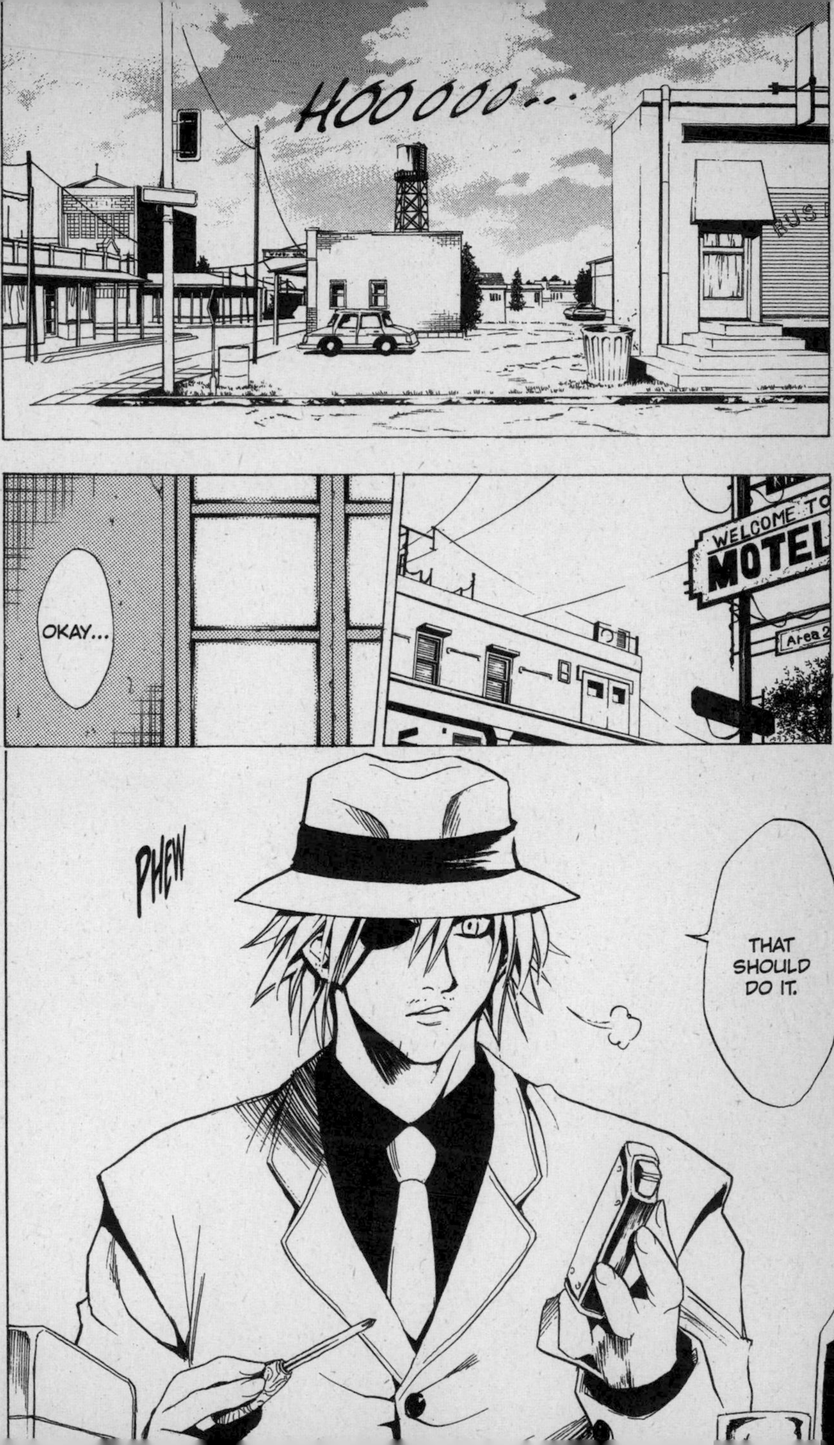
HOOOOO...
WELCOME TO
MOTEL
Area 2
OKAY...
THAT SHOULD DO IT.
PHEW

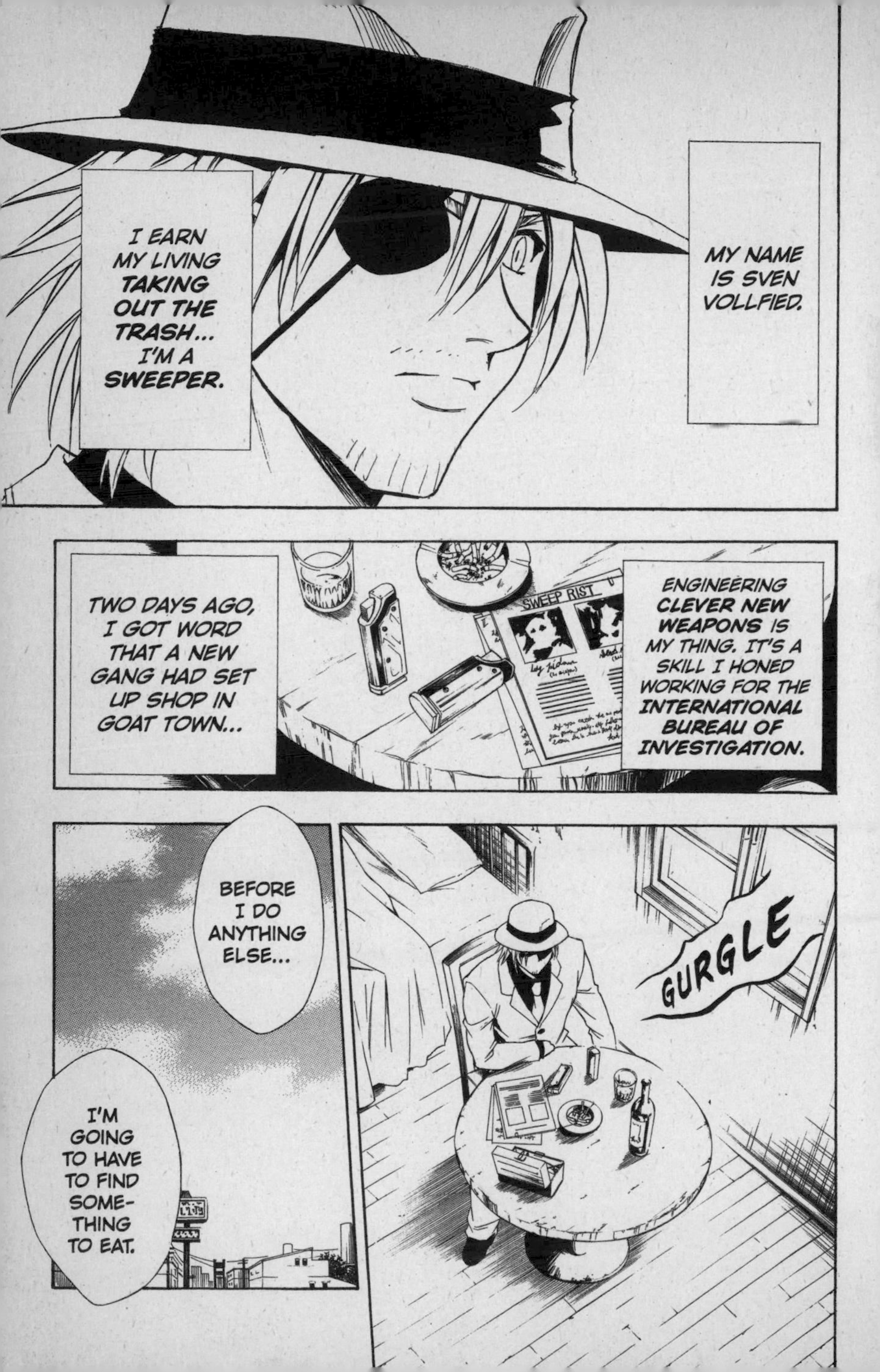
MY NAME IS SVEN VOLLFIED.
I EARN MY LIVING TAKING OUT THE TRASH... I'M A SWEEPER.
ENGINEERING CLEVER NEW WEAPONS IS MY THING. IT'S A SKILL I HONED WORKING FOR THE INTERNATIONAL BUREAU OF INVESTIGATION.
SWEEP RIST
TWO DAYS AGO, I GOT WORD THAT A NEW GANG HAD SET UP SHOP IN GOAT TOWN...
GURGLE
BEFORE I DO ANYTHING ELSE...
I'M GOING TO HAVE TO FIND SOME-THING TO EAT.

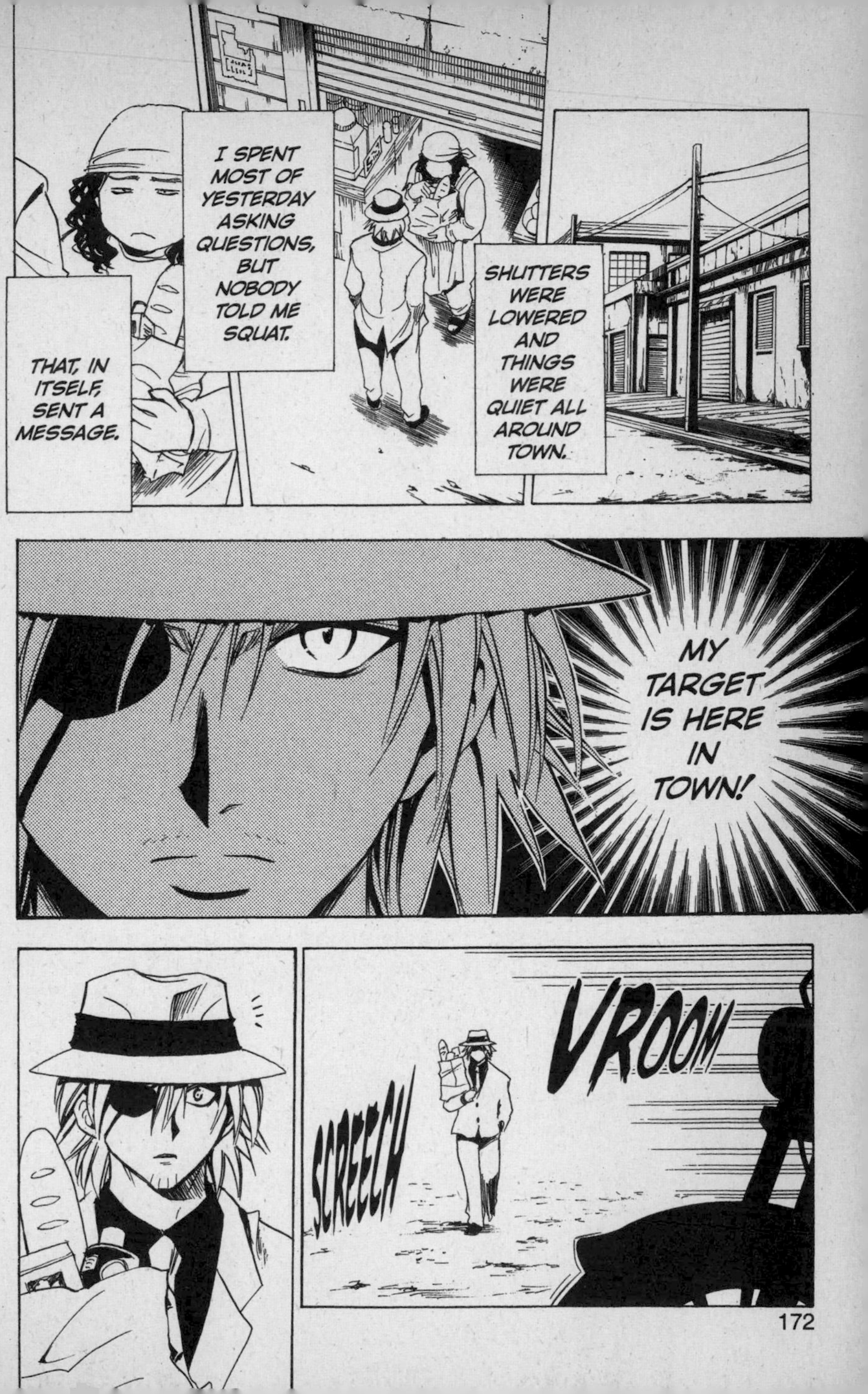
SHUTTERS WERE LOWERED AND THINGS WERE QUIET ALL AROUND TOWN.
I SPENT MOST OF YESTERDAY ASKING QUESTIONS, BUT NOBODY TOLD ME SQUAT.
THAT, IN ITSELF, SENT A MESSAGE.
MY TARGET IS HERE IN TOWN!
VROOM
SCREECH

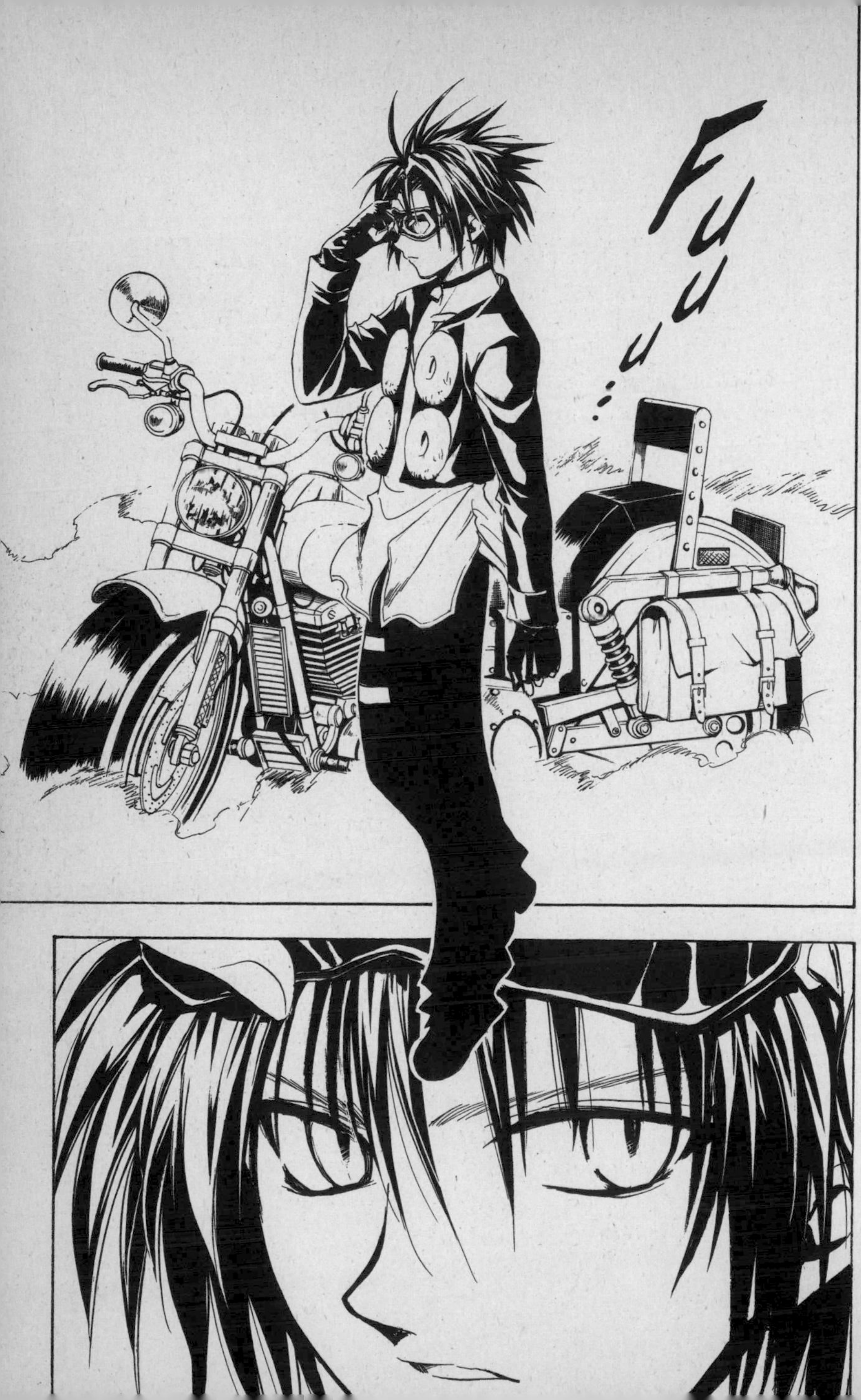
Fuuu...

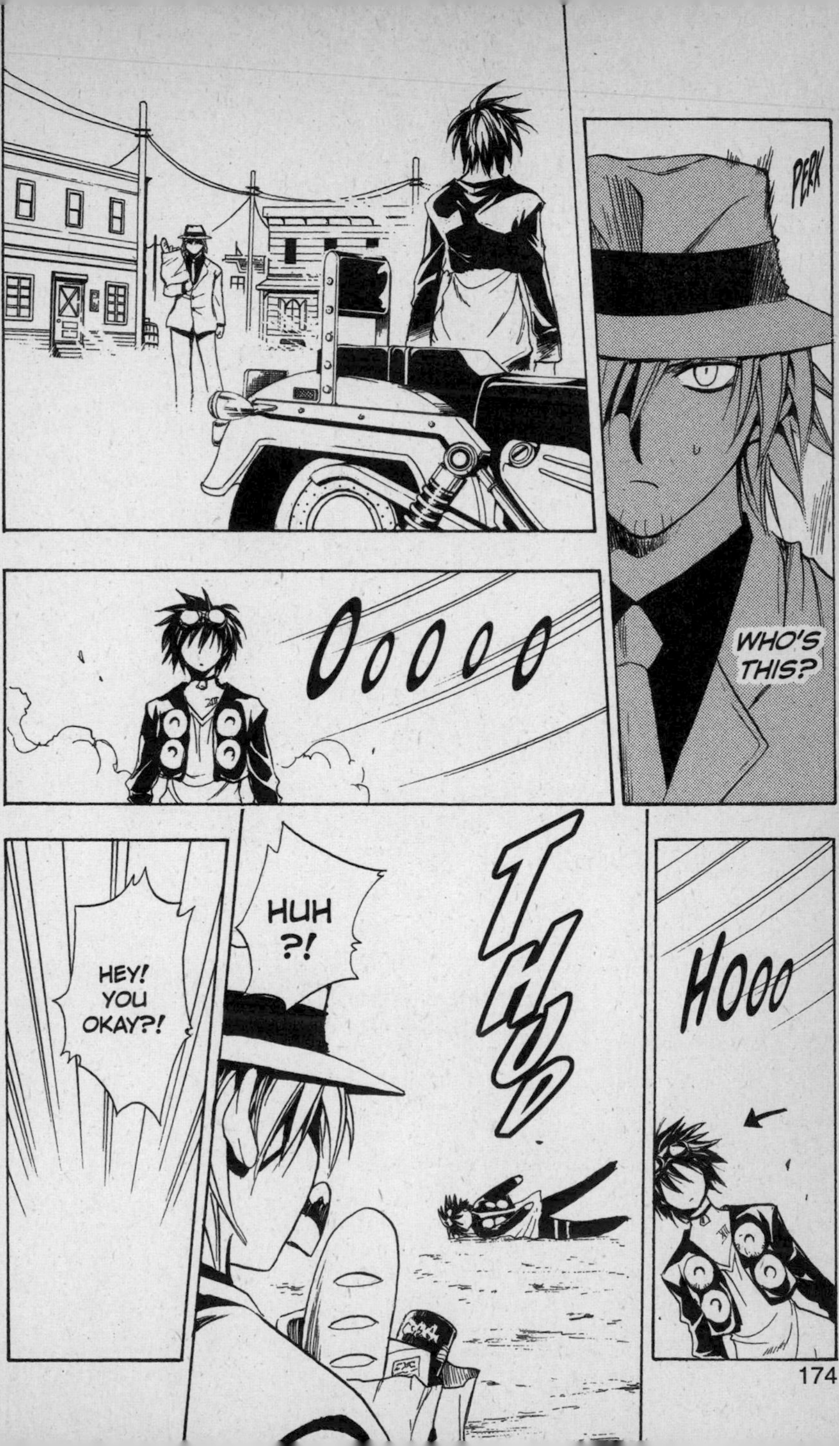
PERK
WHO'S THIS?
OOOOO
HOOO
THUD
HUH?!
HEY! YOU OKAY?!

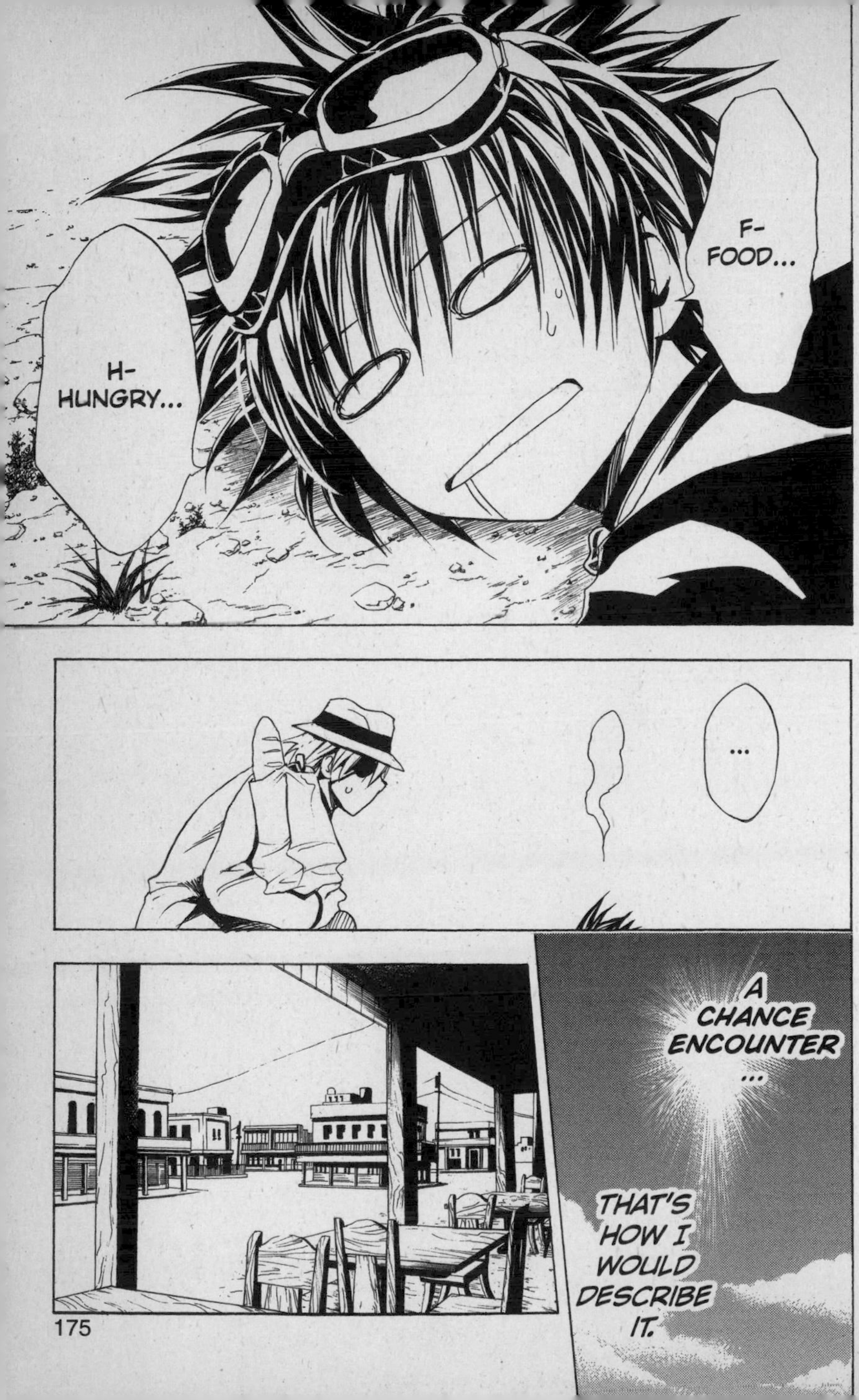
F- FOOD...
H- HUNGRY...
...
A CHANCE ENCOUNTER ...
THAT'S HOW I WOULD DESCRIBE IT.

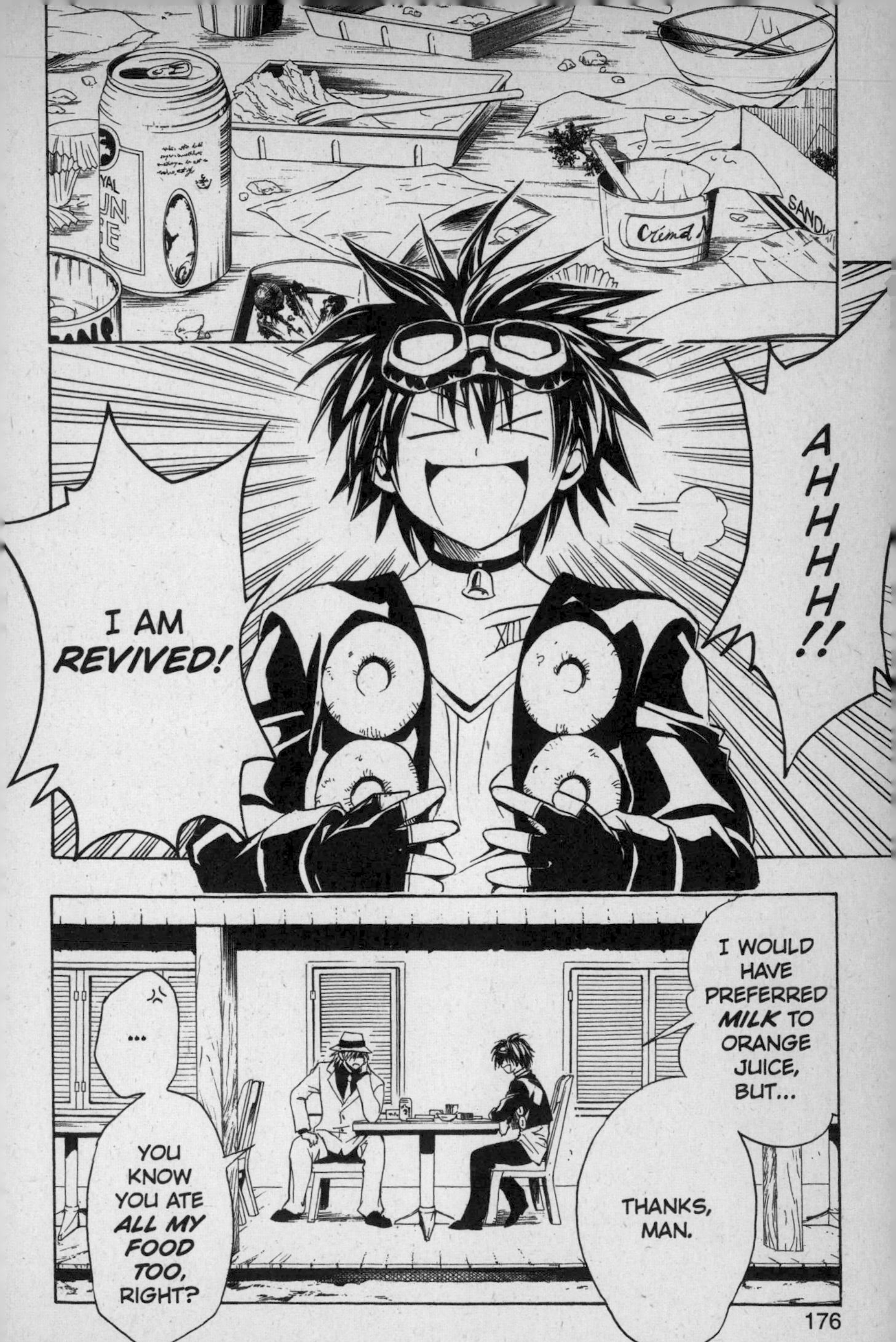
AHHHHH!!
I AM *REVIVED!*
I WOULD HAVE PREFERRED *MILK* TO ORANGE JUICE, BUT...
THANKS, MAN.
...
YOU KNOW YOU ATE *ALL MY FOOD* TOO, RIGHT?

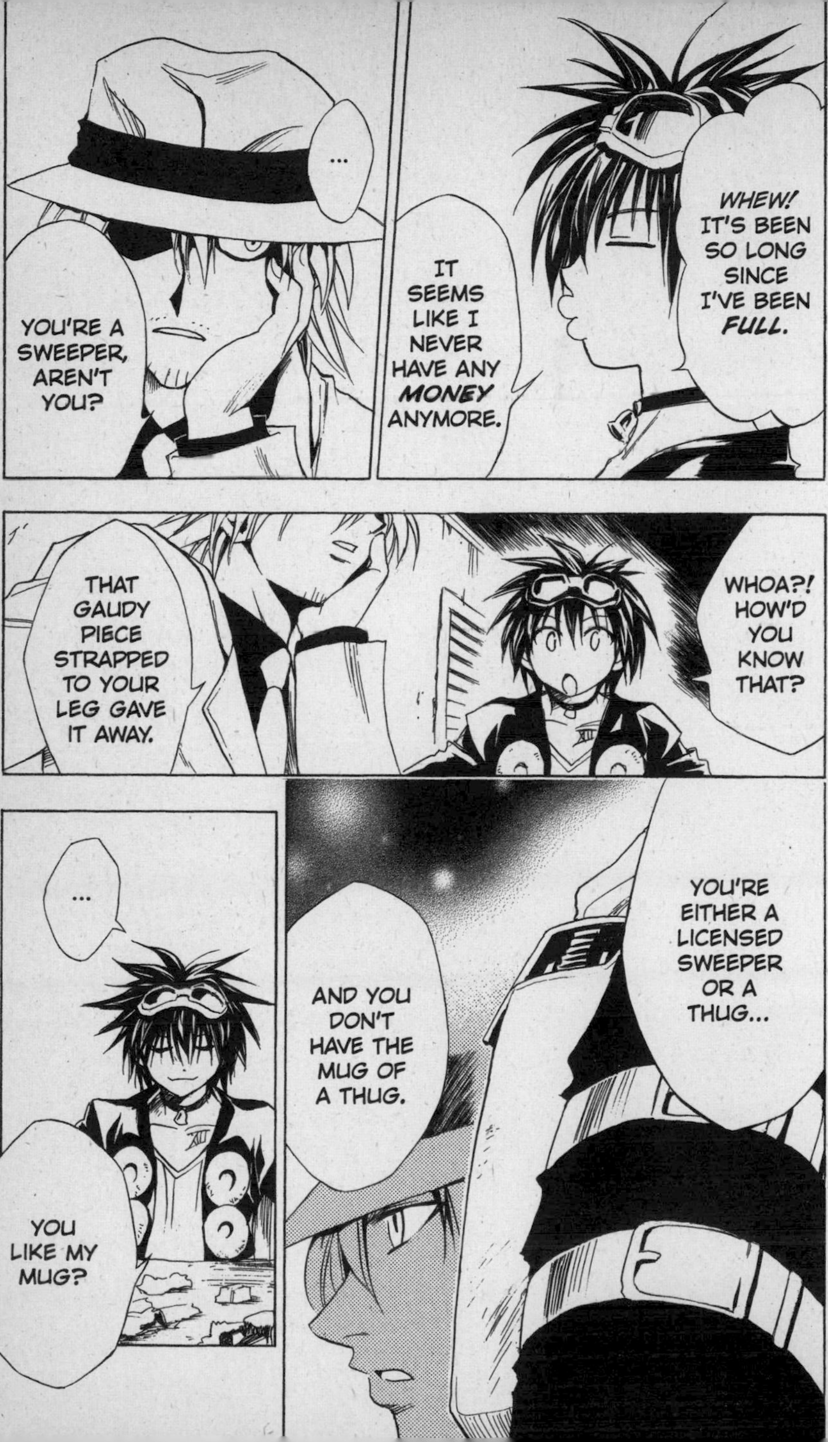
WHEW! IT'S BEEN SO LONG SINCE I'VE BEEN FULL.
IT SEEMS LIKE I NEVER HAVE ANY MONEY ANYMORE.
...
YOU'RE A SWEEPER, AREN'T YOU?
WHOA?! HOW'D YOU KNOW THAT?
THAT GAUDY PIECE STRAPPED TO YOUR LEG GAVE IT AWAY.
YOU'RE EITHER A LICENSED SWEEPER OR A THUG...
AND YOU DON'T HAVE THE MUG OF A THUG.
...
YOU LIKE MY MUG?

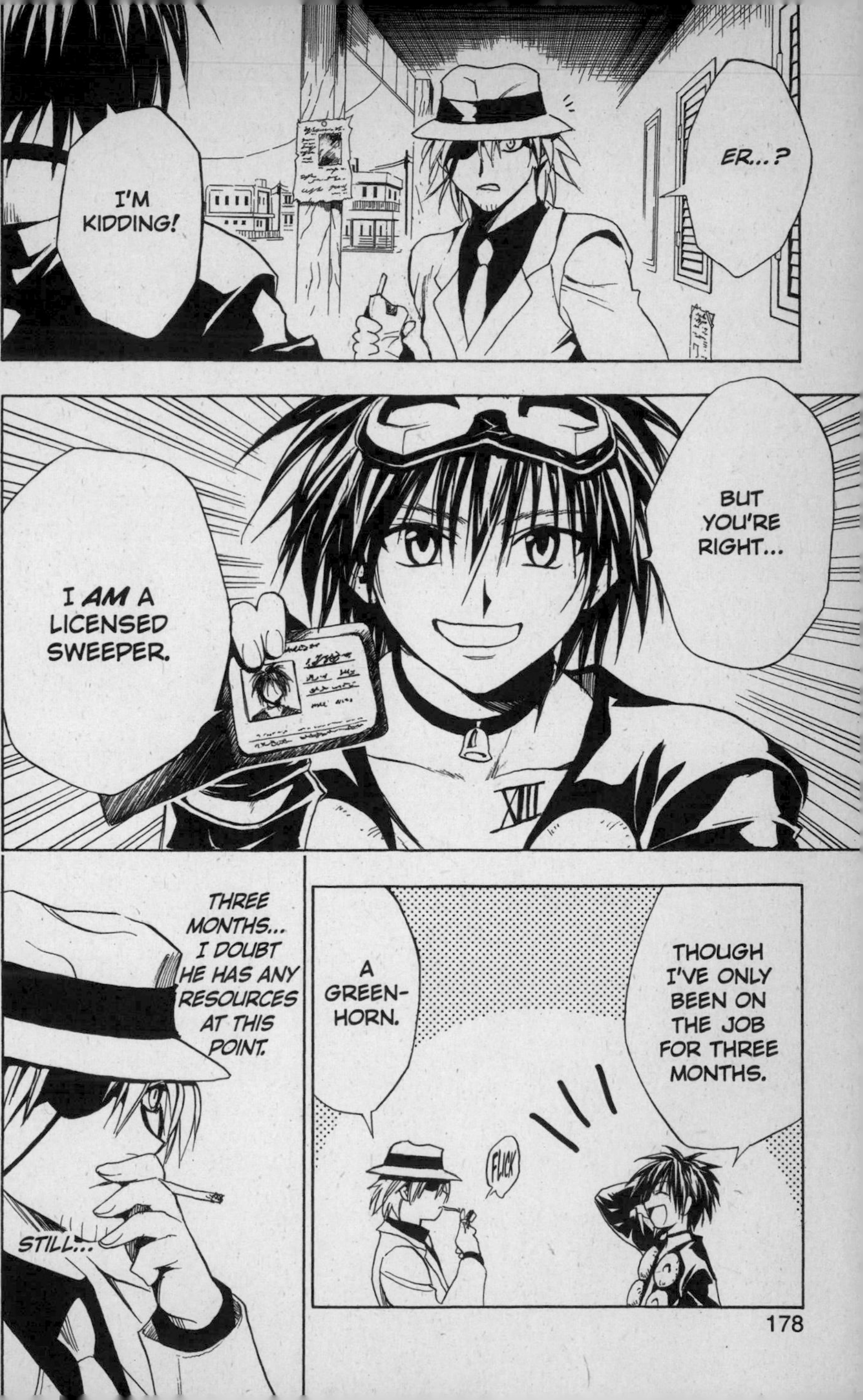

ER...?
I'M KIDDING!
BUT YOU'RE RIGHT...
I *AM* A LICENSED SWEEPER.
THOUGH I'VE ONLY BEEN ON THE JOB FOR THREE MONTHS.
FLICK
A GREENHORN.
THREE MONTHS... I DOUBT HE HAS ANY RESOURCES AT THIS POINT.
STILL...

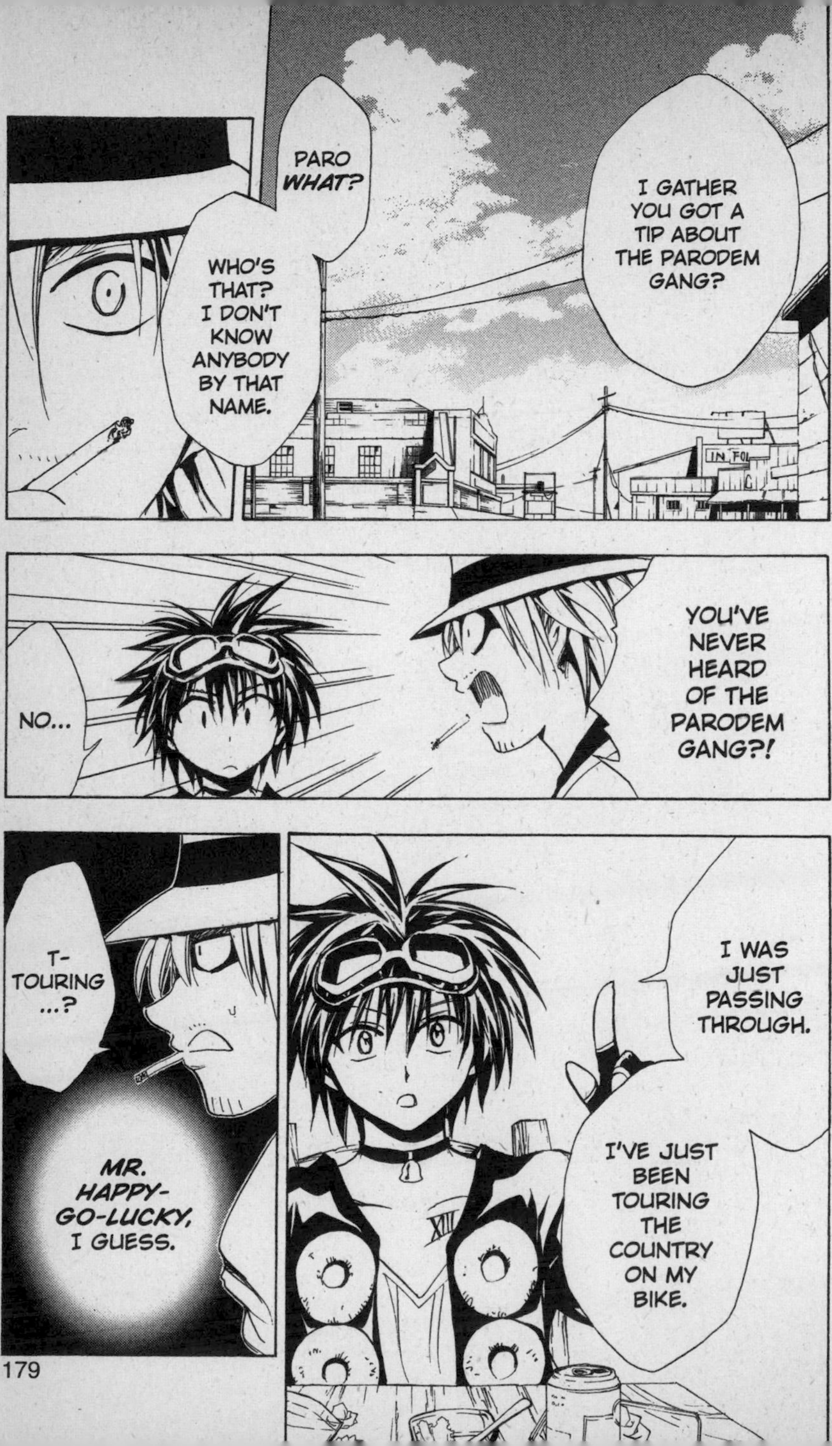
I GATHER YOU GOT A TIP ABOUT THE PARODEM GANG?
PARO *WHAT?*
WHO'S THAT? I DON'T KNOW ANYBODY BY THAT NAME.
YOU'VE NEVER HEARD OF THE PARODEM GANG?!
NO...
I WAS JUST PASSING THROUGH.
I'VE JUST BEEN TOURING THE COUNTRY ON MY BIKE.
T-TOURING ...?
MR. HAPPY-GO-LUCKY, I GUESS.

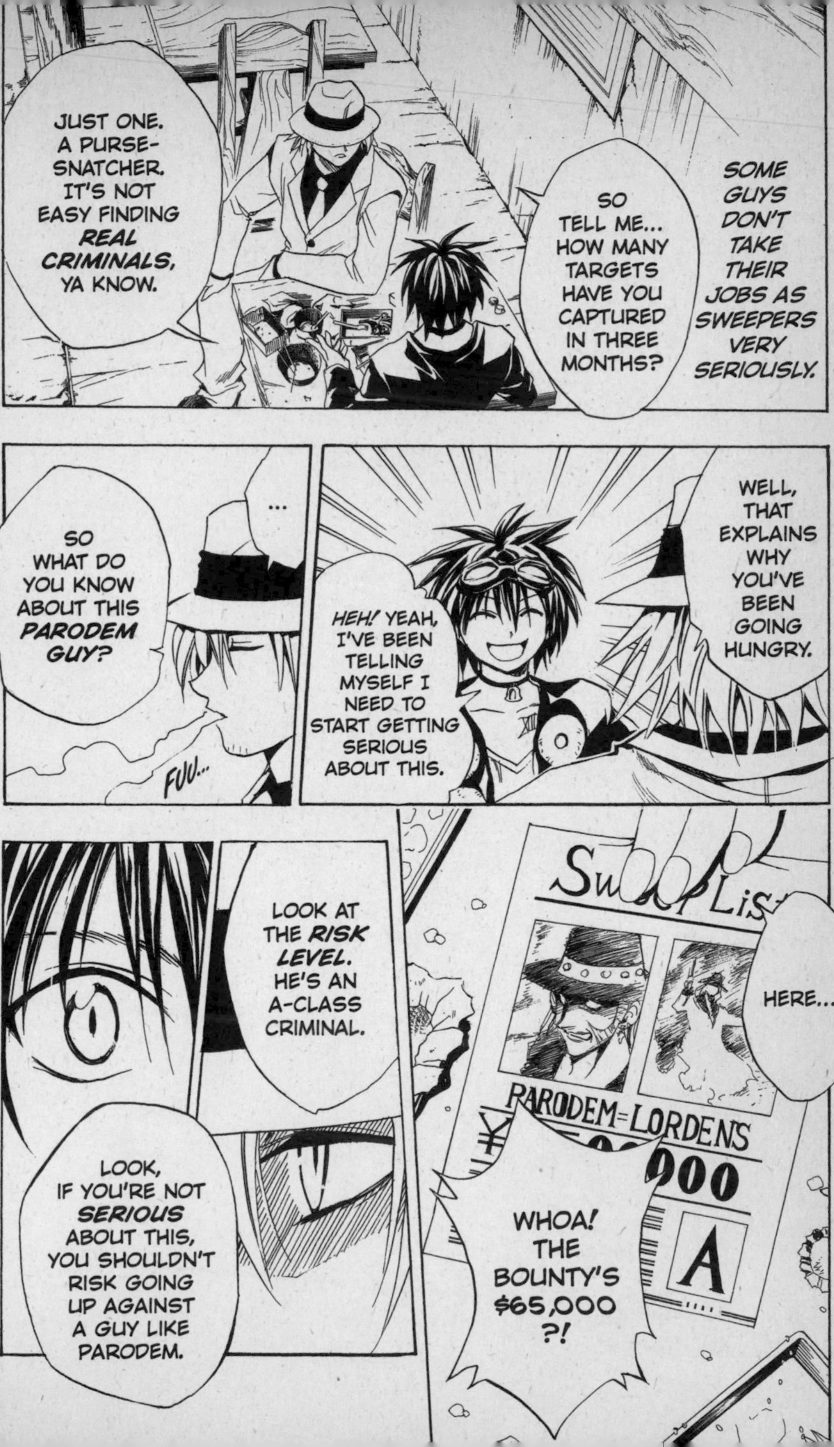
SOME GUYS DON'T TAKE THEIR JOBS AS SWEEPERS VERY SERIOUSLY.
SO TELL ME... HOW MANY TARGETS HAVE YOU CAPTURED IN THREE MONTHS?
JUST ONE. A PURSE-SNATCHER. IT'S NOT EASY FINDING *REAL CRIMINALS,* YA KNOW.
WELL, THAT EXPLAINS WHY YOU'VE BEEN GOING HUNGRY.
HEH! YEAH, I'VE BEEN TELLING MYSELF I NEED TO START GETTING SERIOUS ABOUT THIS.
...
SO WHAT DO YOU KNOW ABOUT THIS *PARODEM GUY?*
FUU...
HERE...
PARODEM=LORDENS
A
WHOA! THE BOUNTY'S $65,000 ?!
LOOK AT THE *RISK LEVEL.* HE'S AN A-CLASS CRIMINAL.
LOOK, IF YOU'RE NOT *SERIOUS* ABOUT THIS, YOU SHOULDN'T RISK GOING UP AGAINST A GUY LIKE PARODEM.

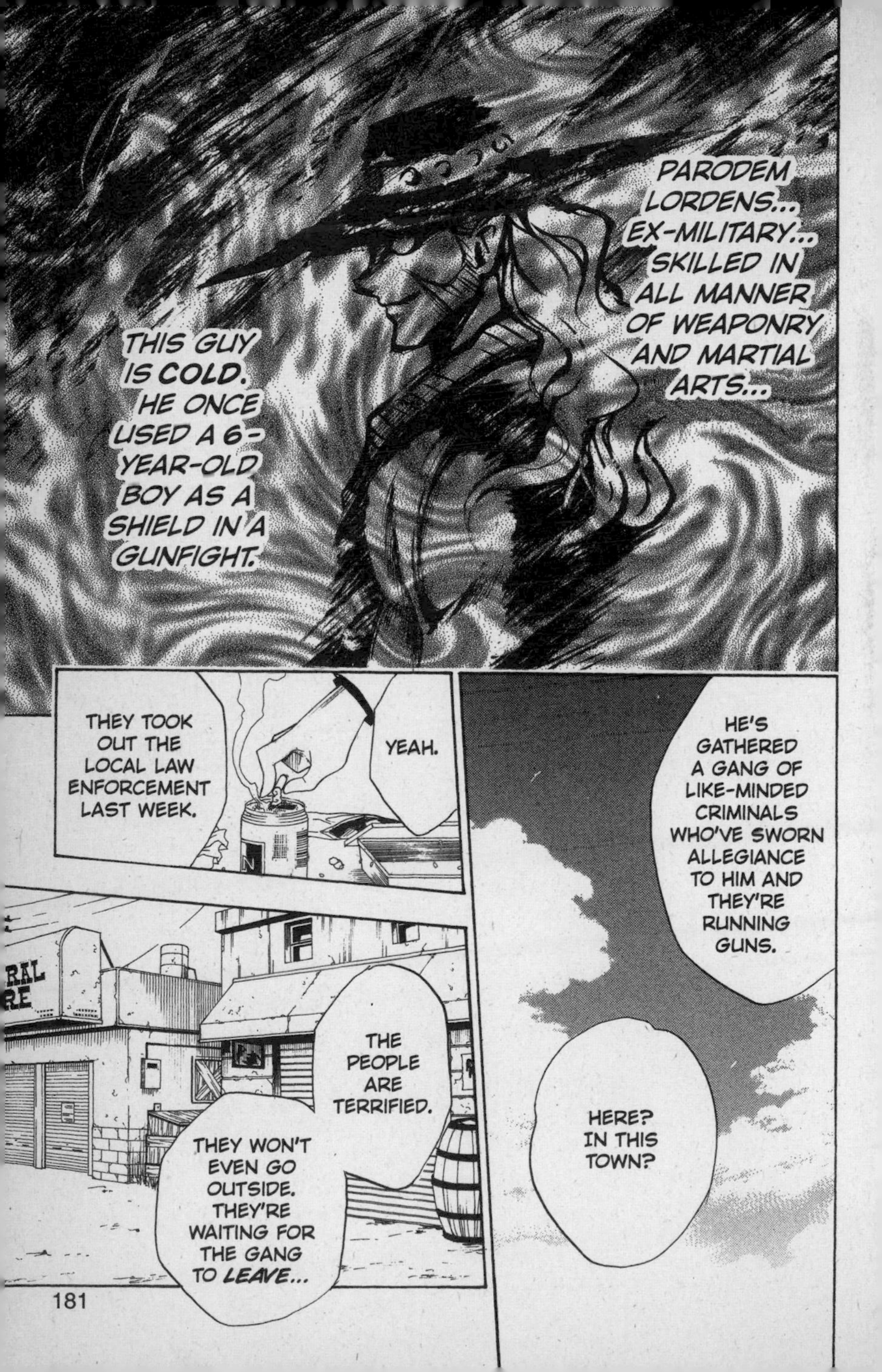
PARODEM LORDENS... EX-MILITARY... SKILLED IN ALL MANNER OF WEAPONRY AND MARTIAL ARTS...
THIS GUY IS COLD. HE ONCE USED A 6-YEAR-OLD BOY AS A SHIELD IN A GUNFIGHT.
HE'S GATHERED A GANG OF LIKE-MINDED CRIMINALS WHO'VE SWORN ALLEGIANCE TO HIM AND THEY'RE RUNNING GUNS.
HERE? IN THIS TOWN?
YEAH.
THEY TOOK OUT THE LOCAL LAW ENFORCEMENT LAST WEEK.
THE PEOPLE ARE TERRIFIED.
THEY WON'T EVEN GO OUTSIDE. THEY'RE WAITING FOR THE GANG TO LEAVE...

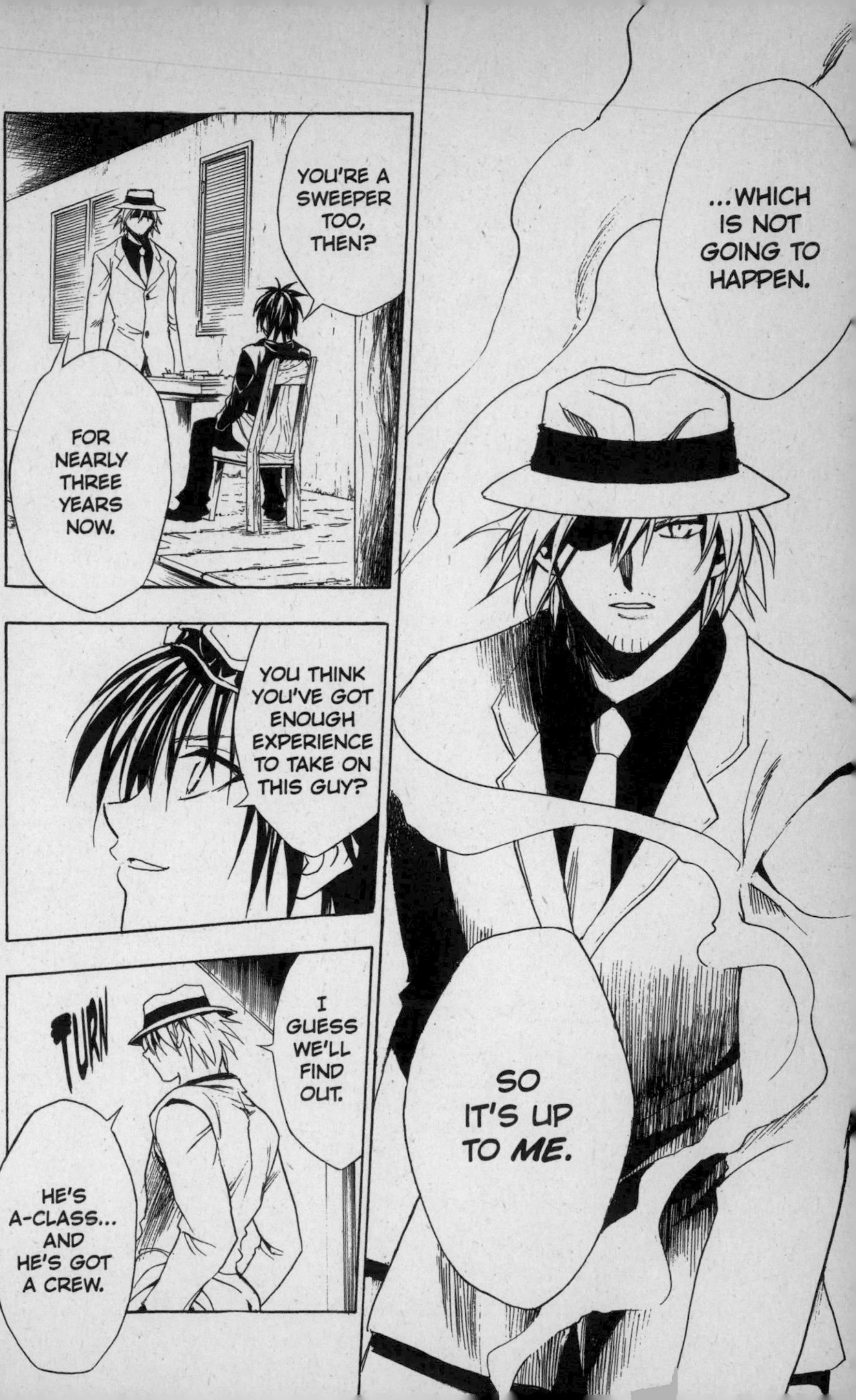
...WHICH IS NOT GOING TO HAPPEN.
SO IT'S UP TO *ME*.
YOU'RE A SWEEPER TOO, THEN?
FOR NEARLY THREE YEARS NOW.
YOU THINK YOU'VE GOT ENOUGH EXPERIENCE TO TAKE ON THIS GUY?
I GUESS WE'LL FIND OUT.
TURN
HE'S A-CLASS... AND HE'S GOT A CREW.

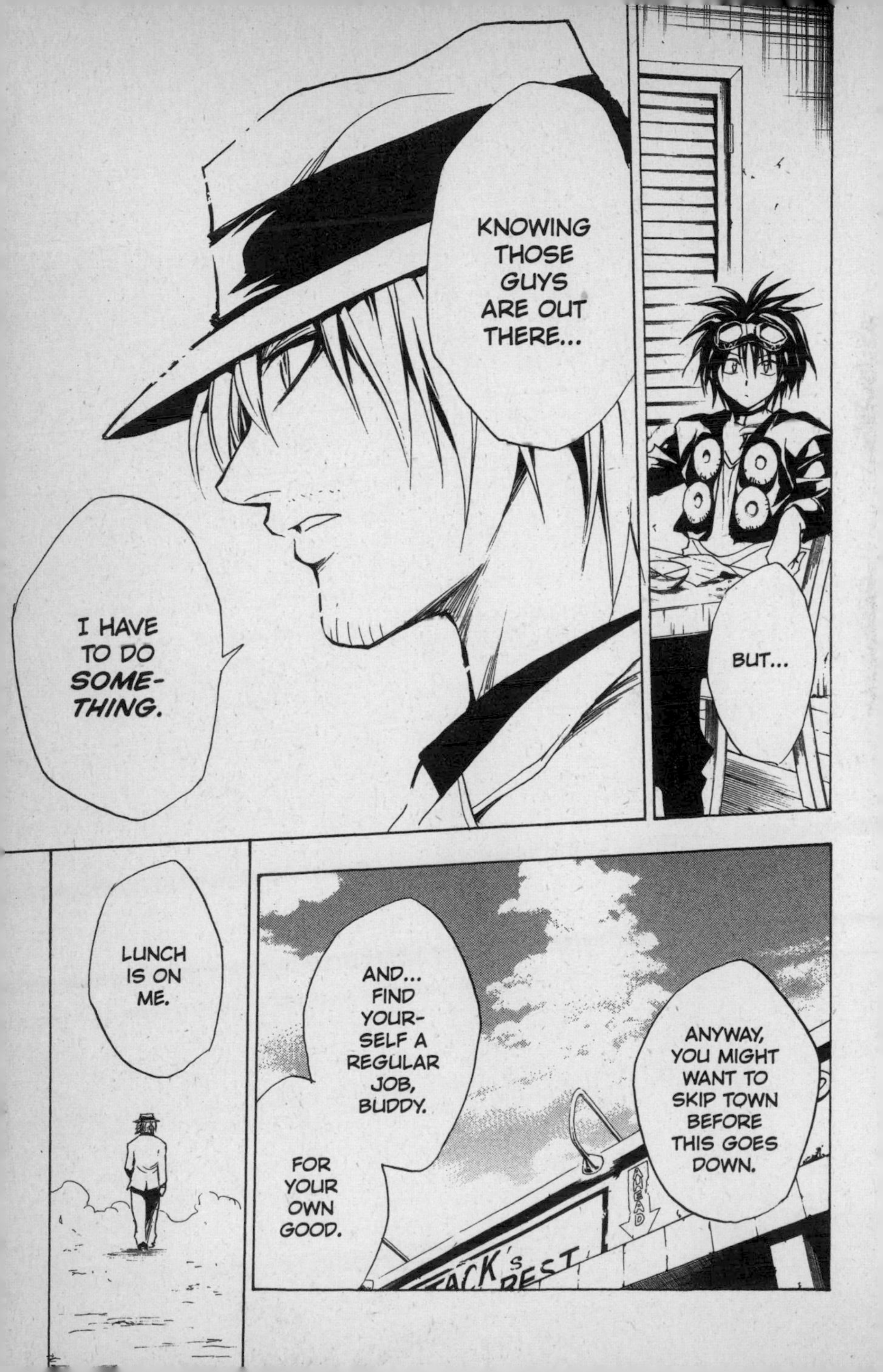
BUT...
KNOWING THOSE GUYS ARE OUT THERE...
I HAVE TO DO *SOME-THING.*
ANYWAY, YOU MIGHT WANT TO SKIP TOWN BEFORE THIS GOES DOWN.
AHEAD
AND... FIND YOUR-SELF A REGULAR JOB, BUDDY.
FOR YOUR OWN GOOD.
LUNCH IS ON ME.

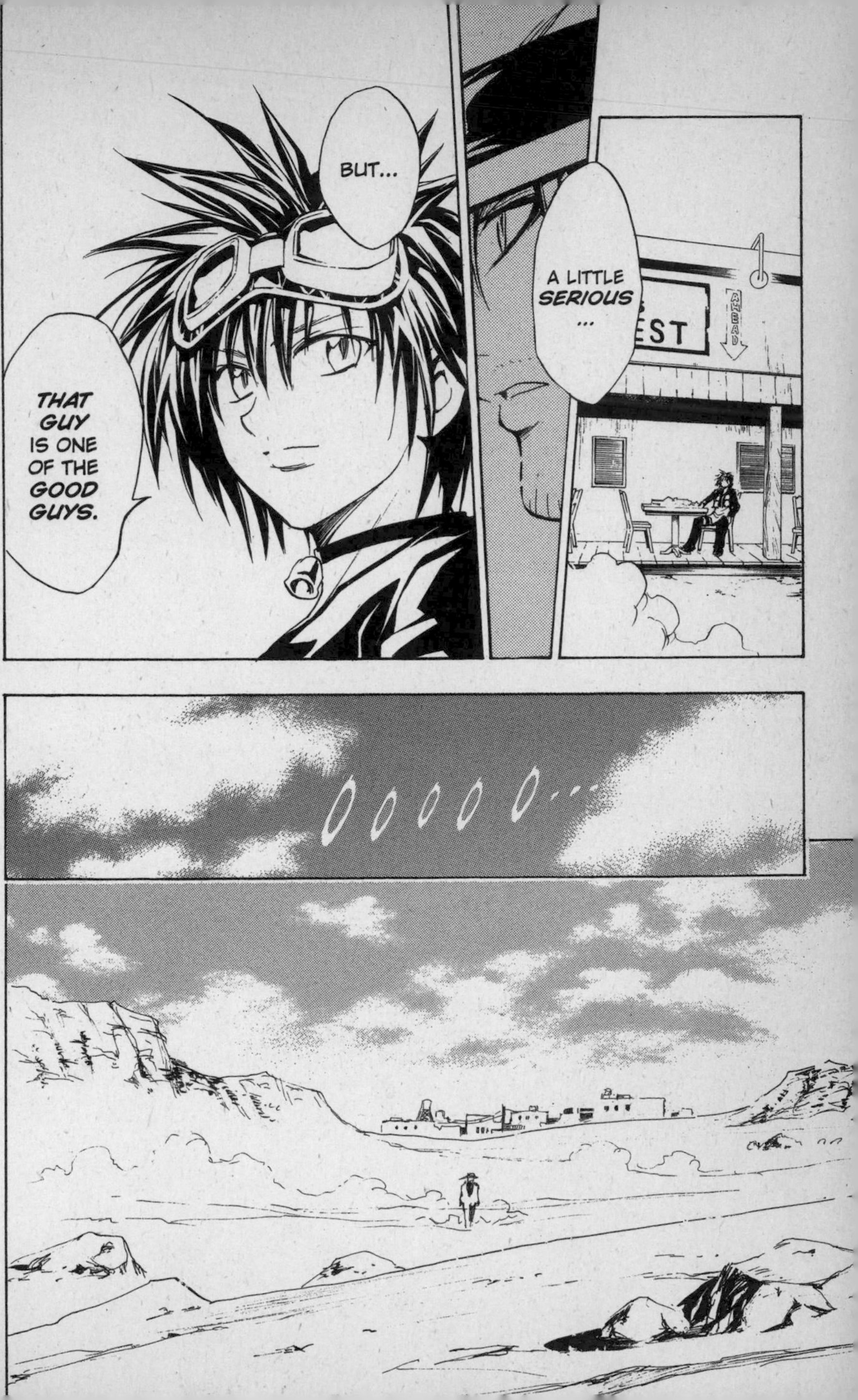
A LITTLE SERIOUS ...
AHEAD
BUT...
THAT GUY IS ONE OF THE GOOD GUYS.
OOOOO...

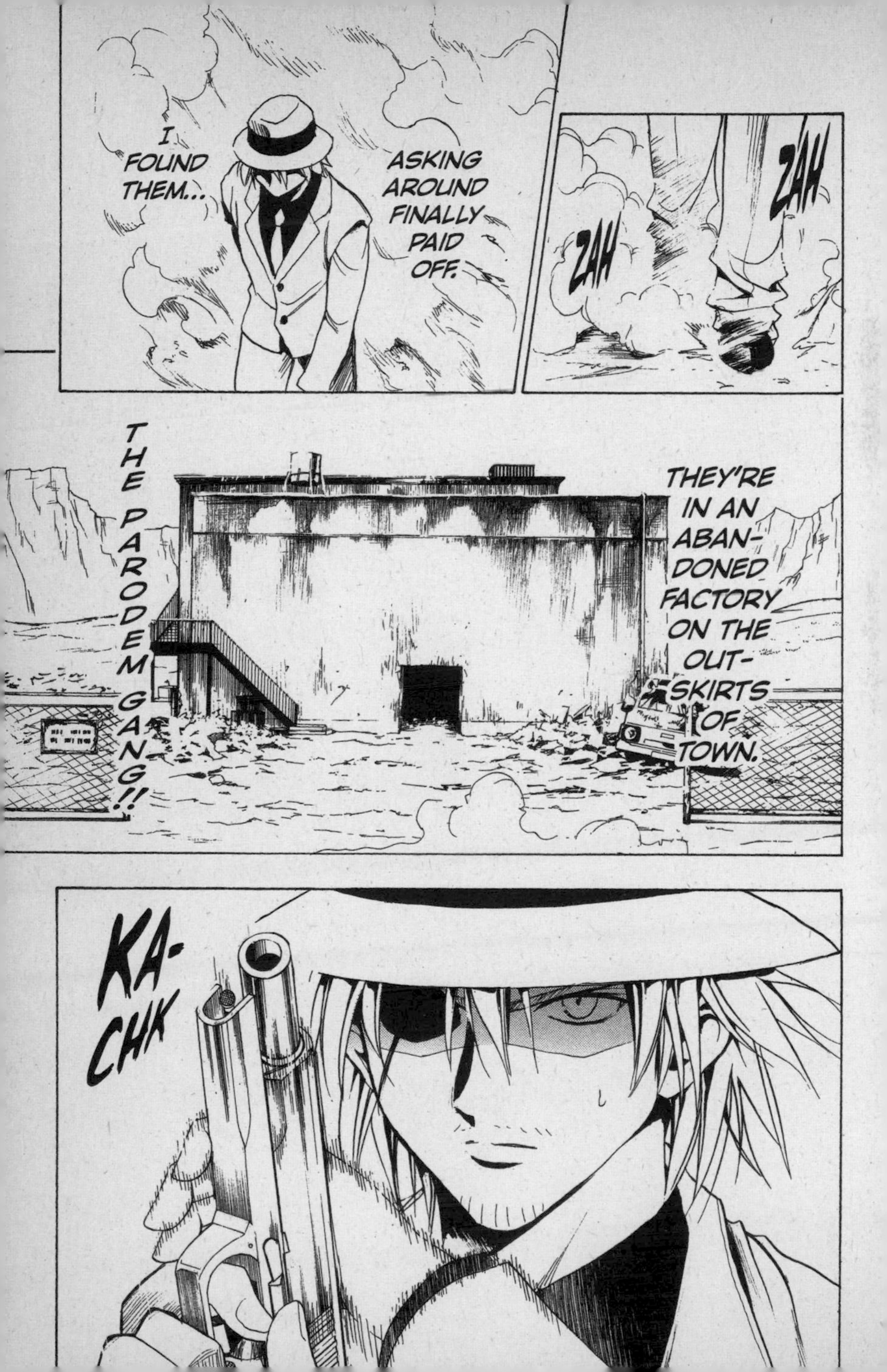
ZAH
ZAH
ASKING AROUND FINALLY PAID OFF.
I FOUND THEM...
THEY'RE IN AN ABAN-DONED FACTORY ON THE OUT-SKIRTS OF TOWN.
THE PARODEM GANG!!
KA-CHK

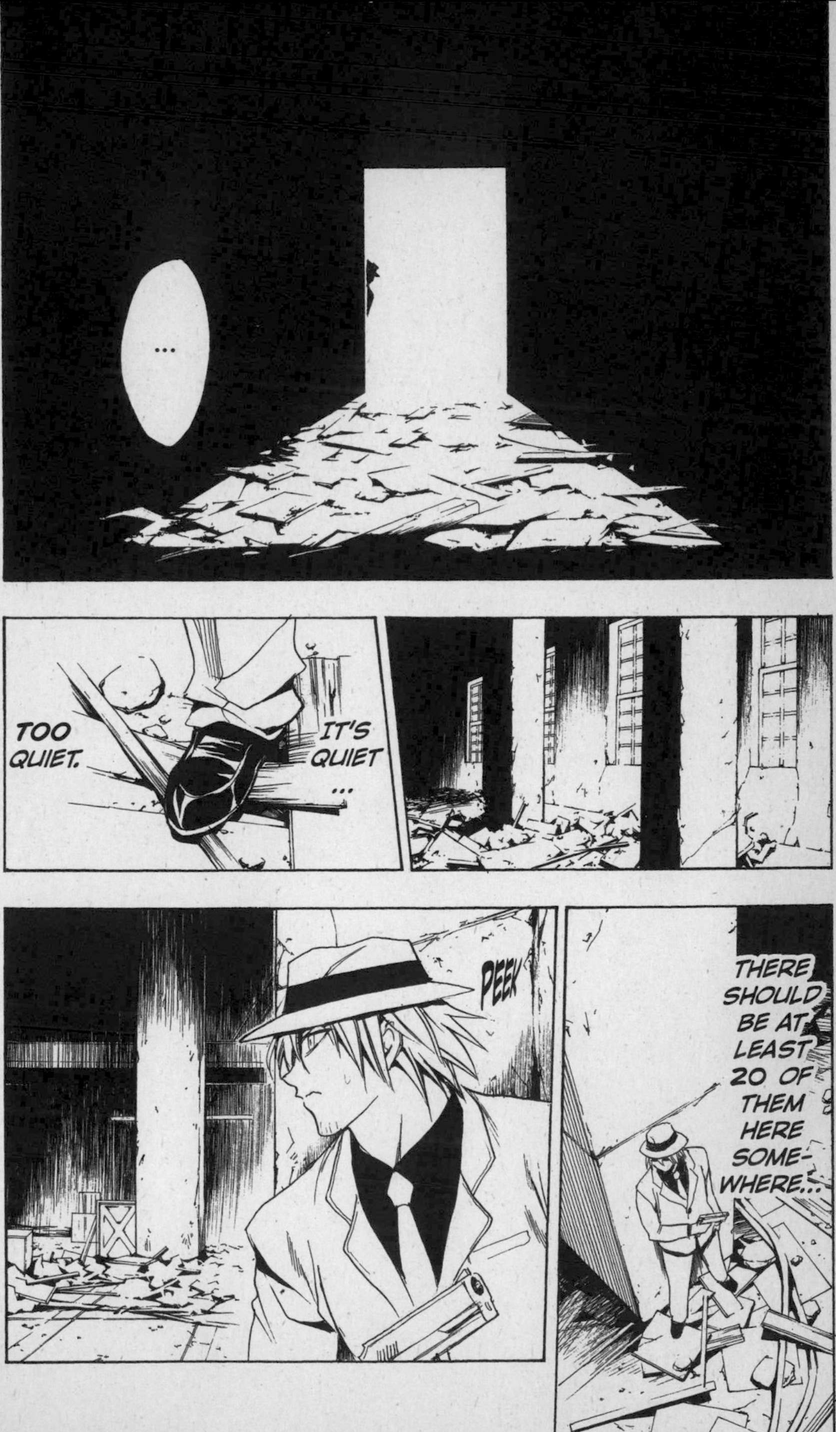
...
IT'S QUIET...
TOO QUIET.
THERE SHOULD BE AT LEAST 20 OF THEM HERE SOME-WHERE...
PEEK

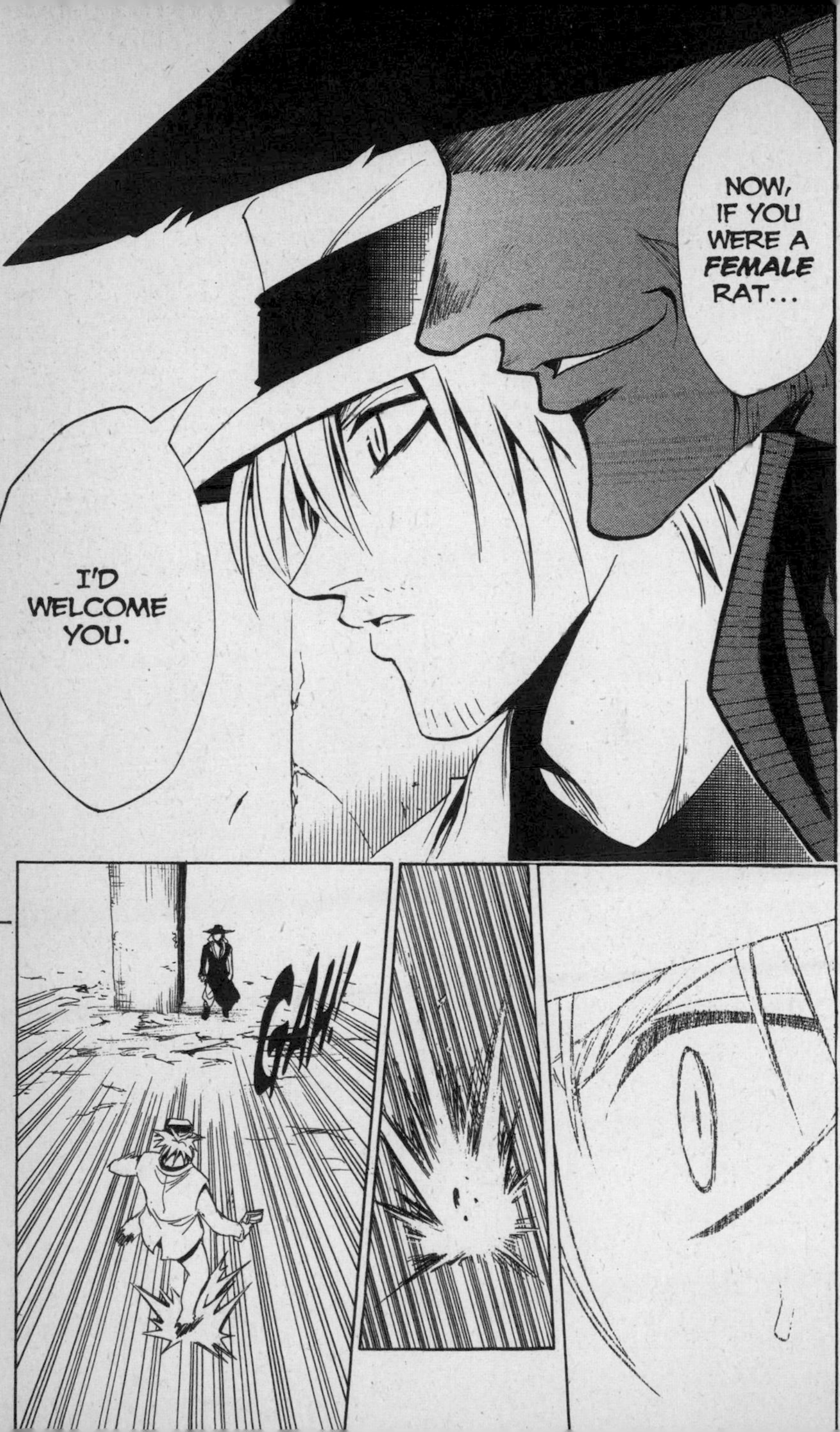
NOW, IF YOU WERE A FEMALE RAT...
I'D WELCOME YOU.
GAH!

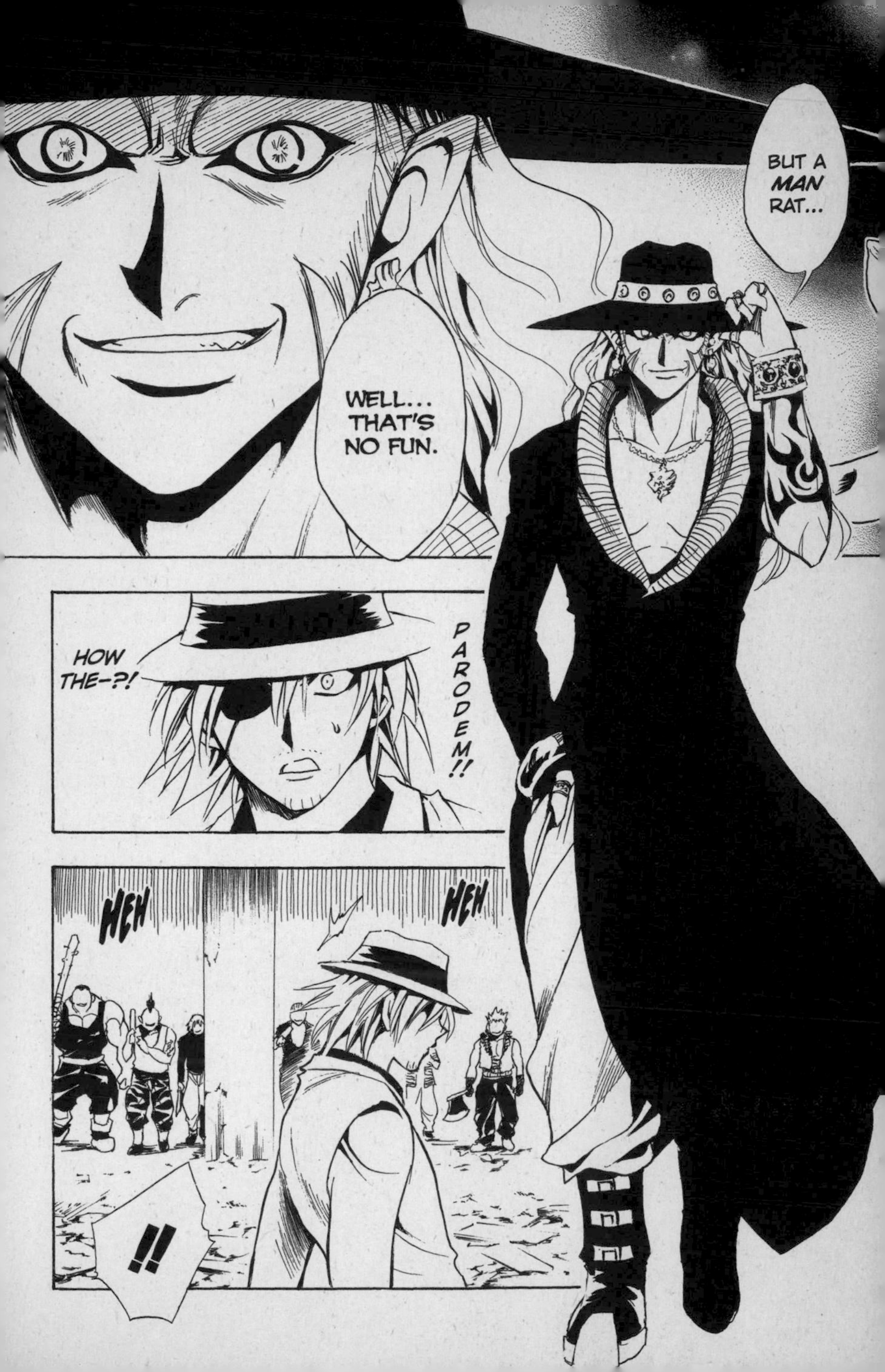
BUT A *MAN* RAT...
WELL... THAT'S NO FUN.
PARODEM!!
HOW THE-?!
HEH
HEH
!!

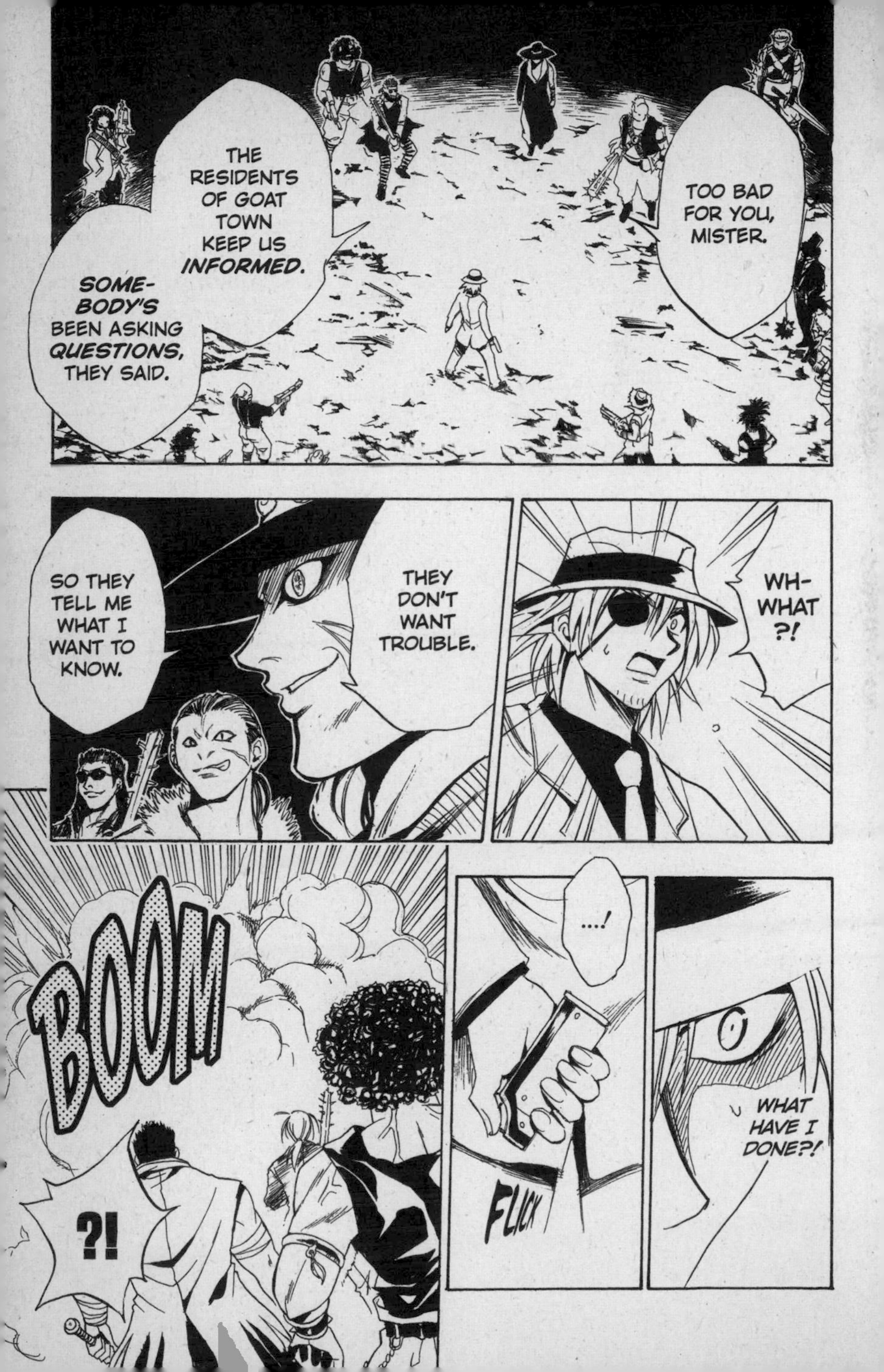
TOO BAD FOR YOU, MISTER.
THE RESIDENTS OF GOAT TOWN KEEP US *INFORMED*.
SOMEBODY'S BEEN ASKING *QUESTIONS*, THEY SAID.
WH-WHAT?!
THEY DON'T WANT TROUBLE.
SO THEY TELL ME WHAT I WANT TO KNOW.
WHAT HAVE I DONE?!
...!
FLICK
BOOM
?!

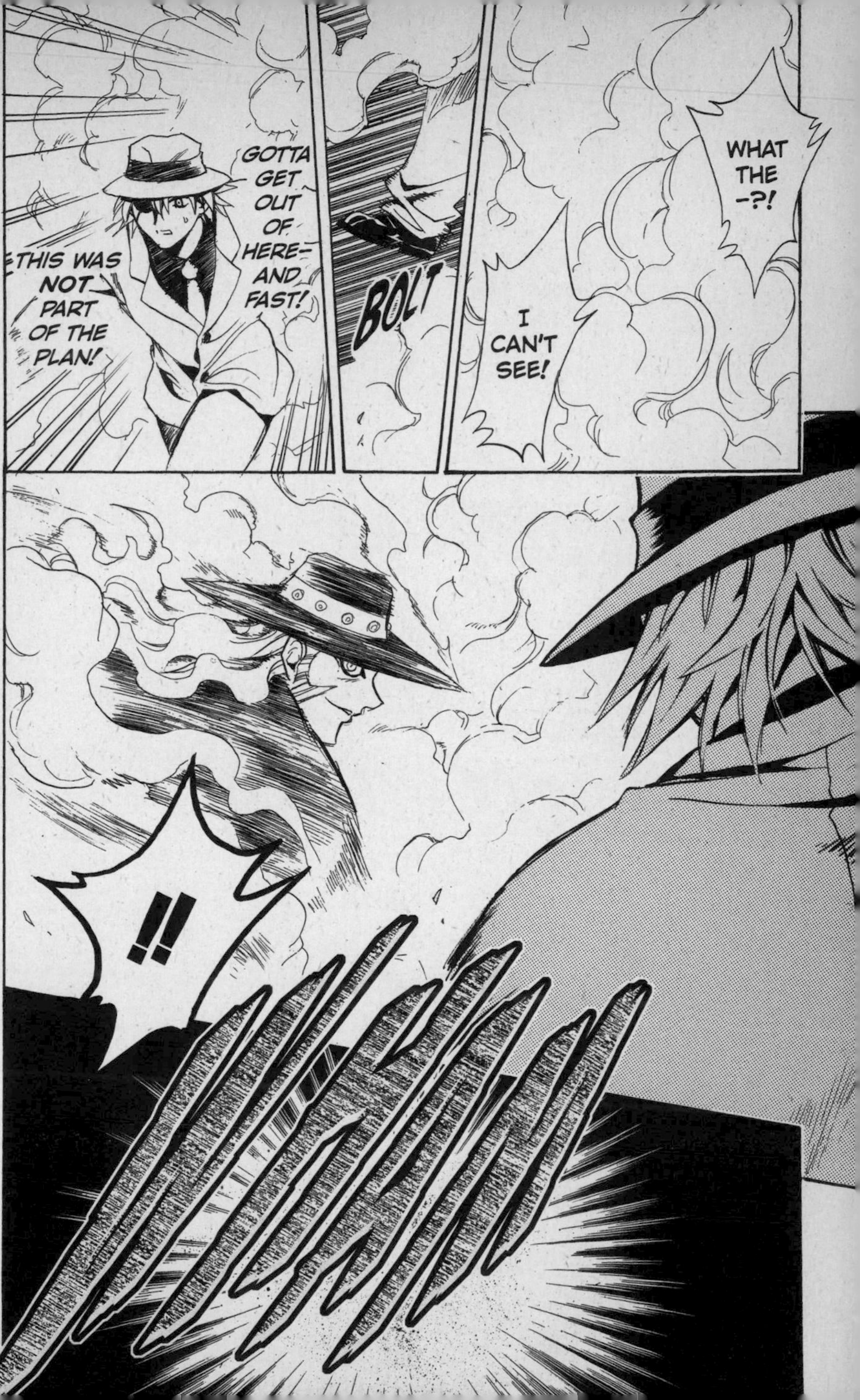
WHAT THE -?!
I CAN'T SEE!
BOLT
GOTTA GET OUT OF HERE—AND FAST!
THIS WAS NOT PART OF THE PLAN!
!!

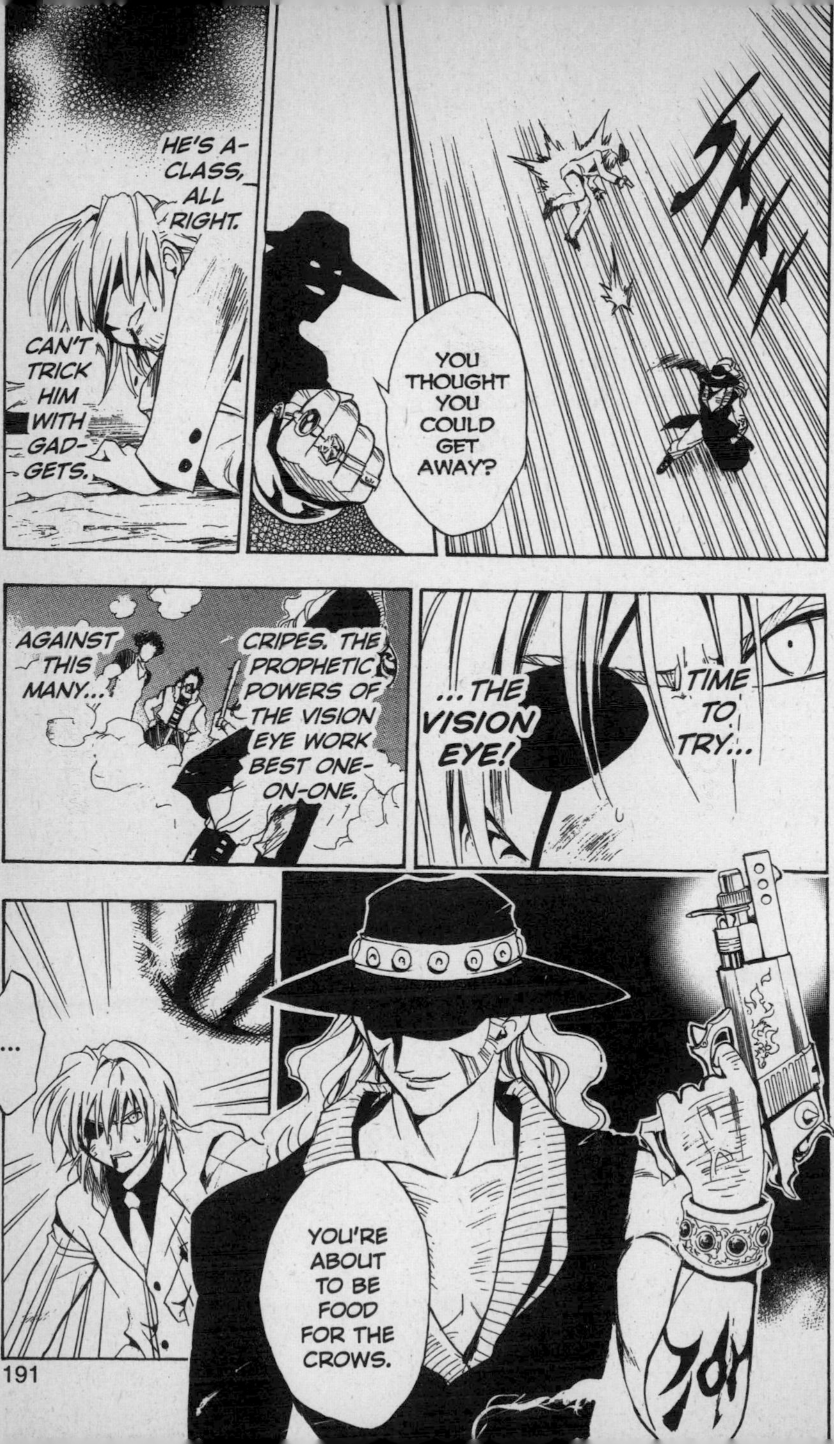
YOU THOUGHT YOU COULD GET AWAY?
HE'S A-CLASS, ALL RIGHT.
CAN'T TRICK HIM WITH GAD-GETS.
TIME TO TRY...
...THE VISION EYE!
CRIPES. THE PROPHETIC POWERS OF THE VISION EYE WORK BEST ONE-ON-ONE.
AGAINST THIS MANY...
YOU'RE ABOUT TO BE FOOD FOR THE CROWS.
...

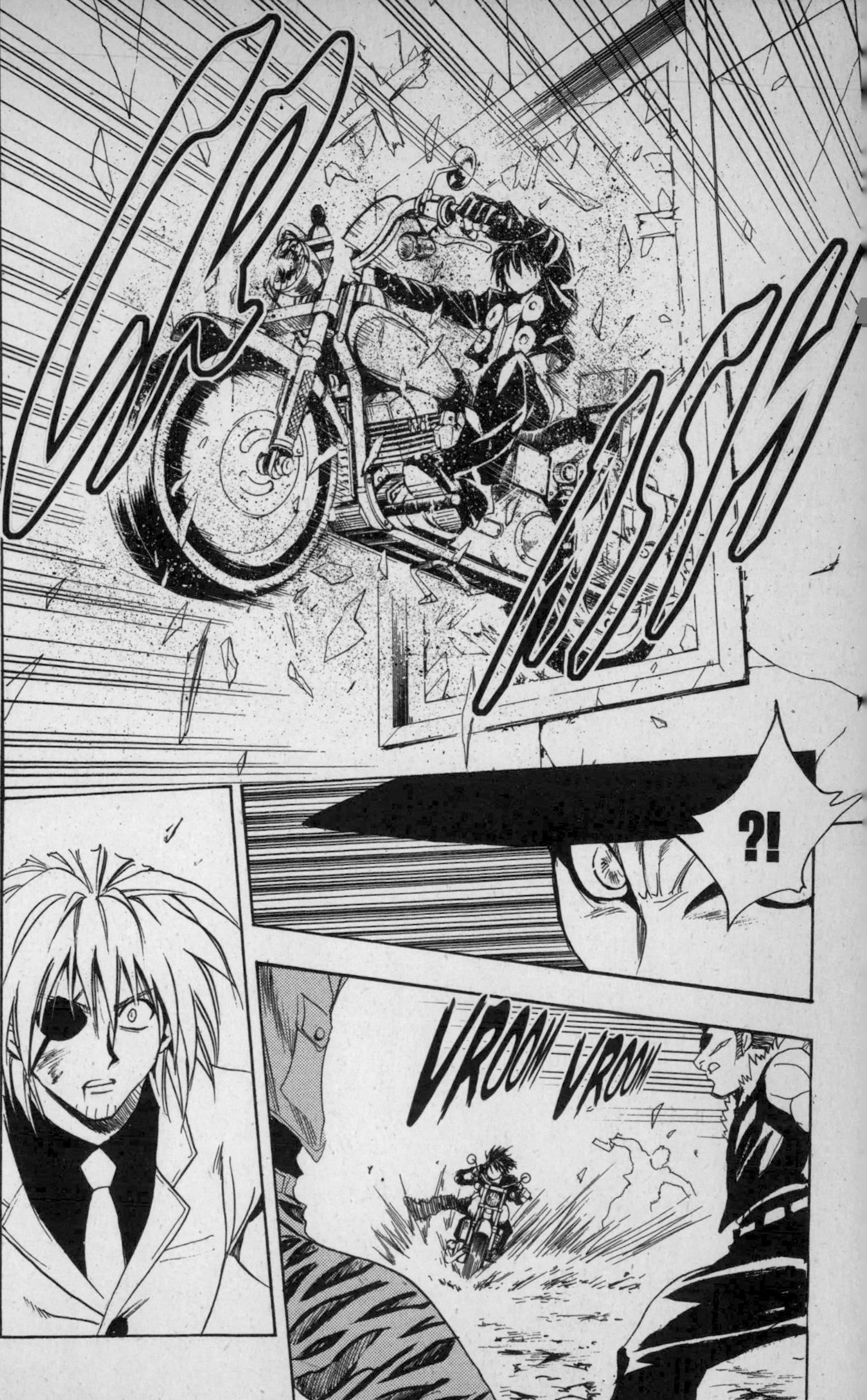
CRASH
?!
VROOM VROOM

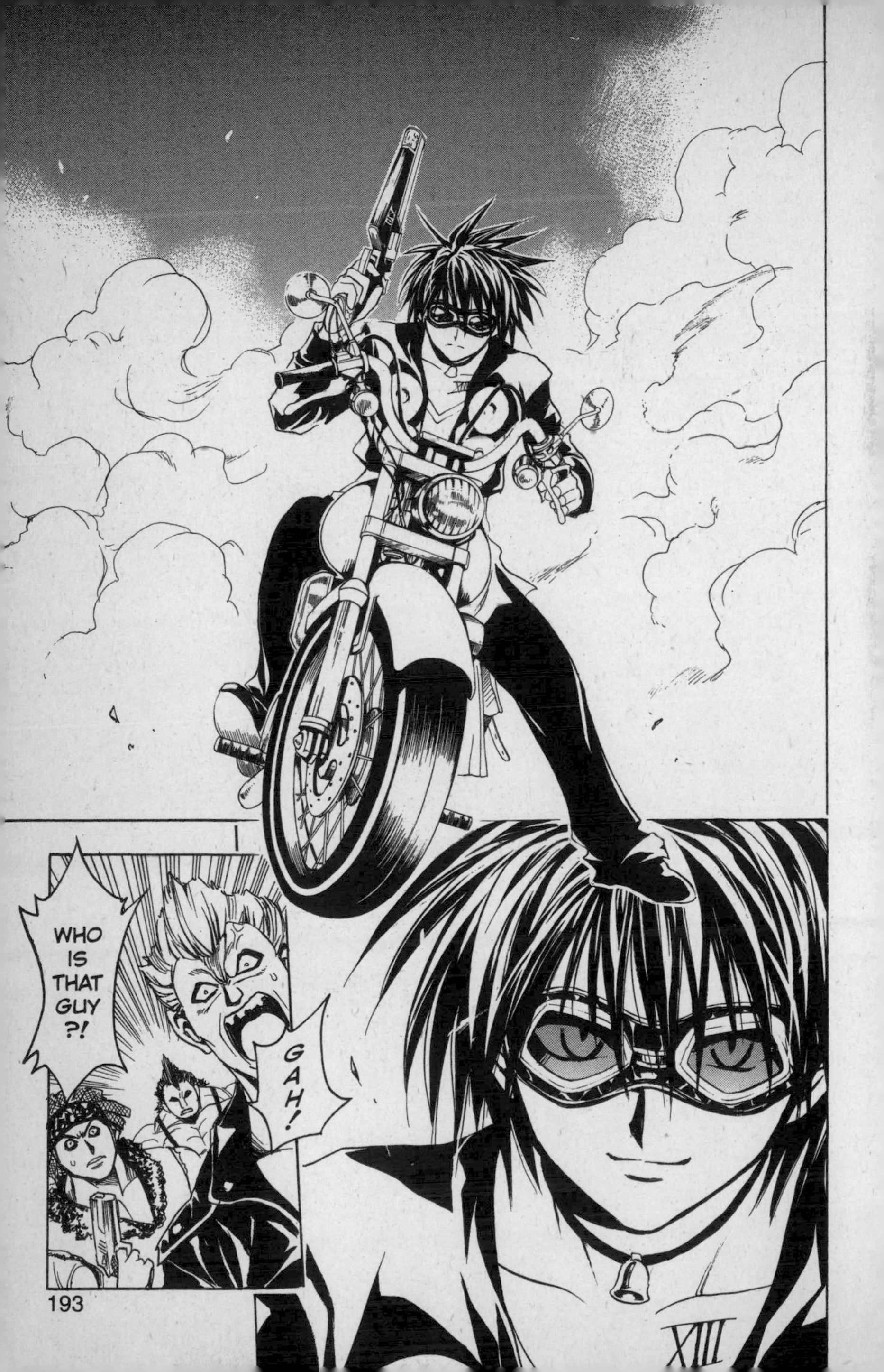
WHO IS THAT GUY ?!
GAH!

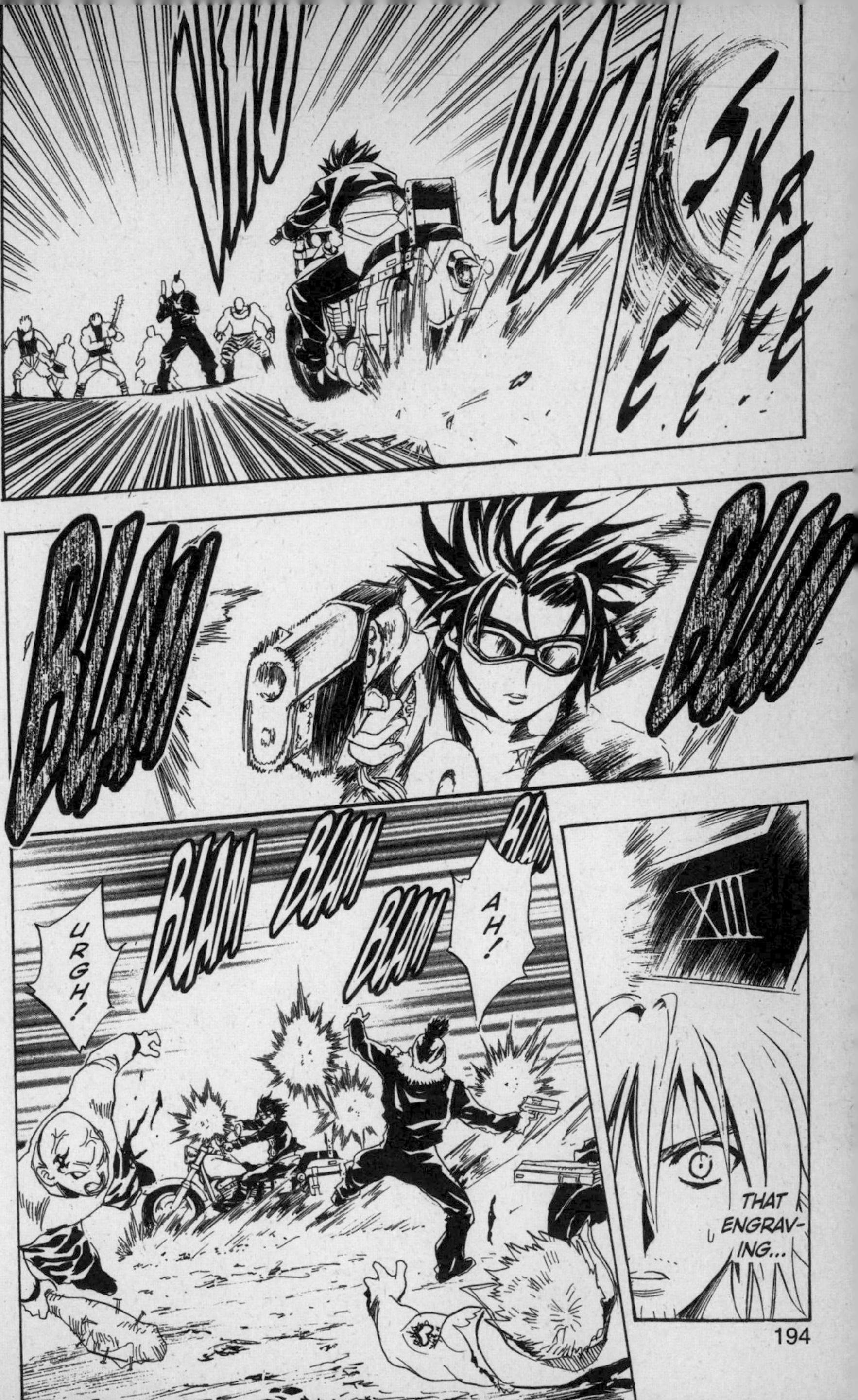
SKREEEE...
BLAM
BLAM
THAT ENGRAV-ING...
BLAM
AH!
BLAM
BLAM
BLAM
BLAM
URGH!

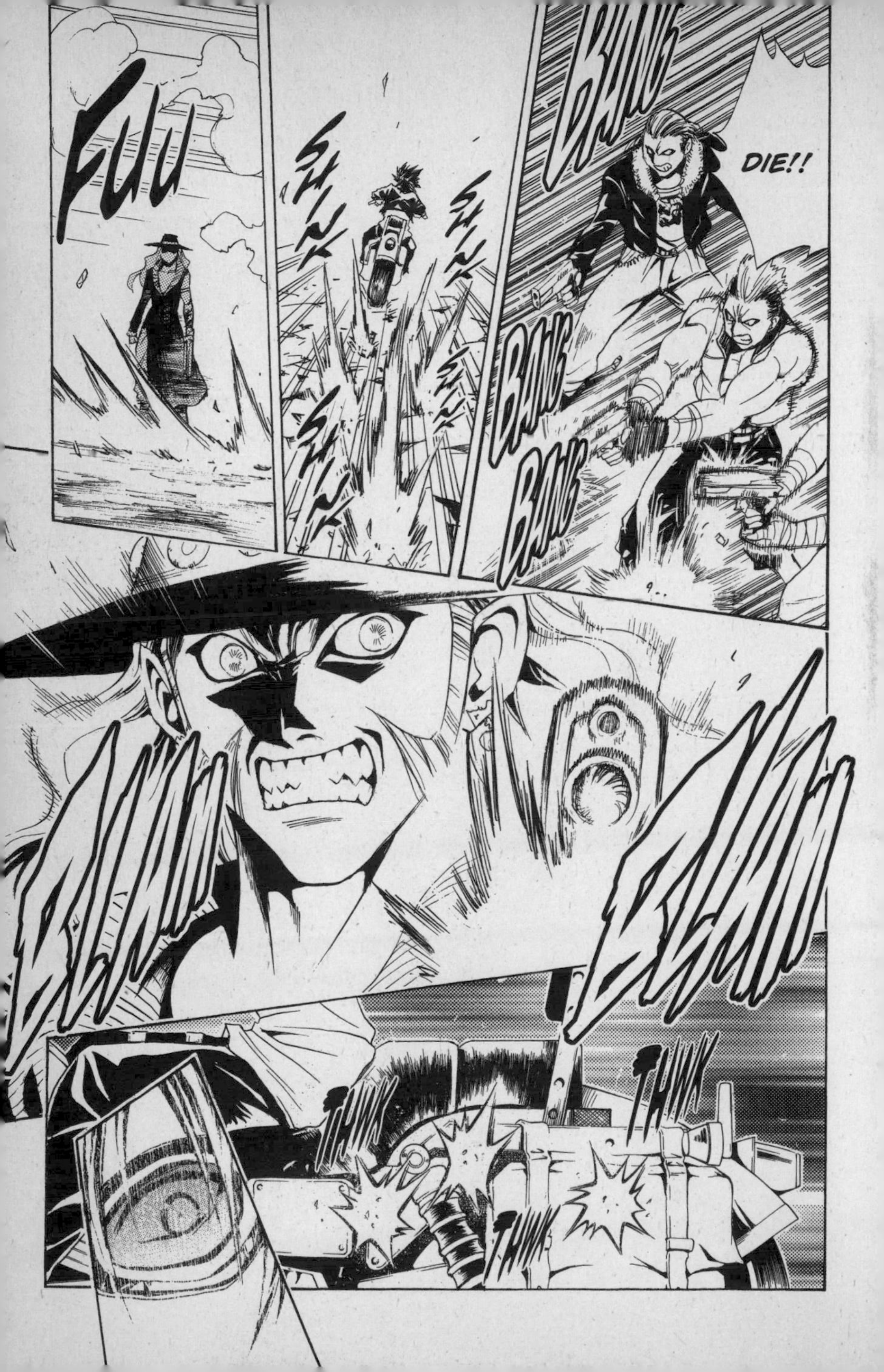
DIE!!
BANG
BANG
THWK
THWK
THWK

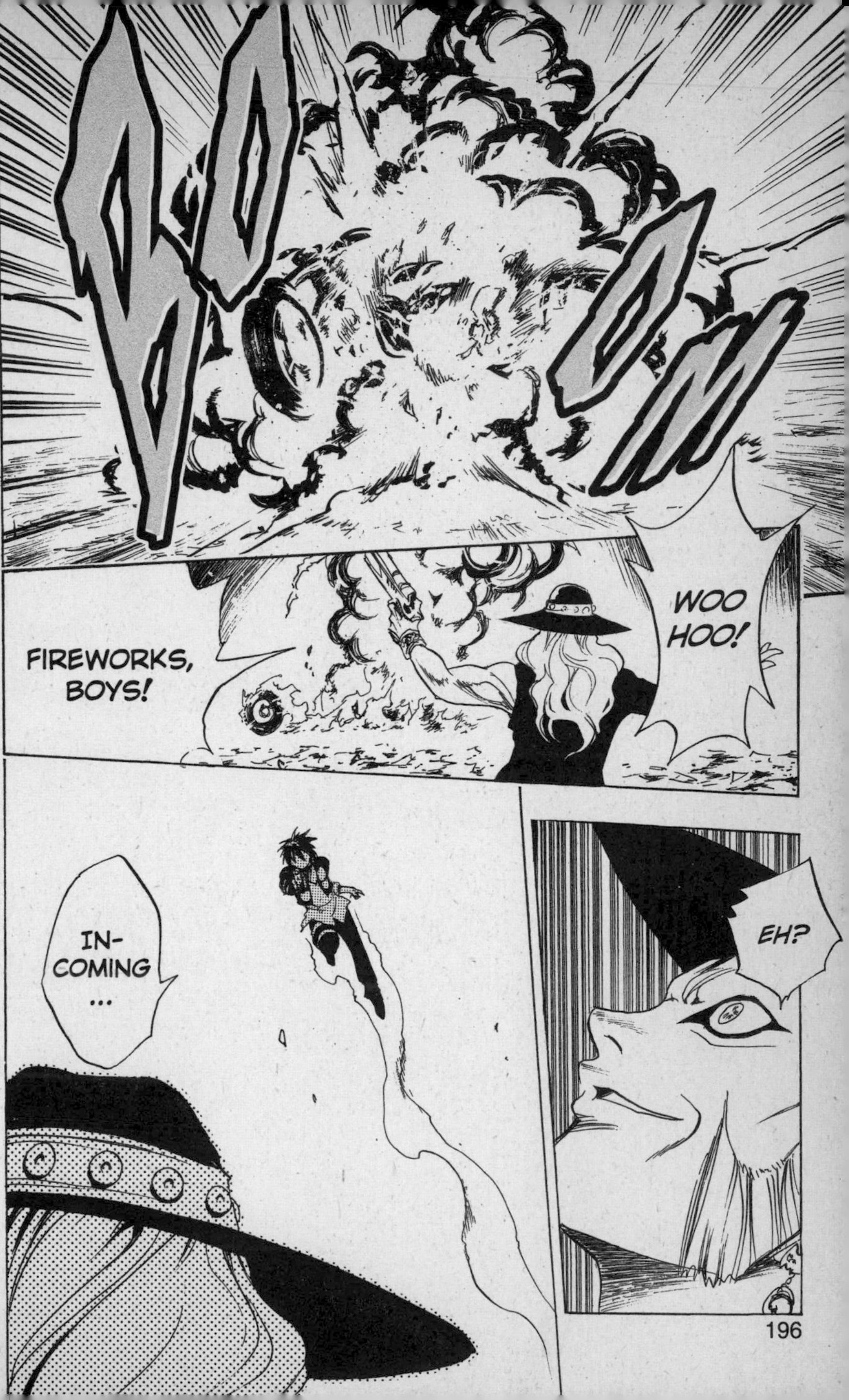
BOOM
WOO HOO!
FIREWORKS, BOYS!
EH?
IN-COMING ...

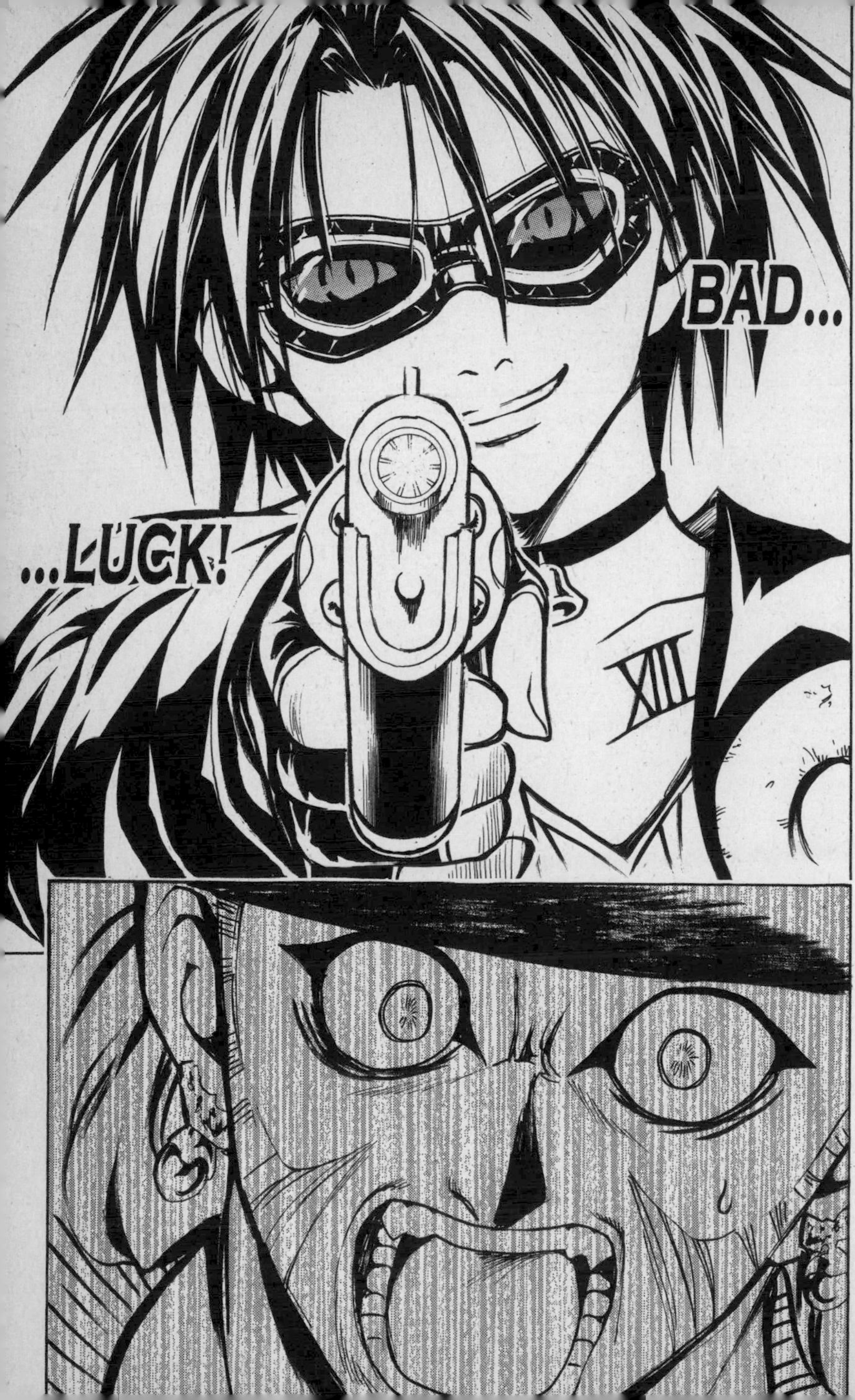
BAD...
...LUCK!

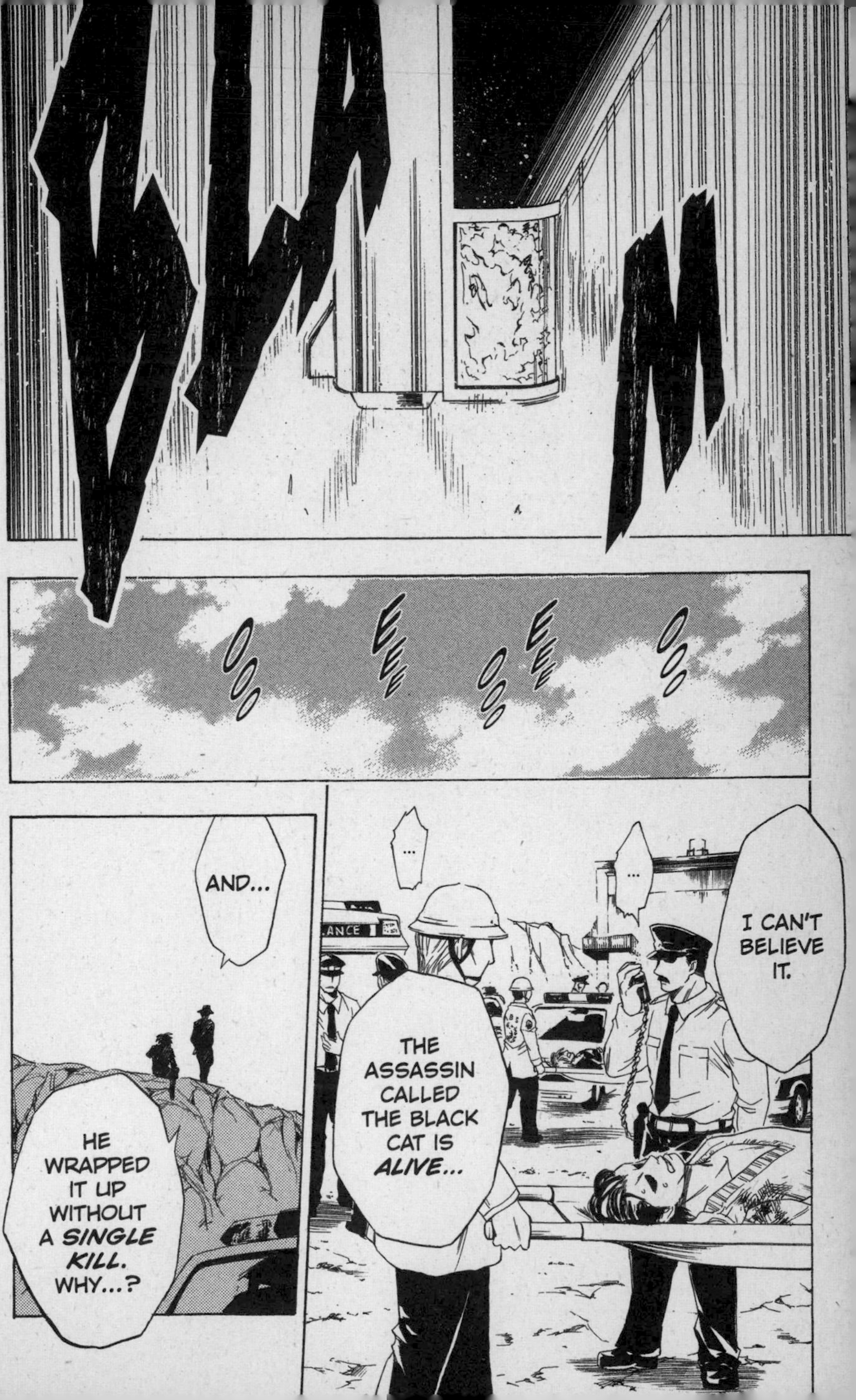
SLAM
OOO EEE OOO EEE OOO
I CAN'T BELIEVE IT.
...
...
THE ASSASSIN CALLED THE BLACK CAT IS *ALIVE...*
AND...
HE WRAPPED IT UP WITHOUT A *SINGLE KILL.* WHY...?

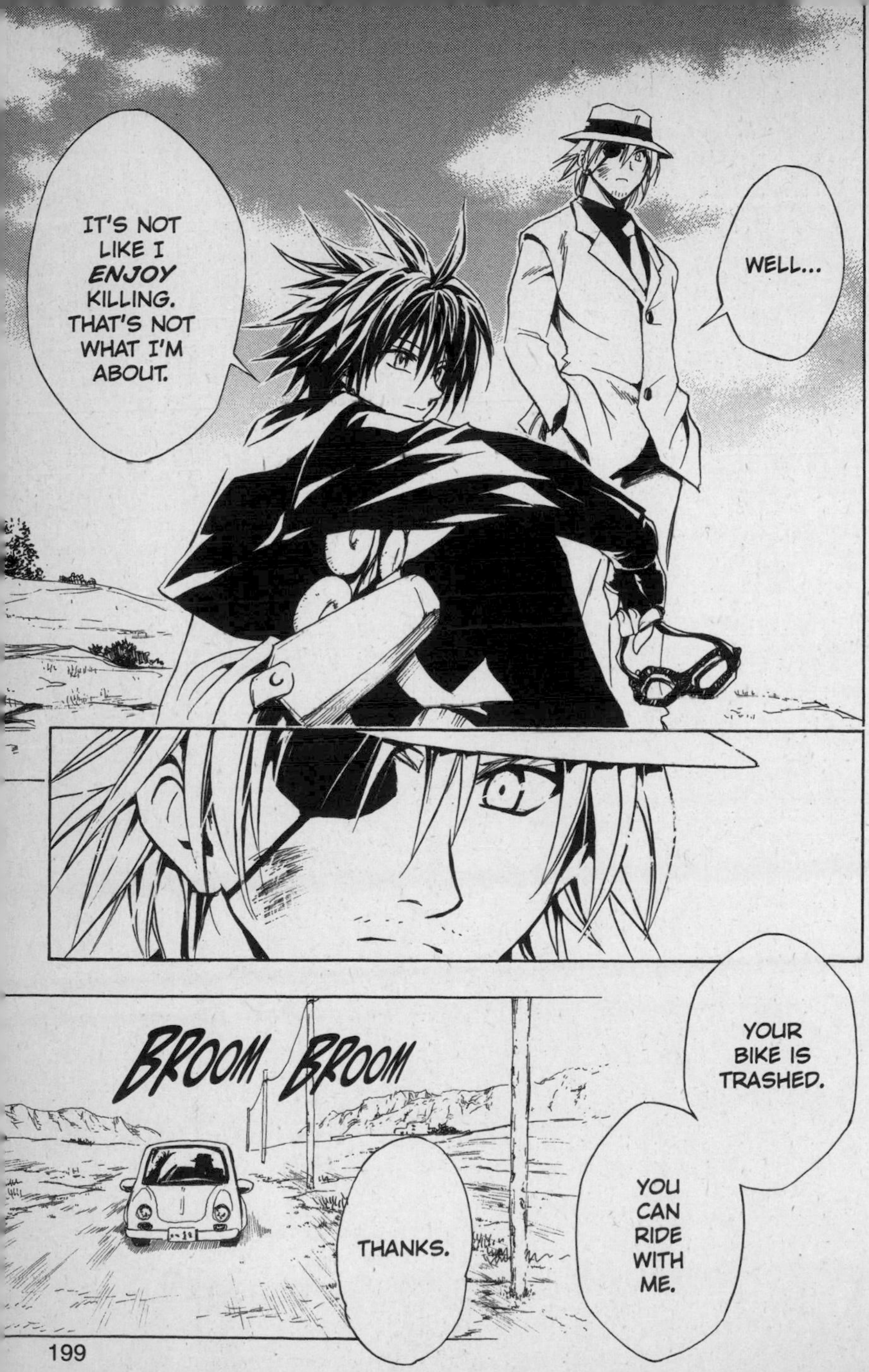
WELL...
IT'S NOT LIKE I *ENJOY* KILLING. THAT'S NOT WHAT I'M ABOUT.
YOUR BIKE IS TRASHED.
YOU CAN RIDE WITH ME.
THANKS.
BROOM BROOM

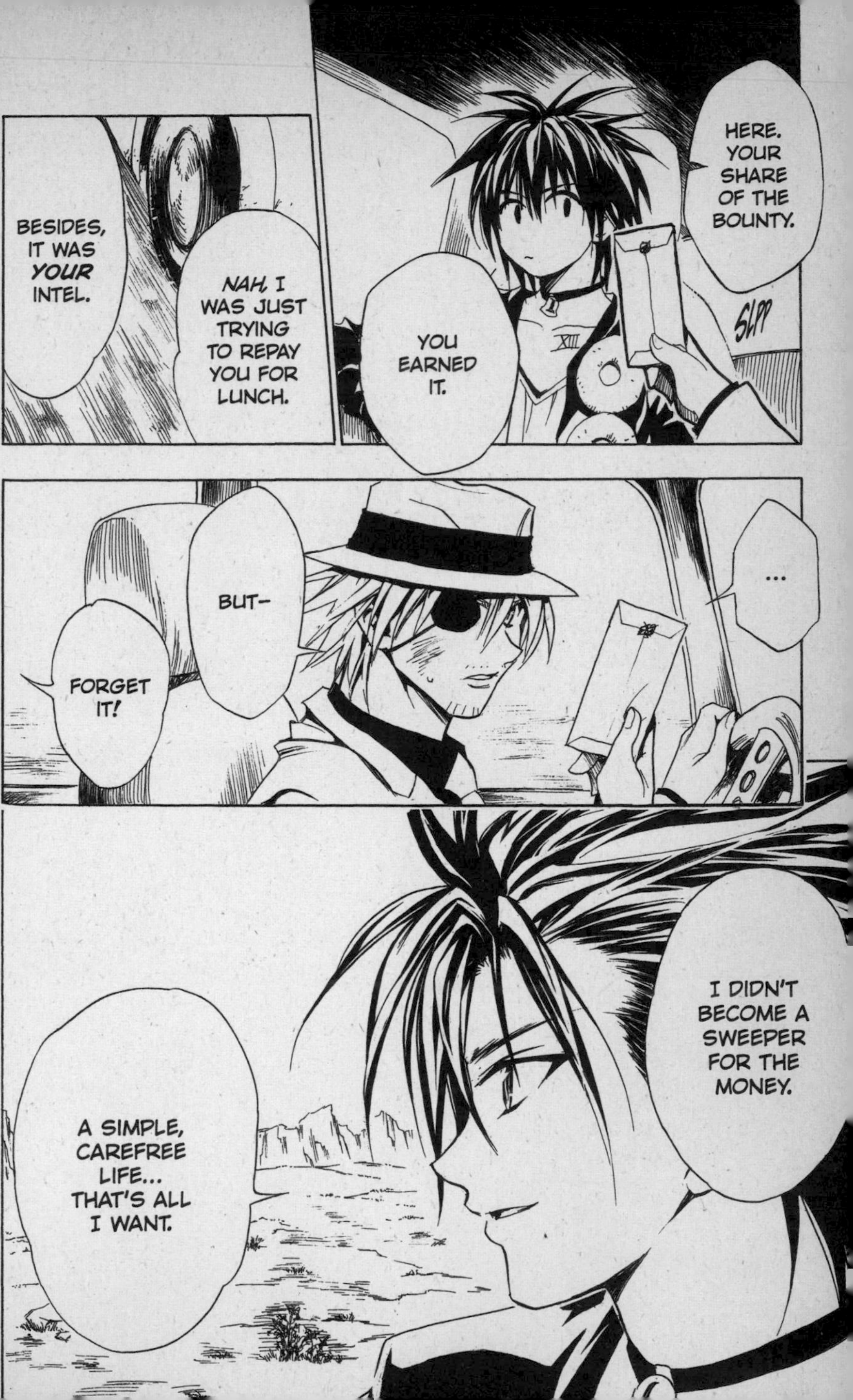
HERE. YOUR SHARE OF THE BOUNTY.
SLPP
YOU EARNED IT.
NAH, I WAS JUST TRYING TO REPAY YOU FOR LUNCH.
BESIDES, IT WAS YOUR INTEL.
...
BUT-
FORGET IT!
I DIDN'T BECOME A SWEEPER FOR THE MONEY.
A SIMPLE, CAREFREE LIFE... THAT'S ALL I WANT.

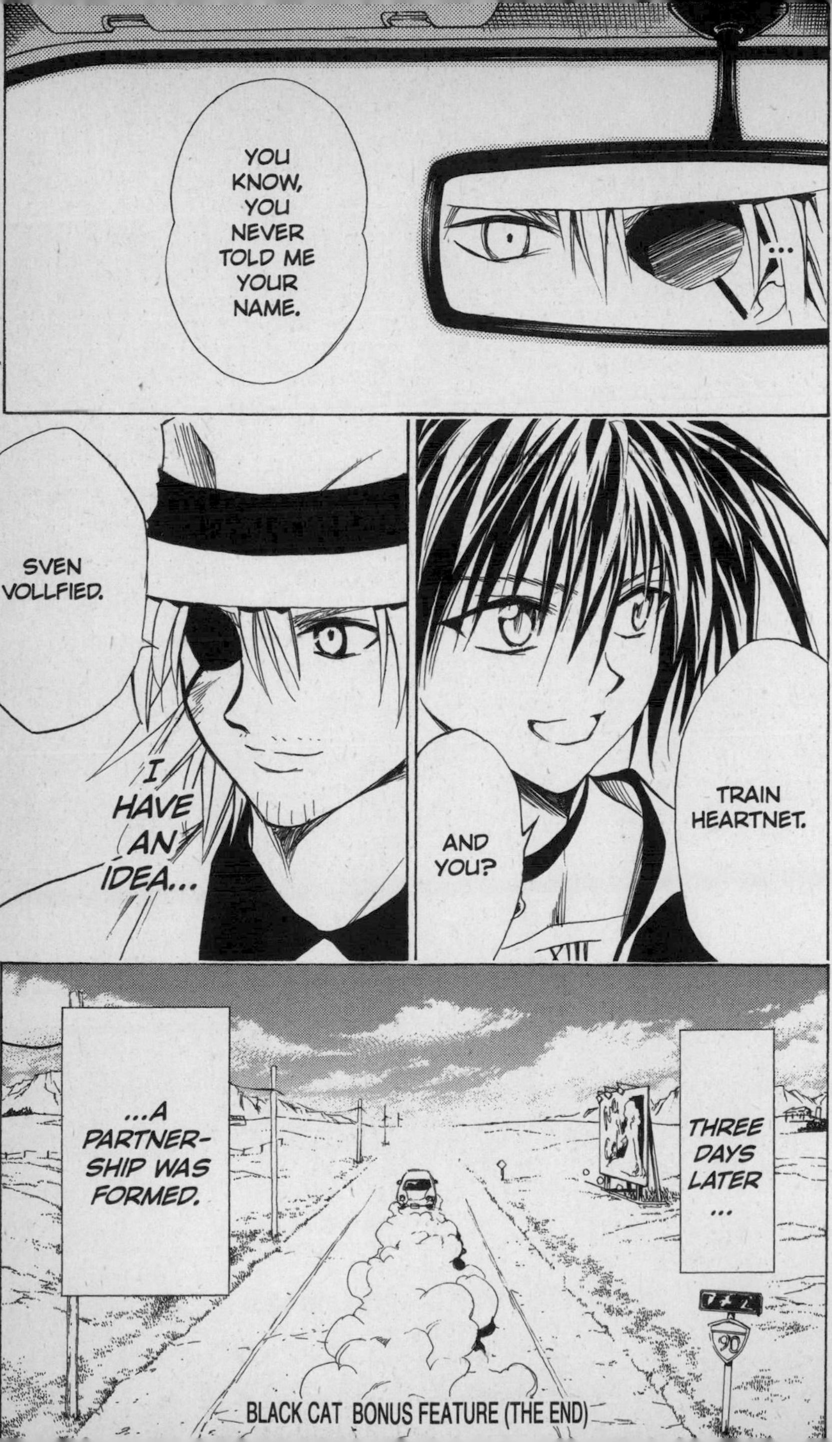
YOU KNOW, YOU NEVER TOLD ME YOUR NAME.
...
TRAIN HEARTNET.
AND YOU?
SVEN VOLLFIED.
I HAVE AN IDEA...
THREE DAYS LATER ...
...A PARTNER-SHIP WAS FORMED.
90
BLACK CAT BONUS FEATURE (THE END)

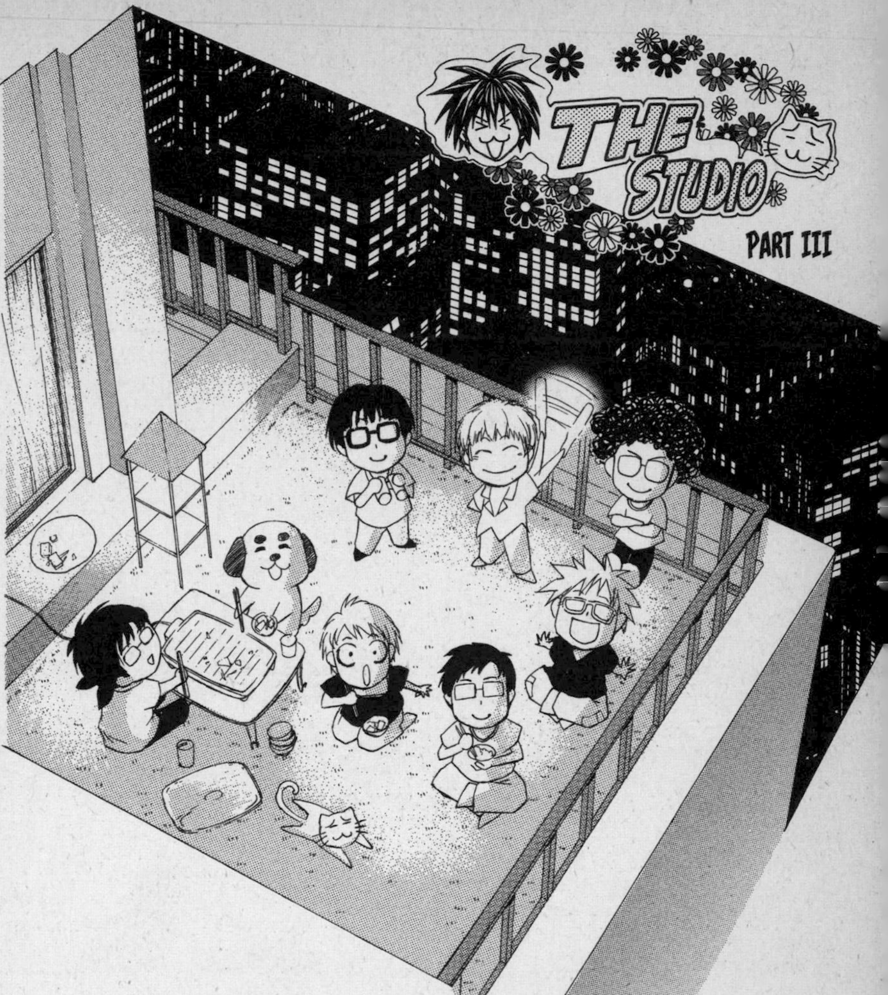
THE STUDIO
PART III

IN THE SUMMER, IT'S BARBECUE. IN THE WINTER, HOT POTS GALORE. SUKIYAKI, KIMCHEE, OKONOMIYAKI PANCAKES... THERE'S ALWAYS A PARTY AT THE BLACK CAT STUDIO. DURING THE SUMMER, WE'RE OUT ON THE TERRACE LOOKING UP AT THE STARS, TAKING TURNS WITH BINOCULARS LOOKING AT THE FERRIS WHEEL IN THE DISTANCE AND WAVING LIGHT STICKS. AS WE NEAR DEADLINE, THE WHOLE STAFF WORKS AT A BREAKNECK PACE IN ANTICIPATION OF GRILLED MEATS. THIS IS HOW BLACK CAT MAKES IT INTO SHONEN JUMP EACH WEEK.

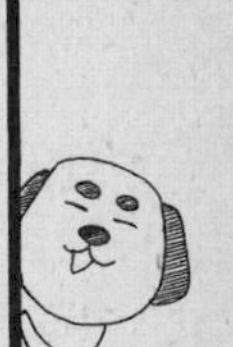

Shiho Kawaki

DANGER IN THE WORKPLACE: THE TOILET SAGA, PART 1

KATSUNORI HIDA

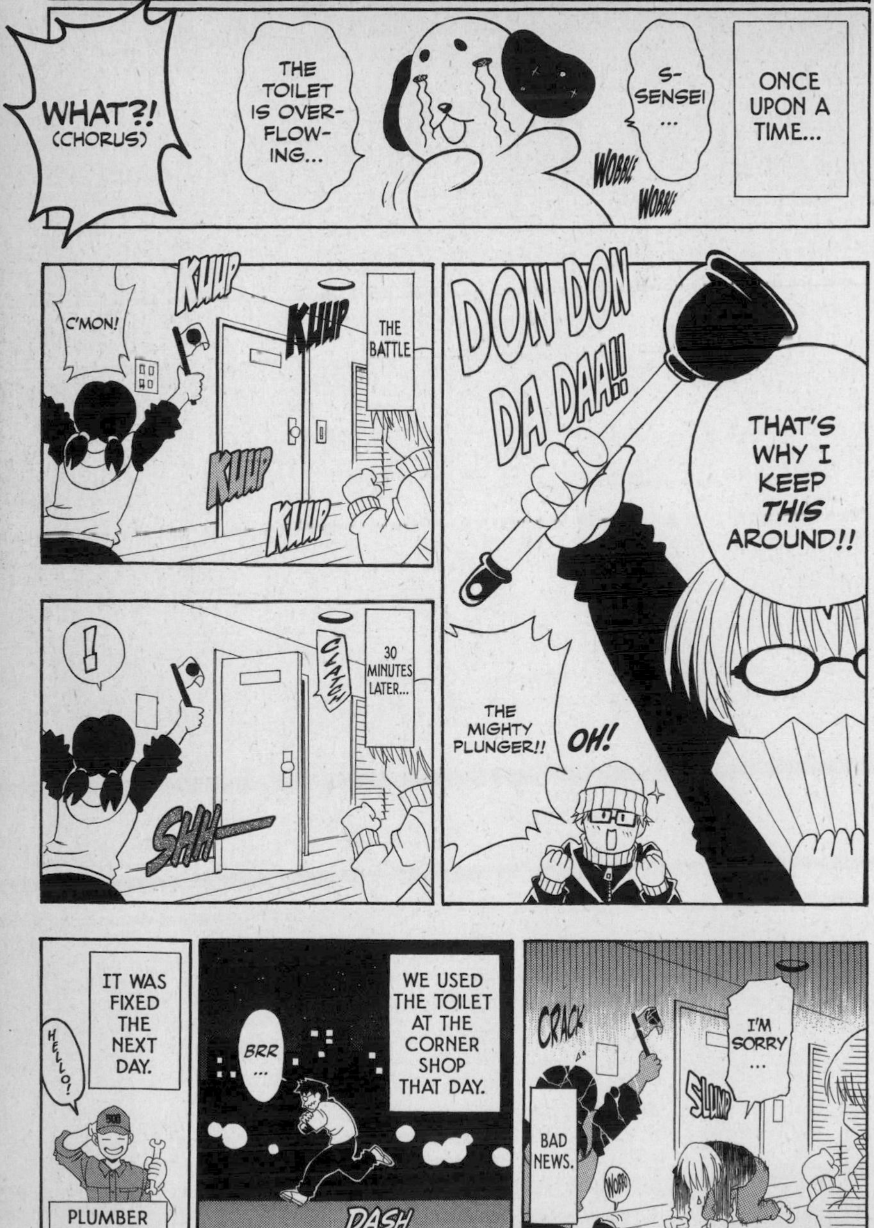

ONCE UPON A TIME...
S-SENSEI ...
WOBBLE
WOBBLE
THE TOILET IS OVER-FLOWING...
WHAT?! (CHORUS)
DON DON DA DAA!!
THAT'S WHY I KEEP *THIS* AROUND!!
OH!
THE MIGHTY PLUNGER!!
THE BATTLE
KUUP
KUUP
C'MON!
KUUP
KUUP
30 MINUTES LATER...
CLATCH
!
SHH
BAD NEWS.
I'M SORRY ...
CRACK
SLUMP
WOBBLE
WE USED THE TOILET AT THE CORNER SHOP THAT DAY.
BRR ...
DASH
IT WAS FIXED THE NEXT DAY.
HELLO?!
PLUMBER

THE POT NAZI BY KOZATO TAI

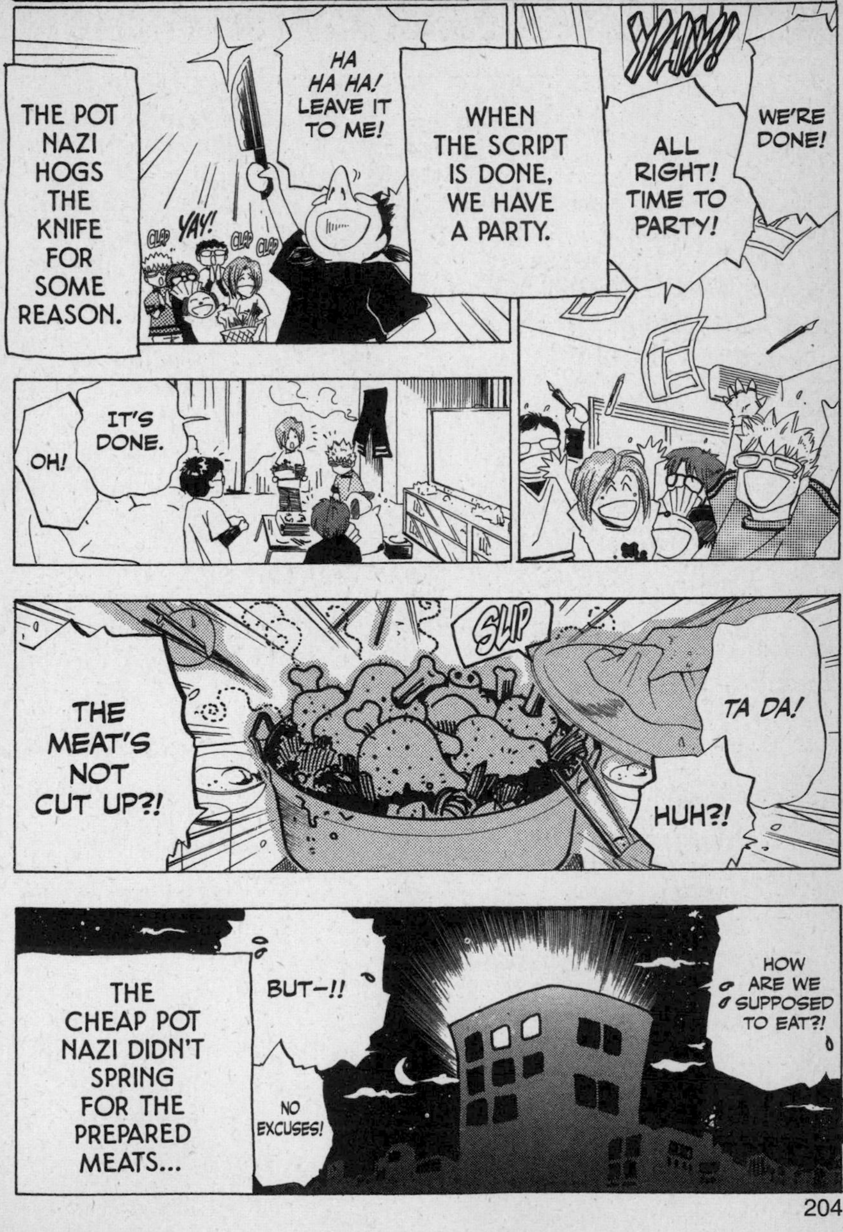
YAY!
WE'RE DONE!
ALL RIGHT! TIME TO PARTY!
WHEN THE SCRIPT IS DONE, WE HAVE A PARTY.
HA HA HA! LEAVE IT TO ME!
YAY!
CLAP CLAP CLAP
THE POT NAZI HOGS THE KNIFE FOR SOME REASON.
IT'S DONE.
OH!
TA DA!
SLIP
HUH?!
THE MEAT'S NOT CUT UP?!
HOW ARE WE SUPPOSED TO EAT?!
BUT—!!
NO EXCUSES!
THE CHEAP POT NAZI DIDN'T SPRING FOR THE PREPARED MEATS...

DANGER IN THE WORKPLACE: THE TOILET SAGA, PART 2

TAKASHI MORIMOTO

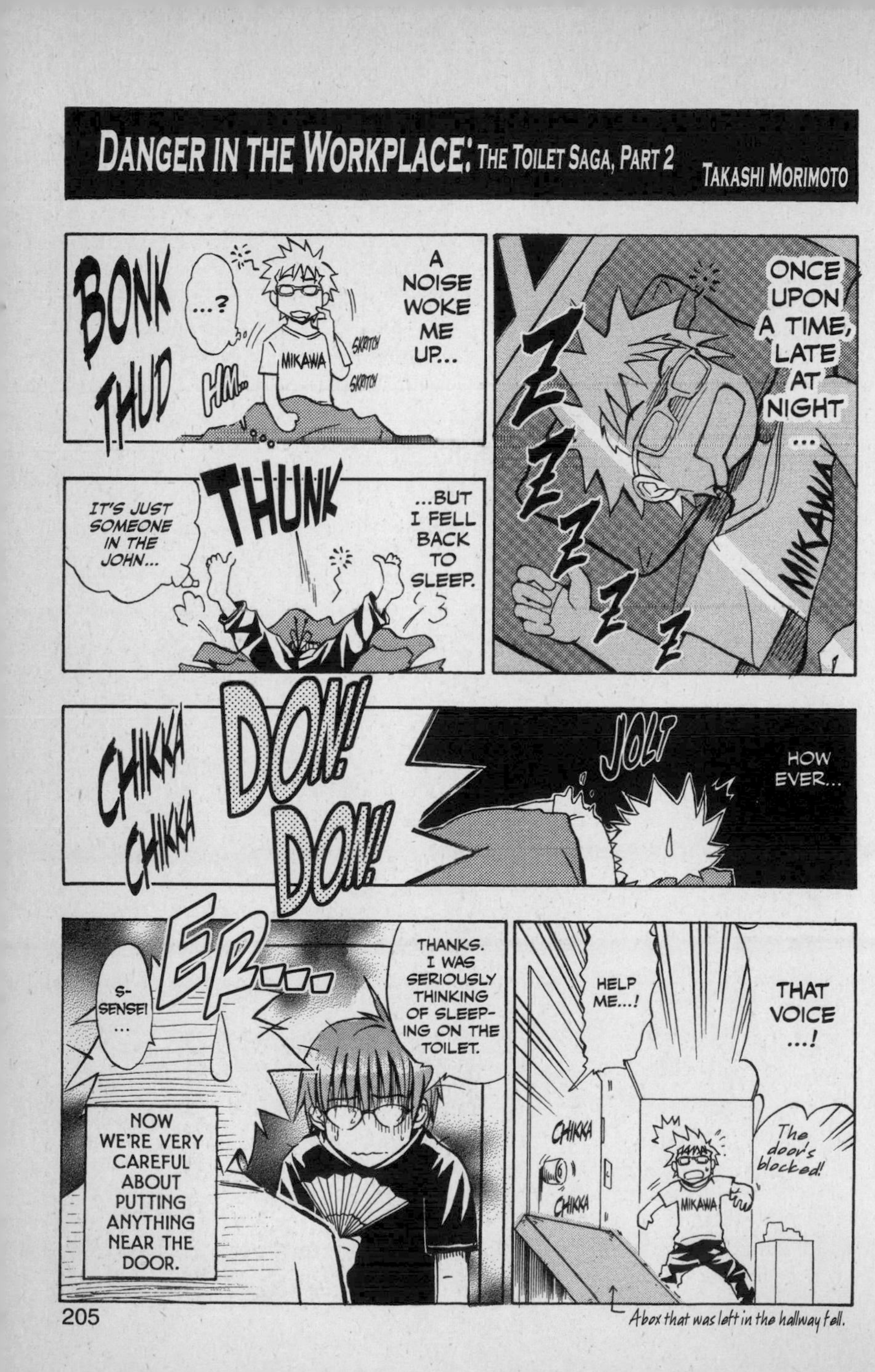
ONCE UPON A TIME, LATE AT NIGHT...
ZZZZZZZ
MIKAWA
A NOISE WOKE ME UP...
SKRITCH SKRITCH
MIKAWA
...?
HM...
BONK THUD
...BUT I FELL BACK TO SLEEP.
THUNK
IT'S JUST SOMEONE IN THE JOHN...
HOW EVER...
JOLT
DON! DON!
CHIKKA CHIKKA
THAT VOICE ...!
HELP ME...!
The door's blocked!
MIKAWA
CHIKKA CHIKKA
THANKS. I WAS SERIOUSLY THINKING OF SLEEP-ING ON THE TOILET.
EP...
S-SENSEI...
NOW WE'RE VERY CAREFUL ABOUT PUTTING ANYTHING NEAR THE DOOR.

A box that was left in the hallway fell.

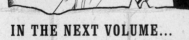

IN THE NEXT VOLUME...

The final battle: Creed versus Train! Creed now possesses an invincible body and his power is accelerating rapidly. Train must gamble on one last bullet to bring his foe down and wipe out their past!!

AVAILABLE MAY 2009!

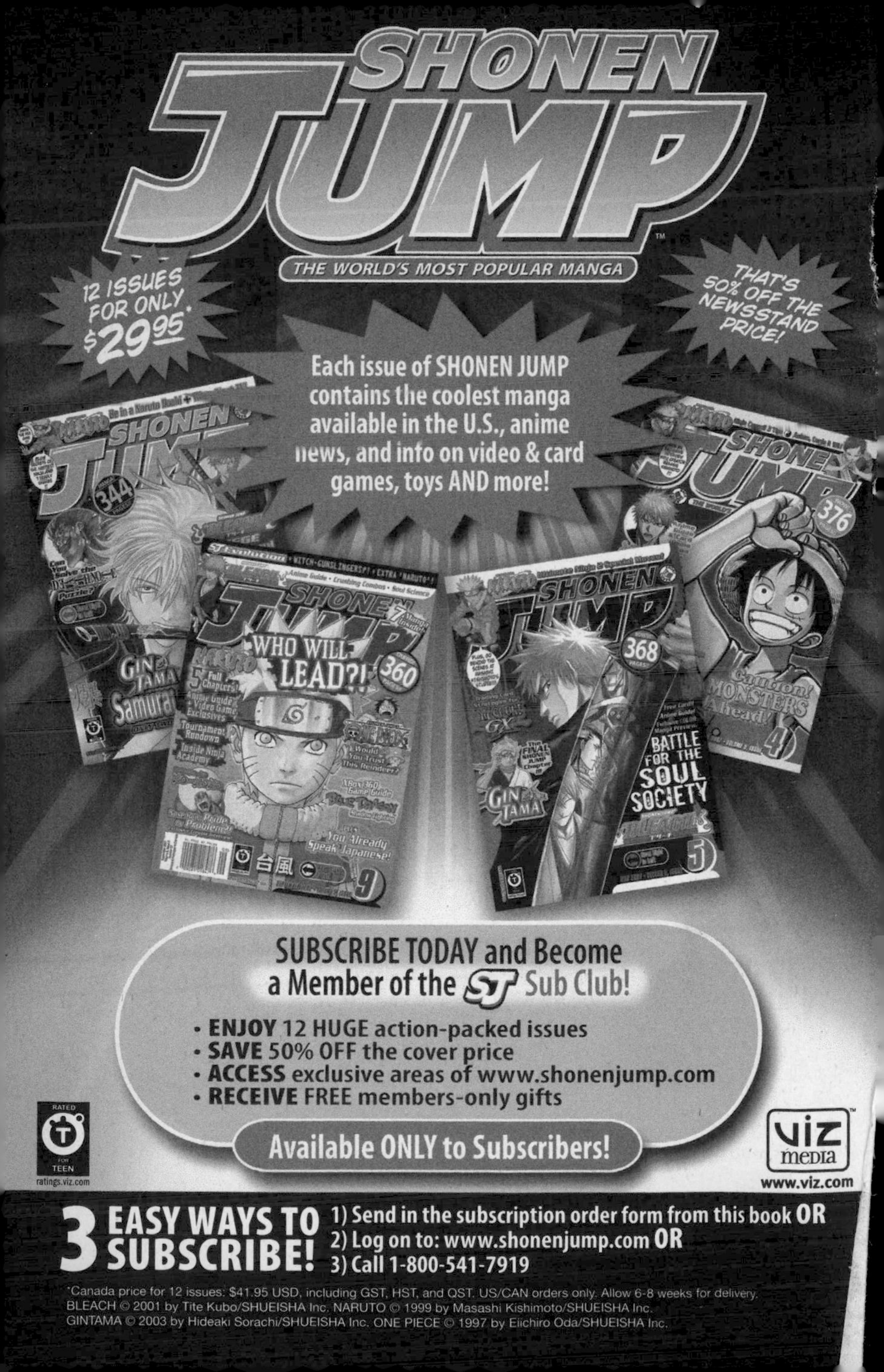
SHONEN JUMP
THE WORLD'S MOST POPULAR MANGA
12 ISSUES FOR ONLY $29.95*
THAT'S 50% OFF THE NEWSSTAND PRICE!
Each issue of SHONEN JUMP contains the coolest manga available in the U.S., anime news, and info on video & card games, toys AND more!
SUBSCRIBE TODAY and Become a Member of the SJ Sub Club!
• ENJOY 12 HUGE action-packed issues
• SAVE 50% OFF the cover price
• ACCESS exclusive areas of www.shonenjump.com
• RECEIVE FREE members-only gifts
Available ONLY to Subscribers!
RATED T FOR TEEN
ratings.viz.com
VIZ media
www.viz.com
3 EASY WAYS TO SUBSCRIBE!
1) Send in the subscription order form from this book OR
2) Log on to: www.shonenjump.com OR
3) Call 1-800-541-7919
*Canada price for 12 issues: $41.95 USD, including GST, HST, and QST. US/CAN orders only. Allow 6-8 weeks for delivery.
BLEACH © 2001 by Tite Kubo/SHUEISHA Inc. NARUTO © 1999 by Masashi Kishimoto/SHUEISHA Inc.
GINTAMA © 2003 by Hideaki Sorachi/SHUEISHA Inc. ONE PIECE © 1997 by Eiichiro Oda/SHUEISHA Inc.